Southern Vietnam under the Reign of Minh Mạng (1820-1841)

Central Policies and Local Response

Choi Byung Wook

Southern Vietnam under the Reign of Minh Mạng (1820-1841)

Central Policies and Local Response

SOUTHEAST ASIA PROGRAM PUBLICATIONS
Southeast Asia Program
Cornell University
Ithaca, New York
2004

Cornell Southeast Asia Program Publications
640 Stewart Avenue, Ithaca, NY 14850-3857

Southeast Asia Program Series Number 20

Printed in the United States of America
Cover Design by Judith Burns, Publications Services, Cornell University

ISBN 0-87727-138-0

CONTENTS

PLATES

ACKNOWLEDGMENTS

This book is based on my PhD dissertation of the same title. While working on this subject, mainly at the Research School of Pacific and Asian Studies, the Australian National University, I was assisted by many persons who deserve thanks. First of all, I wish to thank Professor David Marr, who greatly helped me to complete this work. I will not forget his sincere, patient, energetic, and efficient academic encouragement. I also want to thank Professors Anthony Reid and Mark Elvin. My visits to them with questions relating to both Southeast and Northeast Asia always ended with satisfactory answers and additional learning. I was also lucky to receive advice from Dr. Nola Cooke and Dr. Philip Taylor, who gave me valuable comments on my drafts. Discussions with these respectful colleagues who know my period and region so well were delightful chances to enlarge my knowledge of Vietnam and to develop my ideas. I also thank my friends Dr. David Koh and Dr. Alexander Soucy. Both during the fieldwork period and while we were in Canberra as foreign students doing Vietnamese studies, I was deeply indebted to their friendship, which helped me whenever I felt frustrated. Dr. James Greenbaum was kind enough to spend his time helping me to translate many difficult Chinese terms into English.

I cannot omit mention of the help I received from Professor Phan Huy Lê, former head of the Center of Cooperation for Vietnamese Studies, Hanoi National University. During my fieldwork, he made great efforts to allow me access to valuable documents in the Archives. Dr. Nguyễn Quang Ngọc of the Faculty of History, Hanoi National University, was a very kind scholar to whom I owe a lot for his assistance with both research and daily life in Hanoi. In Saigon, I visited Nguyễn Đình Đầu's office whenever I had questions about southern Vietnam and was always met with his sincere willingness to help me address and answer those questions. I will not forget the help of Professor Nguyễn Phan Quang of the Education University of Ho Chi Minh City. Due to his kind advice, I was able to find the appropriate direction from which to approach persons who would help my research at the local level. Trips to Cai Lậy in Tiền Giang province were also a great joy because I could meet Trương Ngọc Tường there. I deeply appreciate his open-minded attitude, in that he would share priceless documents without any conditions. I also enjoyed visits to Tiền Giang province because I could meet various scholars of southern origin who were working sincerely with their tradition and history. I am especially grateful to Dr. Nguyễn Phúc Nghiệp, historian at the Education College of the Tiền Giang province, who willingly spent time with me as a friend and colleague of the same generation. He introduced me to whomever I wanted to meet for discussion, showed me how to get wherever I wished to go in the Mỹ Tho area for my research, and helped me to find important documents.

I would like to express my appreciation here to Professor Yu Insun at the Department of Asian History in Seoul National University. Under his guidance, I entered this fascinating world of Vietnamese studies twenty years ago. I also deeply thank Professor Oh Keum-Sung at the same department. Ever since I was a freshman in 1981, whenever I encountered conditions that almost made me want to give up academic study, he kindly provided me with valuable advice and encouragement. My thanks also go to the warm, open-minded, liberal, but serious academic atmosphere at the Department of Asian History, Korea University, where I carried out research on nineteenth-century southern Vietnam for my master's thesis under the supervision of Professor Yu Insun, who was working for that department at that time. The research in this lovely department was the first step of my long journey to produce this book.

I would also like to thank Professor Alexander Woodside, Professor Nguyễn Thế Anh, Dr. Đỗ Thiên, Professor Keith Taylor, and other reviewers, who carefully read my work and provided me with precious suggestions to improve it. Without the great and painstaking help of Maxine McArthur in the Research School of Pacific and Asian Studies, the Australian National University, and Dr. Mary Donnelly, Deborah Homsher, and Dr. Michael Wakoff at Cornell University's Southeast Asia Program Publications, I could not have completed this book in English with the context made clear.

The great contribution of my long-term friends, Rhee Jong Sung and Han Jong Woo should also be mentioned here. As two of my closest friends, they were the first persons who knew of my strong interest in Southeast Asian history, and have consistently supported me in various ways for a long time. From Canada and the USA, where they are leading academic careers, though in different fields from mine, they helped me with great pleasure to compose more effective sentences and collect necessary materials for the publication of this book.

I thank my wife Kwon Hye Kyeong and my two sons, Seo Jung and Seo Yong, who put up with the difficulties of the past years, including five years of tough and unstable life as an overseas student family in Australia. They should be the most pleased of all to see the publication of this book because they have most closely observed the work of producing it from beginning to end.

The last, but highest appreciation goes to my parents. Without their patience, support, and encouragement, I could have neither started nor finished this research.

INTRODUCTION

This book aims to explain a series of significant political events that took place in southern Vietnam[1] during the first half of the nineteenth century. From this region, armies marched north to unify Vietnam and produced the Nguyễn dynasty (1802-1945). In 1833, however, a revolt of southerners (popularly called the Lê Văn Khôi revolt) broke out, declaring independent rule for southern Vietnam and lasting two years before being crushed. Ethnic conflicts followed the revolt, further devastating southern Vietnam. Later, in 1859, the French landed in this region, and the southerners' anti-French movement started, fueled by strong loyalist sentiments toward the Huế court.

The political events mentioned above reveal striking inconsistencies in the attitudes of southern Vietnamese towards the central government. In 1802, southerners were heroes of the new dynasty that achieved the amalgamation of the three regions of present-day Vietnam[2] for the first time; but thirty years later, an anti-government revolt erupted, and ended with the central government tightening its grip on the region. It was a dramatic change in status for the southern Vietnamese, who shifted from being winners to losers in three short decades. Southerners not only lost the initiative in central politics, but were also reduced to being virtually colonized by the Huế court in the middle of the 1830s. By the 1850s, however, we find southerners fighting the French invasion and declaring strong loyalty to the Nguyễn king, even though they believed the court had sold out southern Vietnam and abandoned its people. This was another shift for the southern Vietnamese, who transformed themselves from losers to advocates of the central government.

This fluctuation of southern reaction to the central government during this half century was the starting point of my interest in southern Vietnam. While reading the huge volumes of the Huế court chronicle, the *Đại Nam Thực Lục* (Veritable records of Đại Nam), I found that the Nguyễn dynasty rulers were seriously concerned about controlling southern Vietnam during the first half of the nineteenth century. I then began to pay particular attention to the central government's actions in southern Vietnam. During the reign of Minh Mạng (1820-1841), descriptions of the central government's work in southern Vietnam became increasingly frequent, just at the time that tension between Huế and southern Vietnam reached its peak. I wondered if Minh Mạng's actions might have caused the subsequent political vacillations in southern Vietnam.

For an examination of Minh Mạng's policies, we have Alexander Woodside's outstanding 1971 book, *Vietnam and the Chinese Model: A Comparative Study of*

---

[1] In this book, "southern Vietnam" indicates the geographically open region encompassing the lower Mekong delta. This area was called Gia Định or, later, during the first half of the nineteenth century, Nam Kỳ.

[2] North (Miền Bắc), central region (Miền Trung), and south (Miền Nam).

Nguyễn and Ch'ing Civil Government in the First Half of the Nineteenth Century.[3] In this book, Woodside shows the extent to which Chinese elements were imported into Vietnamese administrative and educational units, and how far Sinicization progressed during the first half of the nineteenth century in general and during Minh Mạng's reign in particular: "Vietnamese rulers struggled to ensure that their governments attained a correspondence to the governments of China. The closer their approximation, they believed, the greater would be their effectiveness."[4] With the help of Woodside's Sinicization paradigm, we can gain an insight into the Nguyễn dynasty's institutional outlook. But Woodside's influential concept has also sometimes prevented historians from perceiving the serious efforts of the Huế court to manage its recently unified territory.

Two other scholars have considered the history of early nineteenth-century Vietnam from a different perspective, one that considers the influence of southern regionalism and the deep roots of the new dynasty in former Đàng Trong.[5] In 1990, Philippe Langlet published his important study, *L'Ancienne historiographie d'état au Vietnam,*[6] tracing the influence of the southern past and dynastic ancestral worship on the nineteenth-century Nguyễn ideology of political legitimacy, beginning with the reign of Nguyễn Hoàng, founder of the Nguyễn state, onwards. Nola Cooke has published several articles, arguing from biographical sources that the Nguyễn political elite was strongly influenced by regionalism. In one article, titled "Southern Regionalism and the Composition of the Nguyễn Ruling Elite," she demonstrates "pro-southern (Đàng Trong) bias" among the highest Nguyễn dynasty elites.[7]

Scholars commonly bisect Vietnam, dividing it into south and north (Đàng Trong/Đàng Ngoài), a useful practice insofar as it helps one avoid generalizations about the culturally diverse country of Vietnam and its history. Nevertheless, this bisection does not seem adequate when we are trying to understand regional Vietnamese politics during the first half of the nineteenth century. Regarding this period, a model that shows the trisection of Vietnamese territory (into north, center, and south) is both appropriate and useful. Southern Vietnam, or Gia Định, was one part of the trisection of nineteenth-century Vietnam, and it still exists today under the names of Miền Nam (southern part) or Đồng Bằng Sông Cửu Long (Mekong delta).[8]

---

[3] Alexander Woodside, *Vietnam and the Chinese Model: A Comparative Study of Nguyễn and Ch'ing Civil Government in the First Half of the Nineteenth Century* (Cambridge: Harvard University Press, 1971).

[4] Alexander Woodside, *Vietnam and the Chinese Model*, p. 61.

[5] Vietnamese used the term Đàng Trong for all of the region south of the Gianh River in present Quảng Bình province. The Gianh River formed a natural border, dividing the region of the Nguyễn family (sixteenth through eighteenth centuries) from that of the Trịnh family in northern Vietnam; the Trịnh territory was called Đàng Ngoài.

[6] Philippe Langlet, *L'Ancienne historiographie d'état au Vietnam* (Paris: École Française d'Extrême Orient, 1990).

[7] Nola Cooke, "Southern Regionalism and the Composition of the Nguyen Ruling Elite," *Asian Studies Review* 23,2 (1999): 205-231.

[8] In his excellent analysis of Vietnamese regional differences, Keith Taylor displays six parts of Vietnam—Đồng Kinh, Thanh Hóa-Nghệ An, Thuận Quảng, Bình Định, and Nam Bộ—in historic context. See Keith W. Taylor, "Surface Orientations in Vietnam: Beyond Histories of Nation and Region," *The Journal of Asian Studies* 57,4 (1998). "Nam Bộ" (southern part) is the widely accepted term to indicate the area of Gia Định, while Bắc Bộ and Trung Bộ are used for

Another work of interest, relevant to this period, is Nguyễn Thị Thạnh's dissertation, "The French Conquest of Cochinchina, 1858-1862."[9] Though the thesis is mainly focused on the 1850s-60s, the author also allocates a large part of her analysis to examining the first half of the nineteenth century as background for later events. However, she does not seem to stray from the common view of twentieth-century revolutionary groups, which labeled the regime as one characterized by reactionary feudalism. Nguyễn Thị Thạnh concludes that "the Nguyễn court's political and economic policies made the history of the mid-nineteenth century Vietnam a tragedy."[10] In her discussion of the anti-French movement, she points out that "idealistic intellectuals" led resistance movements, peasants came together to create fighting forces, and "private landlords" financed the resistance in southern Vietnam from 1861 to 1862.[11] There has been a popular, but rather romantic and simplified notion that the Cochinchinese armed opposition to the French was essentially "the reaction of peasants against a foreign presence;"[12] when compared with this notion, certainly Nguyễn Thị Thạnh's argument is more comprehensive. Because of her perspective on the Nguyễn court, however, she contends that intellectuals, peasants, and landlords participated in the anti-French movement only to protect their own interests within southern Vietnam. But I believe that we will find other significant reasons for their engagement if we more seriously examine the Nguyễn court's policies in southern Vietnam during the first half of the nineteenth century.

In Vietnam, an extensive number of works on this southern area have been produced since the beginning of the 1990s. Southern scholars have examined issues regarding Gia Định based on their own view of tradition, observation of historical remains, and discovery of local documents. Among them, Sơn Nam is the most energetic, producing books and articles on the Gia Định people. In particular, his book entitled *Đất Gia Định Xưa* (Land of Gia Dinh in the past)[13] is filled with vivid descriptions of Gia Định life. However, as in Sơn Nam's other works, the author's fixation on the day-to-day lives of Gia Định people places limits on his argument. He is not much concerned with political changes caused by the central government's policies, the reactions of Gia Định people to those policies, and consequent social changes as they related to each stage of the political developments before and after the 1830s, for example.

---

northern part and central part, respectively, in the trisection concept. Pierre Brocheux falsely informs us that "In Vietnamese, the French renamed the region [southern Vietnam] Nam Ky." Pierre Brocheux, *The Mekong Delta: Ecology, Economy, and Revolution, 1860-1960* (Wisconsin: Center for Southeast Asian Studies, 1995), p. 223. But the "Nam Ky" (Nam Kỳ) was an earlier term. It was the Nguyễn court that renamed this region Nam Kỳ after the 1830s administrative reform.

[9] Nguyễn Thị Thạnh, "The French Conquest of Cochinchina, 1858-1862" (PhD dissertation, Cornell University, 1992).

[10] Ibid., p. 106.

[11] Ibid., p. 422.

[12] Milton E. Osborne, *The French Presence in Cochinchina and Cambodia: Rule and Response (1859-1905)* (Bangkok: White Lotus, 1997), p. 65.

[13] *Đất Gia Định Xưa* (Land of Gia Dinh in the past) (Ho Chi Minh City: Nxb Thành Phố Hồ Chí Minh, 1993).

My book examines a very specific form of southern regionalism—the regionalism of Gia Định and Nam Kỳ—and the particular sorts of policies employed by the central government to break down that regional identity and turn it into loyalty towards the dynasty by fully integrating the area into the Nguyễn kingdom.

The first chapter of this book discusses several elements of southern Vietnamese tradition that stemmed from the Gia Định regime of the eighteenth century, based in southern Vietnam. In chapters two and three, I discuss the Gia Định local government (1808-1832), called in Vietnamese Gia Định Thành Tổng Trấn, and examine the central government's conflict with this local regime and the southerners' reaction to the central government. In chapters four through six, I discuss three important policies of Minh Mạng implemented after abolition of the Gia Định local government: *giáo hóa*, or the "cultivation" of southern people; the "Vietnamization" of other ethnic groups, including Chinese; and a new land measurement policy that resulted in an official recognition of private land ownership and land accumulation in southern Vietnam.

Examining these issues achieves three goals. First, we will find the reasons behind many of the political events in southern Vietnam at the time. Second, we can appreciate what the nineteenth-century dynasty achieved in their efforts to pull a peripheral area under central government control before 1859, after which it increasingly appeared as an unsuccessful regime because of its loss of sovereignty to the French. Finally, I hope to provide readers with a way of understanding Vietnam as a nation with specific historical roots, roots that held it together as a geographical and political entity, going back to the early nineteenth century. The Nguyễn dynasty was the first and last unitary state model for post-colonial Vietnam, as it ruled three regions simultaneously. My discussion of the nineteenth-century polity may provide clues to understanding aspects of contemporary Vietnam that involve center versus local interactions and tensions.

My main primary sources can be divided into three categories: documents compiled by the central court; individual observations of southern Vietnam during the first half of the nineteenth century by either foreigners or Vietnamese from other regions; and the southerners' own records, such as family histories, land trade bills, tenant contracts, and wills. I aim to draw a picture of southern Vietnam using these sources, written by a range of people, from court officials to remote southern villagers. Let me introduce some of these sources according to the above three categories.

Đại Nam Thực Lục is a basic source for my research. This official chronicle was compiled by court officials during the nineteenth and twentieth centuries. It contains substantial evidence related to my concerns. *Đại Nam Thực Lục* consists of *Tiền Biên* (earlier period, 1558-1777, 12 volumes), and *Chính Biên* (main period, 1778-1888, 441 volumes). The latter is further subdivided into five periods, each associated with the reign of a king: Nguyễn Phúc Ánh[14] (1762-1820), later known as

---

[14]Inconsistency in writing Vietnamese names that have variations between south (Đàng Trong) and north (Đàng Ngoài) is unavoidable. Basically, I will follow current standard pronunciation. Therefore, I will choose Phúc, Nhân, Nhất, Sinh, Bảo, instead of Phước, Nhơn, Nhứt, Sanh, Bửu, for southern names in cases where names with these characters are found in documents written in Chinese. But I will also allow for popular usage. Today, northerners write the imperial title of the second Nguyễn emperor as Minh Mệnh. But I choose Minh Mạng,

Gia Long (1802-1820, 60 volumes); Minh Mạng (1820-1841, 220 volumes); Thiệu Trị (1841-1847, 72 volumes); Tự Đức (1848-1883, 70 volumes); Dục Đức-Hàm Nghi (1883-1885, 8 volumes); and Đồng Khánh (1885-1888, 11 volumes). The documentation regarding Minh Mạng, especially, is the most detailed and solid, and provides us with much evidence on social and economic matters, as well as the state's ideas and activities. One of the original copies of the *Đại Nam Thực Lục*, along with attached biographies of Nguyễn Vietnam's illustrious figures, collected in *Liệt Truyện*,[15] were brought to Japan in 1933 by a Japanese scholar, Matsumoto Nobuhiro, and were recompiled beginning in 1961 at Keio University. I am using a recompiled edition.

Many parts of the *Đại Nam Thực Lục* were based on Châu Bản Triều Nguyễn (Vermilion Records of the Nguyen Dynasty), which thus figures as a basic complementary source for my study.[16] Central government edicts, reports from local governments, and the suggestions of officials were collected here. As the Châu Bản are currently being held in Hanoi under the very strict control of the Vietnamese authorities, their full extent is not yet known. Unfortunately, I have not been allowed access to these archival documents. However, in 1996 some of the Châu Bản were rediscovered on microfilm in several libraries in the United States; they had been originally given as a gift by the Ngô Đình Diệm government to the Kennedy Administration. This microfilm copy of Châu Bản covers some periods of Gia Long and Minh Mạng, to 1837. In many cases, however, the microfilm is very difficult to read because the characters are too blurred and small. Because of this, I decided to concentrate on those sections most relevant to my research, that is, sections concerning the years 1836 and 1837, following the end of the southerners' revolt. The reports posted by Minh Mạng's officials from each province of southern Vietnam are more numerous and detailed than the earlier reports that reached the capital when southern Vietnam was ruled by Gia Định local leaders, who had decided many matters by themselves.

In the second category, individual records and reminiscences, my sources include Nguyễn Thu's *Hoàn Vũ Kỷ Văn* (Compendium on the [Vietnamese] world),[17] Doãn Uẩn's *Doãn Tướng Công Hoạn Tích* (Minister Doan's chronicle of office),[18] the collection of Phan Thanh Giản's works, *Lương Khê Văn Thảo* (Prose of Luong Khe in

---

because he was more popularly known as Minh Mạng, not only in Vietnam but also overseas. If I can only find names from more recent texts, I will respect the names by which they are called. For example, Trần Thị Sanh was a woman who lived in Gò Công near Saigon during the nineteenth century, but I only encountered her name in twentieth-century writings. I can assume the letter "Sanh" is from the Chinese letter "Sinh," according to contemporary standard pronunciation. In this case, I will not change her name to "Trần Thị Sinh."

[15]The *Liệt Truyện* consist of *Tiền Biên* (1558-1777, 6 vols.) and also *Chính Biên* (1778-1888, 79 vols.). The first part (33 vols.) of *Chính Biên* describes figures who worked with Gia Long and died before Minh Mạng's enthronement in 1820, and the second part (46 vols.) includes the biographies of figures from the Minh Mạng reign.

[16]Châu Bản Triều Nguyễn (Vermilion Records of the Nguyen dynasty) (ANU Library, microfilm reels 60-64 [1836-1837]).

[17]Nguyễn Thu, *Hoàn Vũ Kỷ Văn* (Compendium on the [Vietnamese] world) (n.d. Hanoi: Viện Hán Nôm A 585).

[18]Doãn Uẩn, *Doãn Tướng Công Hoạn Tích* (or *Tuy Tĩnh Tử Tạp Ngôn*) (Minister Doan's chronicle of office, or Tuy Tinh Tu's miscellaneous notes) (1842. Hanoi: Viện Hán Nôm A 2177).

manuscript form), and *Lương Khê Thi Thảo* (Poetry of Luong Khe in manuscript form),[19] Trần Tân Gia's *Bà Tâm Huyền Kính Lục* (An account of compassionate hearts and hanging mirrors),[20] and Trương Quốc Dụng's *Thoái Thực Ký Văn* (After-dinner recollections).[21] Most of them relate the authors' experiences and observations in southern Vietnam. I read these documents in the Hán Nôm Institute in Hanoi. Added to these are the observations of foreigners such as: *Hải Nam Tạp Trứ* (Various records of the land beyond the southern ocean) written by a Chinese scholar, Ts'ai T'ing Lan, who lived in Vietnam in 1835;[22] the published letters of French missionaries; the observations of the American John White, who visited Vietnam in 1819-1820;[23] and the descriptions of John Crawfurd and George Finlayson during their stays in 1822.[24] Taken together, these various accounts help us better to understand Vietnam during the 1820s-30s.

I would also like to introduce a local document from southern Vietnam, *Trương Gia Từ Đường Thế Phả Toàn Tập* (Complete collection of the genealogy of the Truong family's ancestry) (*Trương Gia Thế Phả*, hereafter).[25] I read it in the Hán Nôm Institute in 1997. This collection contains extraordinarily substantial descriptions about a southern family based in a village near Saigon.[26] Compiled in 1886, it deals with seven generations, covering about two centuries, from the eighteenth to the end of the nineteenth century. It describes each person in a way that illuminates southern society during this time: listing each person's occupation, marriage, details on his or her spouse, where each person lived, dates of birth and death (including children), the reason for death, and the place he/she was buried.

Six land trade bills (of 1830-1846), two wills (of 1818, 1857), and one landlord-tenant contract (of 1859) are attached as appendices to this book. These were written by ordinary village people, without the intervention of government officials, and therefore they significantly advance our understanding of southerners' actual practices relating to land ownership, land accumulation, customs of land clearance and trade, and property distribution, as well as the list of possessions, tax, tenant's rent, and so forth.[27]

---

[19]Phan Thanh Giản, *Lương Khê Thi Thảo* (Poetry of Luong Khe in manuscript form) (1876. Hanoi: Viện Hán Nôm VHv 151), and *Lương Khê Văn Thảo* (Prose of Luong Khe in manuscript form) (1876. Hanoi: Viện Hán Nôm A 2125).

[20]Trần Tân Gia, *Bà Tâm Huyền Kính Lục* (An account of compassionate hearts and hanging mirrors) (1897. Hanoi: Viện Hán Nôm A 2027).

[21]Trương Quốc Dụng, *Thoái Thực Ký Văn* (or *Công Ha Ký Văn*) (After-dinner recollections, or recollections beyond the office) (n.d. Hanoi: Viện Hán Nôm A 1499).

[22]Ts'ai T'ing Lan, *Hải Nam Tạp Trứ* (Various records of the land beyond the southern ocean) (1836. Hanoi: Viện Hán Nôm HVv 80).

[23] John White, *A Voyage to Cochin China* (1824. Kuala Lumpur: Oxford University Press, 1972).

[24] John Crawfurd, *Journal of an Embassy from the Governor-General of India to the Courts of Siam and Cochin China* (1828. Singapore: Oxford University Press, 1987) and George Finlayson, *The Mission to Siam and Hue, the Capital of Cochin China, in the Years 1821-22* (1826. Singapore: Oxford University Press, 1988).

[25] *Trương Gia Từ Đường Thế Phả Toàn Tập* (Complete collection of the genealogy of the Truong family ancestry) (1886. Hanoi: Viện Hán Nôm A 3186).

[26] One member of this family was Trương Minh Giảng (1792-1841), the famous Nguyễn official who was in charge of governing Cambodia at the end of Minh Mạng's reign.

[27] I received copies of these documents from a southern scholar, Trương Ngọc Tường, during my fieldwork in 1997.

Additionally, I refer to a series of recent southern monographs, from *Bạc Liêu Xưa và Nay* (Bac Lieu, past and present), published in 1966, to *Gia Định Xưa và Nay* (Gia Dinh, past and present) appearing in 1973, all produced under the author's name of Huỳnh Minh.[28] Considering the vast size and numbers of these monographs, I think they were not written by this one author, but are the result of the collective work of anonymous southern scholars during that period. In my opinion, the content of these monographs is quite solid and reliable. Regarding the content of these books, I am especially interested in the legends, stories, and memories that were collected from southerners during the 1960-1970s. I believe this evidence can also be used to understand southern society of the previous century, as long as each work's content is confirmed by careful examination of the historical context.

---

[28]Huỳnh Minh, *Địa Linh Nhơn Kiệt, Tỉnh Kiến Hoà (Bến Tre)* (Land and people, Kien Hoa Province [Ben Tre]) (Saigon, 1965); *Bạc Liêu Xưa và Nay* (Bac Lieu, past and present) (Saigon, 1966); *Cần Thơ Xưa và Nay* (Can Tho, past and present) (Saigon, 1966); *Vĩnh Long Xưa và Nay* (Vinh Long, past and present) (Saigon, 1967); *Gò Công Xưa và Nay* (Go Cong, past and present) (Saigon, 1969); *Định Tường Xưa và Nay* (Dinh Tuong, past and present) (Saigon, 1969); *Sa Đéc Xưa và Nay* (Sa Dec, past and present) (Saigon, 1971); *Tây Ninh Xưa và Nay* (Tay Ninh, past and present) (Saigon, 1972); and *Gia Định Xưa và Nay* (Gia Dinh, past and present) (Saigon, 1973).

PART I

LOCAL AUTHORITY AND ITS DEMISE

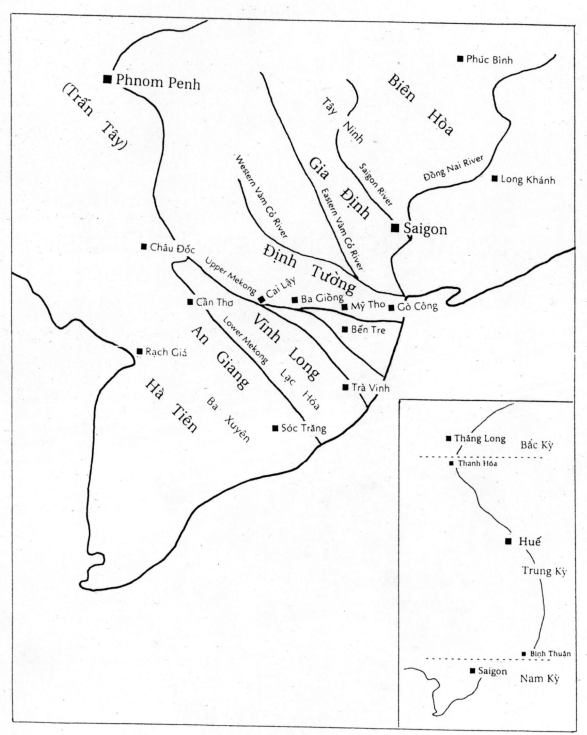

Southern Vietnam: 1840

CHAPTER ONE

THE HERITAGE OF THE GIA ĐỊNH REGIME (1788-1802)

The purpose of this chapter is to consider several aspects of Gia Định prior to the nineteenth century, aspects which are directly related to my argument on nineteenth-century southern Vietnam. To achieve this goal, I will focus on a political organization, namely, the Gia Định regime formed by the initiative of the Gia Định people.

At this stage, this regime has not attracted any serious attention from researchers. This is because it has usually been located in Vietnamese history either at the end of the Nguyễn state (sixteenth through eighteenth centuries), or at the beginning of the Nguyễn dynasty.[1] However, the Gia Định regime obviously had its own features based on Gia Định culture, and understanding the regime will provide us with a clue to understanding nineteenth-century southern Vietnam.

This chapter begins with an overview of the Gia Định regime, which appeared toward the end of the eighteenth century, then focuses on two elements of that regime: relationships among its members and its ethnic diversity. These were the most significant characteristic elements of the regime, and it was these aspects that enabled this local regime to take over the entire territory of Vietnam. At the same time, however, internal relationships and ethnic diversity would also later become the main elements that caused serious friction between Gia Định and the central government during the first half of the nineteenth century.

1. THE FORMATION OF GIA ĐỊNH

Gia Định and Its People

The name of Gia Định[2] first occurred in the history of southern Vietnam in 1698. In that year, a *phủ*, or prefecture, called Gia Định was established to rule the

---

[1] Cao Tự Thanh suggests the years of 1778-1802 should be considered as a separate period. See Cao Tự Thanh, *Nho Giáo ở Gia Định* (Confucianism in Gia Dinh) (Ho Chi Minh City: Nxb Thành Phố Hồ Chí Minh, 1998), p. 48. But this period is only linked with the appearance of Nguyễn Phúc Ánh as the leader of the Nguyễn state army. He also occasionally uses the term "chính quyền Gia Định," or Gia Định regime, in his discussion of this period, but his usage of this term is meant only to indicate broadly Nguyễn Phúc Ánh's group.

[2] The origin of the name Gia Định has not been fully discovered. It is a combination of the Chinese characters "Gia" and "Định." "Gia" means pretty or happy, while "Định" means decide or to pacify. In northern Vietnam, before 1820, one district, one *tổng*, and one *xã*, were all called Gia Định, with the same Chinese characters. See, Dương Thị The et al., *Tên Làng Xã Việt Nam Đầu Thế Kỷ 19— thuộc các tỉnh từ Nghệ Tĩnh trở ra* (Names of Vietnamese villages in the

southern peripheral part of Nguyễn state around present-day Biên Hòa and Saigon. It was from this year, too, that the Nguyễn state mobilized peasants to build villages and organized the tax system of southern Vietnam.[3]

However, it was not until the end of the eighteenth century that Gia Định began to represent the area that corresponds to present southern Vietnam, from Biên Hòa to Hà Tiên. The civil war between the Tây Sơn army and Nguyễn Phúc Ánh's force contributed to this development. In 1771, the Tây Sơn rebellion broke out at Bình Định, a part of the Nguyễn state. This rebellion resulted in a new and different political division of Vietnam. Until that time, for about two centuries, Vietnam had been divided into two parts, separated by the Gianh River in the present Quảng Bình province. Based in a traditional political center, Thăng Long, the Trịnh family had ruled northern Vietnam; territory to the south of the river had been ruled by the Nguyễn family. As the Tây Sơn rebellion grew, the Nguyễn territory was increasingly disrupted by internal turmoil and the Nguyễn king-fled to Gia Định. Taking advantage of this, in 1775 the Trịnh army occupied Phú Xuân, the capital of the Nguyễn family state. In 1777, the Nguyễn state ended when its last king was captured and killed by the Tây Sơn army at Gia Định. A decade

---

beginning of the nineteenth century—places belonging to each province from Nghe An and Ha Tinh northward) (Hanoi: Nxb Khoa Học Xã Hội, 1981), p. 278. Because the name of the Gia Định district caused it to be confused with Gia Định Thành, in 1820 the central government changed the name of the Gia Định district to the Gia Bình district. See Phan Thúc Trực, *Quốc Sử Di Biên* (A transmitted compilation of the state history, hereafter *QSDB*) (n. d. Hong Kong: New Asia Research Institute, 1965), p. 108. But there is no evidence that the Nguyễn state borrowed the name Gia Định from the north, if this name existed at that time, when it named southern Vietnam Gia Định in 1698.

In my opinion, the phrase "Gia Định" in the south not only had the Chinese meanings mentioned above, but also reflected the local word for this region, as did the word "Saigon." "Saigon" represents the influence of the Khmer language. See Trần Văn Giàu et al., *Địa Chí Văn Hóa Thành Phố Hồ Chí Minh* (Cultural gazetteer of Ho Chi Minh City), vol. 1 (Ho Chi Minh City: Nxb Thành Phố Hồ Chí Minh, 1987), pp. 215-224. On the other hand, "Gia Định" also seems to be related to the Malay language, a real possibility if we remember that this region was crowded with Malay language speakers during the seventeenth century. See Trịnh Hoài Đức, *Gia Định Thành Thông Chí* (Gia Dinh gazetteer) (hereafter *GDTTC*) (n.d. Ecole Française d'Extrême-Orient microfilm A. 1561), 4:3. Besides, ethnic minorities belonging to the Malay language family existed in this region before Vietnamese came here. In southern pronunciation, *Gia* is close to *Ya*. In Malay, a word pronounced *ya* (or *ayer*) has the meaning of water, stream, or river. Bình Nguyên Lộc, "Việc mãi nô dưới vòm trời Đông Phố và chủ Đất thật của vùng Đồng Nai" (Being slaves a long time under the sky of Dong Pho and the real owners of Dong Nai region), *Tập San Sử Địa* 19 and 20 (1970): 254. The Vietnamese may have borrowed the Malay pronunciation, or the Malay term, to invent a Chinese name, "Gia Định," to indicate their new land, many parts of which were filled with water. There is another possibility. Professor Anthony Johns suggests we consider the Malay words *dingin* or *hering*, which mean "cool or cold," and "clean or clear," respectively, as they have a pronunciation close to *Định* (from a discussion at the ANU in February 1999). If we remember the rivers in this region such as the Đồng Nai River, the Saigon River, and the Western and Eastern Vàm Cỏ Rivers, which are obviously clearer than the Mekong River, we cannot rule out the possibility that the Vietnamese name, "Gia Định," had to do with the relatively clear (and therefore cool looking) rivers in this region. Or, if we combine these theories, we might suggest that that the name "Gia Định" came from a local name "*Ya* (or *Ayer*) *Dingin* (or *Hering*)" with the meaning of "clear (clean, cool, or cold) water (streams, or rivers)."

[3] *Đại Nam Thực Lục Tiền-Biên* (Primary compilation of the Veritable Records of Imperial Vietnam, premier period) (hereafter *TB*) (1844. Tokyo: Keio Institute of Linguistic Studies, 1961), 7: 14.

later, in 1786, in northern Vietnam, the Tây Sơn also removed the Trịnh family from power. Shortly after, the Tây Sơn general, Nguyễn Huệ, overthrew the Lê dynasty (fifteenth through eighteenth centuries) that had nominally existed under the regentship of the Trịnh family since the sixteenth century. Ch'ing China intervened in this internal disorder in 1788, but Tây Sơn forces succeeded in repulsing the Ch'ing troops from northern Vietnam in 1789. With this victory over the Chinese troops, the Tây Sơn were able to claim exclusive rule not only in the former territory of the Nguyễn family, but also in the territory of the Trịnh family.

But, at the same time, a solid faction led by Nguyễn Phúc Ánh (1762-1820), a prince of the Nguyễn state, later to become king Gia Long (1802-1820), appeared in Gia Định. With the emergence of this faction, Vietnam was divided again: the Tây Sơn held the northern and central regions of Vietnam; and Nguyễn Phúc Ánh controlled territory in Gia Định. This territorial division marked the emergence of Gia Định as a politically independent unit.[4]

Gia Định, the Territory of a Regime

In 1788, Nguyễn Phúc Ánh finally settled in the region around Saigon, after a series of failed attempts to make a bridgehead on southern Vietnam.[5] From this year, Gia Định was regarded as one unit that had resisted inclusion into Tây Sơn territory, and it was from this time that names such as "Gia Định people," "Gia Định soldiers," "Gia Định land," and so forth, began to appear in the history of Vietnam. Nguyễn Phúc Ánh's party changed itself from a mobile military group to a regime with a solid power base in Saigon. One of the significant political actions taken by the regime was the mobilization of civil officials. Disciples of a prominent Gia Định scholar, Võ Trường Toản, participated in Nguyễn Phúc Ánh's party and contributed to the establishment of a new regime.[6] In 1788, the king created Công Đồng Thử, the Council of High Officials, consisting of civil and military subjects.[7] A six-ministry system was formed by this regime.[8] Local

---

[4] In relation to this point, Keith Taylor correctly argues that "Nguyễn Phúc Ánh was the first person to organize Nam Bộ as a region capable of participating successfully in war and politics among Vietnamese speakers." And southern Vietnam was "another Vietnamese speaking surface that began to compete for ascendancy with all the other places inhabited by speakers of the Vietnamese language." Keith Taylor, "Surface Orientations in Vietnam," pp. 966-67.

[5] The Nguyễn dynasty court chronicle claims Nguyễn Phúc Ánh became the Nguyễn state leader in 1778, and took the throne at Saigon in 1780. By 1781, however, he was only a nominal leader under the real power holder, Đỗ Thanh Nhân. Next year, Saigon was occupied by the Tây Sơn. Nguyễn Phúc Ánh was chased by the Tây Sơn army and had no stable power base until 1784, when he left southern Vietnam to take refuge in Bangkok. He came back to Gia Định in that same year with Siamese soldiers, but he was forced to retreat to Bangkok again after his forces, along with the Siamese soldiers, were defeated by the Tây Sơn army. He stayed at Bangkok for three years, until 1788.

[6] *Đại Nam Thực Lục Chính-Biên Đệ Nhất Kỷ* (Primary compilation of the Veritable Records of the first reign of Imperial Vietnam) (hereafter *DNTL1*) (1848. Tokyo: The Institute of Cultural and Linguistic Studies, Keio University, 1968), 3:20a. They included Lê Quang Định, Phạm Đăng Hưng, Trịnh Hoài Đức, Ngô Tòng Châu, and Ngô Nhân Tĩnh.

[7] *DNTL1*, 3:16a. Công Đồng Thử existed during Gia Long's reign (1802-1820) and played almost the same role as Cơ Mật Viện would play later. See *Mục Lục Châu Bản Triều Nguyễn* (Vermilion Record abstracts of the Nguyen Dynasty), vol. 1 (Hue: Hue University, 1960), p. XXXIII.

officials were appointed from 1788,[9] and the head of each commune, or *xã*, was appointed by the regime in the next year.[10] The tax system was organized to insure stable revenue under the command of the civil officials.[11] From 1788, regulations held that half the male population of Gia Định was to be mobilized as soldiers.[12] *Đồn điền*, or military plantations, were formed in 1790 to muster and train not only Vietnamese, but also Chinese settlers and Khmer people.[13] The Gia Định citadel was constructed as a royal residence in the form of Eight Trigrams in 1789; the "royal palace was located in the middle of this citadel"; and the area around this citadel was called "the capital of Gia Định (*Kinh Gia Định*)."[14]

Plate 1. Miniature of the Gia Định citadel in the Saigon National Museum .This very important and valuable miniature shows part of the real structure of the citadel. Credit: the author, 1994.

In fact, during this period Nguyễn Phúc Ánh's defined territory was not restricted to Biên Hòa and the region to its southwest. It included Bình Thuận, Khánh Hòa, and Phú Yên regions to the north, but all of these were more loosely

---

[8] *Đại Nam Chính-Biên Liệt Truyện Sơ Tập* (First collection of the primary compilation of biographies of Imperial Vietnam) (hereafter *LTST*) (1889. Tokyo: Keio Institute of Linguistic Studies, 1962), 11:4b.

[9] *DNTL1*, 3:15b.

[10] Ibid., 4:34b.

[11] Ibid., 4:16.

[12] Ibid., 3:21b.

[13] Ibid., 5:6a; 5:15a.

[14] Ibid., 4:31a-32a.

bound to the central government for one reason or another. The Bình Thuận region was mainly inhabited by the Cham minority at that time, and the other two regions had value only in terms of military operations. Gia Định soldiers hardly had a chance to contact people occupying land beyond the region of Biên Hòa because many of their military operations were not carried out on land, but on the sea. The core region of Nguyễn Phúc Ánh's territory was therefore limited to southern Vietnam. Though Gia Định soldiers occasionally encroached on the regions of Khánh Hòa and Phú Yên, the permanent base of Nguyễn Phúc Ánh's power was concentrated in the region from Biên Hòa to the west.

Nguyễn Phúc Ánh had good reason to restrict his territory to the region of Gia Định: he wished to keep control of its rice. Before he got an opportunity to strike a decisive blow at the Tây Sơn, he never extended his territory beyond Gia Định. Although it was a fertile land, the rice production of Gia Định was not always sufficient to enable Nguyễn Phúc Ánh to feed the population northeast of Biên Hòa. When a suggestion to occupy the region of Bình Thuận was raised in 1792, it was immediately vetoed by Nguyễn Phúc Ánh, for reasons that had to do with the rice supply. According to him, "military operations should be based on the provisions which are located on the enemy side. Now northwards from Bình Thuận the region suffers from annual famines. What will be the benefit in taking it?"[15]

In addition, Gia Định was directly connected with Cambodia and Siam, from which it obtained continuous support as long as diplomatic relations were well maintained. Furthermore, the sea-route around Gia Định provided access to the regions around the Straits of Malacca, where Western military materials were purchased. From 1788, Nguyễn Phúc Ánh started to send missions to this region.[16]

The people of Gia Định were identified as southerners by the Tây Sơn force, too. The southern part of Vietnam was also known as Đồng Nai. A nineteenth-century geographic description reveals the root of the name Đồng Nai: "When Vietnamese reached this region, only herds of deer had lived here before. Thus this land was called Đồng Nai, or the plain [Đồng] of deer [Nai]."[17] Before the name "Gia Định" became popular, the name of Đồng Nai seems to have normally been used in Vietnam and overseas as well[18] to indicate the whole southern area. Gia Định soldiers were usually called Đồng Nai soldiers by Tây Sơn soldiers.[19]

Whether called by the name of Đồng Nai or Gia Định, southern Vietnam from Biên Hòa to Hà Tiên[20] began to be recognized and identified as one polity from the end of the eighteenth century.[21]

---

[15] Ibid., 6:8b.

[16] Ibid., 3:17b.

[17] Nguyễn Thu, *Hoàn Vũ Kỷ Văn* (Compendium on the [Vietnamese] world) (n. d. Hanoi: Viện Hán Nôm A 585) vol. 3.

[18] Southern Vietnam was identified as the land of Đồng Nai by the Chinese court as well. See *Ch'ing Shih Kao Hsiao Chu* (Outline history of the Ch'ing, with annotations) (Taipei: Kuo Shih Kuan, 1990), p. 12103. This identification was adopted by another neighbouring country. To Korean officials during the middle of the nineteenth century, Nguyễn Phúc Ánh was known as "the prince of Dong Nai, or Nong Nai principality" before he beat the Tây Sơn army. Ch'oe Sang Su, *Han'gukkoa Weolnamgoaeui Kwan'gye* (Relations between Korea and Vietnam (Seoul: Hanweolhyeophoe, 1966), p. 150

[19] *DNTL1* 10:37.

[20] From 1707, Hà Tiên became a part of the Nguyễn state due to the submission of Mạc Cửu. But it was treated as a semi-autonomous region ruled by Chinese rulers, the Mạc family. During

2. RELATIONSHIPS AMONG MEMBERS OF THE GIA ĐỊNH REGIME

Power Groups of Gia Định

As far as power holders of each regime are concerned, the leaders of the Gia Định regime showed distinctive characteristics compared to the leaders of Đàng Trong, the Nguyễn state. The Gia Định regime was formed by much the same process as the Đàng Trong regime, that involved the combination of a power group from the north with the local people of the south. However, a critical difference existed between the two regimes in terms of the human element. The core members of the Đàng Trong regime were from Thanh Hóa, the home province of the regime's founder, Nguyễn Hoàng. Information in the official biographies indicates that, outside the court, most leadership positions at the local level were filled with Thanh Hóa men and occasionally royal family members.[22]

In contrast, the Gia Định regime was formed by the initiative of men from Gia Định. If we only rely on the idea of "restoration (*trung hưng*)," which nineteenth-century court historians used to describe the establishment of the Nguyễn dynasty, then this contrast is difficult to imagine. According to historiography based on the concept of "restoration," Nguyễn Phúc Ánh restored the collapsing Nguyễn state, defeated Tây Sơn, unified Vietnam, and established the Nguyễn dynasty. Obviously, the process matches the concept of restoration. But the restoration concept is grounded in the general, and inaccurate, perception that Nguyễn Phúc Ánh was a legitimate or surviving royal prince, who took the throne after the last king of the Nguyễn state was killed by the Tây Sơn, and that he and his subjects mobilized the Gia Định people to fight against the Tây Sơn. This idea encourages historians to regard the formation of the Gia Định regime as being the work of the ruling class, including the royal prince from Huế, and of the mobilized Gia Định people in general. However, this description fails to represent the real nature of the Gia Định regime. To find the reality, we need to investigate how Nguyễn Phúc Ánh recruited his forces.

By the time Nguyễn Phúc Ánh established his permanent base in the region of Gia Định in 1788, his force mainly consisted of four military groups: soldiers who made up the remnants of the Nguyễn state fighting forces, and the three military groups of Đỗ Thanh Nhân, Châu Văn Tiếp, and Võ Tánh. The remnants of the Nguyễn state forces and some of the surviving members of the royal family gave

---

1771-1780, Hà Tiên was completely devastated by Taksin's Siamese troops, and most members of the Mạc family were assassinated. In this situation, a power vacuum developed in Hà Tiên, and as a result, Gia Định forces freely spread their influence into this region. From this time, Hà Tiên was regarded as a part of Gia Định. See *TB*, vol. 6, Mạc Thiên Tử.

[21] Before this region was identified as Gia Định, it was also called Ngũ Dinh, or "five camps." The five camps included three camps (Biên Trấn, Trấn Phiên, and Long Hồ) in the later Gia Định area, ănd another two camps to the north (Bình Khang, and Bình Thuận). Until Nguyễn Phúc Ánh took power in Gia Định, the southern peripheral area had normally been identified as "five camps" which covered former Cham and Khmer regions. The soldiers were called "*ngũ dinh tướng sĩ*," namely "the soldiers of five camps." *TB*, 11:20a. But this name and concept did not last long. As Tây Sơn's power extended to the south covering the region next to Gia Định, both name and concept of the "*ngũ dinh*" disappeared.

[22] Lê Quý Đôn, *Phủ Biên Tạp Lục* (Records of border appeasement) trans. Lê Xuân Giáo (Saigon: Phủ Quốc Vụ Khanh Đặc Trách Văn Hóa, 1973), 3:130. For Thanh Hóa influence on the Nguyễn state, see Nola Cooke, "Regionalism and the Nature of Nguyen Rule in Seventeenth-Century Vietnam," *Journal of Southeast Asian Studies* 29 (1998): 142-157.

their allegiance to Nguyễn Phúc Ánh when his uncle, Duệ Tông (1765-1776), and cousin, Tân Chính Vương (the last king of the Nguyễn state, 1776-1777), were killed in 1777. In truth, however, the size of the above group—soldiers and royals netted from the fallen Nguyễn regime—is hardly worth consideration. By 1776, when Tống Phúc Hợp, the *de facto* leader of the Gia Định five camps, died, the official military system of the Nguyễn state was completely dismantled.

Instead, independent military groups played the most significant roles in fighting against the Tây Sơn, or each other. There were three military groups led by the so-called *"Gia Định Tam Hùng"* (three Gia Định heroes): Đỗ Thanh Nhân, Châu Văn Tiếp, and Võ Tánh. After 1776, Saigon was captured by the Tây Sơn army four times: in 1776, 1777, 1782, and 1783. In the first and second cases, it was recovered by Đỗ Thanh Nhân, in the third by Châu Văn Tiếp, and the permanent recovery of Saigon in 1788 was mainly owing to the contributions of Võ Tánh.

The division of power and resulting fragmentation of the military forces in Gia Định was related to the lack of legitimacy of the last Nguyễn state rulers, Duệ Tông, King Tân Chính, and Nguyễn Phúc Ánh. To understand this matter, it is necessary to remember what happened before Duệ Tông fled to Gia Định in 1775.

Shortly before the death of King Võ in 1765, the question of royal legitimacy had emerged as the main political issue within the Nguyễn state. Because of his eldest son's early death, King Võ chose his ninth son as crown prince. However, this choice proved to be another failure: the new crown prince died soon after. After King Võ died, the succession of the throne was decided by Trương Phúc Loan, a regent of the Nguyễn state at that time. King Võ's sixteenth son was selected by the regent to be king; he was later called Duệ Tông.[23] As a result of this disrupted process of succession, the position of Duệ Tông was quite insecure.

The alternative choice for the succession was King Võ's eldest grandson, the eldest son of King Võ's ninth son, who impressed many powerful people—whether they were Tây Sơn or its opponents—as a likely and legitimate candidate. The Tây Sơn kept trying to declare that they wanted to support the grandson of King Võ, although this alliance was never realized because of the Tây Sơn's larger ambitions and because of the eldest grandson's unwillingness to be supported by Tây Sơn.

Đỗ Thanh Nhân, a leader of one of the powerful independent military groups, also supported the candidacy of the eldest grandson. As soon as Duệ Tông fled to Gia Định, he was pressured to declare the eldest grandson as his successor in 1775, due to strong urging by Đỗ Thanh Nhân, and ultimately he was forced to abdicate his position to the eldest grandson, who became King Tân Chính the following year in Saigon.[24] Đỗ Thanh Nhân was a former Nguyễn state military officer born in Hương Trà near Huế. After he fled to Gia Định, he conscripted three thousand men around Ba Giồng to the north of Mỹ Tho in Định Tường province, and this army, called Đông Sơn, recaptured Saigon in 1776.[25]

At this time, Nguyễn Phúc Ánh was not yet a prominent figure, being only the third son of an unsuccessful second son of King Võ. Nineteenth-century court historians would insist that "Emperor Võ desired [in mind] to make this second son

[23] *TB*, 11:1.

[24] Ibid., 12:1; 12:14.

[25] *LTST*, 27:21b-22a.

succeed him,"[26] but there is no evidence King Võ officially recognized this son as his successor, and so his legitimacy remains questionable. In 1777, the year in which Duệ Tông and King Tân Chính were killed by the Tây Sơn,[27] Nguyễn Phúc Ánh was fifteen years old and did not have any noteworthy patronage.

Đỗ Thanh Nhân chose Nguyễn Phúc Ánh, a fifteen-year-old boy, as his master in 1777. With the support of the Đông Sơn army, Nguyễn Phúc Ánh ascended the throne in 1780. However, it was hardly to be expected that he could draw full loyalty from Đỗ Thanh Nhân, the most powerful commander at that time. Nguyễn Phúc Ánh was only a nominal successor of the Nguyễn state in the eyes of the Đông Sơn leader. Even the court chronicle did not hide Nguyễn Phúc Ánh's humble status at that time.

> The power of life and death came from his [Đỗ Thanh Nhân] hands, the royal budget was cut by Đỗ's decision, but he did not agree to provide anything for royal expenditure [. . .] when emperor [Nguyễn Phúc Ánh] visited his residence, Đỗ did not show any appropriate manner, and his men also arrogantly followed his way.[28]

Nguyễn Phúc Ánh had to seek a way to control the power of Đỗ Thanh Nhân. The result was the assassination of Đỗ Thanh Nhân in 1780.

By killing the general, the prince acquired the power of the Đông Sơn army. The removal of Đỗ Thanh Nhân had an additional meaning: Nguyễn Phúc Ánh was now liberated from the influence of the Huế general and had gained the ability to make direct contact with Gia Định men. Đông Sơn's soldiers, such as Nguyễn Huỳnh Đức, were placed under the direct command of Nguyễn Phúc Ánh. However, he did not succeed in winning full loyalty from the Đông Sơn army. No matter how Nguyễn Phúc Ánh's group tried to justify their assassination of Đỗ Thanh Nhân, they could not persuade all the members of Đông Sơn that the deed had been necessary. Some of them left Nguyễn Phúc Ánh's camp to form individual military groups, and they organized counterattacks against Nguyễn Phúc Ánh.[29] For these southern men, loyalty to their own master was more important than loyalty to the royal family.

Châu Văn Tiếp was another independent military leader based in the highlands of Phú Yên province. As was the case with the Tây Sơn brothers, he used to engage in trade with highland minorities, and indeed was acquainted with the Tây Sơn brothers. When the Tây Sơn brothers' revolt broke out, Châu Văn Tiếp formed his own military faction, largely made up of hill minorities. His main base was in the highlands. By intermittent cooperation with the Tây Sơn to the left, and bargaining with the Nguyễn state officials to the right, he increased his power. His strategic position lay in a region situated between Gia Định and the Tây Sơn, so he was a potential threat to both sides. Because Châu Văn Tiếp had earlier declared his support for the eldest grandson of King Võ, Nguyễn Phúc Ánh had to

---

[26] *TB*, 11:1b.

[27] Ibid., 12:19-20a.

[28] *LTST*, 27:24b-25a.

[29] Ibid., 27:25a.

wait until he took throne in 1780 before he could achieve Châu Văn Tiếp's submission.[30]

Võ Tánh's Kiến Hòa army participated in comparatively later stages of the Gia Định fighting than the armies of Đỗ Thanh Nhân and Châu Văn Tiếp had. Võ Tánh's career prior to his accession as the leader of the army is not clear, nor can we determine the year when he rose to power as a military leader. By looking at his profile recorded in the court biography, one can see that his family had resided in the Gia Định region longer than that of any other meritorious subject, for at least three generations, moving to the Saigon region from Biên Hòa in his grandfather's time. Starting out as a young adventurer, Võ Tánh rose to become a military leader in the Saigon region, and served in Gò Công afterwards.[31]

Unlike Đỗ Thanh Nhân, and Châu Văn Tiếp, Võ Tánh never declared his military loyalty. Until 1788, he had maintained control over a personal territory in the region of Gò Công. After Nguyễn Phúc Ánh left Gia Định in 1784 to move to Siam, Võ Tánh's army was the only force arrayed against the Tây Sơn in Gia Định. In 1787, when Nguyễn Phúc Ánh was preparing to march to Saigon, he suggested cooperation with Võ Tánh. But this upstart prince of Huế did not seem to have any authority in the eyes of Võ Tánh, who was the local military power holder. Nguyễn Phúc Ánh's suggestion was declined. The next year, Võ Tánh decided to participate with Nguyễn Phúc Ánh, but Nguyễn Phúc Ánh still had to show his respect for this military leader. Shortly after Võ Tánh joined Nguyễn Phúc Ánh, Nguyễn Phúc Ánh's sister was given to Võ Tánh as a concubine.[32] We even find reports that, among the members of Võ Tánh's army, a fighter named Võ Văn Lạng refused to bow to Nguyễn Phúc Ánh's wife, saying, "As a general, why do I have to bow to a woman?"[33]

The situation in the Gia Định region at this time was marked by competition among military power groups. Nguyễn Phúc Ánh appears to have been only one amongst a number of local power holders. Besides the military groups led by Đỗ Thanh Nhân, Châu Văn Tiếp, and Võ Tánh, discussed above, there were also Chinese pirates and Western adventurers and missionaries scattered through the region. Many areas isolated by streams and forests were still controlled by local leaders insulated from the broader conflicts. For these leaders, the concept of loyalty to the royal family had not been generally accepted. They could not find any practical motive for giving their allegiance to the royal successor. Nguyễn Phúc Ánh's main role was to manipulate the balance of power within his heterogeneous group. Among the members of different groups, official rank was almost meaningless. For example, the soldier Lê Văn Quân, a former member of Châu Văn Tiếp's group, never accepted the elevated status of Võ Tánh after he was appointed as a commander of the Gia Định regime.[34]

As time passed, the individual armies were reorganized with official titles assigned by the Gia Định regime. For example, the Đông Sơn Army was divided into Left, Right, Front, Rear, and Center Divisions after Đỗ Thanh Nhân was assassinated. But they preserved their characteristic natures as individual armies,

---

[30] Ibid., 6:22b.

[31] Ibid., 6:1.

[32] Ibid., 6:2b.

[33] Ibid., 16:2b.

[34] Ibid., 6:3.

chiefly because of the manner in which soldiers were recruited. Typically, if a person wanted to be an officer in the Gia Định force, he would collect volunteers. He then visited any unit of the Gia Định force until he had struck a deal with the commander of this unit and been assigned a proper position according to his ability, or according to the number of men he brought in. If he was promoted, this usually took place within the division to which he belonged. If he achieved a higher position, he could then move to another division, accompanied by his main staff members and soldiers.

How did a commander increase the number of his own men, then? The most popular way was to recruit his own soldiers directly. He could recruit soldiers by himself, or would accept other volunteers who might visit him, as he had done when he wanted to be an officer. Another way was to muster captives—stray Tây Sơn fighters, minorities, and any deserters who had lost their masters—as soldiers. Under the 1790 regulations of the Gia Định regime, recruitment by individual commanders was promoted. Whoever recruited the soldiers had exclusive right to command them.[35]

The presence of Tây Sơn soldiers who had surrendered and shown themselves willing to join the Gia Định forces was an interesting feature of this army, one that certainly increased its heterogeneity. As long as an enemy showed sincere readiness to submit to the Gia Định forces, he was accepted. If it could be proved that any Tây Sơn captive had been treated arbitrarily, the executioner was to be decapitated in turn.[36] Discrimination against the Tây Sơn fighters who surrendered was rare. Even the ex-commanders of the Tây Sơn were permitted to maintain their former force. Lê Chất, for example, was an ex-commander of the Tây Sơn, but after joining the Gia Định he was still surrounded by his own men.[37] Afterwards, he was promoted to the highest rank of general, and eventually became the governor-general of northern Vietnam.

The Relationship between Nguyễn Phúc Ánh and His Men

Nguyễn Phúc Ánh's soldiers were mainly culled and mobilized from other independent groups, and his own men, those who had fought with him from the beginning, also consisted of figures from various backgrounds. It appears that Nguyễn Phúc Ánh provided opportunities for advancement to men of talent, regardless of their backgrounds. It was not surprising to see a Khmer servant become a meritorious general, as was the case with Nguyễn Văn Tồn. A fisherman could be made a duke for his contribution as a messenger.[38] The king's favorite general, Lê Văn Duyệt, was a eunuch who had been in charge of the royal household before he had an opportunity to display his military talent. A poor boy, Nguyễn Văn Trương, who had once worked tending buffaloes, switched allegiance from the Tây Sơn brothers to Nguyễn Phúc Ánh and eventually rose to become governor of Gia Định.[39]

---

[35] *DNTL1*, 5:11b-12a.

[36] Ibid., 6:27b.

[37] *LTST*, 6:11a.

[38] Nguyễn Văn Mai, *Việt Nam Phong Sử* (A history of the Vietnamese Road) (n.d. Hanoi: Viện Hán Nôm AB 320), p. 76.

[39] *LTST*, 8:1.

While he was engaged in dealing with the different power groups, Nguyễn Phúc Ánh had also to adapt himself to the habits of the Gia Định men. As he demonstrated his leadership, he was able to attract more and more men to his own side. These men were unlike those seen before in the Huế court. As the nineteenth-century court historians pointed out, "there was not a general [mobilized in Gia Định] who knew how to behave properly in front of the emperor [Nguyễn Phúc Ánh]."[40] Among others, Nguyễn Phúc Ánh had to endure Nguyễn Văn Thành, who spent all the money reserved for purchasing military provisions to pay off gambling debts for Gia Định soldiers in Siam.[41] Nguyễn Phúc Ánh was also unable to correct the habits of Lê Văn Duyệt, who often appeared late for court audience because he was watching cockfighting.[42] Until Nguyễn Phúc Ánh intervened, one Gia Định general, Tống Việt Phúc, often openly insulted Pigneau de Béhaine, the local French missionary bishop and close advisor of Nguyễn Phúc Ánh, even though the general knew very well that Pigneau had already been appointed by Nguyễn Phúc Ánh as teacher of the crown prince, Cảnh.[43] Ignorance of or lack of respect for royal authority was found at the village level as well. Once, when Nguyễn Phúc Ánh and his followers visited a village to find food and to hide themselves, the villagers responded with fear rather than assistance. To win their support, Nguyễn Phúc Ánh had to call for the leader of this region, "ông Bõ" (adopted father) to speak with them.[44]

Regarding the flexible, comparatively informal relationship between Nguyễn Phúc Ánh and his men, the court chronicle provides us with another example that almost certainly would not have taken place in a more conventional royal court. In 1803, one year after Nguyễn Phúc Ánh established the new dynasty, he ordered the southern soldiers to take help construct the citadel of the new capital in Huế. In response to this order, his favorite general, Lê Văn Duyệt, expressed strong dissatisfaction:

> When you were in Gia Định, you promised the soldiers to let them return home and take a rest as soon as we overcame the capital. Now we have overcome not only the capital but also the northern region. But they still have to serve in more remote military forts, or have to work in constructing the citadel of the capital [. . .] then, how will you expect the Gia Định people to trust the court in the future?[45]

In response to this complaint, the emperor attempted to reason patiently with his general. But the general firmly repeated his request for the emperor to withdraw the order. The emperor responded with more attempts at persuasion.[46] It is not recorded whether Lê Văn Duyệt was at last convinced by his emperor, but one fact is clear: the disagreement did not adversely affect the relationship between the

---

[40] Ibid., 8:28b.

[41] *LTST*, 21:4.

[42] Huỳnh Minh, *Gia Định Xưa và Nay* (Gia Dinh, Past and Present) (Saigon, 1973), p. 85.

[43] *LTST*, 13:8.

[44] Huỳnh Minh, *Vĩnh Long Xưa và Nay* (Vinh Long, past and present) (Saigon, 1967), pp. 227-28.

[45] *LTST*, 22:10b.

[46] *LTST*, 22:11a.

two at all. This incident reflects the nature of the relationship between Nguyễn Phúc Ánh and his men during the Gia Định regime.

On the whole, the relationship between Nguyễn Phúc Ánh and his men, including those of formerly independent groups, was not as strictly hierarchical as normal relationships between a king and his subjects. The relationship was based on individual loyalty to Nguyễn Phúc Ánh as a military leader in Gia Định, rather than on official loyalty to a former royal prince of the Nguyễn state.

The Attitude towards Christians

In the context of the political relationships of the Gia Định regime, the role of Christianity must also be examined. I will begin by looking at an earlier period, when Gia Định first appeared in the histories of Vietnam. When Vietnamese officials began to take control of the region of Gia Định at the end of the seventeenth century, one of the most troubling phenomena for them was the rapid spread of Christianity in that area. In 1698, the same year that *phủ* Gia Định was established, an action to capture Christians was ordered. In order to rid the country of Western missionaries, all Westerners in the region of Gia Định were to be expelled from Vietnam.[47] Clearly, these events indicate that Christianity was already quite popular in Gia Định before the *phủ* Gia Định was formed. Despite the Nguyễn state's occasional persecutions, however, Christianity continued to spread among the Gia Định population during the eighteenth century. Because i t was a peripheral region of the Nguyễn state, Gia Định became the final destination for many Christians. Especially during the persecution of the 1750s, Gia Định received a large number of Christian refugees who were fleeing from central Vietnam.[48]

The Christian population of Gia Định contributed significantly to the character of the Gia Định regime, which showed itself ready to compromise with and tolerate the Christian missionaries. No doubt, this attitude was also due to the cooperation between Nguyễn Phúc Ánh and Pigneau de Béhaine, a missionary with the Société des Missions Étrangères. From Pigneau, Nguyễn Phúc Ánh hoped to receive material support, manpower, and military knowledge, whereas Pigneau hoped to win the emperor's patronage for his missionary enterprise in Vietnam.

Nonetheless, the two parties were not always ready to grant each other's wishes or even to work out a compromise. Most seriously, they disagreed over matters concerning the traditional Vietnamese ceremonies for respected objects, ceremonies that involved ancestor worship. One example helps illustrate the dilemma. Prince Cảnh, who was Nguyễn Phúc Ánh's eldest son, left for France in 1783, accompanied by Pigneau, and returned to Saigon in 1789, when he was ten years old. During this six years' absence, he had been fully under the influence of Pigneau. From the point of view of Pigneau, this was an excellent opportunity to produce a future Christian king in Vietnam. On his return to Vietnam, Prince Cảnh

---

[47] *TB,* 7:15b.

[48] Nguyễn Văn Hầu, "Sự Thôn Thuộc và Khai Thác Đất Tầm Phong Long—Chặng Cuối Cùng của Cuộc Nam Tiến," (The claiming and opening of Tam Phong Long region—The final stage of southward movement) *Tập San Sử Địa* 19-20 (1970): 13-14.

refused to follow his father's example and bow to their ancestors in the royal shrine. Nguyễn Phúc Ánh and his subjects were in a panic.[49]

How had the alliance between the French missionary and Vietnamese monarch first begun? Nguyễn Phúc Ánh was thirteen years old when he escaped Huế in 1775. It was not easy for the young prince to gain a systematic Confucian education under such circumstances. He was seventeen years old when he met the bishop Pigneau for the first time. We can assume that Pigneau saw the possibility of planting Christian values in this king. In 1779, Pigneau succeeded in establishing a missionary college in the region of Biên Hòa. Before 1782, Nguyễn Phúc Ánh occasionally attended the bishop's sermons with his subjects while he was in Saigon.[50] In return for the king's tolerance and friendship, Pigneau contributed his military knowledge to Nguyễn Phúc Ánh's party. Their relationship grew, and when it came time for Pigneau to set out on his journey to France, Nguyễn Phúc Ánh entrusted his four-year-old eldest son to the bishop as "hostage (*chất*)."[51]

To better understand the context of this event, one must know that civil officials educated in Confucianism[52] had started to play an active role in the Gia Định regime before Pigneau returned from Saigon with the prince, actively seeking to fill the vacancy created by the bishop's departure. In fact, the growing power of the Gia Định Confucian officials had something to do with the six-year absence of Pigneau. After Pigneau returned to Gia Định in 1789, and news of Prince Cảnh's behavior spread, a conflict began behind the scenes. Until his death in 1799, Pigneau stayed close to Prince Cảnh. He was always with the prince as a

---

[49] *Đại Nam Thực Lục Chính-Biên Đệ Nhị Kỷ* (Primary compilation of the Veritable Records of the second reign of Imperial Vietnam) (hereafter *DNTL2*) (1861. Tokyo: Keio Institute of Linguistic Studies, 1963), 196:14a.

[50] Trương Bá Cần, *Công Giáo Đàng Trong: Thời Giám Mục Pigneau (1771-1799)* (Catholicism of Dang Trong: The period of Pigneau de Béhaine) (Ho Chi Minh City: Tủ Sách Đại Kết, 1992), pp. 49-50.

[51] From Nguyễn Phúc Ánh's point of view, his son was a hostage. *DNTL1*, 2:5a.

[52] I do not favor this English vocabulary, but I will use this word because I do not have an appropriate alternative. As with "Christianity" (the religion of Jesus Christ), two English words, Buddhism and Confucianism, were invented using the names of Buddha and Confucius. The name "Buddhism" matches with reality, at least in Northeast Asian countries, where Buddhism is understood as the religion or instructions of Buddha. However, the term "Confucianism" is quite problematic. It carries the strong implication that Confucianism is the ideas of Confucius (K'ung Tzu). Chinese has a corresponding term, "*k'ung chiao*" (K'ung Tzu's instruction). But the term and the consequent meaning of the *k'ung chao* have hardly been used in the neighboring countries that share Chinese letters and "Confucianism." The so-called "Confucianism" has been called *nho giáo* in Vietnam, *yu gyo* in Korea, and *ju kyo* in Japan. These are all different pronunciations of *ru chiao* in the Chinese vocabulary, which has the wider meaning of "the instructions of people who have followed the idea which started from Confucius and Mencius." According to this concept, the people who have followed the idea are not necessarily Chinese. They could be Japanese, Korean, or Vietnamese people who shared the universal ideas of the Northeast Asian classical world. In the case of Vietnam, to use the term "*nho sĩ*" (the scholarly, or educated groups oriented towards *nho giáo*) would be more accurate than using the term "Confucians," "Confucian scholars," or just "scholars" to indicate the wide group of people who learned the value of *nho giáo*. In this book, the terms "Confucianism," and "*nho giáo*," or "Confucians" and "*nho sĩ*" will be used interchangeably, but with certain conditions. For example, I will try to avoid using this problematic term, "Confucianism" or "Confucians" as much as possible. I will also call those persons educated (by *nho giáo* learning) at the local level *nho sĩ* or *sĩ*.

consultant, and Nguyễn Phúc Ánh instructed Cảnh to respect Pigneau as teacher.[53] At the same time, however, Cảnh was being educated by a group of Gia Định Confucian scholars. The key personality in this group was Ngô Tòng Châu, one of the disciples of Võ Trương Toản.[54] He achieved such success that it was reported the Christian missionaries were greatly disappointed with Prince Cảnh after several years.[55]

The relationship between Christian missionaries and Confucian officials of the Gia Định regime was sometimes hostile and tense. In his discussion of Gia Định Confucianism, Cao Tự Thanh pursues this idea,[56] and argues that the king himself, Nguyễn Phúc Ánh, adopted an anti-Christian position. As evidence, he introduces Gia Long's edict called *"hương đường điều lệ,"* promulgated in 1804 to regulate the lives of northern Vietnamese village residents, which includes a regulation on Christianity.[57] As Cao Tự Thanh suggests, it is highly possible that tension existed between Confucian officials and French missionaries during the Gia Định regime.

Despite this tension and Pigneau's influence over the king's eldest son, Nguyễn Phúc Ánh did not take action against Christians. The *"hương đường điều lệ"* is cited by Cao Tự Thanh to show evidence of Gia Long's anti-Christian stance, but if the edict is carefully examined this proves not to be the case. This edict was meant to regulate only the construction and repair of Christian churches in the former Trịnh family territory, or Bắc Hà. Moreover, it also included regulations on other religious traditions, such as Buddhism, Taoism, and sorcery. The regulation on Christian churches was only one element in a series of regulations to restore religious practice.[58]

The general trend for Confucians and Christians during the Gia Định regime was to try to compromise with each other. Though he was not successful, Pigneau appealed to the Vatican, asking that the doctrine forbidding ancestor worship should be reconsidered.[59] In deference to the Christian missionaries, students in the Christian college were exempted from corvée and military service by the Gia Định regime.[60] The freedom of missionary activities was still guaranteed.

Nguyễn Phúc Ánh had to remain flexible towards Christians, as he needed to mobilize all available manpower during the time of war. The Tây Sơn leaders were in the same situation, but they failed to secure Christian support. As a result, Nguyễn Phúc Ánh's Gia Định troops were regarded as akin to crusaders by local Christians. This situation proved most significant when Gia Định troops marched to the north. If a region was occupied by the soldiers of Nguyễn Phúc Ánh along with Christian missionaries, they were enthusiastically welcomed by the local

---

[53] *DNTL1*, 11:16a.

[54] *LTST*, 6:18a.

[55] See Georges Taboulet, *La geste Française en Indochine: histoire par les textes de la France en Indochine des origines à 1914* (Paris: Librairie D'Amérique et D'Orient, Adrien-Maisonneuve, 1955) Tome 1, p. 225.

[56] Cao Tự Thanh, *Nho Giáo ở Gia Định*, p. 81.

[57] Ibid., p. 89.

[58] See *DNTL1*, 23:7b-11a.

[59] Taboulet, *La geste Française en Indochine*, p. 229.

[60] Trương Bá Cần, *Công Giáo Đàng Trong*, p. 126.

Christians. Local Christians figured prominently as leaders of insurrections against the Tây Sơn government whenever Gia Định forces approached their region.[61]

In 1799, Pigneau died of disease in Qui Nhân, and was followed by his erstwhile disciple, Prince Cảnh, two years later. As a consequence, the Christians' opportunity to proselytize among the power holders of the Gia Định regime was greatly reduced by the end of the eighteenth century. But the tolerant policy of Nguyễn Phúc Ánh towards Christians in Gia Định lasted. Christianity continued to spread in Gia Định into the next century under the protection of Nguyễn Phúc Ánh and his men.

3. ETHNIC GROUPS

Glancing at the biography of Gia Long's subjects, we quickly notice the heterogeneity of Nguyễn Phúc Ánh's forces in terms of their nationalities or racial origins. Besides French, Spaniards, British, Lao and Chinese soldiers, Siamese troops, Khmer, Malays, and Chams participated in Nguyễn Phúc Ánh's military operations. Chinese pirates and hill minorities were also members of his forces. All available manpower, it seems, was gathered together into his military by that time. In the history of pre-nineteenth century Vietnam, we cannot find a more ethnically heterogeneous group than that of Nguyễn Phúc Ánh.

The Tây Sơn army was relatively more homogenous, although this was not because the Tây Sơn wished to keep independent of foreign powers. They were also eager to establish an alliance with Siam,[62] and they sent at least one mission to China asking for military support.[63] Chinese pirates and members of the Heaven and Earth Society were to be found in the Tây Sơn's forces,[64] and the Chams of the Bình Định region made some of the best Tây Sơn troops.[65] The difference was that the Gia Định regime secured and extended this plurality, whereas the Tây Sơn failed to do so.

The Gia Định regime maintained its plurality through tolerance of different ethnic groups. Among them, the roles of two main ethnic groups will be examined here: that of the Khmer people and the Chinese settlers. In the history of southern Vietnam, these two ethnic groups were frequently located at the center of important issues. Dealing with these groups would prove to be one of the most challenging tasks facing the Nguyễn dynasty during the next century. To understand the situation in southern Vietnam during the nineteenth century, it is necessary to understand the earlier attitude of the Gia Định regime towards these two ethnic groups.

Khmer People

The basic policy of the Gia Định regime toward the Khmer people guaranteed the Khmer self-government and coexistence. This was a consistent attitude of the

---

[61] *LTST*, 30:49b-50a.

[62] *DNTL1*, 7: 21b.

[63] *LTST*, 30:52b.

[64] Ibid., 30:41b.

[65] Cham vanguards with Chinese hairstyles were described as the most horrible Tây Sơn forces in the eyes of Gia Định soldiers. See *LTST*, 30:3a.

Gia Định regime in relation to different ethnic groups, drastically different from the Nguyễn assimilation policy, which was put into effect towards the end of the Nguyễn reign.

As in other regions dominated by the Vietnamese, a Vietnamese frontier administrative unit called *phủ* was formed in the regions of the Khmer, in Trà Vinh and Sóc Trăng in 1789.[66] But the position as leader or head of this unit was allocated to a Khmer leader. From 1790, *đồn điền*, or military plantations, were opened throughout southern Vietnam. Khmer people were organized into the *đồn điền*, also, from 1791,[67] but their recruits were sent to ethnically distinct military plantations. The main policy of the Gia Định regime was to separate each ethnic group, to allow them to maintain their autonomy, and to protect certain of their rights. For example, in 1791, when Nguyễn Phúc Ánh heard that Vietnamese had encroached on the regions of Trà Vinh and Sóc Trăng and had cleared land there for their own use, he commanded all Vietnamese to cease encroaching on Khmer land and to return all claimed land to the Khmer people.[68]

The primary reason for this policy was a desire not to provoke the Khmer people, but there was another reason as well. It was the idea of Nguyễn Phúc Ánh, that "the Vietnamese and the barbarians must have clear borders," or "*hán di hữu hạn.*"[69] This was not an expression of discrimination in Gia Định, but the expression of his idea that Vietnamese and other ethnic groups had to live separately. The concept of assimilation did not exist for him; the Vietnamese could not enter the regions of other ethnic groups. Later in his reign, in 1815, Vietnamese who had lived in Cambodian territory were ordered to come back because "they would possibly make trouble with Cambodians in the future."[70] Just a few years later, in 1818, Chinese, Khmer, and Malays[71] were recruited to live and clear land around

---

[66] *DNTL1*, 4:8; 4:13a.

[67] See *DNTL1*, 5:15a. The origin of Khmer military plantations was the *đồn Xiêm Binh* that was formed in 1787. In this year, Nguyễn Phúc Ánh came back from Siam to attack Saigon. On the way to Saigon, he mobilized Khmer people in the region of Trà Vinh by the organization of *đồn Xiêm Binh*, and the organization was entrusted to a Khmer general, Nguyễn Văn Tồn. *DNTL1*, 3:6b. The name itself, *đồn Xiêm Binh*, meant "the military post of Siamese soldiers." There is a possibility that the leaders of Gia Định regime wanted to forge Siamese soldiers. Previously, Nguyễn Phúc Ánh fled to Siam in 1784 and came back to Gia Định with three hundred vessels and twenty thousand Siamese soldiers. *DNTL1*, 2:12a. But the Siamese troops were defeated by the Tây Sơn army, and Nguyễn Phúc Ánh had to flee to Bangkok again in 1785. Two years later, Nguyễn Phúc Ánh left Bangkok and returned to Gia Định without Siamese troops. He might have thought that the existence of Siamese troops would be threatening, psychologically at least, to the Tây Sơn army.

[68] *DNTL1*, 5:23.

[69] Ibid., 5:23b.

[70] Ibid., 51:13a.

[71] In nineteenth-century documents, there was a special vocabulary to refer to Malays. It was "*Đồ Bà.*" Certainly, this Chinese word, *Đồ Bà* (*She Po* in Chinese pronunciation) was commonly used by the people of China and Vietnam to indicate Java. See Phan Huy Chú, *Hải Trình Chí Lược* (*Récit sommaire d'un voyage en mer*) (1833), trans. and ed. Phan Huy Lê, Claudine Salmon, and Tạ Trọng Hiệp (Paris: Cahier d'Archipel 25, 1994), p. 130. In southern Vietnam, however, *Đồ Bà* had other meanings. First of all, they were Malays who lived in southern Vietnam, or in Cambodia. Second, *Đồ Bà* was broadly used to indicate Malays. For example, "*Đồ Bà* pirates" were Malay pirates whom Vietnamese occasionally encountered in the coastal area of southern Vietnam, as well as on the maritime route to the region of the Straits of Malacca during the nineteenth century. According to a report from Định Tường province in 1837, "Nguyễn Văn

Châu Đốc. Nguyễn Phúc Ánh (now named emperor Gia Long) warned his officials in charge of this business to "prevent my people from intervening in their lives."[72] This was a central idea of Nguyễn Phúc Ánh's, to which he adhered throughout his reign, and the tradition based on this idea, enabling the relatively peaceful coexistence of ethnic groups, lasted in the land of Gia Định. Nguyễn Phúc Ánh's attitude towards the Khmer people caused his own people to perceive him as an honorable Vietnamese monarch favored by the Khmers. This general belief grew to become a legend, according to which a Khmer woman's ghost occasionally appeared in Nguyễn Phúc Ánh's dream to help him to fight the Tây Sơn (this legend concerns Núi Bà Đen [Black Lady Mountain] in the present Tây Ninh province).[73] Among the Nguyễn kings, to my knowledge, Nguyễn Phúc Ánh was the only one who ever figured in a legend that showed him receiving favors from and being favored by representatives of another ethnic group.

Because of its stable relationship with the Khmer people, the Gia Định regime was able to utilize Khmer manpower effectively. The soldiers of đồn Xiêm Binh constituted an important unit of the Gia Định force. The relationship not only helped the Gia Định regime mobilize human resources, but also provided them with a significant supply of material resources. Timber for constructing vessels was brought from the Khmer areas, such as Đồng Môn, Quang Hóa, and Ba Can in the northern part of southern Vietnam, near Saigon.[74] The stable tax income from the Khmer regions also provided an important revenue source to the Gia Định regime. By achieving the right of tax collection in Sóc Trăng, the regime could secure a long-lasting financial resource; Sóc Trăng was a substantial rice and salt supplier to Cambodia through water transport and had become one of the international trade points of Cambodia by the end of the eighteenth century.[75] In addition, Cambodia continually provided elephants.[76]

Chinese

a) Separation of the Chinese from the Tây Sơn

It was with regard to the Chinese that the Gia Định and Tây Sơn regimes most clearly showed differing attitudes. Despite the Tây Sơn's initial success in securing the cooperation of Chinese settlers, the majority of Chinese settlers eventually sided with the Gia Định force. The massacre of 1782 is occasionally cited as the reason Chinese settlers split from the Tây Sơn. Over ten thousand Chinese, soldiers, civilians, and merchants of Gia Định were killed by Tây Sơn in that

---

Quyền's wife, Huỳnh Thị Thiếp, who lives in Minh Đức village of Kiến Hòa district was attacked by Đồ Bà pirates [*Đồ Bà hải phỉ*] when she left for a trade trip by ship in 1832." Châu Bản Triều Nguyễn (Vermilion Records of the Nguyen dynasty) (ANU Library, microfilm), lunar 29th, July, 1837.

[72] *DNTL1*, 58:10a.

[73] Huỳnh Minh, *Tây Ninh Xưa và Nay* (Tay Ninh, past and present) (Saigon, 1972), p. 46.

[74] *DNTL1*, 3:21a; 5:21b.

[75] *Binh Chế Biểu Sớ* (Memorials and commentaries on the military system) (n.d. Hanoi: Viện Hán Nôm A 1543), p. 71.

[76] *DNTL1*, 8:28b.

action.[77] However, the exact reason for this massacre is not clearly known. Fujiwara Riichiro\ has suggested that the attack had to do with Chinese participation in the Nguyễn Army, and the Tây Sơn's tendency toward nationalism.[78] Vietnamese scholars have also suggested that Chinese exploitation of the Vietnamese had something to do with the division.[79]

I would argue, however, that a more basic reason for Tây Sơn antipathy to Chinese settlers was a result of the Chinese settlers' own operations against the Tây Sơn, especially in Saigon.

To discover the root of Tây Sơn antipathy to Chinese settlers, we need to pay attention to Lý Tài, a Chinese adventurer of this time. Lý Tài was one of the figures who triggered the furious hostility of Tây Sơn against the Chinese in Vietnam. His reason for participating in the Tây Sơn army is not known, but he played a prominent military role in the first stage of the Tây Sơn rebellion. By the time the northern Trịnh army had advanced as far as the Hải Vân Pass, in 1775, two-thirds of Tây Sơn soldiers were commanded by Lý Tài and his Chinese colleague, Tập Định.[80] When, soon after, Tập Định was removed from his position by the eldest of the Tây Sơn's brothers, Lý Tài became the sole leader of the Tây Sơn's Chinese army, called Hòa Nghĩa.

However, perhaps because of his friend Tập Định's removal and his own ambitions, Lý Tài soon left the Tây Sơn party. In 1775, he surrendered to a Nguyễn state general, Tống Phúc Hợp. In the next year, he was introduced to the Nguyễn king Duệ Tông at Saigon. But he encountered opposition from one of Duệ Tông's generals, Đỗ Thanh Nhân. In the eyes of Đỗ Thanh Nhân, a confident man who had begun his career as a genuine Huế military officer, Lý Tài—the former merchant, former Tây Sơn leader, and Chinese—was "like a dog or pig."[81] Before long, Lý Tài left Duệ Tông's camp for the region of Biên Hòa with his Hòa Nghĩa army, and formed another independent military group in the region, claiming that he would support King Võ's eldest grandson.

At the same time, a series of battles started between the Đông Sơn army (of Đỗ Thanh Nhân) and the Hòa Nghĩa army. According to Trịnh Hoài Đức, "he [Lý Tài] additionally recruited *đường nhân*, or Chinese settlers of this region, so the strength of his army became over 8,000 [. . .] again, he collected *minh hương* and *thanh hà* Chinese."[82] This Chinese army was, similar to that of the Manchus, divided into four flag divisions: yellow, red, blue, and white.[83] When the eldest grandson of King Võ entered Saigon in the same year, he was escorted by this Hòa Nghĩa army. When the eldest grandson of King Võ took the throne, Lý Tài became a holder of power. Shortly after, Đỗ Thanh Nhân's Đông Sơn army, which included the king Duệ Tông as well as Nguyễn Phúc Ánh, was defeated by Lý Tài's Hòa Nghĩa army and retreated to Định Tường.

---

[77] Ibid., 1:17a.

[78] Fujiwara Riichiro\, "Vietnamese Dynasties' Policies Toward Chinese Immigrants," *Acta Asiatica* 18 (1970): 60.

[79] Huỳnh Minh, *Gia Định Xưa và Nay*, p. 182.

[80] *LTST*, 30:6.

[81] Ibid., 27:22b.

[82] Trịnh Hoài Đức, *Gia Định Thành Thông Chí*, 5:29. For the terms of *đường nhân, minh hương,* and *thanh hà*, see my discussion of "Terms for Chinese settlers," below.

[83] Ibid.

The next year, in 1777, the second Tây Sơn campaign against Gia Định was launched. Lý Tài's Chinese army was the main force the Tây Sơn army encountered in the region of Saigon. Unlike other power groups in Gia Định at that time, which usually maintained bases in rural areas, Lý Tài's military group was based in urban areas where Chinese settlers were concentrated. By using this location, he would have expected to achieve material Chinese support, such as a supply of manpower and financial assistance. Also, the region being protected by this army was densely populated by Chinese settlers, and later took on the name Chợ Lớn.[84] The Hòa Nghĩa army was defeated by the Tây Sơn in this year, and Lý Tài was subsequently killed by the Đông Sơn army.[85]

The dismantled Hòa Nghĩa army was reorganized under the command of Nguyễn Phúc Ánh. As the Đông Sơn and Hòa Nghĩa armies had previously been in conflict, it would seem this process of assimilation was somewhat unusual. It was made possible when Nguyễn Phúc Ánh had the proud general Đỗ Thanh Nhân murdered in 1781. The removal of Đỗ Thanh Nhân, an anti-Chinese leader, opened a way for Chinese settlers to take part in Nguyễn Phúc Ánh's party. The new Hòa Nghĩa army was used to fight the Tây Sơn, when their third expedition was launched in 1782.[86] Here, the Tây Sơn again met Chinese troops as a main force following the second expedition to Gia Định. Both in 1777 and 1782, I assume the Chinese community in Saigon contributed to the Hòa Nghĩa army in many forms.

These events form the background to the massacre of 1782. Angered by the death of one of his close friends in a battle around Saigon that had been initiated by the Chinese Hòa Nghĩa army, Nguyễn Văn Nhạc, one of the Tây Sơn brothers, decided to clean out Chinese settlers from his territory in 1782. It did not matter to him whether the Hòa Nghĩa soldiers had been under the command of Lý Tài or of Nguyễn Phúc Ánh; all that mattered was the Hòa Nghĩa members were Chinese. It is very likely that the Tây Sơn brothers believed the Hòa Nghĩa soldiers had been supported by the Chinese settlers in Saigon. I believe that Nguyễn Văn Nhạc's massacre took place because he wished to wipe out the Chinese community of Saigon that had been the most serious obstacle to his capture of this city. In reality, the 1782 massacre was a decisive event for the Chinese settlers and caused those who escaped to stand resolutely against the Tây Sơn.

---

[84] According to Nguyễn Thế Anh, it was from 1813 that this place began to be called Chợ Lớn, "Big Market." Nguyễn Thế Anh, *Kinh Tế và Xã Hội Việt Nam Dưới Các Vua Triều Nguyễn* (Vietnam's economy and society under kings of the Nguyen dynasty) (Saigon: Lửa Thiêng 1971), p. 47. In most nineteenth-century Vietnamese documents, this place is referred to as "Saigon." Thus, any "Saigon" in my writing indicates the region around present Chợ Lớn. Saigon was extended to the east after Nguyễn Phúc Ánh recovered it in 1788. The Gia Định citadel constructed in 1789 was at the east side of old Saigon. It was the region called Bến Nghé, the region of the center of present Ho Chi Minh City. By the end of the eighteenth century, Sài Gòn and Bến Nghé were regarded as separate regions. In one of Nguyễn Phúc Ánh's letters to French missionaries in 1788, the two regions were mentioned separately: "I defeated Tây Sơn, and recovered Ba giồng, Sài gòn, Bến nghé, Đồng nai, Bà rịa." Tạ Chí Đại Trường, "Những Bức Thư Chữ Nôm của Nguyễn Ánh Do Giáo Sư Cadière Sưu Tập" (Chu Nom letters of Nguyen Phuc Anh collected by Father Cadiere), *Tập San Sử Địa* 11 (1968): 121.

[85] *LTST*, 27:23a.

[86] *DNTL1*, 1:17a.

b) Terms for Chinese settlers

As terms to indicate Chinese settlers in Vietnam, *"đường nhân"* (T'ang people), *"thanh nhân"* (Ch'ing people), *"khách nhân"* (visiting people), *"thanh thương"* (Ch'ing merchants), and *"minh hương xã nhân"* (*minh hương* society members) were used variously during the nineteenth century. The Chinese maintained their own associations (*bang*, and *xã*[87]) in Vietnam, and their own identity as well. The *khách nhân* and the *thanh nhân* were Chinese settlers who maintained their own outlook. The phrase *thanh nhân* was most commonly used to indicate the Chinese immigrants who settled in Vietnam during the eighteenth and nineteenth centuries.[88] *Đường nhân* was a broader term indicating, not necessarily Chinese immigrants, but anyone of Chinese identity.[89] Generally, this was the phrase the Vietnamese used when referring to the Chinese. Among these kinds of Chinese, *minh hương* and *thanh nhân* were the two groups of Chinese who played important roles in Vietnamese history from the end of the eighteenth century.

c) Minh Hương: Ming Loyalist Chinese Refugees

When in 1679 the Nguyễn state provided three thousand Ming Chinese refugees with Gia Định land, it proved to be a watershed in the history of Chinese immigrants and the Gia Định region. From this time, the center of Chinese residence moved to Saigon from Hội An. After the Ming Chinese refugees settled in the Gia Định region, especially in Mỹ Tho and Biên Hòa, these two regions were developed as commercial centers in which "Chinese, Westerners, Japanese, and Malay traders were bustling."[90] Throughout the eighteenth century, the Chinese settlers gradually moved up to the Saigon river basin until they found a permanent place to settle in Saigon.

In fact, it was the Chinese who played the most important role as a cultural vanguard spreading Northeast Asian culture, or diluting the Khmer influence, in the region of Gia Định. No doubt there were Vietnamese who had permeated this region before the Chinese refugees arrived in Gia Định in 1679,[91] but Vietnamese

---

[87] Though the word *xã* is used in Vietnam usually for an administrative unit, its popular meaning in other Classic Chinese culture countries is "society," or "associations." This split of usage probably resulted in confusion in Vietnam. *Minh hương xã* in Gia Định mainly indicated the association of *minh hương*, similar to the *bang* of other Chinese, whereas it normally indicated a commune or residential area in other regions such as Hội An. See Huỳnh Minh, *Bạc Liêu Xưa và Nay* (Bac Lieu, past and present) (Saigon, 1966), p. 138.

[88] Woodside identifies this term as meaning "Chinese people in China." Woodside, *Vietnam and the Chinese Model*, p. 19. In rare cases, especially in the descriptions of the eighteenth century, his definition is right. For example, in a description of 1790, the court chronicle *Thực Lục* says "*thanh nhân* mobilized Lưỡng Quảng [Quảng Đông (Kuang Tung) and Quảng Tây (Kuang Hsi)] soldiers to attack Tây Sơn." *DNTL1*, 5:2a. In this case the *thanh nhân* was evidently the "Chinese people in China." But it is only one of several special cases. Common usage of *thanh nhân* indicated Chinese settlers in Vietnam. See also my discussion on these Chinese settlers in chapter two.

[89] See Ts'ai T'ing Lan, *Hải Nam Tạp Trứ* (Various records of the land beyond the southern ocean) (1836. Hanoi: Viện Hán Nôm HVv 80), p. 7.

[90] *TB*, 5:22b.

[91] In 1833, Nguyễn Bảo claimed that in 1647 the Nguyễn state found Vietnamese peasants had already immigrated and lived in the region of Biên Hòa. Nguyễn Bảo, *Sử Cục Loại Biên* (Editions from the history bureau) (1833. Hanoi: Viện Hán Nôm A 9), 8:4. Nguyễn Đình Đầu shows

settlement was characterized by the long-term and continuous immigration of small groups from the central region, while Chinese immigration involved larger groups and proved to be more potent in transforming the culture and economy of the region from typically Khmer to more typically Chinese and, ultimately, Vietnamese. As the Huế court observed, when the Ming refugees first arrived in Vietnam, the fertile land around Saigon was still "the territory of Cambodia."[92]

Considering the fact that the number of registered Vietnamese families had grown to over forty thousand when the *phủ* Gia Định was formed in 1698,[93] it can be assumed that Chinese settlement had contributed to attracting more Vietnamese immigration during the preceding two decades, 1679-1698. As nineteenth-century court historians admitted, "After [Ming refugees settled in Mỹ Tho and Biên Hòa,] the region around Saigon began to be more and more influenced by *hán phong*."[94] According to nineteenth-century usage, *hán phong* refers to Vietnamese custom, including the Vietnamese way of life, clothing, language, and so forth. It also indicates the common cultural elements shared by Northeast Asian peoples, such as Confucianism, Mahayana Buddhism, and Classical Chinese writing.[95] Within less than twenty years after the Chinese immigrants settled on the Gia Định land, *phủ* Gia Định was established. In the same year, a *minh hương xã* society was formed from the Ming refugees who had lived in Saigon, and *thanh hà xã* were formed from another group of Ming refugees who had settled in Biên Hòa.[96]

d) Minh Hương Identity

Originally, Ming refugees were mainly single soldiers, so that they usually married Vietnamese woman. Consequently, the members of *minh hương* had mixed Vietnamese parentage in many cases.[97]

But, in fact, their identity as Chinese and identification with patriarchal China remained strong. The three thousand Ming refugees had been part of one of the groups in China most strongly resolved to protect "Chinese" China against the "barbarian" influences of the Manchu Ch'ing. Ming refugees identified themselves more passionately as "pure" Chinese than would be true of the later Ch'ing Chinese immigrants, who had already experienced and accepted the Manchu outlook in matters such as clothing and hair style. The Ming dynasty was also one of the Chinese dynasties that was established by pure Chinese and maintained Sinocentric perceptions of the world. It is hardly to be imagined that these refugees would willingly forget their identity as Chinese in a "barbarian" country, i.e.

Vietnamese began to be found earlier in Gia Định region from the sixteenth century. Nguyễn Đình Đầu, *Chế Độ Công Điền Công Thổ Trong Lịch Sử Khẩn Hoang Lập Ấp ở Nam Kỳ Lục Tỉnh* (The public land system in the history of opening land and establishing villages in the Six Provinces of southern Vietnam) (Hanoi: Hội Sử Học Việt Nam, 1992), p. 31.

[92] *TB*, 5:22a.

[93] Ibid., 7:14a.

[94] Ibid., 5:22b-23a.

[95] In relation to the issue of *hán phong*, see Chapter Five.

[96] *TB*, 7:14b. Afterwards, the name of *thanh hà xã* disappeared. Instead, the *minh hương xã* was commonly used to indicate any Ming refugee association.

[97] Fujiwara Riichiro, *Tonanajiashi no Kenkyu* (Study on Southeast Asian history) (Kyoto: Hozokan, 1986), pp. 263-64.

Vietnam. Influenced by their Vietnamese mothers, in particular, and by Vietnam in general, some children of *minh hương* could have lost their sense of identity as people of Chinese origin, but as long as they were members registered on *minh hương xã*, it meant they were keeping their formal identity as Chinese descendants.

There is evidence that helps us assess the strength of the *minh hương* members' identification with their fatherland. Today, at 380 Trần Hưng Đạo Street, District 5, Saigon, there is a shrine dedicated to Gia Thịnh Minh Hương. The tablet of Chu Yuan Chang (founder of the Ming dynasty) is located at the center of the altar. To the left there are tablets of Trịnh Hoài Đức and Ngô Nhân Tĩnh,[98] to the right, tablets of Trần Thượng Xuyên (a leader of Ming refugees who settled in Biên Hòa), and Nguyễn Hữu Cảnh (the first governor of the *phủ* Gia Định, Vietnamese), who had a close relationship with the *minh hương*. On a wooden pillar in the shrine there is an impressive poem written by Trịnh Hoài Đức (1765-1825), a *minh hương* from Fu Chien: "The fragrance has fulfilled heaven and earth, it has spread to the land of Vietnam. The dragon settles down deeply and promotes literature."[99] These people showed their readiness to join Vietnamese society by wearing Vietnamese costume, speaking in Vietnamese, and living in Vietnamese ways, yet they still maintained their distinct origin and identity as Chinese.

Plate 2. Gia Thịnh Đường. Sign on the Gia Thịnh Minh Hương Association Hall. The small letters (*minh huong* in Chinese) on the left indicate that this was written before Minh Mạng ordered that the letter "*huong*" (fragrance or incense) be changed to another Chinese letter with the same pronunciation, but with the meaning "country" or "local," in order to reduce the prestige of *minh hương* Chinese.
Credit: the author, 1997.

---

[98] Both of them were members of *minh hương*, and participated in the Gia Định regime.

[99] "Hương mãn kiền khôn hình Việt địa, long bàn thường cứ thịnh văn chương." The fragrance has dual implications, referring to *minh hương* and the fragrance of Ming China, whereas the dragon indicates China or the Chinese.

However, their *minh hương* identity did not prevent Gia Định leaders from recruiting them into powerful positions. Due to their acquaintance with Vietnamese society, *minh hương* were recruited into the high official level of the Gia Định regime. Especially, the members of Bình Dương Thi Xã[100] held influential positions at the center of the Gia Định regime. It was during the Gia Định regime that *minh hương* Chinese started to play roles as active decision makers at the court level.

e) Thanh Nhân — Ch'ing People

Another group of Chinese settlers in Vietnam were called *thanh nhân*. They publicly declared they were Chinese, but they originated from the Manchurian-dominated state of Ch'ing China. Thus, they resembled the Ch'ing Chinese, with Manchurian pigtail and costume. They resisted assimilation, and barely tried to learn Vietnamese. They had their own associations, called *bang*, according to their regional origins in China. *Thanh nhân* played an important role in Vietnamese history during the next century.

After Lý Tài's army was dismantled in 1777, and the subsequent massacre of Chinese settlers in 1782, it is difficult to find any influential figure identified as *thanh nhân* in any group of power holders in Gia Định. The situation was the same during the period of the Gia Định regime. The *thanh nhân* were mobilized as soldiers according to the number of each *bang* in Gia Định from the year of 1789. The Chinese in the more peripheral areas, such as Trà Vinh, Sóc Trăng, and Hà Tiên, were organized into military plantation units.[101]

The most prominent Chinese role in the Gia Định regime involved providing supplies and equipment. From 1789, Chinese traded iron, black lead, and sulphur to Gia Định in exchange for rice, cotton fabric, and raw silk.[102] As the frontier of Gia Định territory expanded to the north, the region began to experience instability in rice prices. To relieve the situation, rice had to be imported from Siam. When the Gia Định leaders decided to import rice, in 1791, they found that they needed to rely on *minh hương* Chinese to do so.[103]

Other Ethnic Groups

Besides the Khmer and the Chinese, there were other ethnic minority groups in the Gia Định regime. Certain numbers of Malay soldiers operated under the command of the Gia Định force.[104] About one thousand members of another unspecified ethnic minority in Biên Hòa also took part in the Gia Định force.[105] It

---

[100] This was a club named after the district Bình Dương around Saigon. It was called "Sơn Hội," too. It was a club of literary Chinese whose pen names ended with the letter Sơn (mountain). Lê Quang Định, Trịnh Hoài Đức, Ngô Nhân Tĩnh, Huỳnh Ngọc Uẩn, and Diệp Minh Phụng were members of this club. See Nam Xuân Thọ, *Võ Trường Toản* [biography] (Saigon: Tân Việt, 1957), p. 46.

[101] *DNTL1*, 5:15a.

[102] Ibid., 4:12b; 8:5.

[103] Ibid., 5:23a.

[104] Ibid., 6:36a.

[105] *DNTL2*, 64:27b.

was due to the Gia Định regime's peaceful and successful dealings with ethnic minorities that it was able to exploit the detour route to Nghệ An via the region of Laos in 1802.[106] Though they met with furious antipathy from the Cham during the first stage of their advance, the Gia Định force was able to placate the Cham people by withdrawing the assimilation policy that had been imposed earlier by the Nguyễn state.

Cambodian, Siamese, and Western soldiers were recruited from outside Vietnam. Five thousand Cambodian soldiers advanced to the region of Quảng Nam side by side with the Gia Định force in 1800,[107] and twenty thousand Siamese soldiers landed on Gia Định to support Nguyễn Phúc Ánh in 1784. There is also evidence that Westerners were working for Nguyễn Phúc Ánh from no later than 1780.[108]

Acquiring material supplies from outside Vietnam was a vital matter for the Gia Định military, and Siam was an indispensable supplier. Whenever famines loomed in the region, the Gia Định regime turned first to Siam to supply rice. Iron and sulphur for military purposes were imported from Siam as well.[109] Siamese tobacco was one of the most valuable luxuries distributed to Gia Định soldiers.[110] In return, Gia Định products such as cotton fabrics[111] and rice were exported to Siam.[112] With the assistance of Westerners, the men of Gia Định regime exploited the routes to the Straits of Malacca, Batavia, the Philippines, and Bengal.[113] From 1788 to 1801, Gia Định emissaries sailed to these regions with the northeastern monsoon almost every year, and the most advanced munitions were supplied from these regions to Gia Định.

CONCLUSION

I have examined the Gia Định regime and several of its elements. Gia Định emerged as an independent unit from the 1770s, and the Gia Định regime was formed from 1788. It relied on the initiative of the Gia Định people. Nguyễn Phúc Ánh stood at the center of this regime. He did not achieve leadership as the result of his legitimacy as a royal successor, but by dint of his own capability to attract the allegiance and participation of independent military groups of Gia Định, and other kinds of Gia Định peoples as well.

His attitude was undoubtedly shaped by his experiences growing up. Though he was born in Huế, he was thirteen years old when he left his home town to travel to Gia Định. His personality was mainly formed in Gia Định and through contact with the people of that region, contact that must certainly have helped him learn how to deal with the heterogeneous population.[114] The relationship between him

---

[106] Ibid., 16:10a.

[107] Ibid., 12:13a; 12:20a.

[108] *LTST*, 28:7.

[109] *DNTL1*, 9:31b.

[110] Ibid., 12:27b.

[111] Ibid., 9:31.

[112] Ibid., 4:10b; 6:37b; 9:31.

[113] Ibid., 6:35a.

[114] His successor, Minh Mạng, experienced the opposite transition. He was born in Gia Định, but was raised in Huế after he turned eleven years old.

and his men was individual rather than official. He abandoned the Nguyễn state's traditional anti-Christian policy and continued to win support from Gia Định Christians. Ethnic diversity was also one of the characteristic features of this regime.

Until different men from the central and the northern regions appeared as power holders in the Huế court from the third decade of the next century, the characteristic features of Gia Định lasted in that region. In the next chapter, we will see how the heritage of the Gia Định regime manifested itself in southern Vietnam, and how it caused conflicts with the central government, and eventually provoked a serious clash between southern Vietnam and the central government.

CHAPTER TWO

THE GIA ĐỊNH GOVERNMENT (1808-1832), AND LÊ VĂN DUYỆT

The southern region of Vietnam was again identified by the name of Gia Định after the founding of the Nguyễn dynasty in 1802. As argued in Chapter One, the Gia Định regime was a local unit with strong local characteristics, for southerners had formed their own identity as Gia Định people and soldiers under the regime in southern Vietnam, which for many years had existed as a separate, distinctive region.

After 1802, however, the southerners became ruling elites in the Huế court headed by Nguyễn Phúc Ánh, and found themselves responsible for governing all parts of Vietnam as a single, unified territory—a challenge that required new approaches to government. It was not only the matter of ruling an expanded territory, but also of unifying three distinct major units: the former territory of the Trịnh family in the north; the core region of the Nguyễn state in the central region; and Gia Định in the south.

To rule the newly unified territory, Gia Long[1] chose to govern much of the country indirectly, by delegating authority to representatives located far from the capital. Four military camps (*dinh*): Quảng Bắc, Quảng Trị, Quảng Bình, and Quảng Nam near the capital Huế and eight local military provinces (*trấn*), situated in a region that stretched from present Ninh Bình to Bình Thuận, were under the direct rule of the Huế court, whereas the eleven military provinces of northern Vietnam and the five military provinces of southern Vietnam were administered by the highest ranking generals. The northern region was called Bắc Thành; the southern region was called Gia Định Thành. The administrative unit covering northern Vietnam was Bắc Thành Tổng Trấn, and the unit covering southern

---

[1] Imperial title of Nguyễn Phúc Ánh during 1802–1820. This imperial title signified that he rose in Gia Định and achieved the unification at Thăng Long. See Ts'ai T'ing Lan, *Hải Nam Tạp Trứ* (Various records of the land beyond the southern ocean) (1836. Hanoi: Viện Hán Nôm HVv 80), p. 31; Nguyễn Gia Cát, *Đại Nam Hoàng Triều Bi Nhu Quận Công Phương Tích Lục* (The record of outstanding achievements of the Commandery Duke Bi Nhu) (1897. Hanoi: Viện Hán Nôm A 1178), p. 9. Originally, the Chinese character "Long" of Thăng Long was the character meaning dragon. In 1805 (or in 1803. See Phan Thúc Trực, *Quốc Sử Di Biên* [A transmitted compilation of the state history, hereafter *QSDB*] [n. d. Hong Kong: New Asia Research Institute, 1965], p. 30), however, the character "Long" (dragon) in the city's name was replaced by another character with the same pronunciation "Long" (rising or prospering). *Đại Nam Thực Lục Chính-Biên Đệ Nhất Kỷ* (Primary compilation of the Veritable Records of the first reign of Imperial Vietnam) (hereafter *DNTL1*) (1848. Tokyo: The Institute of Cultural and Linguistic Studies, Keio University, 1968), 27:7b. I think the reason for this replacement was because the character "Long" (dragon) implied king, but the king did not reside here anymore. Nguyễn Phúc Ánh became emperor in 1806, therefore his imperial title may have been created from the two characters signifying Gia Định and the altered name of Thăng Long.

Vietnam was called Gia Định Thành Tổng Trấn (*tổng trấn* means "to rule all military provinces [*trấn*]"). The head of Gia Định Thành was called Gia Định Thành Tổng Trấn Quan, governor-general of Gia Định Thành. The territory of this new entity, Gia Định Thành, was identical to the territory of the former Gia Định regime, while the central and northern regions experienced a little reshaping.[2] As a result of the Nguyễn dynasty's decision to govern its expansive territories indirectly, the heritage of the Gia Định regime was able to survive the next three decades in southern Vietnam.

Studies on Gia Định Thành are few, despite its significance for an understanding of Nguyễn dynastic politics. To my knowledge, "Tìm Hiểu Một Điểm Liên Quan Đến Nguyên Nhân Cuộc Bạo Động Lê-Văn Khôi - Vấn Đề Lê Văn Duyệt (Understanding one point relating to the cause of the Lê Văn Khôi insurrection—The problem of Lê Văn Duyệt)," written by Nguyễn Phan Quang, Đặng Huy Văn, and Chu Thiên, is the first academic work to study the Gia Định government. As its title reveals, however, the work focuses on Lê Văn Duyệt and his Gia Định government only in order to study Lê Văn Khôi's revolt, and the main purpose of the discussion is to show the linkage between Lê Văn Duyệt, a governor-general of Gia Định Thành, and Lê Văn Khôi's revolt and to find evidence that clarifies the causes of this revolt. The authors describe Lê Văn Duyệt as Minh Mạng's political enemy, who opposed Minh Mạng's succession to the throne of Gia Long, and who established his own power base in Gia Định in order to better resist the new government.[3] This argument will be discussed in section one of this chapter.

Shimao Minoru's important article titled "Meimeiki (1820-1840) Betonamu no Nankichiho Tochi ni Kansuru Ichi Kosatsu" (A study on Vietnamese rule of the South during the reign of Minh Mạng), raises questions and deals with many important issues concerning the nature of the governor-general of Gia Định Thành. It focuses on the nature of Lê Văn Duyệt's group, his personal army, and the commercial nature and openness of Lê Văn Duyệt's power. But each element is discussed in relation to Lê Văn Duyệt, the person, rather than in relation to the characteristic features of the Gia Định regime. Consequently, this author's argument chiefly deals with Minh Mạng's efforts to remove a local power holder and minimize his influence in southern Vietnam. For example, Shimao says that Minh Mạng tried to dismantle Lê Văn Duyệt's powerful network of alliances with the "private/individual army [*shiheishudan*]" and Chinese merchants after Lê Văn Duyệt died.[4] But the author does not provide us with answers to the basic question of why Lê Văn Duyệt maintained the individual army and established connections with Chinese merchants in the first place.

To understand clearly the character of Lê Văn Duyệt's group in particular and of Gia Định Thành in general, it is necessary to examine the wider aspect of this

---

[2] Especially the regions of Thanh Hóa and Nghệ An. During the two previous centuries, those two regions had been part of northern Vietnam under the rule of the Trịnh family, but they belonged to the central region from the nineteenth century.

[3] Nguyễn Phan Quang et al., "Tìm hiểu một điểm liên quan đến nguyên nhân cuộc bạo động Lê Văn Khôi—vấn đề Lê Văn Duyệt" (Understanding one point relating to the cause of the Le Van Khoi insurrection—The problem of Le Van Duyet), *Nghiên Cứu Lịch Sử* (hereafter *NCLS*) 105 (1967): 27.

[4] Shimao Minoru, "Meimeiki (1820-1840) Betonamu no Nankichiho Tochi ni Kansuru Ichi Kosatsu" (A study on Vietnamese rule of the South during the reign of Minh Mang), *Keio Gishokudaigoku Gengobunka Kenkyusho Kiyo* (Tokyo, 1991): 187.

alliance's power, which was based in Gia Định. Lê Văn Duyệt's political profile, his relation with central government, Minh Mạng's policy, political change in the central government, the differences between Gia Long and Minh Mạng, southern Vietnam's status in nineteenth-century Vietnam, the social and economic situation of southern Vietnam, the change in the outside world relative to Vietnam from the nineteenth century—all these topics need to be examined in order to understand Lê Văn Duyệt and Gia Định Thành.

In 1993, I discussed Minh Mạng's enthronement and Lê Văn Duyệt; tension between Minh Mạng and Lê Văn Duyệt; and civil officials' occupation of influential Gia Định positions after the Gia Định Thành was divided into six provinces. I paid attention to the different attitudes of Minh Mạng and Lê Văn Duyệt towards Christians, convicts, and Chinese settlers residing in Gia Định who later became the core members of Lê Văn Khôi's revolt, and I concluded that those discrepancies sprang from the different attitudes of the first and second generations.[5] The shortcoming of my work, however, was its failure to trace the origins of the ideas that the first generation accepted and held in common. At the same time, I overlooked the local southerners' role in the political tension between the central government and Gia Định Thành, and in the revolt as well.

In this chapter, two main issues will be discussed. First, I will consider the nature of Gia Định Thành Tổng Trấn, or the Gia Định government. Though this was not a fully independent regime as its predecessor had been, it did function as a semi-autonomous local authority exclusively in charge of ruling southern Vietnam. By examining the nature of Gia Định Thành Tổng Trấn, we may find how southern Vietnam maintained its own local identity during the first three decades of the nineteenth century. Second, I will examine discrepancies between the attitudes of the southern authority and the central government concerning the heritage of the Gia Định regime, discrepancies that created tension between the capital and the outlying region. At the center of this tension was a southern man, Lê Văn Duyệt. By studying his leadership in southern Vietnam, and the reactions of the central court eager to subdue and uproot the local heritage of the south, we will see how the tension between southern Vietnam and the central court increased during the third decade of the nineteenth century.

1. GIA ĐỊNH GOVERNMENT: GIA ĐỊNH THÀNH TỔNG TRẤN

The Name

The original meaning of the word *thành* is "castle"; this word was eventually used to refer to cities in China, Korea, and Japan, which shared a history of classic Chinese usage. In Vietnam, however, the meaning of *thành* expanded to indicate a huge region governed by a military authority. In other words, the Vietnamese used *thành* to identify a large area which had been recently attached to, or subsumed by, an existing territory, so that military administration seemed to be necessary to

---

[5] Choi, Byung Wook, "Wanjo Ch'ogieui Kajeongseongch'ongjin: Myeongmyeongjewa Ch'ongjin'gwan Yeomunyeol'eui Kwan'gyereul Chungsimeuro" (Gia Dinh thanh tong tran, and relations between Minh Mang and Le Van Duyet, in the early Nguyen Dynasty), (MA thesis, Korea University, 1993), p. 56.

rule this newly appropriated area. Gia Định Thành was the region of Gia Định under military rule.[6]

Formation of the Southern Government

Gia Định Thành Tổng Trấn was formed in 1808, five years after the formation of the Bắc Thành Tổng Trấn by the Huế government. Leadership of the administration was delegated to military generals and strengthened by the role of Chinese settlers. A Gia Định man, Nguyễn Văn Nhân, was appointed the first governor-general of Gia Định Thành, and a member of the *minh hương* association of southern Vietnam, Trịnh Hoài Đức, was named as hiệp Tổng Trấn, or assistant governor-general.[7]

No extant records describe the powers of the Gia Định Thành Tổng Trấn Quan when that administrative unit was formed in 1808, but a clue to the situation can be found in the description of the powers of the Bắc Thành Tổng Trấn Quan when Nguyễn Văn Thành was appointed to this position in 1803:

> He has his own rights to rule eleven military provinces; to decide lawsuits; and to appoint and dismiss officials at his own will. It is enough only to report to the court after acting at his own discretion.[8]

We might assume that the Gia Định Thành Tổng Trấn Quan's original powers were similar to those of his northern counterpart.

However, evidence suggests they were in fact even more substantial, as Gia Định's governor-general was also responsible for inspecting and controlling a neighboring country, Cambodia, and for maintaining the southern region as an economic treasure and reliable source of agricultural and forest products, as well as trade goods. In 1820, Minh Mạng granted Lê Văn Duyệt, the Gia Định governor-general, rights to conduct all frontier business and collect profits at his own discretion.[9] Therefore, land clearance, the construction of communication routes, and overseas trade were under the Tổng Trấn Quan's control in Gia Định.

Tổng Trấn Quan and his Locality

It needs to be emphasized that most of the governors-general, the vice governors-general, and the assistant governors-general of Gia Định Thành were southerners in origin. There were three governors-general, four vice governors-general, and two assistant governors-general of Gia Định Thành during its twenty-

---

[6] After the Vietnamese government completely annexed Cambodia in 1835, another *thành* appeared in the Cambodian territory called Trấn Tây Thành. Trấn Tây means pacification of the west, namely Cambodia.

[7] *DNTL1*, 36:11a.

[8] Ibid., 18:31a.

[9] *Đại Nam Thực Lục Chính-Biên Đệ Nhị Kỷ* (Primary compilation of the Veritable Records of the second reign of Imperial Vietnam) (hereafter *DNTL2*) (1861. Tokyo: Keio Institute of Linguistic Studies, 1963), 3:3a.

four-year existence. The first Tổng Trấn Quan, Nguyễn Văn Nhân,[10] was from An Giang province. Nguyễn Huỳnh Đức[11] and Lê Văn Duyệt were from Định Tường province. Among the four vice governors-general of Gia Định Thành, we can identify the birthplaces of two persons, Trương Tiến Bảo and Trần Văn Năng. The former was from Vĩnh Long province (southern Vietnam), while the latter was from Khánh Hòa province of the central region. Two assistant governors-general, Trịnh Hoài Đức and Ngô Nhân Tĩnh, were from Biên Hòa and Phiên An provinces, respectively, of southern Vietnam.

On the other hand, the governors-general of Bắc Thành Tổng Trấn were all from outside the northern area, that is, from the central or southern regions. The origins of the four governors-general of Bắc Thành are identified in the records: Nguyễn Văn Thành was from Phiên An, Nguyễn Huỳnh Đức from Định Tường, Lê Chất from Bình Định, and Trương Văn Minh from Thanh Hóa. Among the four governors-general, two men originated from Gia Định and two hailed from the central region. No northerners were appointed to high positions in southern or in northern Vietnam because, with a few exceptions, northerners had not played significant roles in the earlier Gia Định regime. The fact that the delegated rulers of northern Vietnam usually did not share origins with the people they governed prevented officials from forming strong local alliances. Indeed, records show that the rulers of Bắc Thành were sometimes disregarded or even disdained by the people under their authority. When Lê Chất was in charge of Bắc Thành in 1821, he accused a local official called Lê Duy Thanh of receiving bribes. According to regulations, punishment had to be decided by the governor-general of Bắc Thành, but Lê Duy Thanh appealed directly to the central court, appealing for the king's favor, ignoring the authority of Lê Chất.[12]

Power Base 1: Civil Officials

Just below the top ranks of Gia Định government, there were four local ministries called *tào*, dealing with finance (*hộ tào*), warfare (*binh tào*), justice (*hình tào*), and construction (*công tào*). Each local ministry was supposed to be linked with one of the six Boards at the center: Lại Bộ (Board of personnel), Hộ Bộ (Board of finance), Lễ Bộ (Board of rites), Binh Bộ (Board of warfare), Hình Bộ (Board of justice), and Công Bộ (Board of construction). But these administrative arrangements did not always function as planned. If we carefully examine records detailing personnel changes and the appointments of local high-ranking officials, we discover the interesting fact that civil officials in Gia Định Thành functioned outside the control of the central Boards and maintained much stronger connections with governors-general of Gia Định Thành.

At the central court, there were administrators identified as *tham tri* (second rank, second class), and *thiêm sự* (third rank, first class), assigned to positions under each *thượng thư* (head of a Board, second rank, first class). As a rule, a high-

---

[10] He was appointed to the same position again in 1819. See *Đại Nam Chính-Biên Liệt Truyện Sơ Tập* (First collection of the primary compilation of biographies of Imperial Vietnam) (hereafter *LTST*) vol. 7, Nguyễn Văn Nhân (1889. Tokyo: Keio Institute of Linguistic Studies, 1962).

[11] He worked as the governor-general of Gia Định Thành for three years from 1816. See *LTST*, vol. 7, Nguyễn Huỳnh Đức.

[12] Ibid., 24:10.

ranking official of a central board was to be appointed to a position at the local ministry, so that, for instance, a person who held the title of *tham tri* of a central board would become the head of a local ministry of Gia Định Thành. However, in actual practice, a single bureaucrat generally took charge of more than one field at the local level. A personnel management list of 1813 reveals this pattern. According to this list, a *tham tri* of the Board of Construction, named Nguyễn Khắc Thiệu, became the head of the local ministries of construction and of finance, while a *tham tri* of the Board of Justice, Lê Bá Phẩm, took responsibility for both justice and warfare in Gia Định Thành.[13] In each local ministry, the *tham tri* could expect to be assisted by a *thiêm sự*, but here again, we find that in actual practice a *thiêm sự*, like his superior, the *tham tri*, could also be appointed to two local ministries at once. Interestingly, a *thiêm sự* was not appointed to two local ministries with the same *tham tri*, so that this was not a simple patronage arrangement. For clarification, let us consider a personnel management list of 1821. When a *tham tri* of the Board of Warfare, Nguyễn Xuân Thục, was appointed to direct the local ministries of finance and of construction, a *thiêm sự* of the Board of Justice, named Trần Hữu Châu, was appointed to assist the heads of local ministries of justice and of construction. In this case, Trần Hữu Châu was supervised by Nguyễn Xuân Thục in the local ministry of construction, at the same time that he was also supervised by the head of the local ministry of justice. In another example, a *thiêm sự* of the Board of Finance, Ngô Quang Đức, who was to work in the local ministries of finance and warfare, assisted his boss Nguyễn Xuân Thục in the local ministry of finance, but also reported to another boss, Trần Văn Tuân, in the local ministry of warfare of Gia Định.[14]

It is not clear why the Nguyễn dynasty, from the Gia Long reign to the beginning of the Minh Mạng reign, used this system to provide local civil officials. The major reason was probably because the number of trained civil officials was insufficient, and the system described above may have therefore been unavoidable, since there was simply no other way to provide local government with trained civil officials. At any rate, this complex relationship made it relatively difficult for the heads of the central Six Boards to control their staff at the local level. In contrast, the governor-general of Gia Định Thành held a position that enabled him to contact the heads of local ministries and their staff directly. This personnel system was therefore an element that led the higher-ranking local officials to rely on the governor-general of Gia Định Thành rather than on the central government.

The right of the governor-general to appoint and dismiss local officials according to his own will served to strengthen this bond. On many occasions, local officials were not dispatched from the central court at all, but were selected and appointed by the governor-general; the fact that they formally received their titles from central boards was relatively insignificant. Again, evidence for this arrangement can be found in the personnel management list of 1821. Nguyễn Hữu Nghị was appointed to direct the local ministry of justice of Gia Định Thành Tổng Trấn, and Nguyễn Đức Hội was given the title of *thiêm sự*, assigned to assist Nguyễn Hữu Nghị. Yet Nguyễn Hữu Nghị had been a secretary in the Vĩnh Thanh (later Vĩnh Long) military province of Gia Định, while Nguyễn Đức Hội had been

---

[13] *DNTL1*: 47:18b.

[14] *DNTL2*, 2:22a; 7:14a.

a financial secretary of the Gia Định Thành Tổng Trấn.[15] Nguyễn Hữu Nghị, in reality, had served as an individual retainer to Lê Văn Duyệt, and this experience could have helped him to earn this promotion.[16] Another example is the case of Trần Nhất Vĩnh, who had also been a retainer of Lê Văn Duyệt's; records show he accompanied Lê Văn Duyệt to Gia Định in 1820 as a secretary and stayed there for ten years, during which time he was in charge of the local ministries of finance and construction.[17]

All lower officials—those who in ranks below the levels of *tham tri* and *thiêm sự*—were recruited on the spot. Power over them was totally entrusted to the governor-general. In 1821, for example, the governor-general of Gia Định Thành selected 219 men as administrative officials from the sons of government rank holders in Gia Định.[18] Clearly, individual relationships with the governor-general constituted an important factor for those who hoped to gain positions in local government. Ultimately, the administrative line in Gia Định was mainly filled with men who had stronger connections with the governor-general than with the central government.

Minh Mạng attempted to circumvent the obstructionism of Gia Định authority and administrative system at the beginning of his reign. In 1821, Minh Mạng dispatched two of his men, one from Nghệ An, to positions as education officials of Gia Định Thành.[19] But his men completely failed to accomplish their missions in the southerners' land. Though they stayed in Gia Định for two years, all their efforts to take charge were blocked by local officials. When one of these men, Nguyễn Đăng Sở, returned to Huế in 1823, Minh Mạng heard him complain that, "The emperor's order [on the matter of education and selection of educated men] was delivered from *thành* to *trấn*, and from *trấn* to *phủ* and *huyện*, but nobody asked [me]."[20]

Power Base 2: Military Members

Shimao claims that the individual nature of Lê Văn Duyệt's military forces was formed during the 1820s.[21] However, the peculiar and distinctive characteristics he notes were not limited to Lê Văn Duyệt's military forces, but affected all the Gia Định generals and were part of the heritage of Gia Định.

Tả Quân (Left Division) is an alternate name for Lê Văn Duyệt in Vietnam. Tả Quân is, no doubt, an abbreviation of the phrase: "the commander of Tả Quân." Why is this man popularly called Tả Quân if, in fact, he also held two notably more prestigious and influential positions, as Tổng Trấn Quan, his highest civil title, and as the commander of the royal guards, which was the highest military position available?

---

[15] Ibid., 7:14.

[16] *LTST*, 22:18b-19a.

[17] For more on Trần Nhất Vĩnh, see the next chapter.

[18] *Mục Lục Châu Bản Triều Nguyễn* (Vermilion record abstracts of the Nguyen Dynasty, Minh Mang reign to 1823), vol. 2 (Hue: Hue University, 1962), p. 28.

[19] *DNTL2*, 8:10b.

[20] Ibid., 23:1b.

[21] Shimao, "Meimeiki (1820-1840) Betonamu no Nankichiho Tochi ni Kansuru Ichi Kosatsu," pp. 178-79.

The people's identification of Lê Văn Duyệt as "Tả Quân" reveals something about the personal nature of the Left Division. In the previous chapter, I mentioned that Lê Văn Duyệt's first action, when he was approved to participate in military work in 1787, was to recruit individually his own soldiers. Subsequently, he and his men were mustered into the Left Division.[22] Eventually, in 1802, he was promoted to become the commander of the Left Division, and it was this division, under his command, that captured Thăng Long the same year. In fact, regarding Gia Định generals allied to the Gia Định regime, it was a common practice for the soldiers and populace to call a general by the name of the army he commanded. Today, at the entrance to General Nguyễn Huỳnh Đức's shrine in Long An province, one can see a board at the entrance gate which says "Tiền Quân Miếu" (Shrine of the Front Division). Even though Nguyễn Huỳnh Đức would later accept higher positions of authority—becoming governor-general of both Gia Định Thành and Bắc Thành—he is most often identified as the commander of the Front Division. Another example is Nguyễn Văn Thành, the first governor-general of Bắc Thành, whose nickname was Trung Quân (Center Division).

Until 1802, the territories controlled by commanders such military units as Left Division, Front Division, Center Division and so on, were almost fixed. Each commander headed a power group based in his own individual division. Power games, conspiracies, and regimental social activities were common. Of these, the commanders of the Center Division (Nguyễn Văn Thành) and the Left Division (Lê Văn Duyệt) were the most powerful figures, and they sparred with each other from the beginning of the Nguyễn dynasty. Relationships among the soldiers were also in flux. A soldier who was disappointed in his attempts to win guaranteed patronage from a military leader might switch sides, even shifting allegiance to his former master's opponent, in order to seek revenge.[23] But sometimes these turncoats could not be trusted, for soldiers had been known to join the opposition because they hoped for an opportunity to assassinate their master's chief rivals.[24]

In addition to his own army, there were other factors to increase the governor-general's power. Even after the formation of the Nguyễn dynasty, military campaigns were continuous because revolts were commonplace, especially in the regions of central and northern Vietnam. Throughout the military campaigns, manpower was constantly recruited. Ex-convicts, ex-bandits, surrendered insurgents, and ethnic minorities were absorbed into the forces of military generals. Lê Văn Khôi, a member of an ethnic minority in Cao Bằng, was such a case. While Lê Văn Duyệt was engaged in pacifying insurgents of the regions of Nghệ An, Thanh Hóa, and Ninh Bình in 1819, Lê Văn Khôi joined Lê Văn Duyệt's force with his own

---

[22] *LTST*, 22:2a.

[23] Nguyễn Hữu Nghị had been the retainer of Nguyễn Văn Thành. Afterwards, he became the retainer of Lê Văn Duyệt, and he helped Lê Văn Duyệt to destroy Nguyễn Văn Thành in 1816. See *LTST*, 22:18b-19a.

[24] A soldier called Hữu belonged to the Center Division of Nguyễn Văn Thành. He was caught in Lê Văn Duyệt's camp by the soldiers of the Left Division. Lê Văn Duyệt claimed that this soldier confessed he had been ordered by Nguyễn Văn Thành to poison Lê Văn Duyệt. *LTST*, 22:19b. The veracity of Lê Văn Duyệt's accusation cannot be proven, of course, but this record does provide evidence that any member of each Division could be regarded as a potential opponent by the soldiers of other divisions.

soldiers. Having established an individual relationship with Lê Văn Duyệt, he was able to start his military career with a government title.[25]

Under this system of individual recruitment, soldiers were provided to the commander of each Division. If a general was appointed as the governor-general of Gia Định Thành, he was accompanied by his own soldiers. Saigon must have been crowded with soldiers and retainers of the Front Division when Nguyễn Huỳnh Đức was made governor-general of Gia Định Thành in 1816, just as it was surely crowded with the members of the Left Division when Lê Văn Duyệt was governor-general of that same region during 1812-1813 and 1820-1832.

Gia Định and Cambodia

Apart from the five military provinces of southern Vietnam—Biên Hòa, Phiên An (Gia Định later), Vĩnh Thanh (Vĩnh Long later), Định Tường, and Hà Tiên—the Gia Định Thành Tổng Trấn also held jurisdiction over Cambodia. When Vietnam fell into turmoil during the period of the Tây Sơn rebellion, Cambodia came under the patronage of Siam. Later, when the Nguyễn dynasty was established, Cambodia became a tributary of Vietnam at the request of the Cambodian king, Ang Chan. When, in 1812, Ang Chan's younger brother, supported by Siam, challenged Ang Chan for control of Cambodia, the king fled to Gia Định Thành. At that time, Lê Văn Duyệt was appointed as Gia Định Thành Tổng Trấn Quan, and he entered Cambodian territory accompanied by the Cambodian king, whom he subsequently reinstated.

From this time, Cambodia was under the protection of the Vietnamese emperor. "Bảo Hộ Chân Lạp," or the Protectorship of Chân Lạp (Cambodia), a bureaucratic position in charge of controlling Cambodia, was under the direct command of Gia Định Thành. Usually, matters related to Cambodia were decided by the governor-general of Gia Định. The right to "protect" the Cambodian king was another element that buttressed the prestige of the governor-general in Gia Định Thành.

Lê Văn Duyệt (1763-1832)

Among the three governors-general of Gia Định Thành, Lê Văn Duyệt is the most prominent. His term as the governor-general was longer than the terms of his two counterparts, Nguyễn Văn Nhân and Nguyễn Huỳnh Đức. During 1812-1813, he briefly worked as the governor-general of Gia Định Thành. From the beginning of Minh Mạng's reign in 1820, Lê Văn Duyệt devoted himself to ruling Gia Định until his death in 1832.

a) Lê Văn Duyệt and Southerners

No matter whether they are indigenous Vietnamese or Chinese settlers, Buddhists or Christians, residents of Saigon have long paid enthusiastic tribute to one favorite southern, local hero—Lê Văn Duyệt—whose gorgeous shrine is located

---

[25] *Đại Nam Chính-Biên Liệt Truyện Nhị Tập* (Second collection of the primary compilation of biographies of Imperial Vietnam) (hereafter *LTNT*) (1909. Tokyo: The Institute of Cultural and Linguistic Studies, Keio University, 1981), 45:1.

on Đinh Tiên Hoàng Street[26] in Bình Thạnh District. You will not be able to find any other place in Hue or Hanoi where the residents, regardless of ethnic or religious backgrounds, regard their own local hero with such reverence.

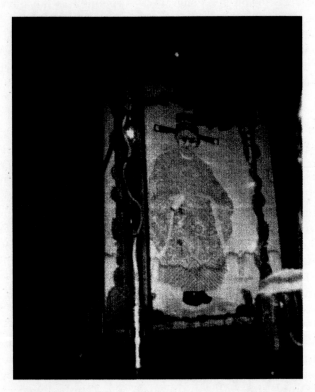

Plate 3. Portrait of Lê Văn Duyệt, found in his shrine. Although this portrait was certainly not drawn during his lifetime, it reflects southerners' image of him very well. Credit: the author, 1994.

Lê Văn Duyệt was generally described as a stern personality. Records report that ordinary officials and soldiers were not able to speak with him directly, and even his colleagues often dared not address him because he was so stern.[27] Evaluations of his character in later court biographies are more critical. After Tây Sơn forces killed his favorite colleague, Tống Viết Phúc, in 1801, Lê Văn Duyệt was reportedly overcome by an almost insane rage, that reportedly drove him to kill any Tây Sơn soldiers he encountered, until at last he was admonished by Nguyễn Phúc Ánh for his ferocity. A Confucian official from Nghệ An, Phan Thúc Trực, tried to describe Lê Văn Duyệt's personality after Lê died. According to him, Lê Văn Duyệt beat dogs to death and decapitated high-ranking local officials arbitrarily. His eccentric habits were recorded as well: he raised thirty hill minority people to

---

[26] Its previous name was Lê Văn Duyệt Street, until the name was changed after the 1975 unification.

[27] *Lê Công Văn Duyệt Sự Trạng* (Accounts of matters for Le Van Duyet) (n.d. Hanoi: Viện Hán Nôm A 540), p. 12.

become his servants, and kept one hundred chickens and one hundred dogs. Whenever he returned home, he had one tiger and fifty dogs follow him.[28]

Yet Lê Văn Duyệt's personality is described much more moderately whenever he is mentioned in descriptions of southern Vietnam. Michel Đức Chaigneau, who visited Saigon in 1825, stated: "He [Lê Văn Duyệt] has great talent both in battle and administration. People fear him, but he is heartily loved by people here because he is fair."[29] According to the stories of southern Vietnam, it was Lê Văn Duyệt who appeared in the dream of their 1860s anti-French leader, Nguyễn Trung Trực, to instruct him how to defeat the enemy.[30] Southern Vietnamese remember Lê Văn Duyệt as a dignified high-ranking general, yet one who also remained close to their own heritage. It is said that, like the common Vietnamese, he loved cockfighting so much that he delivered a long speech about the merits of this recreation in front of Emperor Gia Long, in the manner of a joke. He was also said to be an enthusiastic spectator of southern folk drama, *hát bội*,[31] and he reportedly protected local goddess spirits.[32] A vivid observation by a British visitor to Saigon in 1822 confirms the governor-general's humble style:

> His dress is not merely plain, but almost sordid, and to the sight as mean as that of the poorest persons [. . .] The mandarins appeared to be perfectly at their ease in the presence of the Governor [Lê Văn Duyệt], exhibiting neither fear nor awe of any kind.[33]

Lê Văn Duyệt's popularity had to do with the fact that he began with nothing, for his parents were ordinary peasants of Gia Định. As was common amongst Gia Định people, his family had moved to Gia Định from a central region, Quảng Ngãi. According to the court biography, his genitals were indistinct from the time of his birth. He became a eunuch when he was seventeen years old.[34] Seven years later, his military talent enabled him to gain unexpected success, and from then on he won every battle without fail. When the Nguyễn dynasty was formed in 1802, he became one of the most influential opinion leaders in the Huế court.[35]

---

[28] *QSDB*, pp. 68-69.

[29] Cited from Jean Silvestre, "L'insurrection de Gia-Dinh, la révolte de Khoi (1832-1834)," *Revue Indochinoise* 7-8 (1915): 18.

[30] Thái Bạch, *Bốn Vị Anh Hùng, Kháng Chiến Miền Nam* (Four heroes of the southern resistance movements), vol. 2 (Saigon: Tủ Sách Sông-Mới, 1957), p. 12.

[31] Huỳnh Minh, *Gia Định Xưa và Nay* (Gia Dinh, past and present) (Saigon, 1973), pp. 186-87.

[32] Huỳnh Minh, *Vĩnh Long Xưa và Nay* (Vinh Long, past and present) (Saigon, 1967), p. 43.

[33] George Finlayson, *The Mission to Siam and Hue, the Capital of Cochin China, in the Years 1821-22* (1826. Singapore: Oxford University Press, 1988), pp. 319-20.

[34] The British visitor of 1822 further reports: "The Governor of Saigon is reputed an eunuch, and his appearance in some degree countenances that notion. He is apparently about fifty years of age, has an intelligent look, and may be esteemed to possess considerable activity both of mind and body: his face is round and soft, his features flabby and wrinkled; he has no beard, and bears considerable resemblance to an old woman: his voice, too, is shrill and feminine." Finlayson, *The Mission to Siam and Hue*, p. 319.

[35] See *LTST*, vol. 22, Lê Văn Duyệt .

b) Lê Văn Duyệt and Minh Mạng's Enthronement

The Problem of Royal Succession

As a powerful figure at court in the early 1800s, Lê Văn Duyệt was necessarily involved in the designation of the crown prince. Since the previous crown prince, Cảnh, had died in 1801, just one year before the formation of the Nguyễn dynasty, the nomination of a new prince was a pressing issue.

Nguyễn Phan Quang, who has studied Lê Văn Khôi's revolt (1833-1835), suggests that Lê Văn Duyệt opposed Gia Long's choice of Minh Mạng as crown prince, and that Minh Mạng eventually posted him far away, to Gia Định, for this reason.[36] This would lead one to conclude that conflict between Minh Mạng and Lê Văn Duyệt was basically the result of political factionalism, and that Lê Văn Khôi's revolt was another significant outcome of this factionalism.[37] If we accept his assumption, then Minh Mạng's twenty-one years (1820-1841) of involvement in southern Vietnam should be understood only as a series of actions to eliminate his political opponent.

In my opinion, this basic premise—that Lê Văn Duyệt opposed Gia Long's designation of Minh Mạng as crown prince—ought to be questioned, even though Nguyễn Phan Quang's interpretation of the contentious relationship between Vietnam's new king and one of his most powerful generals has been widely accepted by scholars inside and outside of Vietnam.[38] There is, admittedly, evidence to support his theory. Lê Văn Duyệt reportedly pressured Gia Long to choose his eldest grandson, former crown prince Cảnh's eldest son, as crown prince in 1810.[39] A letter written by Mgr. Jean Louis Taberd in 1830 says that French missionaries also had a vivid memory that Lê Văn Duyệt had opposed the appointment of Minh Mạng as crown prince.[40] I think the belief that Lê Văn Duyệt opposed Minh Mạng's succession to Gia Long stems from these pieces of evidence.

However, this evidence does not tell us who it was that Lê Văn Duyệt advocated at the time Gia Long made his final decision in 1816 or later, because Phan Thúc Trực's account only concerns Lê Văn Duyệt's opinion in 1810 and Mgr. Taberd did not make clear *when* Lê Văn Duyệt opposed Gia Long's choice of Minh Mạng. Ralph Smith's approach to this issue is cautious. Even though he admits Lê Văn Duyệt may have protested against Gia Long's election of Minh Mạng, he also

---

[36] Nguyễn Phan Quang et al., "Tìm Hiểu Một Điểm Liên Quan Đến Nguyên Nhân Cuộc Bạo Động Lê-Văn Khôi—Vấn Đề Lê Văn Duyệt," p. 27; Nguyễn Phan Quang, *Cuộc Khởi Binh Lê Văn Khôi ở Gia Định (1833-1835)* (Le Van Khoi's raising an army) (Ho Chi Minh City: Nxb Thành Phố Hồ Chí Minh, 1991), p. 36.

[37] Nguyễn Phan Quang, *Cuộc Khởi Binh Lê Văn Khôi ở Gia Định (1833-1835)*, pp. 38-39.

[38] See Woodside, *Vietnam and the Chinese Model*, pp. 284-85; Alastair Lamb, ed., *The Mandarin Road to Old Hue: Narratives of Anglo-Vietnamese Diplomacy from the Seventeenth Century to the Eve of the French Conquest* (CT: Archon Books, 1970), p. 283; Mark McLeod, *The Vietnamese Response to French Intervention, 1862-1874* (New York: Praeger, 1991), p. 24; Claudia Michele Thompson, "A Negotiated Dichotomy: Vietnamese Medicine and the Intersection of Vietnamese Acceptance and Resistance to Chinese Cultural Influence," (PhD dissertation, University of Washington, 1998), p. 31.

[39] *QSDB*, p. 68.

[40] Georges Taboulet, *La geste Française en Indochine: Histoire par les textes de la France en Indochine des origines à 1914*, Tome 1 (Paris: Librairie D'Amérique et D'Orient, Adrien-Maisonneuve, 1955), p. 325.

notes the fact that in 1820 "[Lê Văn Duyệt] was entrusted by Gia-Long with responsibility for the succession, together with the president of the Board of Rites, Phạm Đăng Hưng"[41]; this evidence suggests that the general had not fallen out of favor with the court by 1820 or been alienated from those influential persons who were most involved in the succession decisions.

Gia Long's decision to appoint his successor was made in 1816. By that time there were two prominent candidates for the throne: Gia Long's fourth son, (later Minh Mạng), and his eldest grandson, former crown prince Cảnh's eldest son. As Gia Long's second and third sons had both died before 1802, the top priority was given to the fourth among his living sons. The eldest grandson was already eighteen when the final nomination was made in 1816, while the fourth son was twenty-six years old. Eventually, Gia Long chose his fourth son as successor.[42] From Gia Long's point of view, it was better to appoint a mature successor than to trust a younger prince who might be easily controlled by older, influential subjects. When Gia Long learned that Nguyễn Văn Thành was supporting the candidacy of his eldest grandson in 1815, he expressed his displeasure as follows: "The reason for him [Nguyễn Văn Thành] to want to support the little one is because he wants to take the chance of being able to easily control [the little one] in the future."[43] Gia Long must have remembered that he himself had been frequently challenged by Đỗ Thanh Nhân after he took the throne as a fifteen-year-old boy.

However, Gia Long's decision in favor of the fourth son was opposed by a group of his subjects. When the intention of Gia Long to designate his fourth son as crown prince became known, "great dispute broke out as bees buzz."[44] This internal dispute between the factions supporting the fourth son and those supporting the eldest grandson seems to have lasted for a long time. Even on the eve of the new king's succession in the beginning of 1820, "many of the nobles were secretly opposed to the established succession, and a renewal of bloody civil war was expected."[45]

The Contribution of Lê Văn Duyệt

Based on the evidence, I believe that Lê Văn Duyệt supported the candidacy of the fourth son of Gia Long, while Nguyễn Văn Thành headed the opposition at the time Gia Long made his final decision.[46] Lê Văn Duyệt had favored the eldest grandson in principle, according to evidence in the *Quốc Sử Di Biên* of Phan Thúc Trực, but he expressed that opinion in 1810. However, it appears that he changed

---

[41] Ralph B. Smith, "Politics and Society in Viet-Nam During the Early Nguyen Period (1802-1862)," *Journal of the Royal Asiatic Society* 2 (1974): 154.

[42] In the history of Vietnam, there were three elements that were supposed to determine royal succession: the candidate had to come from the direct paternal line; be male; and be the oldest son (primogeniture). The third element was often ignored. See Nguyễn Minh Tường, *Cải Cách Hành Chính Dưới Thời Minh Mệnh (1820-1840)* (Administrative reform under the reign of Minh Mang) (Hanoi: Khoa Học Xã Hội, 1996), p. 48.

[43] *DNTL1*, 51:16b.

[44] *QSDB*, p. 92.

[45] John White, *A Voyage to Cochin China* (1824. Kuala Lumpur: Oxford University Press, 1972), pp. 266-68.

[46] In the court biography of Nguyễn Văn Thành, we can find evidence that until 1816 he consistently insisted that the eldest grandson should be appointed as Gia Long's successor. *LTST*, 21:34.

his mind after he perceived Gia Long's real intention, and he certainly had enough time to change his opinion by 1816.

In fact, Gia Long's final decision to choose his fourth son owed something to Lê Văn Duyệt's contribution. Several months earlier, there had been a critical incident which must have inclined the king to this decision: Nguyễn Văn Thuyên, the son of Nguyễn Văn Thành, had been accused and tried for plotting a rebellion to insure the succession of Gia Long's eldest grandson. It was Lê Văn Duyệt who exposed this plot, and he was in charge of investigating this affair.[47] Lê Văn Duyệt might well have expected that exposing this plot (whether real or fictitious we cannot know) would have two results: one, the eldest grandson would be damaged in the competition to be the next emperor; and two, Nguyễn Văn Thành, the most active advocate of the eldest grandson, would be eliminated. Following the incident, Nguyễn Văn Thành drank poison, and Gia Long appointed his fourth son as the crown prince two months later.

Compensation for Lê Văn Duyệt's contribution was generous. During the remaining four years of Gia Long's reign, Lê Văn Duyệt rose to the highest rank at the court. Only Lê Văn Duyệt and another Gia Định civil official, Phạm Đăng Hưng, were allowed at Gia Long's bedside when he was near death, and only they heard his last words. The dying king granted Lê Văn Duyệt command over five royal regiments. At this point, Lê Văn Duyệt was appointed governor-general of Gia Định Thành by Minh Mạng.

Strengthening the Authority of Minh Mạng

For several years after Minh Mạng took the throne, his relations with Lê Văn Duyệt were extremely warm. Minh Mạng showed his trust towards the old general, and Lê Văn Duyệt successfully secured his new master's favor. At the beginning, Lê Văn Duyệt scored noteworthy achievements in Gia Định. He skillfully quelled a turbulent insurrection caused by Khmer people; his persistent work brought to light ten thousand new taxpayers, a source of substantial revenue for the court; and under his supervision the renovation of the Vĩnh Tế Canal was completed in 1823. In recognition, Lê Văn Duyệt received an honorable jade belt from the emperor, and his adopted son was chosen to be Minh Mạng's son-in-law.[48]

The most dramatic event illustrating Lê Văn Duyệt's loyalty to Minh Mạng took place in 1824. Lê Văn Duyệt secretly reported to Minh Mạng the incestuous relationship between the eldest grandson of Gia Long and his mother, the widow of Prince Cảnh. Lê Văn Duyệt then willingly accepted the role of killing Prince Cảnh's wife by drowning.[49] The result, of course, was complete destruction of any claim to the throne by the eldest grandson.[50]

---

[47] *QSDB*, p. 90; *LTST*, 22:18b-20a.

[48] *LTST*, 23:4a; 6a.

[49] Ibid., 23:7b-8a. A different document says that Minh Mạng already knew of the matter that Lê Văn Duyệt reported. See *Lê Công Văn Duyệt Sự Trạng*, p. 27. Either way, it is important that Lê Văn Duyệt reported the matter himself and took responsibility for killing Prince Cảnh's widow.

[50] Nevertheless, the legitimacy of the Prince Cảnh hereditary line lasted longer. Though his eldest son committed suicide in 1829, it was said that he or any of his sons was still regarded as the possible alternative to Minh Mạng by the participants in the Lê Văn Khôi revolt. See Nguyễn Phan Quang, "Thêm mấy điểm về cuộc bạo động Lê Văn Khôi (1833-1835)," (Several additional points concerning Le Van Khoi's revolt), *NCLS* 147 (1972): 41. When Khmer revolts

The New Atmosphere of the Huế Court

Although Lê Văn Duyệt contributed to stabilizing the new king's position, he did not seem to have been entirely successful in adjusting himself to the mood of the new court controlled by Minh Mạng. The basic problem was that the personality of Minh Mạng was quite different from that of his father. According to the experience of J. B. Chaigneau, one of Gia Long's French military officers, Gia Long was "frank and you could count on what he said," whereas Minh Mạng was a person who "does not say what he thinks."[51] Gia Long's character was largely shaped by his military experience, the many years when he was surrounded by Gia Định generals, while Minh Mạng's character was formed by years of interactions with civil officials in Huế.[52] When Lê Văn Duyệt visited Huế in 1824, he felt the court had changed under the new king during his absence. As Minh Mạng's position became increasingly stable and secure, Lê Văn Duyệt, in particular, and the Gia Định group of generals overall, had to realize that circumstances were changing. Civil officials from the northern and the central regions were welcomed into the political center of power from the beginning of Minh Mạng's reign. Lê Văn Duyệt's manner—marked by the informality and idiosyncrasies of an old southern general—began to be criticized by the young, courtly officials as coarse and ignorant.[53] For the older generation of Gia Định generals, the central court was no longer a comfortable place. Lê Văn Duyệt's and Lê Chất's mutual opinion of the new atmosphere at court was recorded in 1824, when Lê Văn Duyệt visited Huế:

> The court recruits civil officials and wants to make a proper ruling system with them. Both of us have risen in the world from a military background. We only know straight expression and quick action, thus violating manners or official rules, sometimes. We are originally different from them. We had better give up our positions [. . .] to avoid possible mistakes.[54]

Following this declaration, the two generals tendered their resignations, but these were not accepted. Lê Văn Duyệt wanted to discontinue his work as governor-general of Gia Định and stay at the capital. However, it would have been dangerous for the courtiers to allow influential military leaders to remain so near

---

devastated southern Vietnam after 1841, the court was astonished to find a man could attract thousands of Khmer people and southern Vietnamese to join an insurrection against Minh Mạng's dynasty by declaring himself as a son of Prince Cảnh. *Đại Nam Thực Lục Chính-Biên Đệ Tam Kỷ* (Primary compilation of the veritable records of the third reign of Imperial Vietnam) (hereafter *DNTL3*) (1894. Tokyo: Institute of Cultural and Linguistic Studies, Keio University, 1977), 14:19b.

[51] Taboulet, *La geste Française en Indochine*, p. 295.

[52] For example, Đặng Đức Siêu (1750–1810), a Confucian from the central region, was Minh Mạng's principal teacher. Nguyễn Minh Tường, *Cải Cách Hành Chính Dưới Thời Minh Mệnh*, p. 40. Đặng Đức Siêu's biography shows that he was from a Confucian family based on Bình Định province for several generations during the Nguyễn state. Đặng Đức Siêu was educated in Phú Xuân, the capital of Nguyễn state, and passed the Nguyễn state's regional examination in 1766. See *LTST*, vol. 10, Đặng Đức Siêu.

[53] *QSDB*, p. 68.

[54] *LTST*, 23:8.

the center of power. Throughout the history of Vietnam, there had always been two alternatives for royal courts in their dealings with the military power holders: one was to let them remain in the capital, the other was to remove them from the political center. Military power holders who were allowed to remain in the capital include Ngô Quyền and Lê Hoàn in the tenth century; Lý Công Uẩn in the eleventh century; Hồ Quý Ly in the fourteenth century; Lê Lợi's Thanh Hóa men in the fifteenth century; and Mạc Đăng Dung in the sixteenth century. In each of these cases, the result was usurpation or a court coup. On the other hand, Nguyễn Hoàng was sent far from court. Either one of these options could have led to possible disaster for Minh Mạng's court, but the latter could guarantee a safer situation as long as the central government was confident and did not fear weakening the local military and its own defenses.

2. DISAGREEMENT BETWEEN MINH MẠNG AND LÊ VĂN DUYỆT ON THE ELEMENTS OF THE GIA ĐỊNH HERITAGE

In this section, we will discuss several issues concerning Gia Định during the first three decades of the nineteenth century, focusing especially on the roles of certain "outsiders," namely Christians, northern convicts, and Chinese settlers. Christians and Chinese settlers had made important contributions to the Gia Định regime. Convicts did not share that history, for they were a new element that first became engaged in Gia Định society beginning in the nineteenth century, when the territories of Vietnam were unified. Nonetheless, we will find that the status of the northern convicts who migrated to the south was influenced and effectively heightened by the heritage of the Gia Định regime, which had always tended to be more inclusive than exclusive. Christians, northern convicts, and Chinese settlers would prove to be important elements in Gia Định society under Gia Định Thành Tổng Trấn, whereas from Minh Mạng's point of view they were merely potential threats to state order. These differences in attitude between Minh Mạng and Lê Văn Duyệt would cause sharp conflicts between the court and Gia Định Thành.

Different Responses to Christians

As was the case during the Gia Định regime, the period of Gia Định Thành in southern Vietnam was characterized by peaceful coexistence among members of the various religions, including Christianity. A visitor to Saigon in 1819 or in 1820 would have found examples of the popularity of Christianity. A Christian church stood in the center of Chợ Lớn.[55] The visitors might have been impressed by the tomb of Pigneau that was a "masonry tomb in the best style of Onamese [Vietnamese] architecture,"[56] located in the north-west of Gia Định citadel. He or she might have encountered a foreign missionary strolling on Saigon streets with a red face caused by wine. Whenever he wanted to smoke, his assistant, usually a native convert, would run to hand him his pipe. Of course, the foreign Christian missionary spoke fluent Vietnamese.[57] His status as a Christian convert would not

---

[55] White, *A Voyage to Cochin China*, p. 233.

[56] Ibid., p. 275.

[57] Ibid., p. 273.

prevent an older Vietnamese man from admitting publicly that he was rich, influential, and an intimate friend of the governor-general of Gia Định.[58] It was during this period in south Vietnam's history that a young French priest, Joseph Marchand, was invited to a local church which had been built in the previous century by native Christians;[59] no local government officials attempted to prevent his arrival.

However, anxiety was spreading among the Christians towards the end of Gia Long's reign because of the rising certainty that Gia Long's fourth son, Minh Mạng, would succeed to the throne. At the beginning of 1820, John White observed:

> [. . .] towards Christians and foreigners, it is to be feared, that a system of expulsion from the kingdom, or of extermination, will be adopted, as he is sworn enemy to both those descriptions of persons. Indeed, so great have been the fears of the French in Onam [Vietnam] of late, as the present monarch advances in years, and begins to feel the infirmities of age[60] [. . .] A few days previous to our quitting Saigon, Father Joseph begged of us [for] some wine and flour, for a particular purpose, [. . .] He informed us, that as the king had frequently been indisposed of late, and in the event of his death, an extermination of the Christians was feared, the wine and flour were designed as elements to be used at the celebration of the eucharist, of which he intended to partake with his converts at their last extremity.[61]

What was the nature of Minh Mạng's antagonistic attitude towards Christians that frightened them even before he took the throne?

Minh Mạng's antipathy to Christianity rested on three concerns. First, he meant to protect ancestor worship. He must have remembered the behavior of his eldest brother, who after long association with a French missionary refused to bow in homage to the altars of his ancestors. As Minh Mạng was ten years younger than Prince Cảnh, he would not have directly witnessed his brother's act of resistance, but it is certain that he heard about this matter from the people who surrounded him from his childhood, and it appears that his "memory" of the incident remained with him throughout his life.[62] His second concern was the irrationality of some parts of the Old Testament, from his point of view, based on the strict Neo-Confucian concept that emphasizes cause and result. The third problem was misinformation he received and accepted concerning Christianity.

Minh Mạng's emotional antipathy towards Christians did not prevent him from gaining access to the writings of Christianity. It is not clear what kind of books he read to understand this religion, but he might well have been exposed to versions of Christian literature translated by the Western missionaries into Nôm and Chinese, or books brought from China. At any rate, this curious king read some parts of the Bible, and reportedly found many of the Bible's stories impossible to believe. He was not markedly parochial or constitutionally suspicious of all things

---

[58] Ibid., p. 317.

[59] Thạch Phương et al., *Địa Chí Bến Tre* (Gazetteer of Ben Tre Province) (Hanoi: Nxb Khoa Học Xã Hội, 1999), p. 554.

[60] White, *A Voyage to Cochin China*, p. 267.

[61] Ibid., p. 346.

[62] DNTL2, 196:14a.

foreign. He respected the scientific materials and discoveries of the Western world; Western geography, politics, history, and military strategy were the matters of interest for him. When he was informed that the naval forces of America and Britain were much superior to that of Vietnam, he was willing to learn about these things.[63] His government purchased steam ships from overseas and repeatedly attempted to convert them into warships.[64] What's more, he was ready to extend Vietnam's economic and academic reach. The number of purchasing missions to Southeast Asian island regions peaked during his reign, and the court sent some young students to these regions to study foreign languages and mechanical skills.[65] However, this king found the Biblical stories of Noah's Ark and the Tower of Babel to be *"vô kê"* (unfounded)" and *"vô lý"* (irrational).[66] He could not accept them.

Regarding the third element, misinformation, it is necessary to consider not only the king's attitude, but the attitudes of his officials as well, for a number of his court officials were radically opposed to and distrustful of Christianity. Thus they all influenced each other with misinformation. It is possible that some of this misinformation seemed credible in the light of the West's technological skill, which must sometimes have seemed to verge on magic, but in fact the most frightening rumors had little to do with the Christians' technology, for they focused much more on alleged Christian barbarism. One of Minh Mạng's favorite officials, Phan Bá Đạt, the holder of a doctoral degree, who originated from Hà Tĩnh, in the central region, reported horrors allegedly committed by Christians in order to convince Minh Mạng to tighten the anti-Christianity edict. The court chronicles make it clear how this Vietnamese scholar understood Christian practice "through a veil of Confucian rationalism." Phan Bá Đạt insisted (in 1835) that his statement was based on the testimony of a French missionary called Marchand. He told the king how Western doctors removed the eyes from human bodies and dried them to produce a medicine for coughs, and claimed that, according to his sources, Western Christians followed the same practice in Vietnam. Furthermore, according to Phan Bá Đạt, Christians liked to stage odd dramas; they would send a man and women to live together in a single room, separated only by a wall, and then kill them once their sexual desire was sufficiently aroused. By mixing the dead bodies of the couple with water, they made pieces of cake, which was given to the people to eat in every Christian ceremony. As a result of these rituals, people became addicted to the religion, so that even if they wished to convert, they could not leave it.[67]

Misinformation of this sort increased the court's prejudice against Christianity and, occasionally, caused serious worry to Minh Mạng. For example, he believed that Jesus Christ declared "if any Western brother countries try to invade each other, all the rest of the countries would attack them." To dispute this imaginary

---

[63] Ibid., 192:6a.

[64] Ibid., 214:18; *DNTL3*, 40:21.

[65] Ibid., 162:18b-19a; 187:3a.

[66] Woodside, *Vietnam and the Chinese Model*, pp. 287-89; *DNTL2*, 202:6b.

[67] Woodside, *Vietnam and the Chinese Model*, p. 287; *DNTL2*, 164:1b-2a. A famous northern scholar, Phạm Đình Hổ, claimed, in his book *Tang Thương Ngẫu Lục* (Tang Thuong's occasional records) (1836. Hanoi: Viện Hán Nôm A 218), that Western Christians were descendants of a male *con chó* or dog who had married a female human.

doctrine, Minh Mạng racked his brains in a meeting of his subjects in 1838 to justify the idea that *"cửu phân tất hợp"* (Being divided long, should be amalgamated) applies equally in the West and the East.[68] For Minh Mạng, who had taken Cambodia three years earlier, Jesus' instruction must have seemed to threaten his empire's security, since he had violated Jesus' alleged command and so had to expect that other countries, faithful to Christ's instruction, might now attack Vietnam in response.

Besides the three elements mentioned above, another factor increased Minh Mạng's antipathy towards Christianity. It had to do with his efforts to collect knowledge about the Western countries and their activities in Southeast Asian countries during this time. As mentioned above, promising young civil officials were dispatched to the Southeast Asian island regions during this period, among them the notable Phan Thanh Giản, Lý Văn Phức, Nguyễn Tri Phương, and Phan Huy Chú. Compared with their Confucian colleagues in China, Korea, and Japan, Vietnamese Confucian intellectuals were more concerned with observing Western countries in Asia. What they observed was the briskly maneuvering Western powers inspired by the imperialism of the nineteenth century.

The attitude of Phan Huy Chú illustrates the usual reaction of Vietnamese intellectuals to experiences in the island Southeast Asian countries. When he visited Singapore and Batavia in 1832, he was overwhelmed by Western goods, materials, and the efficient legal and military systems. He even confessed that Westerners had superior skills in working certain materials that could be compared with the skills of the Chinese. But he was most strongly impressed by the serious competition he witnessed among Christian Western countries, each of which sought to increase its own influence in these regions, and the potential threat this competition posed to his own country.[69] The young Vietnamese intellectuals observed that the threatening Western powers always supported Christianity, and their reports may very well have created fear in the capital, which in turn increased the court's hostility towards Christianity.

At this time, Christianity was popular in Gia Định, and Western missionaries gathered around Lê Văn Duyệt, whom they seemed to trust as a kind of protector. One of these was a French missionary named Régereau, who had secretly landed in Đà Nẵng in 1825. Under the anti-Christianity edict of early 1825, banning the entrance of Western missionaries into Vietnam, he should have been arrested,[70] but he fled to Gia Định and was able to lead a normal life there.

In 1826, Minh Mạng prohibited all missionary work in Vietnam, and he ordered all missionaries sent to Huế to engage in the translation of foreign writings into Vietnamese;[71] they were not allowed to proselytize among the people. In fact, this order was aimed only at the missionaries of southern Vietnam. Subsequent to the edict, only three missionaries appeared in Huế, and these were all men who had been based in Gia Định: Taberd, François-Isidore Gagelin, and Odorico (a

---

[68] *DNTL2*, 192:7b-9a.

[69] Phan Huy Chú, *Hải Trình Chí Lược* (Récit sommaire d'un voyage en mer) (1833), trans. and ed. Phan Huy Lê, Claudine Salmon, and Tạ Trọng Hiệp (Paris: Cahier d'Archipel 25, 1994), pp. 201-2 and 208.

[70] Phan Phát Huồn, *Việt Nam Giáo Sử* (History of Christianity in Vietnam) (Saigon: Cứu Thế Tùng Thư, 1965), p. 279.

[71] *DNTL2*, 47:15.

Franciscan). Taberd complained that they could not find any other priests from the other regions of Vietnam.[72] Obviously Minh Mạng's intention was to separate these men from Lê Văn Duyệt.

A report of Taberd to Paris says that Lê Văn Duyệt expressed his opinion of Minh Mạng's anti-Christian policy in this way: "The king does not remember the services performed by missionaries. They gave us rice when we were hungry, they gave us cloth when we were cold [. . .] the king is repaying charity with ingratitude."[73] This report, however, needs to be cautiously interpreted, for it is not actually direct and trustworthy evidence of Lê Văn Duyệt's reaction. If this opinion was spoken in a private dialogue between Lê Văn Duyệt and Taberd, Duyệt might indeed have said these words, but Taberd alleges that Lê Văn Duyệt wrote this statement in a letter to him. A letter was indisputable recorded evidence, and surely the experienced Lê Văn Duyệt was not so dull as to write direct, personal criticism of the king in a private letter to Taberd. In the same report, Taberd claimed that Lê Văn Duyệt had collected Nguyễn Phúc Ánh's letters to Pigneau, and he implied that Lê Văn Duyệt was preparing to show these letters, containing evidence of Pigneau's contribution to Vietnam, to Minh Mạng.[74] In truth, these letters were given by Taberd to Lê Văn Duyệt when Lê Văn Duyệt came to Huế.[75]

The Christian scholar Adrien Charles Launay, who compiled the records of the Missions Étrangères in the late nineteenth century, wrote that Lê Văn Duyệt reportedly questioned Minh Mạng's anti-Christian policy in these words:

> How could we persecute the European teachers? The rice [they gave us] is still in our teeth! Who helped the late king to take back this kingdom? Your Majesty seems to lose it again. The Tây Sơn persecuted this religion, so they were destroyed. The King of Pegu [Burma] expelled the missionaries, so he lost his position [. . .] Bishop Pigneau's tomb is still here! No, the king cannot do this while I am alive; Your Majesty can do whatever he wants to do after my death.[76]

The above record should also be interpreted cautiously, not as a direct quote from Lê Văn Duyệt, but as an illustration of how French missionaries regarded Lê Văn Duyệt's attitude.

We can glean pieces of valuable information from the above records. From Taberd's report, we can gather that Christian missionaries regarded Lê Văn Duyệt as sympathetic to themselves. Unless they had experienced favorable treatment in Gia Định, they would not have left such record. In fact, Lê Văn Duyệt's attitude to Christian missionaries really was favorable. When the king's order sent the Western missionaries to Huế, Régereau stayed behind in Gia Định by permission of

---

[72] Taboulet, *La geste Française en Indochine*, pp. 326-27.

[73] Ibid., p. 325.

[74] Ibid., p. 325.

[75] Tạ Chí Đại Trường, "Những Bức Thư Chữ Nôm của Nguyễn Ánh Do Giáo Sư Cadière Sưu Tập" (Chu Nom letters of Nguyen Phuc Anh collected by Father Cadiere), *Tập Sản Sử Địa* 11 (1968): 105.

[76] Adrien Charles Launay, *Histoire générale de la Société des Missions Etrangères* Tome 2 (Paris: Téqui, Libraire-Editeur, 1894), p. 535.

Lê Văn Duyệt.[77] If Régereau had been sent to Huế, it was highly possible that he would have been arrested, because he was a person sought by the central government. Under the protection of Lê Văn Duyệt, Régereau resided at Gia Định until at least 1831.[78] During this same period, in 1826, another missionary named Gagelin left his impression of Gia Định's religious atmosphere:

> Dong Nai [Gia Định] is exempt from the brutality of persecution that has been common in all parts of this kingdom. Here, the exercise of religion is not only tolerant but also as free as it can be. Unlike in other provinces, Christians [here] are not inquisitorial about superstitions at all, neither do the people who believe in superstitions oppose them [Christians].[79]

Next we consider the perception of the Christian missionaries revealed in Launay's description, which can be interpreted as a record of the thoughts of Christian missionaries. Launay's summary makes it clear that they were proud of their contribution to the founding of the Nguyễn dynasty; they believed they had given Vietnamese many gifts of food; and they might have believed that God would insure the Nguyễn dynasty met the same fate as Tây Sơn and Burma unless it maintained a friendly relationship with its Christian missionaries. As a core member of the Gia Định regime that had relied on the support of the Christians, Lê Văn Duyệt might well have shared these opinions, as we know that emperor Gia Long did, for during his reign hostile action towards the Christianity was not seen in Vietnam. Under the rule of Lê Văn Duyệt, no Christians were persecuted or executed in Gia Định despite the central government's pressure.

Minh Mạng was not so sanguine about the Christian influence, for he observed that Asian countries—notably India and various Southeast Asian countries—which had allowed contact with Western powers had been subsequently colonized, while different Confucian countries that tightly restricted Christianity were still safe. Christianity had been persecuted from the first half of the eighteenth century in China, from the end of the eighteenth century in Korea, and from the seventeenth century in Japan. From his officials who occasionally paid visits to China, Minh Mạng must have heard what had happened to Christians in these countries, and he may have been attempting to follow their examples.

In regard to the Burmese-British war referred to in the "Lê Văn Duyệt's appeal," cited by Launay, Minh Mạng again had his own opinion, which differed from the interpretations of Christian missionaries. While the missionaries, and possibly Lê Văn Duyệt, thought the Burmese experience ought to teach Vietnam that it was dangerous to persecute Christians, Minh Mạng regarded it as a proof of the Westerners' desire for territorial expansion. He feared that Western military expansion would extend into neighboring Southeast Asian countries. Discussing the Burmese-British war with the members of Siam's mission to the Huế court in 1824,

---

[77] Taboulet, *La geste Française en Indochine*, p. 327; A letter of Gagelin written Feb. 1828. From *Annales de L'association de la Propagation de la Foi* 21 (July 1830).

[78] In his letter written in March, 1831, Régereau claimed that he had listened to 1,349 confessions, baptized ten adults, presided over fifteen marriages and organized catechism six times during 1830. A letter of Régereau, *Annales de L'association de la Propagation de la Foi* 34 (October 1833).

[79] A letter of Gagelin written in Dec. 1826. From *Annales de L'association de la Propagation de la Foi* 17 (May 1829).

Minh Mạng expressed his concern that Siam itself would be threatened if Britain won. He knew well that Siam and Burma had been hostile rivals for generations. Despite this fact, he claimed the situation would become more dangerous for Siam if Burma was invaded by the British, because Siam would then be living with a more threatening and powerful neighbor on her western border.[80]

Towards the end of Lê Văn Duyệt's rule in Gia Định, the restriction on missionary activities was tightened. Taberd managed to escape to Siam when Lê Văn Duyệt died in 1832, but his two colleagues, Gagelin and Odorico, who had come to Huế with him, were executed.

Convicts

The first half of the nineteenth century saw the emergence of a new element of the population of southern Vietnam: convicts in exile from the northern and central regions. Thanh Thuận, An Thuận, Hồi Lương, and Bắc Thuận were the four main convict groups. Lê Văn Duyệt utilized their manpower, mustering many as soldiers, and even appointing some as officials in Gia Định—a normal practice that he learned from Gia Long.[81] But Minh Mạng showed a strong suspicion of this practice, which he regarded it as an obvious violation of the state rule. We need to pay attention to these four convict groups, because they constituted an important element that formed part of the diverse Gia Định population during the period of Gia Định Thành.

Thanh Thuận and An Thuận were troops made up of former insurgents (including ethnic minorities) who had participated in insurrections in the Thanh Hóa and Nghệ An regions during the 1810s. The Thanh Thuận and An Thuận battalions were formed by Lê Văn Duyệt and given names that identified the regional origins of their members.[82] Since the word *thuận*, used in both names, means "obedience," the new titles signified that the former bandits of Thanh Hóa and Nghệ An had sworn obedience to the government in general, and to Lê Văn Duyệt in particular. When Lê Văn Duyệt went to Saigon in 1820, these battalions accompanied him.

To understand the other two groups, Hồi Lương and Bắc Thuận, we must first consider Vietnamese systems of exile punishment and military conscription, which were closely linked. One of the common forms of punishment during the first half of the nineteenth century in Vietnam was exile. Generally, criminals from the northern region were exiled to southern Vietnam, and vice versa.[83] Yet the numbers of exiles in the two regions were extremely unbalanced, due, in part, to imbalances in population. It appears that normally more crimes were committed in the central and northern regions than in Gia Định, so that the circulation of exiles flowed most strongly from north to south. Secondly, the unbalanced number of exiles was due to an unequal number of insurrections. According to Phan Thúc Trực's descriptions in *Quốc Sử Di Biên*, most insurrections during the thirty years between 1802 and 1833 took place in Bắc Thành, the region of northern Vietnam. As a matter of fact, no insurrections by Vietnamese occurred in Gia Định before the time of Lê Văn Khôi's

---

[80] *DNTL2*, 28:17b-18a.

[81] See *LTST*, 22:21b; 23b-24a.

[82] Ibid., 22:25a.

[83] *DNTL2*, 27:20-22a.

revolt in 1833. Consequently the influx of exiled criminals from the north into Gia Định was much larger.

This method of punishment was intended not only to penalize criminals and rid the north of potential troublemakers, but also to facilitate the clearing and agricultural development of land in Gia Định. According to the rule of 1807, portions of uncultivated land, as well as seeds, buffalos, and tools for cultivation, were given to the exiled convicts. More importantly, the convicts' wives and children were allowed to go with them. The criminals could never return to their homes.[84]

However, not all convicted exiles found Gia Định to be a land where they were doomed to work until death to serve out their sentences; for some convicts, it offered them opportunities to begin new lives as normal commoners. In 1824, even those exiles who had not completed their compulsory period of labor had their sentences revoked. These were the convicts of northern origin. Ten Hồi Lương platoons were made up of 462 of these criminals, and they were paid a monthly wage.[85] The word *hồi* means "to return," or "to go back," and the word *lương* means "goodness," or "common people," so that the name Hồi Lương refers to the troop made up of former criminals, now pardoned. By this stage, in the mid-1820s, Hồi Lương soldiers had gained a status equal to that of Thanh Thuận and An Thuận troops.

Nguyễn Văn Trắm was one of the Hồi Lương leaders during Lê Văn Khôi's revolt. He had been exiled to Gia Định from Hưng Yên province of northern Vietnam.[86] After Lê Văn Khôi died of disease in 1834, Nguyễn Văn Trắm took command of the rebel army to lead a full resistance against the central court. He remains one of the legendary heroes of Gia Định. Among the southern Vietnamese in the countryside, he has become the symbol of a strict figure who can give direction to unruly youths.[87]

How could the Bắc Thuận soldiers be defined? From its name, we can conclude that this troop was made up of lawbreakers of northern Vietnamese origin. Literally, these were the insurgents of Bắc Thành who agreed to end their rebellion and pledge obedience to the government. Originally, in 1824, the Bắc Thuận troop was made up of the non-registered male residents of the Bắc Thành area.[88] Non-registered people were those who lived outside the villages, and who therefore were not subject to the conscription quotas that the government used to muster a prescribed number of soldiers from each village. Non-registered residents living outside the confines of the villages were recruited, rather than conscripted, into the Vietnamese military. The Bắc Thuận troop was formed in this way.

The Bắc Thuận members had to complete a specified term of compulsory service—either military or labor service—in southern Vietnam and were therefore compelled to move to southern Vietnam. On the way to the south and back to the north, a number of these travelers deserted,[89] so that recruitment of non-registered

---

[84] *DNTL1*, 31:14.

[85] *DNTL2*, 30:12a.

[86] *LTNT*, 45:3b.

[87] Huỳnh Minh, *Gia Định Xưa và Nay*, p. 176.

[88] *DNTL2*, 37:20a; *QSDB*, p. 145.

[89] In 1824, for example, over three hundred of two thousand Bắc Thuận soldiers were lost on the way from Bắc Thành to Huế. *DNTL2*, 29:2b-3a. In 1829, 2,000 of 2,500 Bắc Thuận and one

men in Bắc Thành was an ongoing process, constantly repeated. Other elements were brought into Bắc Thuận as a result, and we can learn something of those elements i f we examine the composition of the Thanh Thuận and the An Thuận troops in 1824. As mentioned above, these two troops were originally formed from ex-bandits from Thanh Hóa and Nghệ An, but in time the components of those troops changed to include: 1) released criminals, 2) surrendered rebels, 3) runaway soldiers from Thanh Thuận, and An Thuận who had decamped when they had been in Gia Định, and 4) non-registered people.[90] In short, recruitment was not restricted to a certain group, and the addition of new elements described above effectively reorganized these troops over time. I think this general method was also used in the ongoing recruitment of soldiers for Bắc Thuận, which was generally regarded as a troop made up of "exiled lawbreakers."[91]

Consequently, both the soldiers of Hồi Lương and the Bắc Thuận share certain distinctive characteristics: they were soldier-lawbreaker-northerners. The Thanh Thuận and the An Thuận could be classified similarly insofar as they were composed of lawbreakers who became soldiers in the Gia Định.

Gia Định was a land where these convicts had a good chance to climb to a higher social position. Some of them maintained close relations with Gia Định power groups. For instance, immediately after Lê Văn Khôi 's revolt broke out, Nguyễn Văn Trắm of the above-mentioned Hồi Lương troop took a position as the second highest military leader.[92] Considering that many former Gia Định officials participated in the revolt, he could not have been appointed to such a high position unless he had already gained access to the main power center of Gia Định.

Lê Văn Duyệt's policy was to utilize the manpower of the ex-convicts even at the level of administrative units. We note Lê Văn Duyệt's request in 1829:

> Each of Gia Định's ministries, six lower administrative units [*phòng*], and the region of Hà Tiên do not have enough officials, but have too much work to do. Please allow me to select some persons who are able to write and calculate among the An Thuận and the Hồi Lương troops and to enlist them at the rank of the lower local officials [*vị nhập lưu thư lại*].[93]

Was it Lê Văn Duyệt's intention to strengthen his own power through the use of convicts? If so, there was no reason for him to make his suggestion publicly to the king. From Lê Văn Duyệt's point of view, utilizing the manpower of the lawbreakers was a normal response, not surprising for a man of his generation, a man who had decades of experience in warfare. In the Gia Định regime under Nguyễn Phúc Ánh, there had been no group that was more disruptive to state rule than the Tây Sơn participants, yet they were accepted into the Gia Định regime so long as they publicly submitted to its authority. In much the same manner, if a former opponent proved himself to be talented within a certain field, he could be appointed to any appropriate position; no internal, exclusive, hierarchal "ladder"

---

thousand other northern soldiers were lost when they returned from Gia Định to Bắc Thành. *DNTL2*, 61:35b-36a.

[90] *DNTL2*, 26:14.

[91] Ibid., 109:3b.

[92] *LTNT*, 45:3.

[93] *DNTL2*, 58:3a.

impeded his accession to a more elevated appointment within the Gia Định regime. Châu Văn Tiếp, Võ Tánh, and especially Lê Chất were such cases, as noted in chapter one.

For Minh Mạng and his officials, Lê Văn Duyệt's proposal was unacceptable. If they allowed the northern convicts to enter the administrative system, "it is like releasing a monkey to climb up a tree," according to Minh Mạng, who reacted to the proposal with fury.[94] This practice of rewarding capable men, regardless of their pasts, must have shocked Minh Mạng and his officials. The practice was part of the Gia Định heritage, but it was essentially opposed to the prestige of state rule.

Chinese Settlers and Rice Smuggling

Fujiwara has already analyzed the connection between the Chinese and the smuggling of rice and opium during the Nguyễn dynasty.[95] His evidence suggests that the Chinese were very likely to have been involved in the smuggling of these goods.[96] In the context of my discussion, the implications of this thesis require further elaboration. Firstly, we must consider the links between rice and opium smuggling and southern Vietnamese capability in the field of commerce. Secondly, this issue should be examined as it relates to the Nguyễn dynasty's basic policy towards Chinese settlers, because in fact the central government's strong opposition to rice and opium smuggling was motivated, in part, by its intent to separate Chinese settlers from Gia Định's power group.

a) Gia Định Rice

The balance between supplies and consumption of rice in the northern and central regions of Vietnam was dependent on southern rice. This situation began in the nineteenth century, when southern rice played a key role in the state economy. In the previous century, of course, Gia Định was known as a fertile land which produced much rice. Its productivity and the variety of its rice were known even in the United States, which was seeking appropriate rice seed for its new land to the west.[97] But it is hard to believe that Gia Định rice was an active element in overseas trade during the previous century. The supply of rice during this time was not always enough to feed the population. That was why, as mentioned in chapter one, Nguyễn Phúc Ánh was reluctant to advance to the region northeast of Biên Hòa in 1792, because if he subdued that territory, he would then be required to use part of Gia Định's rice supply to feed the people there.[98] During this period, there were even cases of rice being imported from Siam.[99]

Several conditions had to be met in order for Gia Định to produce rice sufficient for its own people and a surplus for overseas trade. First, southern Vietnam had to wait until the next century, when the immigration not only from the central region

---

[94] Ibid.

[95] Fujiwara, *Tonanajiashi no Kenkyu*, pp. 283-302.

[96] Ibid., p. 300.

[97] Robert Hopkins Miller, *The United States and Vietnam, 1787-1941* (Washington DC: National Defense University Press, 1990), p. xv.

[98] DNTL1, 6:8b.

[99] Ibid., 9:31b.

but also from the northern territory increased, and additional cultivation of lands in the south generated a corresponding increase in productivity. Second, southern Vietnam had to wait until a stable authority, Gia Định Thành Tổng Trấn, appeared to encourage the production of rice. Third was the matter of markets in the region. Big markets started to open up in the early nineteenth century, when the Southeast Asian island regions began to expand economically, especially with the active incursion of the British imperial forces. Demand for rice drastically increased with the formation of Singapore in 1819.

To the eyes of a northern Vietnamese, Doãn Uẩn, who came from a core region of Red River delta (Nam Định province), the land of Gia Định in the 1830s appeared to be a paradise for peasants:

> At the time of seeding the rice, they just use a bamboo stick to remove the watery weeds on rice fields. Once they seed rice, they pick weeds only once or twice. They hardly expend any labor in plowing or picking weeds. Once they seed, they never take care of the field, but neither do they ever meet flood and drought. During July, August, and September [lunar], they seed, and through October, November, and December [lunar], reap one harvest after another. Once the harvest is done, they leave the bunches of rice on the rice fields. Around February and March [lunar], they bring the buffalo to tread the bunches, and merely pick up the grains. They can do this because rain is rare from winter to spring. In sum, the fields are fertile and grains are rich. Forest resources and fishery products are numerous.[100]

The central court was seriously concerned about the price of rice in Gia Định. Until 1827, Gia Định officials had to report their prices twice a month, while other areas reported once a month.[101] In 1804, soon after the unification, 500,000 *cân* of rice[102] were exported to the Philippines,[103] but this was a special case, for normally the exportation of rice was strictly forbidden, and even foreign traders were unable to acquire it. Each vessel departing from the country was allowed to load a certain quantity of rice for provisions, in proportion to the number of her crew and the anticipated length of her passage, but no more. The penalty for violating these regulations was decapitation.[104]

b) Gia Định Rice for Overseas Trade

The price of rice continued to increase during Minh Mạng's early rule. According to Nguyễn Thế Anh's account, the price rose during the years 1825 to 1829-1830 by

---

[100] Doãn Uẩn, *Doãn Tướng Công Hoạn Tích* (or *Tuy Tĩnh Tử Tạp Ngôn*) (Minister Doan's chronicle of office, or Tuy Tinh Tu's miscellaneous notes) (1842. Hanoi: Viện Hán Nôm A 2177), pp. 13-14.

[101] *DNTL2*, 45:12b.

[102] 1 *cân* was 0.604 kg. See Đỗ Bang, *Kinh Tế Thương Nghiệp Việt Nam Dưới Triều Nguyễn* (The commercial economy of Vietnam during the Nguyen dynasty) (Hue: Nxb Thuận Hóa, 1996), p. 21. 500,000 *cân* was over 300 tons.

[103] *DNTL1*, 23:18a.

[104] White, *A Voyage to Cochin China*, p. 234.

50 percent to 100 percent in the northern territory.[105] The situation in southern Vietnam was similar. A report from Gia Định in 1829 informs us that the rice price climbed sharply towards the end of the 1820s: "Previously, the rice price was very low. The price of one *phương* [38.5 liters] of rice was not higher than 5-6 *mạch* [5/10 – 6/10 *quan*]. These days, however, the rice price hardly drops down under 1 *quan*."[106] The court suspected that this situation was caused in large part by illegal rice exports flowing out of Gia Định:

> The larger land, Gia Định, has very fertile soil and produces more grain than in any other region [in Vietnam]. Until now, the northern area from Bình Định northwards has been dependent on southern rice. Once the rice price of Gia Định jumped, the rest of the regions followed. Smuggling rice outside is a serious affair related to the management of the state economy.[107]

Where did the smuggled Gia Định rice circulate? It was destined most often for southern China, Cambodia, Siam and the regions of island Southeast Asia. Island Southeast Asia was the most popular destination.

According to Minh Mạng, rice in Vietnam cost only about half the price of rice available in foreign countries where it was most expensive.[108] (He may have been using information gathered from his subjects who had been sent to China or to various island Southeast Asian countries.) For this reason, Gia Định rice, though illegal, was attractive to foreign markets. But the lower price was not the only factor encouraging Vietnamese to smuggle and sell rice in these regions. Foreign goods such as knives, swords, muskets, metal tea pots, serge, flannel, broadcloth, calico, and linen lured Vietnamese to trade with the Western colonies.

In normal trading, the profit earned from a single round trip between Vietnam and Singapore, for instance, could amount to 200–400 percent over costs.[109] But if traders dealt in illegal goods, such as rice and opium, the profit was much higher. Opium was the most profitable of the goods to be obtained from the British colonies in island Southeast Asia. Generally, China figured as the main market for British opium during the first half of the nineteenth century. Occasionally, however, British opium could be provided to Vietnamese traders at a cheaper price when the export of opium to the Chinese market was frustrated.[110] Gia Định was the main place of entry for opium into Vietnam. In 1832, shortly before Lê Văn Duyệt died, Minh Mạng complained about the situation:

---

[105] Nguyễn Thế Anh, "Quelques aspects économiques et sociaux du problème du riz au Vietnam dans la prèmier moitié du 19 siècle," *Bulletin de la Société des Études Indochinoises* Tome 42, no. 1-2 (1967): 9.

[106] *DNTL2*, 61:6.

[107] Ibid., 26:10.

[108] Ibid., 79:26b.

[109] Edward Brown, *Cochin-China, and my experience of it. A Seaman's Narrative of His Adventures and Sufferings during a Captivity among Chinese Pirates, on the Coast of Cochin-China, and Afterwards during a journey on Foot Across that Country, in the years 1857-1858* (1861. Taipei: Ch'eng Wen Publishing Company, 1971), pp. 198-99.

[110] *DNTL2*, 201:24b.

As Gia Định Thành neglected to patrol the sea, cunning people secretly carry away rice and sell it [. . .] Basically, rice is very important for my people, so i t should not be sold outside Vietnam [. . . the cunning people] return with opium to make more profit. This situation is most serious in Gia Định.[111]

c) Suspect: Chinese or Vietnamese?

Lê Văn Duyệt offered his own analysis of the factors that were increasing the price of rice throughout Vietnam. He gave three reasons for the increased price: *gian thương* (cunning merchants) were secretly buying up rice; *thanh thuyền đáp khách* (Chinese passengers) were consuming more; and *đại dịch thuyền* (rice transportation junks on behalf of government) were illegally trading rice.[112]

"Chinese passengers" referred to Chinese emigrants on Chinese-owned and Chinese-crewed junks from mainland China. At this time, Gia Định was one of the most attractive destinations for Chinese emigrants. According to a report from Gia Định Thành, the officials of Gia Định Thành had been overwhelmed by the increasing number of these immigrants. In 1826, it was reported that the region absorbed three thousand new families of Chinese immigrants,[113] which meant that the region now had approximately fifteen thousand new mouths to feed. Chinese immigrants to southern Vietnam usually brought their families. They were generally not peasants, but people from the merchant class and poor city dwellers,[114] which is why they usually chose jobs in the urban area rather than settling as rice farmers. Though they might sometimes become farmers, they were inclined to grow items such as vegetables and fruit for the urban market. Thus, the increase of Chinese immigrants in Vietnam led to an increase of rice consumers, rather than producers.

The Gia Định government was concerned about this influx of Chinese immigrants, not only because they worried about the consumption of their rice supplies, but also because they suspected that the ships carrying these immigrants were loaded with illegal trade goods, notably opium. Though the following is a list of such goods from 1857, a few decades after the period under discussion here, i t provides an insight into the items brought into Vietnam by Chinese immigrants: tea, beans, wheat, lead, Chinese coins, and opium.[115] Opium flowed into Gia Định not only from island Southeast Asia, but also from China. That was why Lê Văn Duyệt made the accusation that "the *thanh thuyền đáp khách* are luring Gia Định people to smoke opium."[116]

Next, the cunning traders, the "*gian thương* who were buying up rice" in Gia Định, might have been Chinese settlers, either *thanh nhân* or *minh hương*, but their ranks also might have included local Vietnamese eager for profit. This latter supposition can be backed up by examining Lê Văn Duyệt's third factor: illegal rice transportation. Local Vietnamese were the masters of the junks sent to transport

---

[111] Ibid., 79:27.

[112] Ibid., 61:6b-7a.

[113] Ibid., 40:17b.

[114] Mạc Đường, *Vấn Đề Dân Tộc ở Đồng Bằng Sông Cửu Long* (Ethnic issues in the Mekong Delta) (Ho Chi Minh City: Nxb Khoa Học Xã Hội, 1992), p. 60.

[115] Brown, *Cochin-China, and my experience of it*, p. 82.

[116] DNTL2, 61:7a.

rice. Rice was supposed to be transported to different regions within Vietnam to balance supply and demand; these vessels circulated mainly from Gia Định to the central and northern regions. Basically, government junks were responsible for this task, but the work was also entrusted to private junk owners.[117] It can hardly be expected that the price paid by the government was always satisfactory to the junk masters. Once a junk was moving to a destination, free from the watchful eyes in the harbor, we can imagine that the master might decide to conduct business in a different place where he could get a bigger profit. For example, it was more profitable to sell the rice to Chinese traders who could be found in the far seas. In later years, the junks ventured even farther. When a court official took a position in the administrative unit of the province of Vĩnh Long after 1832, he found that transportation junks had been going to the regions of island Southeast Asia, Kuang Tung, and Hai Nan.[118] According to the observation of John Crawfurd, who encountered thirteen small junks on his way to Huế, the capacity of each junk was "from five to seven hundred *piculs* burden."[119] From Lê Văn Duyệt's point of view, recorded in the 1829 report, the masters of these junks transporting rice, all local Vietnamese, were the people who should be suspected of conducting the illegal rice trade.

As long as rice was a profitable item and transportation was monopolized by local Vietnamese, it was unavoidable that these Vietnamese should attempt to buy up rice, too. That is the reason why the *gian thương* could be Vietnamese as well as Chinese settlers.

d) Commercial Activities of the Gia Định Vietnamese

Lê Văn Duyệt's diagnosis reveals a clue to a possible transformation in the economy of Gia Định. I believe that the Vietnamese were gaining in the field of commerce from the beginning of the nineteenth century, a situation that differed markedly from the eighteenth century, when the commerce of Gia Định had come

---

[117] In 1836, 3 *quan* was paid if one *thống* (57 *phương* 9 *thăng*) of rice was carried by *đại dịch thuyền* from Gia Định to Huế. Châu Bản Triều Nguyễn (Vermilion Records of the Nguyen dynasty) (ANU Library, microfilm reels 60-64 [1836-1837]), lunar January 25, 1836.

[118] *DNTL2*, 167:15b-16a.

[119] John Crawfurd, *Journal of an Embassy from the Governor-General of India to the Courts of Siam and Cochin China* (1828. Singapore: OUP, 1987), p. 230. It was 250-350 dollars' worth of goods. According to John White's experience during 1819–1820 in Saigon, high quality rice was one Spanish dollar per one *picul* (roughly 60 kg). White, *A Voyage to Cochin China*, p. 322. John Crawfurd noted the same cost in 1822. See Crawfurd, *Journal of an Embassy from the Governor-General of India to the Courts of Siam and Cochin China*, p. 226. However, I do not believe it represented the real market price because probably a higher price was offered to the foreigners by merchants or brokers. The real market price did not exceed half the price they paid during that time, according to the report from Gia Định. *DNTL2*, 61:6. Towards the middle of the 1820s, the price of rice rose. Through his analysis of Châu Bản stored in the National Archives in Hanoi, Phan Huy Lê provides us with the rice price in 1825 and in 1826. In Gia Định, the rice price was 1.2 *mân* or *quan* per *phương* (28.5 kg) in 1825, and 0.9 *mân* per *phương* in 1826. Phan Huy Lê, "Châu Bản Triều Nguyễn và Châu Bản Năm Minh Mệnh 6-7" (Vermillion record of the Nguyen dynasty during 1825-1826) (manuscript), p. 33.

* 1 *quan* = 1 *mân* = 50 cents = 10 *tiền* = 10 *mạch* = 600 *đồng*. White, *A Voyage to Cochin China*, p. 241. But the value of Vietnamese currency against the Spanish dollar dropped by one third by 1833. See Phan Huy Chú, *Hải Trình Chí Lược*, p. 188.

to be dominated by the Chinese. Without reliance on the Chinese, Nguyễn Phúc Ánh's faction could not have achieved final victory over the Tây Sơn.

Chinese dominance in commerce lasted until the next century. Western missions in the nineteenth century, such as those led by John White, John Crawfurd, and his follower, George Finlayson, found that the Chinese were actively engaged in commerce in Saigon during 1819–1822. Visitors often remarked on the active Chinese role in trade, comparing it with the role of the Vietnamese, who were reportedly less capable in these pursuits. According to such witnesses, the streets were filled with lively Chinese vendors and arrays of Chinese products for sale:

> These industrious and enterprising people are the butchers, the tailors, the confectioners, and the pedlars of Cochin China: they are met with in every bazaar, and in every street [. . .] they are also the bankers, and money-changers [. . .] Many of the cooking utensils, and a principal part of the clothing of the Onamese [Vietnamese], are brought from China, from whence they also have their porcelain, tea, many of their drugs and medicines, cabinet-work, and, in short, almost every article of convenience which they possess.[120]

However, there are some things we must take into account when considering Western visitors' descriptions of Saigon in the nineteenth century. First, the Saigon they observed did not comprise the same area as present day Saigon, but was the region of Big Market, Chợ Lớn, to the west of twentieth-century Saigon, as discussed in the previous chapter. It was the Saïgon where "the *hội quán* [buildings of the Chinese associations] of Phúc Châu [Fu Chou], Quảng Đông [Kuang Tung], Trào Châu [Ch'ao Chou], Ôn Lăng [Wen Ling], Chương Châu [Chang Chou] are located."[121] This fact would have helped convince the Western visitors that the Chinese dominated trade throughout Vietnam.[122]

The second problem with their descriptions was the limitations on their experience in Vietnam. Whether in Saigon or Chợ Lớn, they spent all their time in the urban areas, where Chinese vendors were most likely to be encountered. To comprehend the real situation regarding commerce and trade, not only in urban, but also in rural areas, we need to rely on evidence from the following decade. After court officials took over Gia Định in 1832, they found and reported that numbers of people in Gia Định had been pursuing *"mạt nghiệp"* (the lowest occupation), meaning trade or commerce. The most popular means of transport in Gia Định was by water; there were no taxes on trade by water, and evidence suggests that many indigenous Vietnamese traders navigated these routes. In 1835, when the central government launched its own policy in the recently pacified land of Gia Định, a central official named Trương Phúc Cương reported what he saw in the region to the west of the Upper Mekong River (Tiền Giang):

---

[120] White, *A Voyage to Cochin China*, pp. 261-62.

[121] *GDTTC*, 6:18.

[122] The areas of the city that mainly comprise Saigon today began to be developed from the end of the eighteenth century, when Nguyễn Phúc Ánh established his citadel, which was to be the city's administrative and military center, to the east of the older neighborhoods. By the time of Crawfurd's mission, this region was called Bến Nghé. In that area, the members of the mission encountered well-planned streets: "The plan of the streets is superior to that of many European capitals." Finlayson, *The Mission to Siam and Hue*, p. 305.

Six provinces of southern Vietnam have fertile land, but people are idle and many of them have professions [of commerce] by means of ships and boats. Thus, fertile land is abandoned. Until now, no tax has been charged on the trade ships [with the exception of the trade ship to Cambodia]. If we charge these ships, the people can be called back from the lowest occupation to farming.[123]

In short, we can conclude that a high proportion of Gia Định's Vietnamese population, in addition to Chinese settlers, engaged in commerce. During the first half of the nineteenth century, residential areas to the west of Saigon were divided by streams. According to Doãn Uẩn's observation in 1833: "of the land of southern Vietnam, only the region around Saigon is solid. In the other regions, you will see water if you only dig into the ground one *thước* [about 30cm]. Streams cross like the warp and weft of cloth. There is no land access between villages. Once you go out of the gate, you cannot reach different villages without using boats."[124] Residential areas were scattered and isolated from each other. Once the rainy season came, each residential area was also inundated. Thus people had to rely on a supply of goods from the outside. It was a condition that made trade by boats essential in Gia Định.

Even in the region of Saigon, where the Chinese dominated commerce, there were active Vietnamese merchants; the Vietnamese controlled trade in large amounts of sugar in 1819–1820, for example. When John White sought to purchase goods to load his ships in 1819, Vietnamese female merchants approached him, offering goods such as sugar, silk, cotton, gamboges, and other articles for sale. He found that these articles were 50 to 100 percent more expensive than usual. To avoid the inflated price, this American tried to procure sugar via a different route, possibly from the Chinese merchants who had connections with a Chinese high-ranking official in Gia Định Thành Tổng Trấn. White describes the furious reaction of the Vietnamese merchants against this Chinese official. The merchants insisted that their privileges had been interfered with.[125]

There is also evidence that local Vietnamese merchants had already accumulated enough maritime experience to navigate to the island regions of Southeast Asia by themselves. John White concluded, from his observations around Saigon, that Vietnamese maritime skills had reached significantly high standards: "It is perhaps, of all the powers in Asia, the best adapted to maritime adventure [. . .] the Vietnamese rivaling even the Chinese as sailors."[126] When Minh Mạng wanted to resume the state-run trade based in Huế,[127] he was startled because his man insisted on using Gia Định vessels for a safe journey to the Straits of Malacca.[128] These examples reveal the superiority of Gia Định's maritime experience compared with the expertise available in any other region of Vietnam.

---

[123] *DNTL2*, 159:13.

[124] Doãn Uẩn, *Doãn Tướng Công Hoạn Tích*, pp. 13 and 15.

[125] White, *A Voyage to Cochin China*, pp. 208, 245, 246-47, 271; 332.

[126] Ibid., p. 265.

[127] This operation had stopped in 1801. See Ch'en Chingho, "Gencho Shoki no 'Kashukomu' ni Tsuite" (Comments on 'The Official affairs of the Ha Chau [Regions below Vietnam], *Sodaiajiakenkyu* 11 (1990): 75-6.

[128] *DNTL2*, 16:18b-19a.

In time, the Gia Định Vietnamese came to travel as a matter of course between southern Vietnam and the island regions of Southeast Asia such as the Straits of Malacca, Batavia, Singapore, and the Philippines. It appears that Vietnamese sailors were frequently encountered in the waters around these locations, for during the 1820s through 1830s, documents from these regions left records on "junks from Cochinchina."[129] Some of these "junks from Cochinchina" may have been the vessels of Chinese settlers in Vietnam, which means that these reports cannot give us a clear picture of Vietnamese, as opposed to Chinese, trade at this time. For such information, records by the Vietnamese are more reliable. Local Vietnamese were occasionally discovered trading in the regions of island Southeast Asia by the officials of the state-run trade missions: "Once they [Vietnamese private ships] saw state vessels, they scattered to the four winds [. . .] In exchange for rice, what they brought back was opium."[130]

Gia Định Vietnamese commercial ability was demonstrated in state-run trade. If we carefully review the court chronicles of the reigns from Minh Mạng to Tự Đức, one name—Đào Trí Phú—appears frequently during this period in connection with matters of foreign trade with the Western world. This man's original name was Đào Trí Kính, but it was changed to the eccentric Đào Trí Phú, which means "accumulation of wealth." He came from the district of Long Thành in the region of Biên Hòa, and was a Gia Định graduate, *cử nhân*, of 1825.[131] He met his end in 1854, being torn to pieces after he was convicted of participating in the failed coup by Hồng Bảo, Tự Đức's elder brother. The court chronicle's description, therefore, is not friendly. Nevertheless, Đào Trí Phú's contribution to the state-run trade is apparent in the record. He was the most important central official in charge of purchasing foreign goods from the regions of island Southeast Asia and the eastern part of the Indian subcontinent. He who can be called the Nguyễn dynasty's "state businessman," was accomplished in foreign languages, and, according to the court chronicle, had accumulated great wealth in his frequent trips overseas.[132] Because of his talents at business and foreign languages, he mainly worked at the Board of Finance at the central government. It was he who introduced steam ships to Vietnam after he commanded his first trip to Batavia in 1839.[133] He is described as being so accurate and careful that, working through the night, he was able to complete an account book without any mistakes, even when he was smoking opium,

---

[129] Wong Lin Ken, "The Trade of Singapore," *Journal of the Malayan Branch of the Royal Asiatic Society* 33,192 (1960): 155; Crawfurd, *Journal of an Embassy from the Governor-General of India to the Courts of Siam and Cochin China*, p. 226.

[130] *DNTL2*, 166:33b.

[131] Cao Tự Thanh, *Nho Giáo ở Gia Định* (Confucianism in Gia Dinh) (Ho Chi Minh City: Nxb Thành Phố Hồ Chí Minh, 1998), pp. 124-25; Cao Xuân Dục, *Quốc Triều Hương Khoa Lục* (Record of regional examination graduates under the current dynasty) (hereafter *QTHKL*), trans. Nguyễn Thúy Nga and Nguyễn Thị Lâm (n.d. Ho Chi Minh City: Nxb Thành Phố Hồ Chí Minh, 1993), p. 151.

[132] *DNTL3*, 41:8a.

[133] Choi, Byung Wook, "Shipgusegi Cheonban (1823-1847) Betnameui Tongnamashia Kwanseon Muyeok" (Vietnamese court vessel trade in Southeast Asia during the first half of the nineteenth century), *Dongyang Sahak Yongu* (Journal of Asian Historical Studies) 70 (2000): 181-2.

a favorite indulgence when he traveled overseas.[134] When he was involved in Hồng Bảo's plot, he tried to use his own commercial network overseas to procure military support from outside.[135] Đào Trí Phú was an exemplary Gia Định man with a talent for commerce.

Considering the circumstances mentioned above, Lê Văn Duyệt's analysis becomes increasingly convincing. The illegal rice and opium trade was run not only by Chinese, but also by local Vietnamese. Even the court officials agreed with his assessment.[136] Nonetheless, Minh Mạng and his men fixed their eyes more on the Chinese settlers. In 1827, the *thanh nhân* group of Gia Định asked for permission to participate in the rice transportation business. This request seems to have been granted by Lê Văn Duyệt in Gia Định, but it was refused by the central court because "the cunning *thanh nhân* are secretly trading rice with Chinese merchants in the far islands."[137]

e) Chinese in Gia Định Thành

Many Chinese settlers were involved in ruling Gia Định Thành, as had also been true during the Gia Định regime. Trịnh Hoài Đức and Ngô Nhân Tĩnh were in the top leadership positions of Gia Định Thành. Nguyễn Hữu Nghị, another *thanh nhân*,[138] who had been a retainer of Lê Văn Duyệt's since he was stationed in Huế during Gia Long's reign, also played an important role in the government. After Lê Văn Duyệt was appointed as the governor-general of Gia Định, Nguyễn Hữu Nghị also moved to Gia Định to accompany him. Soon after he relocated, he was appointed as the head of the local ministry of justice in Gia Định Thành Tổng Trấn.[139]

Another influential Chinese was Lưu Tín, a rich merchant, born not in China, but in Hội An Vietnam. As did many of his expatriate countrymen who had emigrated from China to Vietnam, he kept his identity as Chinese. When he was twenty years old, he visited the land of his ancestors in China. After his business trips to the north, south, and China, he eventually decided to settle in Gia Định, where his business prospered.[140] The prosperity of his business was both the cause and result of his relations with Lê Văn Duyệt. As was normal during the Gia Định regime and during Gia Định Thành, the personal relationship between this enterprising young man and Lê Văn Duyệt developed into an official relationship.

---

[134] Trần Tân Gia, *Bà Tâm Huyền Kính Lục* (An account of compassionate hearts and hanging mirrors) (1897. Hanoi: Viện Hán Nôm A 2027), p. 102.

[135] Ibid., p. 103.

[136] *DNTL2*, 167:15b-16b. For the ethnic Vietnamese merchants in the field of overseas trade in the nineteenth century, see Choi, Byung Wook, "Shipgusegi Chungban Nambu Betnameui Taeoemuyeokgoa Betnam Sang'incheung' eui Hyeongseong" (The Rise of Vietnamese Overseas Traders during the middle of the nineteenth century), *Dongyang Sahak Yongu* (Journal of Asian Historical Studies) 78 (2002).

[137] *DNTL2*, 46:28b-29a.

[138] *Lê Công Văn Duyệt Sự Trạng*, p. 16.

[139] *DNTL2*, 7:14a.

[140] Đinh Xuân Lâm, Nguyễn Phan Quang, "Bốn Bang Thư, Một Tài Liệu Có Giá Trị Về Cuộc Khởi Nghĩa Lê Văn Khôi (1833-1835)" (Bon Bang's statement, a valuable document about Le Van Khoi's revolt), *NCLS* 178 (1978): 77.

First, Lưu Tín was adopted as a son by Lê Văn Duyệt.[141] Next, he was appointed as a member of Hành Nhân Ty, the organization in charge of the foreign trade of Gia Định Thành.[142] Possibly, as Shimao claims, Lê Văn Duyệt's group received financial support from Chinese merchants like Lưu Tín.[143] Certainly it cannot be denied that the Chinese immigrants in Gia Định enjoyed favorable treatment from the local government, thanks to their connections with ethnic Chinese who were appointed as influential Vietnamese officials, including these men like Trịnh Hoài Đức and Lưu Tín.

Moreover, ethnic Chinese officials were directly involved in commercial activities. According to John White's observation during his stay (1819–1820), "the acting governor of the Gia Định was a petty dealer in sugar and other merchandise, and was leagued with other petty dealers."[144] John White kept his own Chinese agent for the same business.[145] It might have been impossible for John White to recognize that the acting governor was a *minh hương* member. A court biography informs us that the acting governor was Trịnh Hoài Đức, who was in charge of the Gia Định Thành when the governor-general, Nguyễn Văn Nhân, was absent visiting Huế.[146]

The many contributions and strong influence of Chinese officials and merchants in Gia Định Thành inclined the southerners to shield these allies from unwanted restrictions imposed by the central government in Huế. We can see this process at work if we consider the imposition—and avoidance—of state taxes. When new immigrants landed in Gia Định in the nineteenth century, they were visited by the heads of local Chinese associations according to their respective origins in China. The majority of the new immigrants belonged to a *bang*, the chief association of the *thanh nhân*, while some of them were accepted into a *minh hương* association instead; that is why, on their arrival, the new immigrants were commonly visited by the leaders of *thanh nhân* associations together with heads of *minh hương* associations.[147] But the majority of the immigrants were organized as members of *thanh nhân* associations. Their names were also registered on the list of *bang*. After this stage, newcomers could hide themselves in *bang* associations. Most immigrants quickly settled down in the new land under the protection of the association they belonged to. Though the following case dates from the twentieth century, the story of Quách Đàm, introduced by Hoàng Anh, will help us to understand how Chinese immigrants settled down in Gia Định.

---

[141] Ibid.

[142] *LTST*, 45:2a.

[143] Shimao, "Meimeiki (1820-1840) Betonamu no Nankichiho Tochi ni Kansuru Ichi Kosatsu," p. 180.

[144] White, *A Voyage to Cochin China*, p. 287.

[145] Ibid., p. 332.

[146] *LTST*, 11:6a.

[147] *Khâm Định Đại Nam Hội Điển Sự Lệ* (Official compendium of institutions and usages of Imperial Vietnam) (hereafter *KDDNHDSL*) (1851. Hanoi: Viện Hán Nôm VHv 1570), *thanh nhân*, p. 5. This is important evidence that the members of *minh hương* were not always Ming refugees' descendants during the nineteenth century. From 1843, the children of *thanh nhân* Chinese were also to be registered as members of *minh hương*. See chapter five of this book.

His family left their homeland for Vietnam with empty hands. With the financial help of friends from the same homeland, he did business in collecting discarded materials such as duck feathers, empty bottles, and crushed metal, [. . .]. Afterwards he moved to another business to trade in buffalo leather, the gills and the bladders of fish, and rice. Among these, his main commodity was rice. It was not only for domestic use but also for export. He usually sent his people to every place in the six provinces of southern Vietnam in order to collect rice, and store it in his warehouses located in Chợ Lớn. After waiting for the price to rise, he sold it off.[148]

The problem discovered by Lê Văn Duyệt was that the new immigrants, whose economic conditions were loosely reported by the associations to which they belonged, were too often exempt from tax payments as a result. Usually, the newcomers were registered as *cung cố* (extremely poor employees) or *vô vật lực giả* (people without property), both categories that left them exempt from taxation. What's more, they were seldom converted to taxpayers even though they might quickly achieve a more a stable life by accumulating property in the new land.[149] Responding to the situation, the Gia Định Thành suggested that they would charge 6.5 *quan* in taxes for the ordinary *thanh nhân*, and that they would exempt the "empty-handed" *thanh nhân* from taxation. Lê Văn Duyệt's suggestion reached the Huế court in 1827,[150] but it did not please Minh Mạng, who saw that it would be difficult to identify "the empty handed," and that this ambiguity would provide the *thanh nhân* with more opportunities to avoid taxes. Minh Mạng's argument was more logical and realistic in terms of rounding up the tax payers: "I know the newcomers are really poor, but my paradise will not let them remain poor, then they will be able to pay tax."[151] Minh Mạng's idea was that new Chinese immigrants should be charged the full amount in principle. Half the amount was to be charged to those who were judged as extremely poor for three years. Afterwards, they would be expected to pay the full amount. This decision was delivered to Gia Định.

But, before long, Minh Mạng and his men discovered that this rule was not being applied to the *thanh nhân* in Gia Định. The so-called "extremely poor *thanh nhân*" were being exempted from paying tax in Gia Định. From 1830, when Minh Mạng and his officials began to take power over Gia Định, their rule was

---

[148] Hoàng Anh, "Chợ Bình Tây Xưa" (Binh Tay Market in the past), *Xưa và Nay* no. 36B (Ho Chi Minh City, 1997): 9.

[149] *DNTL2*, 40:17b-18a.

[150] Ibid., 40:18a. In fact, Gia Định's suggestion was quite favorable to the *thanh nhân*. First of all, their tax was lower than that of *minh hương*. According to the rule of 1826, one *minh hương* member's tax was 2 *lượng* of silver. The exact price of silver in 1826 is not known. But it is possible to figure out roughly the silver price of that year by referring to the exact prices of two other times: the price (of silver) was 3 *quan* per 1 *lượng* in 1824, and it rose to 4.7 *quan* per 1 *lượng* in 1828. See *DNTL2*, 23:15b; 54:24a. The amount of the tax charged to the *thanh nhân* seems to have been calculated from the silver price of 1827, and the amount was almost equal to that of *minh hương*. But the amount of the *thanh nhân*'s tax was supposed to be less, because Vietnamese currency kept losing its value against silver. Fujiwara, *Tonanajiashi no Kenkyu*, p. 341. In 1845, the price of 1 *lượng* of silver rose to 9 *quan* in Hà Tiên province. *DNTL3*, 56:18a.

[151] *DNTL2*, 40:18a.

implemented more consistently throughout the south. In the Hà Tiên region, this amount of tax levied on *thanh nhân* rose steeply to nearly triple its original sum.[152]

Though the central government banned sea route rice transportation by Chinese, the Chinese settlers did not give up this enormously profitable business. As long as the alliances between Chinese associations and the ruling group of the Gia Định Thành were maintained, Chinese settlers must have found various means to escape the government's ban. They could register their junks under the names of their Vietnamese colleagues, including their Vietnamese wives or concubines. Since most ships in the Gia Định region were registered under women's names,[153] this was a real possibility. Another strategy was to transport rice with forged permission documents, a practice which required the active collusion of Gia Định Thành officials. A case of this sort was uncovered by one of Minh Mạng's officials in 1837; it turned out that a *thanh nhân* had been doing his business this way for ten years.[154]

Minh Mạng's intention was to eradicate Chinese influence on the economy of Gia Định in particular, and on the economy of Vietnam in general. Every year state vessels sailed to the regions of island Southeast Asia or to the eastern part of India and Kuang Tung to purchase necessary goods. By government order, Chinese were completely excluded from these trips.[155] As mentioned before, Chinese were also prohibited from transporting rice by sea; their request to participate in this business was refused by the court in 1827, though it had been approved by the Gia Định government. The request was made again ten years later, but this time the result was more disastrous to the Chinese immigrants. Whether *thanh nhân* or *minh hương*, they were permanently prohibited from making or purchasing ships for sea travel. In other words, the Chinese immigrants were banned from maritime trade forever.[156] Minh Mạng's basic view was: "Chinese settlers [*thanh nhân*] are not reliable."[157]

CONCLUSION

Gia Định Thành Tổng Trấn was the administrative unit that ruled Gia Định. From 1808 to 1832, there were three governors-general of Gia Định, all of them Gia Định men. Broad rights were given to the governors-general, such as the rights to rule the whole region of Gia Định, to control Cambodia, to decide law suits, to make appointments or dismiss local officials, and to collect profits and conduct all business on the frontier. Land clearance, construction of transport, and overseas trade were also under the governor-general's own control. He filled influential

---

[152] Ibid., 173:13a.

[153] Ibid., 183:42b.

[154] Ibid., 179:29b.

[155] Instead, there are pieces of evidence that Westerners were hired as important crew members. Phan Thanh Giản informs us that a Portuguese called "An Ton" was commanding one vessel of the mission Phan took on a trip to Batavia in 1830. Phan Thanh Giản, *Lương Khê Thi Thảo* (Poetry of Luong Khe in manuscript form) (1876. Hanoi: Viện Hán Nôm VHv 151), 10:170. In 1837, Minh Mạng directed a monthly salary be paid to a Western helmsman hired for a vessel called "Linh Phượng." The monthly salary of this man was fifty Spanish dollars. Châu Bản Triều Nguyễn, lunar October 5, 1837.

[156] DNTL2, 177:27b-28a.

[157] Ibid., 218:24a.

positions with southerners or with his own individual retainers. In other words, Gia Định was a semi-autonomous territory in the south until an historic reform was implemented by the central government in 1832.

Among the three governors-general of Gia Định, Lê Văn Duyệt was the most prominent. His term as governor-general was longer than either term of the other two governors-general, Nguyễn Văn Nhân and Nguyễn Huỳnh Đức. He was appointed governor-general of Gia Định twice. His first term was during the reign of Gia Long, but this appointment was relatively brief (1812-1813). His more important term started at the beginning of Minh Mạng's reign. He ruled Gia Định from 1820 until his death in 1832. He was one of Minh Mạng's greatest supporters when Minh Mạng was designated the successor of Gia Long in 1816. But he was too faithful to the heritage of the Gia Định regime that had been formed during the civil war. During the rule of Lê Văn Duyệt, Christians and Chinese settlers actively played central roles in the Gia Định ruling circles, just as they had done in the Gia Định regime of the previous century. Power stemmed from personal relationships between individuals, so that even ex-convicts were often recruited to join the group of men in power.

During the 1820s, political tension was generated between Minh Mạng and Lê Văn Duyệt by their different policies towards these three groups. Although there was continuity in Gia Định, there was also a shift at the center of politics in Vietnam from 1820, when Minh Mạng took the throne. The Gia Định people and Gia Định's relatively egalitarian heritage had been dominant during the reign of his father. But, from the beginning of Minh Mạng's reign, men from the central and northern regions began to replace the people of Gia Định. They were mainly armed with Confucian knowledge, and guided by Vietnam-centric ideas. This second generation of the Nguyễn dynasty wanted to eliminate the special culture of the Gia Định regime from the land of Gia Định. Elements in the character of the Gia Định had helped to unify the territory earlier, but, according to the second generation's point of view, these same elements now threatened to undermine that unity.

CHAPTER THREE

DISMANTLING SOUTHERN POWER

From the point of view of Minh Mạng and his men, the land of Gia Định was thoroughly sheltered by Lê Văn Duyệt's prestige. It was a place where Christians were publicly declaring and practicing their religion without any restriction; convicts were leading normal lives; and it was the land in which Chinese were freely exercising their commercial talent at the expense of the king's subjects' wealth and health. On one hand, the central court rejected all recommendations from Lê Văn Duyệt favoring those people (Christians, convicts, and Chinese immigrants). On the other hand, the central court found itself unable to implement effective actions restricting these populations in the land of Gia Định.

Plate 4. Hue Royal Palace Gate. One of the most impressive parts of the Hue palace. It conveys the prestige of the central court. Credit: the author, 1994.

In contrast, Bắc Thành (northern Vietnam) was on the way to being dismantled by the central government. After the death of Nguyễn Văn Thành, the first governor-general and a Gia Định man, in 1816, the power of the governor-general of Bắc Thành quickly declined. When Minh Mạng took the throne, the governor-general of Bắc Thành was Lê Chất (from Bình Định, in the central region). He was not as politically astute as Lê Văn Duyệt,[1] and died just after his resignation in 1826. The next governor-general, Trương Văn Minh, another native of Gia Định, left his position after two years,[2] leaving the position of the governor-general of the Bắc Thành vacant for several years. Finally, a civil official, Lê Đại Cương (from Bình Định), was appointed vice governor-general in 1831 and instructed to begin dismantling and dividing Bắc Thành into provinces.[3] This administrative reform was completed by the end of that year.

In this chapter, two main issues will be discussed. First, I will examine how the central government undermined the authority of the Gia Định ruler. It was a cautious process, designed to reduce local power step by step. Secondly, I will examine how local personnel were replaced with representatives more closely aligned with the government in Huế. This involved a substitution of Lê Văn Duyệt's men by Minh Mạng's men, and a replacement of Gia Định men by men from the central and northern regions. Finally, I will discuss the Gia Định revolt which followed these changes.

1. THE ABOLITION OF GIA ĐỊNH

The Undermining of Gia Định Authority

Compared with the situation in Bắc Thành, where the Huế government was able to implement its policies with little difficulty, Gia Định presented a much more serious challenge. Lê Văn Duyệt's authority and prestige were substantial, and any attempts to undercut that authority would require caution and dexterity. Minh Mạng's chosen method involved eliminating some elements on which Lê Văn Duyệt's power relied. The first victims were core staff members of the higher rank in the Gia Định Thành. The second target was Lê Văn Duyệt's position of authority over Cambodia. Next, the king set out to weaken Lê Văn Duyệt's military forces, and only after these steps were completed, did he seek direct control over Gia Định. In the long run, Christians, convicts, Chinese settlers, and southerners in general became targets of the central government.

a) Removing Members of Lê Văn Duyệt's Own Staff

Regarding the first of the king's strategies, Trần Nhất Vĩnh's case provides an example. In 1823, one of Lê Văn Duyệt's most influential staff members, Trần Nhất Vĩnh, was denounced by one of Minh Mạng's young officials for illegal rice trading and running a brothel. Lê Văn Duyệt was able to vindicate his deputy and put a stop to the proceedings, and in his fury he even pressed further, demanding that

---

[1] See Phan Thúc Trực, *Quốc Sử Di Biên* (A transmitted compilation of the state history, hereafter *QSDB*) (n. d. Hong Kong: New Asia Research Institute, 1965), p. 160; *Đại Nam Chính-Biên Liệt Truyện Sơ Tập* (First collection of the primary compilation of biographies of Imperial Vietnam) (hereafter *LTST*) (1889. Tokyo: Keio Institute of Linguistic Studies, 1962), 24:12.

[2] Ibid., p. 178.

[3] Ibid., p. 204.

Minh Mạng execute the accuser for having made a false charge. As a result, Minh Mạng found himself powerless to take any action against Trần.[4]

In 1828, Minh Mạng and Lê Văn Duyệt again confronted each other. In the personnel changes of that year, Trần Nhất Vĩnh, the same official who had previously been accused of misdeeds and vindicated, was forced to move to a position in Bắc Thành, where before long he was put into prison. As expected, Lê Văn Duyệt tried to defend his former official, but this time he could not resist Minh Mạng's power.[5] Worse for Lê Văn Duyệt, Nguyễn Khoa Minh, one of Minh Mạng's men, took Trần Nhất Vĩnh's position in Gia Định.[6] It was a signal that positions in Gia Định Thành would be occupied by Minh Mạng's men from now on, whenever openings occurred.

b) Protector of Cambodia

Changes in the Protectorship of Cambodia (Bảo Hộ Chân Lạp) took place next. The famous Nguyễn Văn Thoại, who had been protector from 1820 under the command of Lê Văn Duyệt, died in 1829. Taking it for granted that he had the right to name a successor to the position, Lê Văn Duyệt recommended one of his colleagues, Nguyễn Văn Xuân. However, his suggestion was deliberately rejected and another general was selected and appointed by Minh Mạng personally. At the same time, one of the king's civil officials, Bùi Minh Đức, was given the same title, as Protector of Cambodia, and instructed to cooperate with the general.[7] Consequently, the power of the protectorate was divided between Bùi Minh Đức and the general. But the balance of power between these two men was quickly unsettled, for Minh Mạng elected to grant Bùi Minh Đức an additional position, as minister of the Board of War, so that now his titles outweighed those of the general.[8] By this means, the position of protector was removed entirely from Lê Văn Duyệt's control, and linked directly to the central government through the agency of civil officials.

c) Military Forces

In order to gain military control over Gia Định, Minh Mạng chose his own general, Nguyễn Văn Quê, and dispatched him to the southern region in 1831. Before long, Lê Văn Duyệt's main military force was dismantled. His core forces, such as the Tả Bảo and Minh Nghĩa brigades, were forced to leave Gia Định for Huế and Quảng Ngãi provinces.[9] In addition, this new general was given the right to intervene in Lê Văn Duyệt's own work as governor-general. From that time, any

---

[4] *Đại Nam Thực Lục Chính-Biên Đệ Nhị Kỷ* (Primary compilation of the veritable records of the second reign of Imperial Vietnam) (hereafter *DNTL2*) (1861. Tokyo: Keio Institute of Linguistic Studies, 1963), 27:3b; 162:7.

[5] Ibid., 52:19; *LTST*, 23:12b-13a.

[6] *Đại Nam Chính-Biên Liệt Truyện Nhị Tập* (Second collection of the primary compilation of biographies of Imperial Vietnam) (hereafter *LTNT*) (1909. Tokyo: The Institute of Cultural and Linguistic Studies, Keio University, 1981), 14:5b-6.

[7] *LTST*, 23:14b.

[8] *DNTL2*, 62:3.

[9] Ibid., 82:24.

report from Gia Định would not be accepted by the court unless it was signed by Minh Mạng's general. But the power of this military appointee was not absolute in the region, for before he could act, the general had to secure the approval of the heads of three local ministries that were already run by Minh Mạng's appointees.[10] Minh Mạng no longer wanted to tolerate the superiority of military officials over civil officials, as had previously been the case. He and his court officials wished to establish the authority of civil over military government throughout Vietnam; their decision to form new administrative units in Gia Định figured as another part of this larger effort.

The changes increasingly disturbed the Gia Định people, and they grew anxious as central civil officials occupied positions in Gia Định Thành. These central officials created many problems because of their ignorance of the region and its people. When the central officials dispatched to Gia Định did not respect the decisions of the head of Phiên An, a military province, local people became deeply dissatisfied with them. Discord erupted among ranking officials of Phiên An province in 1831. The military governor (*trấn thủ*) and his two civil officials, one of whom was Nguyễn Thừa Giảng (who had passed the regional examination of Thừa Thiên in 1821) could not reach agreement on some local litigation cases. Earlier, the military governor would have simply made the final decision in each case, as he had final authority, but now the civil and military officials faced an impasse. This sort of discord had not occurred before the infiltration of central officials into local levels of Gia Định Thành, and it was denounced by the local people.[11] Central officials appointed by Huế also found it difficult to deal with Cambodia and Cambodians. So awkward were his interactions with Cambodians that the new protector of Cambodia, Bùi Minh Đức, quickly lost his position following furious accusations by Cambodian officials whom he had irritated.[12]

The End of Gia Định

After Lê Văn Duyệt died in 1832, Gia Định Thành Tổng Trấn was immediately dismantled and reorganized. Five former military areas, called *trấn*, were changed into five provinces called *tỉnh*, and An Giang province was created between Vĩnh Long and Hà Tiên. Thus, six provinces were established in the former Gia Định Thành territory: *tỉnh* Biên Hòa, *tỉnh* Phiên An (or Gia Định[13]), *tỉnh* Định Tường, *tỉnh* Vĩnh Long,[14] *tỉnh* An Giang, and *tỉnh* Hà Tiên. Now, Gia Định began to be called Nam Kỳ (southern region), to match the names of Trung Kỳ (central region) and Bắc Kỳ (northern region). It was also popularly called Lục Tỉnh (six provinces), or Lục Tỉnh Nam Kỳ (the six provinces of Nam Kỳ).

The next step of the central government was to attack the groups in Gia Định that had formerly lived under the protection of Lê Văn Duyệt. The first blow fell immediately after the death of Lê Văn Duyệt, when Minh Mạng decreed a total prohibition of Christianity. From 1833, the government actively began to suppress

---

[10] Ibid., 72:11a; 82:4b.

[11] Ibid., 73:15a.

[12] Ibid., 106:13a.

[13] In 1833, the name of Phiên An was changed to Gia Định. Ibid., 102:4b.

[14] The name of Vĩnh Long appeared just before the reform. The former name of this region was Vĩnh Thanh. Ibid., 78:34b.

Christians throughout Vietnam. Churches were destroyed, and Christians were forced to step on the cross, an action meant to prove that they renounced their religion. Members of the Missions Étrangères in southern Vietnam faced a final decision between two options: martyrdom or escape from Vietnam. The total ban on Christianity drove some southern Vietnamese Christians to escape Gia Định. Phan Văn Minh (1815–1853), for example, an eighteen-year-old student of Bishop Taberd, had been learning Christian doctrines and Latin in Gia Định. He fled to the mission college at Penang and eventually became a vicar.[15]

In the same year, the ex-northern convicts in Gia Định, many of whom had started new lives, now found that they were being returned to their former status. The members of the Hồi Lương, who had been in the process of becoming southerners, were now to be removed from new settlements in every province. By decision of the government, they were to be transferred to the outermost frontier, where they would be mixed in with real convicts.[16]

As Chinese influence in Gia Định had been restrained by state policy over the previous decade, no special action was needed against Chinese settlers at this stage. However, the new government officials were convinced that Chinese settlers were still at the center of illegal trade activities, and now these Chinese settlers in southern Vietnam were within direct reach of court officials. This may have been the first time that government officials tried to launch a tough inspection into the Chinese commercial network involving illegal trade.[17]

In addition to tightening restrictions on and surveillance of those groups that Lê Văn Duyệt had tolerated, and even favored, the government turned its eye on the governor-general himself, as the court began to look for any crimes that the late Lê Văn Duyệt might have committed. All possible cases were manipulated to provide evidence of Lê Văn Duyệt's faults. Minh Mạng secretly ordered one of his civil officials, Bạch Xuân Nguyên, to unearth Lê Văn Duyệt's misdeeds, list them, and collect witnesses to confirm them.[18] For example, construction of the large Saigon citadel, with spaces for storing ammunition, and local construction of ships, were now designated as "crimes" and presented as obvious evidence that Lê Văn Duyệt had intended to "resist the central court."[19]

2. REPLACEMENT OF PERSONNEL

Domination by Civil Officials

Under Minh Mạng's new provincial administrative structure, a single governor-general (*tổng đốc*) administered two provinces; he was stationed in the larger of the two provinces.[20] A provincial governor (*tuần phủ*) headed each province. Under the

---

[15] Huỳnh Minh, *Vĩnh Long Xưa và Nay* (Vinh Long, past and present) (Saigon, 1967), p. 260.

[16] *DNTL2*, 67:13-14a; 95:6b.

[17] After Gia Định Thành Tổng Trấn was abolished, central officials found out that some of Lê Văn Duyệt's soldiers had illegally cut timber and traded it. They knew the main purchasers of the illegally cut timber were Chinese settlers of Gia Định. *LTNT*, 45:1b.

[18] *LTST*, 23:16b-17a.

[19] Ibid., 23:20a.

[20] Biên Hòa/Phiên An; Định Tường/Vĩnh Long; and An Giang/Hà Tiên. Governors-general were located in Phiên An, Vĩnh Long, and An Giang.

command of the *tuần phủ* were three other officials: a provincial administration commissioner (*bố chính*), a surveillance commissioner (*án sát*), and a military commander (*lãnh binh*).

In fact, however, the *bố chính* was the *de facto* head of each province. There were two reasons for this. First, the position of governor-general, almost always filled by a military general, was political rather than executive in this administration. Second, the position of *tuần phủ* was rarely filled.

The governor-general was supposed to sit in the larger of the two provinces entrusted to him, and the *tuần phủ* was meant to be only a nominal position. Smaller provinces were fully under the control of the *bố chính*. Even in the larger provinces where the governor-generals were stationed, the *bố chính* might still be the primary decision-maker, at work behind the comparatively ineffectual governor-general. We note, for instance, that when the court was requested to grant permission for the arrest of Lê Văn Khôi in 1832, this request was posed by two officials together: the governor-general, Nguyễn Văn Quê, and the *bố chính* of Phiên An province, Bạch Xuân Nguyên.[21] Actually, Nguyễn Văn Quê was involved in few real official duties in Saigon; he only worked in his office two or three times a month, and all important matters concerning Phiên An province were decided by the *bố chính*.[22] The positions of *bố chính* and *án sát* were filled by Minh Mạng's young civil officials who were responsible for taking over Gia Định Thành. Only one southern governor-general position was filled by a civil official: Lê Đại Cương. Lê started his career during the reign of Gia Long and enjoyed rapid promotion after Minh Mạng took power. His jurisdiction included An Giang and Hà Tiên, but with the additional responsibility of control over Cambodia. For the nominal positions of governor-general in the other four provinces, it was enough to appoint military generals.

At the start of this significant administrative reform, a *tuần phủ* was appointed only in An Giang province, according to the personnel management roster of 1832 (see Table 1, below). Afterwards, the title of *tuần phủ* appeared from time to time in the records whenever a province needed an additional high-ranking official. The reason why the *tuần phủ* was appointed only in An Giang province was because this province was newly created, and its rulers had the additional responsibility of managing Cambodia, situations that apparently convinced Huế that more representatives would be needed in this region. It is clear that the three positions of *bố chính*, *án sát*, and *lãnh binh* were most important in the administration of each province in Nam Kỳ.

Before the administrative reform, each military province had also been governed by officials in three main positions, which paralleled the organization of the Gia Định Thành Tổng Trấn. At the top, was a governor's (*trấn thủ*) post, which was filled by a general. Next came an assistant governor (*hiệp trấn*) and another person ranked below the assistant governor (*tham hiệp*); both of these latter positions were filled by civil officials. Just as the *trấn thủ*, the *hiệp trấn*, and the *tham hiệp* had constituted the three main positions of the military province, the *bố chính*, the *án sát*, and the *lãnh binh* were the three main positions of the new province, but with one significant difference: the hierarchical positions of the general and two civil officials were reversed. Table 1 shows the personnel

---

[21] *LTNT*, 45:1b.

[22] Ibid., 100:11b.

management situation of 1832, which reveals the hierarchical shifts between military officials and civil officials.

Table 1: Personnel Management of Southern Officials in 1832[23]

			Title		
	Tổng đốc	*Tuần phủ*	*Bố chính*	*Án sát*	*Lãnh binh*
Province					
Biên Hòa	**Nguyễn Văn Quê**		**Vũ Quýnh** #*hiệp trấn*, Biên Hòa	**Lê Văn Lễ** #*tham hiệp*, Biên Hòa (1821)	**Hồ Kim Truyền** #brigadier, Rear Division
Phiên An	–		**Bạch Xuân Nguyên** #head of Ministry of Law in Gia Định Thành	**Nguyễn Chương Đạt** #*tham hiệp*, Phiên An (1819)	**Nguyễn Quê** #governor, Bình Hòa
Định Tường	**Lê Phúc Bảo**		**Tô Trân** #*hiệp trấn*, Vĩnh Long (1827)	**Ngô Bá Tuấn** #*tham hiệp*, Vĩnh Long (1821)	**Nguyễn Văn Chính** #vice brigadier, Thần Cơ Division
Vĩnh Long	–		**Phạm Phúc Thiệu** #*hiệp trấn*, Vĩnh Long	**Vũ Đức Khuê** #*tham hiệp*, Vĩnh Long (1821)	**Nguyễn Văn Hợp** #governor, Phú Yên
An Giang	**Lê Đại Cương**	**Ngô Bá Nhân**	**Nguyễn Văn Bính** #*án sát*, Thanh Hóa (1821)	**Bùi Văn Lý** #*lang trung*, Board of Justice (1821)	**Lê Văn Thường** #governor, Quảng Ngãi

---

[23] *DNTL2*, 85:20b-22a; *QTHKL*.

Hà Tiên	–			Phạm Xuân Bích #*hiệp trấn*, Hà Tiên (1821)	Trần Văn Quan #*tham hiệp*, Hà Tiên	Nguyễn Quang Lộc #brigadier, Left Division

#: previous position; ( ): year in which the regional examination was passed

As the above table shows, the three *lãnh binh* of Phiên An, Vĩnh Long, and An Giang had formerly been governors of *trấn* in the central region. At the same time, the former military governors of Hà Tiên, Định Tường, and Vĩnh Long were moved to take up the positions of *lãnh binh* in the provinces of Quảng Ngãi, Bình Định, and Bình Thuận.[24] At this point, the previous governors had to come under the command of the *de facto* power holders, the *bố chính* and the *án sát*, because their role was restricted to the field of military affairs in the province. The *hiệp trấn* and the *tham hiệp* had been under the command of the governor before the administrative reform. Most of those men chosen to become *bố chính* and *án sát* had been *hiệp trấn* and *tham hiệp*, respectively, of the previous local administrative units (*trấn*) of Gia Định Thành. Just as the *hiệp tổng trấn* of Gia Định Thành had been the assistant governor-general of Gia Định Thành Tổng Trấn, so the *hiệp trấn* and *tham hiệp* were the civil officials who cooperated with the military governor of each *trấn*.

A second significant pattern apparent in the personnel changes of 1832 was that the important positions in the southern provinces were now occupied mainly by civil officials who had passed the state examinations. Amongst the twelve *bố chính* and *án sát*, eight were graduates who had earned regional examination titles (*cử nhân*), and two, Tô Trân and Vũ Đức Khuê, held doctorates (*tiến sĩ*). Most of them had passed the state examination at the start of Minh Mạng's reign: six of the eight men graduated in 1821, the first year during Minh Mạng's reign when the state examinations were scheduled throughout the country.

The Problem of Regionalism

Further examination of the 1832 personnel changes reveals another one of the king's motives: the elimination of regionalism. Table 2 below shows that, not counting the three men whose places of origin are unidentified, there was not a single southerner appointed as either *bố chính* or *án sát* in the south. Among the nine whose origins are identified *bố chính* and *án sát*, three were from the Red River delta, while six were from the central region. If we categorize them according to whether they came from former Lê/Trịnh Đàng Ngoài (from Hà Tĩnh north) or former Nguyễn Đàng Trong (Quảng Bình south), then five men were from Đàng Ngoài and four from Đàng Trong region, but all from outside Gia Định. Among the governors-general, only Lê Đại Cương's home is identified. He was from Bình Định in the center. Therefore, the old system of Gia Định being ruled by Gia Định men did not exist any more; positions of power in Gia Định were now occupied by men from the central and northern regions.

---

[24] Ibid., 85:19b-20b.

Table 2: Birthplaces of Southern Officials in 1832[25]

		Title		
	Tổng đốc	*Tuần phủ*	*Bố chính*	*Án sát*
Province				
Biên Hòa	Nguyễn Văn Quê		Vũ Quýnh	Lê Văn Lễ *Thừa Thiên (C)
Phiên An	–		Bạch Xuân Nguyên	Nguyễn Chương Đạt *Nghệ An (C)
Định Tường	Lê Phúc Bảo		Tô Trân *Bắc Ninh (N)	Ngô Bá Tuấn *Quảng Bình (C)
Vĩnh Long	–		Phạm Phúc Thiệu	Vũ Đức Khuê *Hải Dương (N)
An Giang	Lê Đại Cương *Bình Định (C)	Ngô Bá Nhân *Quảng Trị (C)	Nguyễn Văn Bính *Bắc Ninh (N)	Bùi Văn Lý *Thừa Thiên (C)
Hà Tiên	–		Phạm Xuân Bích *Thanh Hóa (C)	Trần Văn Quan *Thừa Thiên (C)

* birthplace (C: central Vietnam, N: northern Vietnam)

It can be argued that this pattern of appointments does not provide us with clear evidence of the king's intentions to subjugate Gia Định because, in Confucian countries generally, according to the normal regulations, called *hồi ty* (proscription against serving in one's native area), a man from a certain region was not supposed to be appointed to an administrative post in the same region. This was intended to discourage local power alliances. In principle, this was the case in Vietnam, too.[26] As the personnel management changes of 1832 show,[27] the court was cautiously obeying this principle, as far as we can determine. It seems to have happened in the new provinces from Quảng Bình province to the north, after the Bắc Thành Tổng Trấn was dismantled. There is not enough information to identify the regional origins of all officials. The main reason is that there were too few state examination graduates: among the thirty-six *tuần phủ*, *bố chính*, and *án sát*, only fourteen were laureates. Even though the origin of one person, Nguyễn Đức Nhuận,

---

[25] *DNTL2*, 85:20b-22a; *QTHKL*; Cao Xuân Dục, *Quốc Triều Đăng Khoa Lục* (Record of metropolitan examination graduates under the current dynasty) (hereafter *QTDKL*), trans. Lê Mạnh Liêu (n.d. Saigon: Trung Tâm Học Liệu, Bộ Văn Hóa Giáo Dục Thanh Niên, 1961); Viện Sử Học, trans., *Đại Nam Nhất Thống Chí* (Dai Nam gazetteer) (hereafter *DNNTC*) (Huế: Thuận Hóa, 1992).

[26] Nguyễn Sĩ Giác, trans., *Đại Nam Điển Lệ Toát Yếu* (A summary of the statutes of Imperial Vietnam) (hereafter *TY*) (1909. Ho Chi Minh City: Nxb Thành Phố Hồ Chí Minh, 1994), p. 122.

[27] *DNTL2*, 76:25b-30a.

can be added if we refer to a court biography, *Liệt Truyện Nhị Tập*, it is still impossible to know the exact distribution of administrators according to their regional background. However, at least among the fifteen men for whom we have evidence, we can say that none was appointed to his own province. Most of the northern *tuần phủ, bố chính*, and *án sát* were men from the central region, while those sent to govern the central region were from the north. Following is a table of regional backgrounds of northern and central officials who were appointed in 1831.

Table 3: Personnel Management of 1831 in Northern and Central Regions[28]

	Title			
	Tổng đốc	*Tuần phủ*	*Bố chính*	*Án sát*
Province				
Quảng Bình	Đoàn Văn Trưởng *An Giang		Nguyễn Công Thuyện	Vũ Thân
Quảng Trị	–	Trần Danh Bưu *Bắc Ninh (1819)		Trịnh Quang Khanh
Nghệ An	Tạ Quang Cự *Thừa Thiên		Hà Thúc Lương	Lê Đan Quê
Hà Tĩnh	–	Nguyễn Danh Giáp		Nguyễn Sĩ Bảng *Nam Định (1813)
Thanh Hóa	Lê Văn Quý		Nguyễn Đăng Giai *Quảng Bình (1825)	Nguỵ Khắc Tuân *Hà Tĩnh (1821)
Hà Nội	Lê Văn Hiếu *Gia Định		Nguyễn Văn Điệp	Bùi Nguyên Thọ *Biên Hòa (1821)
Ninh Bình	–	Hồ Hưu		Trần Lê Hoán
Nam Định	Huỳnh Kim Xán *Quảng Bình		Nguyễn Khắc Giai *Gia Định (1821)	Lê Dục Đức *Thanh Hóa (1819)
Hưng Yên	–	Nguyễn Đức Nhuận *Thanh Hóa		Nguyễn Đại Phong
Hải Dương	Nguyễn Kim Bảng *Thừa Thiên		Hoàng Tế Mỹ *Hà Nội (1825)	Phan Hiển Đạt

[28] *DNTL2*, 76:25b-30a; *LTNT; QTHKL; DNNTC.*

Quảng Yên	–		Lê Đạo Quảng *Thanh Hóa (1813)	Nguyễn Đôn Tố
Sơn Tây	Lê Đại Cương *Bình Định		Lê Nguyên Hy *Nghệ An (1813)	Nguyễn Thế Nho
Hưng Hóa	–	Hoàng Quốc Điều *Nghệ An (1813)		Ngô Huy Tuấn
Thuyên Quang	–		Nguyễn Hữu Khuê	Nguyễn Thường Trân
Bắc Ninh	Nguyễn Đình Thiện *Thanh Hóa		Nguyễn Khắc Biểu *Thừa Thiên (1819)	Doãn Văn Xuân *Thừa Thiên (1819)
Thái Nguyên	–		Trần Thiên Tải	Nguyễn Dư
Lạng Sơn		Hoàng Văn Quyền		Nguyễn Đình Chưởng
Cao Bằng			Dương Tam Bổ	Nguyễn Huy Khoát

*: birthplace; ( ): year in which the regional examination was passed

At the same time, however, there is evidence to show that the situation in Gia Định, regarding the origins of its bureaucrats, was subtly, but significantly, different from the situations in the northern and central regions. Further north, a man from a certain region could still be appointed to the same general region, though not to the province of his birth. For example, a man from Hà Tĩnh, Nguy Khắc Tuần, was appointed as *án sát* of Thanh Hóa province, and a man from Hà Nội, Hoàng Tế Mỹ, was posted as *bố chính* in Hải Dương province. In contrast, similar cases were not found in the 1832 records of personnel appointments in Gia Định. An extreme case was that of Nguyễn Song Thanh. Nguyễn Thế Anh cited this case as evidence proving that the Nguyễn dynasty tended to follow Confucian *hồi ty* principles,[29] but in fact this case can be used better to illustrate the special case in Gia Định.

With the help of the *Quốc Triều Hương Khoa Lục* and the *Đại Nam Nhất Thống Chí*, we can identify Nguyễn Song Thanh as a man from the central province of Bình Thuận. In 1837, he was recommended by the court officials to become *bố chính* in Định Tường province. This appointment was at first accepted by Minh Mạng, but the decision was hastily changed when the king discovered that Nguyễn Song Thanh used to study in Gia Định. Minh Mạng justified his reversal by citing the principle that "any official who has been born in, has ever lived in, has ever studied in, or has a mother or wife who has been born in a certain region, can not be appointed to the same region."[30] But Nguyễn Song Thanh was subsequently

[29]Nguyễn Thế Anh, *Kinh Tế và Xã Hội Việt Nam Dưới Các Vua Triều Nguyễn* (Vietnam's economy and society under kings of the Nguyen dynasty) (Saigon: Lửa Thiêng, 1971), p. 76.
[30] *DNTL2*, 181:31a.

appointed as *bố chính* of Bình Định province in the central region. In other words, Minh Mạng only followed the principle of *hồi ty* strictly when it applied to the southern region.

When the 1833 revolt broke out in the south, the rebels' first victims were Minh Mạng's men. Bạch Xuân Nguyên was immediately killed by rebels seeking revenge for the court's harsh posthumous treatment of Lê Văn Duyệt.[31] Phạm Xuân Bích, a state examination graduate of 1821, and Trần Văn Quan, who commenced his official career in 1824, chose to die rather than renounce allegiance to their king.[32] The animosity of southerners towards these men quickly developed into resistance against the authority of Minh Mạng, the monarch who stood behind them.

Plate 5. Entrance to Lê Văn Duyệt's shrine. In the 1830s, Lê Văn Khôi had a central official, Bạch Xuân Nguyên, beheaded in this shrine as part of a sacrificial rite for Lê Văn Duyệt.
Credit: the author, 1994.

---

[31] When Lê Văn Khôi and his followers captured Bạch Xuân Nguyên, they brought him to Lê Văn Duyệt's wife first and justified their action as follows: "We and Bạch Xuân Nguyên originally have no reason to hate each other. But Xuân Nguyên uncovered past matters too severely, and has said that if he could not dig up Duyệt's bones, he could not rest. As Lê Văn Duyệt's subjects, we could not endure it." They asked her to allow them to offer Bạch Xuân Nguyên as a sacrifice in a sacrificial rite for Lê Văn Duyệt. Duyệt's wife strongly opposed their action against the central officials. But the sacrificial rite was performed by beheading Xuân in Lê Văn Duyệt's shrine. See *LTST*, 23:18b; *LTNT*, 45:3a.

[32] See *LTNT*, 40:16b-17b.

3. REVOLT[33]

According to one source, in the Saigon region alone thousands of people joined the rebel army in less than ten days after the start of the insurrection. They were stirred to action by the call to reject the legitimacy of the Nguyễn dynasty and avenge their benefactor, Lê Văn Duyệt.[34] As soon as the revolt broke out in the Saigon citadel in lunar May of 1833, it quickly spread to different provinces. Within three months, all fortresses of the six provincial centers had been captured by rebels.

Undoubtedly, the main forces that led the revolt were the Christians, the ex-convicts, and the Chinese settlers who had suffered from Minh Mạng's hostile interventions. After the quelling of the revolt, there were six leaders who were sent to Huế to be executed. Among them was the French missionary Marchand, accused of being the leader of Christian participants. Another was Nguyễn Văn Trấm, leader of the Hồi Lương, who had taken command of the revolt after Lê Văn Khôi died in 1834. A third was Lưu Tín, a *thanh nhân* Chinese who had actively organized the Chinese settlers to join the insurrection when the rebellion erupted.[35]

Ultimately, the Lê Văn Khôi revolt would seriously damage the Gia Định Christian communities in Vietnam. Many Christians were killed, captured, or forced to move away from their home villages, and a number of others fled Vietnam. Court sources said that at least two thousand Gia Định Christians took refuge in Siam during the turmoil.[36] The second group, ex-convicts who had immigrated from the north to the south, would be completely eliminated by the end of the revolt. In 1837, the government decreed that northern convicts were no longer to be exiled to southern Vietnam.[37] Since convicts from southern Vietnam were supposed to be exiled to Cambodia after 1835 (the year when Cambodia became a part of Vietnam), in the late 1830s Gia Định found itself relatively free of convicted lawbreakers for the first time in decades. As for the Chinese, in 1833, just before the rebels entered the citadel of Gia Định to stage their final defense, the royal army swept through the Chợ Lớn Chinese settlement, which was located in a region the Chinese rebels had adopted as their central military base. Over one thousand Chinese settlers were killed or captured in Chợ Lớn alone, and their property confiscated. Any Chinese regarded as a participant in the rebellion had four fingers of his right hand cut off before being exiled, and his property confiscated, even if he had surrendered.[38]

Although three groups had constituted the core of the revolt, they were not the only participants. Once the insurrection began, a wide range of people joined in. Minh Mạng would express his bitterness over the fact that so few local officials or soldiers proved loyal to Huế, for "there was no one who died with his fortress

---

[33] In this section, I mainly discuss the participants of the revolt. For the detailed process of revolt, see *LTNT*, vol. 45, Lê Văn Khôi; *Khâm Định Tiểu Bình Lưỡng Kỳ Nghịch Phỉ Phương Lược* (1836. Hanoi: Viện Hán Nôm VHv 2701); Nguyễn Phan Quang, *Cuộc Khởi Binh Lê Văn Khôi ở Gia Định (1833-1835)* (Le Van Khoi's raising an army) (Ho Chi Minh City: Nxb Thành Phố Hồ Chí Minh, 1991).

[34] *LTNT*, 45:4a.

[35] Ibid., 45:3b; 26b.

[36] *DNTL2*, 198:3b.

[37] Ibid., 180:15a.

[38] Ibid., 103:21-22; 104:7a.

when each province fell."[39] Low-ranking local officials who had been recruited from Gia Định often switched allegiance to the rebels and helped create the administrative units of the revolutionary government. For example, Nguyễn Văn Mân had been an official of the ninth rank in An Giang. As he was fluent in the Siamese language, he agreed to travel to Siam to seek military aid for Lê Văn Khôi.[40] Đinh Phiên, who took charge of the Board of Rites in the rebel government, had been an educational official, or *giáo thụ* (seventh rank first class) of the Tân Bình prefecture of Gia Định Thành.[41] Rebel officials Nguyễn Văn Nghị, Bùi Văn Thuận, and Đào Duy Phúc had been seventh-rank first-class officials, or *tự vụ*, in the local ministries of warfare and finance in Gia Định Thành Tổng Trấn.[42] In the province of Vĩnh Long, we find a case where a central official was pressured by villagers to take their side. Phạm Phúc Thiệu was *bố chính* of Vĩnh Long province. When he was defeated by the insurgents' forces, he escaped the capital of Vĩnh Long and hid himself in a village. He might have attempted to mobilize the villagers, as many of his colleagues did, but instead the villagers forced him to join them in the revolt.[43] The sons and grandsons of meritorious generals of Gia Định also participated in the rebellion.[44]

Minh Mạng's edict of 1835 illustrates the extent of Gia Định participation in the Lê Văn Khôi revolt:

> When the revolt took place, there were some who fought with the court against the bandits. But we saw abominable men, too. There were those who committed wickedness, taking advantage of the disaster, standing at the bandit's side; those who took government property; who threatened villages, using the rebels' power; who brought elephants to take part in the revolt; and who captured head officials and joined the revolt. Chinese settlers [*thanh nhân*] and Christians were also participants. The number of rebels, like herds of foxes and dogs, grew daily, and the revolt became an extremely serious problem. Now the revolt has been pacified at the expense of three year's time and the efforts of my soldiers. Looking back on it, I cannot hide my vexation. When the revolt started, the number of the Hồi Lương and the Bắc Thuận was thirty-five. Though certain criminals were added to them, the number of participants did not exceed two hundred. If only the gathering of blind followers had been prevented, the participants in the revolt must have been as easily wiped out as scattering fireflies. If so, how was the disaster able to extend through the six provinces and resist the court for three years? [. . .] You southerners, the people of Nam Kỳ, are said to have followed the revolt because you were severely maltreated [by the government officials] or were forced to join [by the revolt participants]. But why didn't you surrender when

---

[39] *Minh-Mệnh Chính-Yếu* (Abstract of policies of Minh Mang) (hereafter *MMCY*), trans. by Ủy Ban Dịch Thuật Phú Quốc Vụ Khanh đặc-trách Văn-hoá (1897. Saigon: 1972-74), 12:21b.

[40] *DNTL2*, 102:24b.

[41] *LTNT*, 45:3b-4a.

[42] Ibid., 45:7-8a; *DNTL2*, 102:12a.

[43] *DNTL2*, 102:12a.

[44] Ibid.,190:6b.

the court army arrived there, instead spending your last moments with the bandits in the citadel? How regrettable it is![45]

While in this passage Christians, ex-convicts from the north, and Chinese settlers are cited as the three most important groups leading the revolt, the king identifies many others as well, including those who "took government property," "threatened the villagers," or "captured the high-ranking local officials."

Those who "threatened the villagers" were probably men who had been living in and held some authority at the village level. A report on the revolt participants provides us with one piece of evidence concerning the identities of the people who allegedly "threatened the villagers." Nguyễn Văn Huân had been a village notable of Gia Định province. Once the revolt broke out, he and his sons "happily" joined it. One of his duties was to persuade the people in his village to cooperate with the rebels, who wished to register the villagers according to their own method.[46] "Participants who captured their head officials," as described by the king in his statement, most likely refers to local people like to those who had pressed the government officials to join the revolt in Vĩnh Long province. These were also the "blind followers" who claimed to have been maltreated by government officials, as Minh Mạng noted with disapproval in his edict.

The royal army recovered five provinces by the end of 1833, forcing the rebels to retreat to the Saigon citadel. Minh Mạng had to wait until 1835 to see his generals capture the Saigon citadel. With the end of Lê Văn Khôi's revolt, the grip of the central government became tighter than ever before. Thousands of people were killed by the royal army. According to a record of the court, at least 1,200 men and women, regardless of their ages, were captured and buried alive in a mass grave near Saigon citadel when it fell.[47] Based on a report from Gia Định province, the number of prisoners incarcerated for their involvement in the rebellion was 1,360 in 1836 for this province alone.[48] Lê Văn Duyệt's tomb was flattened by the order of Minh Mạng, as the dead general was accused of having first planted the seeds of revolt.[49]

For a while, southern Vietnam was terrorized by these mass murders and the continuing liquidation of rebel participants. A report to the king reveals that deadly intimidation by government forces persisted at the village level until at least 1837. Incidents are described in the reports: for example, during one search for remnants of the opposition, the royal forces arrested fifty villagers of Bình Xuân village in Gia Định province and took them into custody.[50] One can surmise that such actions must have made the people of southern Vietnam feel they were living in a colony under alien rulers and armed forces. Indeed, one of Minh Mạng's men even insisted on a radical method to repress the population—which he considered

---

[45] Ibid., 158:5b-6a.

[46] Châu Bản Triều Nguyễn (Vermilion Records of the Nguyen dynasty) (ANU Library, microfilm reels 60-64 [1836-1837]), lunar July 20, 1837.

[47] *LTNT*, 45:26.

[48] Ibid., 18:8a.

[49] *LTST*, 23:25b-26a. He was reinstated from 1848.

[50] Châu Bản Triều Nguyễn, lunar July 20, 1837.

unreliable—permanently, by stationing military forces from outside of Gia Định in the region on a long-term basis. His master agreed to this proposal.[51]

AFTERMATH

Though the revolt was quelled, southern Vietnam remained tense for some time. The southerners' resistance to the ongoing presence of Minh Mạng's soldiers and officials, though repressed, was occasionally expressed in various forms, and the central government had to struggle to avoid igniting another explosion of popular resentment in the region. During the reign of Tự Đức (1848-1883), a high official, Trương Quốc Dụng,[52] was startled when he discovered how his colleagues had had to behave following the rebellion in southern Vietnam. He heard that all of the officials from the northern or central regions dispatched by the court to Nam Kỳ had been so wary of the sentiments of Gia Định people that they had willingly violated the general rules of the state. One of their tactics was to pay the highest respect to Lê Văn Duyệt whenever they passed his flattened tomb, the tomb of a person who had been executed posthumously by the court. Otherwise, they risked death as a consequence, according to a story recorded by Trương Quốc Dụng in his book, *Thoái Thực Ký Văn*.

Tổng đốc Nguyễn Đức Hoạt[53] and *bố chính* Nguyễn Văn Cử Sĩ[54] of Gia Định province died of disease one after another in a few months. When *phó lãnh binh* (deputy commander) Giả Quang Mật visited [Huế], I asked him about what happened to Nguyễn *đốc* [*tổng đốc* Nguyễn]. Mật replied that he could not understand the disease. One day, Nguyễn *đốc* was on the way back to his office from a trip with cavalry and the elephant army. He was about to pass the tomb of Lê Văn Duyệt. An officer said that all officials usually showed their politeness by lowering their flags and ceasing to beat the drums. To this suggestion, he [Nguyễn Đức Hoạt] responded that he himself was the governor-general, he was marching on official business with the cavalry escort, and that the action the officer recommended was only an amusing habit. He kept going. After he returned to his residence, he was sick from that night. He was in an abnormal mental state. A couple of days later, when an office servant

---

[51] *DNTL2*, 189:10b-11a.

[52] Trương Quốc Dụng (1797-1864) was a doctoral degree holder, *tiến sĩ*. He was born in Hà Tĩnh province. He passed the local examination in 1825, and succeeded in the court examination in 1829. See *LTNT*, vol. 29, Trương Quốc Dụng; Cao Xuân Dục, *Quốc Triều Hương Khoa Lục* (Record of regional examination graduates under the current dynasty) (hereafter *QTHKL*), trans. Nguyễn Thúy Nga and Nguyễn Thị Lâm (n.d. Ho Chi Minh City: Nxb Thành Phố Hồ Chí Minh, 1993), p. 140.

[53] He was born in Thừa Thiên around Huế, and passed the local state examination in 1825. See *QTHKL*, p. 138.

[54] The name of Nguyễn Cử Sĩ is not found in the different books such as *Quốc Triều Hương Khoa Lục*, *Đại Nam Thực Lục*, and *Liệt Truyện Nhị Tập*. In a different record, *Hát Đông Thư Dị*, however, we can find the same story, and the name of the *bố chính* here is Nguyễn Văn Cử. *Hát Đông Thư Dị* (Hat Dong's records of curiosities) (n.d. Hanoi: Viện Hán Nôm VHc 01749), p. 33. And his name was recorded as Nguyễn Cử in the *Liệt Truyện Nhị Tập*. Though *Liệt Truyện Nhị Tập* does not mention this matter, it says that he worked in Gia Định at the beginning of the Tự Đức reign. *LTNT*, 30:2a. He was born in Hanoi, and passed the local state examination in 1831. *QTHKL*, 171.

woke up in the morning, he found a stick standing in the middle of the office court. They could not find out where the stick came from. When this matter of the stick was reported to the *bố chính* Nguyễn Văn Cụ, he replied that he [Lê Văn Duyệt] had broken the law, so how did he [Lê Văn Duyệt] deserve to be respected? After saying this, Nguyễn Văn Cụ also fell sick as the *tổng đốc* had.[55]

In these tense circumstances, the central court took further actions in Gia Định. It resolved to convert the outlying land of Gia Định into an integral part of Vietnam: Nam Kỳ in reality as well as in name.

---

[55]Trương Quốc Dụng, *Thoái Thực Ký Văn* (or *Công Ha Ký Văn*) (After-dinner recollections, or recollections beyond the office) (n.d. Hanoi: Viện Hán Nôm A 1499), p. 115.

PART II

THE NEW ETHOS UNDER MINH MẠNG

CHAPTER FOUR

MINH MẠNG'S "CULTIVATION" (*GIÁO HÓA*) OF SOUTHERNERS

As I discussed in chapter three, the administrative reform of 1832 brought the area of Gia Định under direct rule by the central government. The Gia Định Thành Tổng Trấn was dismantled, and immediately afterwards the Gia Định people arose in revolt against the Huế court. The successful pacification of this insurrection led to the dilution of the Gia Định regime's heritage in southern Vietnam. Activities by Christians were drastically curtailed. Within the ruling group, networks of individual relationships were replaced by the government's bureaucracy. Chinese settlers were forced to isolate themselves from commercial activities in which they excelled, as well as from politics. Most of all, Gia Định people were excluded from top ruling positions in their own land, and these high-ranking positions were filled, instead, with Minh Mạng's men from the regions of central and northern Vietnam. When Gia Định Thành Tổng Trấn was dismantled, the name of Gia Định, which since 1698 had identified the region stretching from Biên Hòa to Hà Tiên as an entity, a land with its own significant character, was reduced to a mere provincial designation.

In Part II, I will discuss the strenuous efforts of the central government to convert the land of Gia Định into a part of Vietnam and to convert the Gia Định people into model citizens of Vietnam, as it was envisioned by the court at Huế. Minh Mạng's basic idea was to cultivate (*giáo hóa*) the Gia Định people. His intent is made clear in an edict issued immediately after the pacification of Lê Văn Khôi's revolt:

> The southern land is far from the capital, but it is neither a hidden valley nor a deep forest. If it is enlightened [by our efforts], southern Vietnam will be brightened before long [. . .] Each person has to realize what is the proper way. You must improve yourselves by filial piety [*hiếu*], sympathy [*dễ*], loyalty [*trung*], and trust [*tín*].[1]

---

[1] *Đại Nam Thực Lục Chính-Biên Đệ Nhị Kỳ* (Primary compilation of the veritable records of the second reign of Imperial Vietnam) (hereafter *DNTL2*) (1861. Tokyo: Keio Institute of Linguistic Studies, 1963), 158:6b-7a.

In this chapter, I will discuss Minh Mạng's attitude towards southerners, and the ways in which he used educational institutions in southern Vietnam to try to increase southerners' respect for the authority of the central government.

1. MINH MẠNG'S IMPRESSIONS OF SOUTHERNERS

Another quotation from the above edict shows how Minh Mạng viewed southerners.

> During the last two hundred years under the authority of the court, the way of life has been innocent, and there has not been any deceitfulness among people. At the time of the last emperor [Gia Long], all of you contributed to the restoration with money and soldiers. Recently, however, because the greedy and vicious Huỳnh Công Lý[2] and the arrogant Lê Văn Duyệt ruled this region without thinking of teaching people the right way, they led people to be contaminated by improper manners. As a consequence, you became accustomed to ignoring higher authority. *Sĩ* [literati] have fallen into laziness, people's behavior has become arrogant, and you have become addicted to extravagance. Your way of entertainment is lecherous [*dâm đãng*], you are attracted by opium, despise the value of rice, and are luxurious with clothes. You yourself said your land was the farthest frontier, so that you only knew the existence of a frontier leader, but did not know the existence of the central court [. . .] [This] corrupt atmosphere led to the Khôi revolt. Though it was caused by the awkwardness of Nguyễn Văn Quế[3] and by the cruelty of Bạch Xuân Nguyên, the growth of the problem from the bud they planted to the full flower of disaster was inevitable.[4]

Minh Mạng's most significant opinion about southerners can be found in one sentence of this citation: "You yourself said your land was the farthest frontier, so that you only knew the existence of a frontier leader, but did not know the existence of the central court." Gia Định had been a peripheral area of Nguyễn state and existed as an independent unit for over four decades, from the time of the Gia Định regime until the beginning of the 1830s. Therefore, the Gia Định people tended to prefer their own leaders. Minh Mạng's task was to establish the principle of a direct line of authority from him to southern society.

But Minh Mạng's desire to cultivate southerners also derived from his perception of other elements defining their character, such as those noted in the quote above. He regarded the southerners as "contaminated," and attributed this contamination to Lê Văn Duyệt's misguided leadership. But in fact southerners had possessed for centuries these stubborn characteristics that Minh Mạng interpreted negatively and despised.

---

[2] A vice-governor-general of Gia Định. He held this position when Lê Văn Duyệt was appointed governor-general of Gia Định in 1820.

[3] The first governor-general of Gia Định and Biên Hòa provinces in 1832.

[4] *DNTL2*, 158:4b-5b.

The Pursuit of Commerce

Minh Mạng condemned southerners for "despising the value of rice," by which he meant that too many people in the south were engaged in trade, rather than in agriculture. In some sense, this might have been true, because the production of rice was not as difficult in the south as in the other regions of Vietnam and therefore required fewer farmers. More importantly, this tendency relates to the popularity of commerce in Gia Định. *Gia Định Thành Thông Chí* by Trịnh Hoài Đức (1765-1825), details the development of commerce, especially in the two districts called Bình Dương and Tân Long in the Saigon area. "The population is dense, markets are linked to each other, houses are located side by side, the languages of Phúc Kiến [Fu Chien], Quảng Đông [Kuang Tung], Trào Châu [Ch'ao Chou], Hải Nam [Hai Nan], the West, and Siam are used as means of communication."[5]

Sources make it clear that many southerners worked in the field of commerce. Of the population in the districts of Thuận An and Phúc Lộc, "one was a merchant while nine were peasants," according to *Gia Định Thành Thông Chí*.[6] In the history of the Trương family, titled *Trương Gia Thế Phả*, we are told that some of the peasants ceased farming rice and became engaged in market-oriented agriculture.[7] Thứ (1762-1843) was a peasant, and he had three sons, all of whom were peasants as well, but we find that the eldest son, called Thạnh (1785-1834), invested in vegetables (p. 8), a more profitable crop than rice. Thạnh seems to have accumulated a certain amount of wealth from this business, and earned a village leadership title of *thủ bản*.[8] Because his village was located in the present Bình Dương district of Saigon area,[9] I believe his business must have had connections with markets such as those described in Trịnh Hoài Đức's narrative. In fact, market-oriented pursuits were not new to the family, because Thứ's own father (1725-1778), Thạnh's grandfather, had also cultivated vegetables, rather than rice, after migrating from Bình Định to this village in the south and marrying a girl from a neighboring village called Bình Phúc (p. 2).

The popular practices of smoking opium and wearing luxurious clothes, and the other allegedly extravagant habits of Gia Định people pointed out by Minh Mạng, were undoubtedly signs of well-developed trade and the prosperous economic situation of Gia Định compared with other regions of Vietnam. In *Gia Định Thành Thông Chí*, Trịnh Hoài Đức describes Saigon as a bustling port city, host to ships and junks from many countries, where all varieties of goods poured in, and writes that the luxurious habits of the populace were general even among literati (*sĩ*).[10]

---

[5] Trịnh Hoài Đức, *Gia Định Thành Thông Chí* (Gia Dinh gazetteer) (hereafter *GDTTC*) (n.d. École Française d'Extrême Orient microfilm A 1561), 4:11.

[6] Ibid., 4:12.

[7] *Trương Gia Từ Đường Thế Phả Toàn Tập* (Complete collection of the genealogy of the Truong family ancestry) (1886. Hanoi: Viện Hán Nôm A 3186).

[8] *Thủ bản*: an administrative position in charge of village finance. See Alfred Schreiner, *Les Institutions Annamites en Basse-Cochinchine avant la Conquête Française*, Tome 2 (Saigon: Claude & Cie, 1901), p. 26.

[9] The name of his village is Hành Thông. This village was located beside the present Gò Vấp market in Ho Chi Minh City. It is at the northeast side of this city.

[10] *GDTTC*, 4:11.

At the very least, this observation was true of the situation in Gia Định until 1820.[11] For additional evidence of the region's character, we refer to the narrative of Lê Quang Định (1751-1811), a colleague of Trịnh Hoài Đức's, who informs us of the habits of southern *sĩ* in his book, *Đại Việt Nhất Thông Dư Địa Chí*: "The custom of *sĩ* in Phiên An is luxurious, and they like splendid things. Traders flock to this region. Large numbers of ships and junks stand closely together."[12] As Lê's book was written before 1806,[13] it is obvious that the allegedly extravagant indulgences of Gia Định had little to do with Lê Văn Duyệt's rule, for these marks of prosperity had obviously existed in Gia Định from the previous century.

The luxurious practices of the *sĩ* would not have been possible without a certain income, and that income is thought to have been earned by direct or indirect involvement with business. In chapter two, we already noted that Trịnh Hoài Đức himself was also linked with commercial business.

"Contaminated Ethics"

We cannot be certain exactly what Minh Mạng referred to when, in his edict, he criticized southerners by declaring, "Your way of entertainment is lecherous." Since he had only lived in Gia Định until he was eleven years of age, the likelihood that he had much direct experience with "lecherous entertainment" is small. Nevertheless, he expressed this judgment of the southern Vietnamese intermittently throughout his reign. To Minh Mạng, Gia Định was an ethically contaminated land where "even women smoke opium."[14] Since the edict of 1835 was intended as official instruction to southerners, the language here is relatively restrained, but in reports of his discussions with his own men we can find his personal views on southerners more frankly expressed. Speaking with his officials in 1832, he is reported to have said: "These days I hear they [southerners] smoke opium, sing rowdily, gamble, dispute, and like the most brutal violence. These habits inevitably lead to robbery and burglary. As the women are licentious, their behavior is more disgusting. Husbands are already dissipated, then how can they ask for the fidelity of their wives?"[15]

---

[11] It is not clear when the *Gia Định Thành Thông Chí* was written, but we can conclude it was written after the Gia Định Thành was formed in 1808 because the title of this book includes the phrase "Gia Định Thành," and we know it was written before 1820 because Trịnh Hoài Đức sent three volumes of this book to the Huế court this year. *DNTL2*, 3:6b. Recently, Dương Bảo Vận argued that this book was written in 1820. See Dương Bảo Vận, "Một vài nghiên cứu về sách Gia Định Thành Thông Chí" (Some research into the book Gia Dinh Thanh Thong Chi), *Xưa và Nay* no. 53B (Ho Chi Minh City, 1998), p. 18.

[12] From Nguyễn Thu, *Hoàn Vũ Kỷ Văn* (Compendium on the [Vietnamese] world) (n.d. Hanoi: Viện Hán Nôm A 585), vol. 3.

[13] *Đại Nam Chính-Biên Liệt Truyện Sơ Tập* (First collection of the primary compilation of biographies of Imperial Vietnam) (hereafter *LTST*) (1889. Tokyo: Keio Institute of Linguistic Studies, 1962), 11:2a.

[14] *DNTL2*, 158:22a.

[15] *Minh-Mệnh Chính-Yếu* (Abstract of policies of Minh Mang) (hereafter *MMCY*), trans. by Ủy Ban Dịch Thuật Phú Quốc Vụ Khanh đặc-trách Văn-hoá (1897. Saigon: 1972-4), 13:19a.

The fidelity of women, meant to be a characteristic Vietnamese virtue, was important to Minh Mạng, who was convinced that the people of Gia Định failed to meet his own high standards. His attitudes are made clear by his response to a court case involving a Gia Định woman with the family name of Dương, whose husband was ill and household deeply in debt. Dương reportedly resisted the sexual advances of an unscrupulous creditor and was stabbed and killed by him as a result. According to the narrative in *Đại Nam Thực Lục*, the officials of Gia Định Thành reported this matter to court in 1829, and members of the Board of Rites agreed to honor this woman as a model of fidelity. Responding to this suggestion, Minh Mạng said: "The women of Gia Định are usually very licentious. It is not improper to encourage good behavior [in Gia Định] by this example. But [this example] cannot be a good enough model for people in other regions."[16]

This woman's history is not found in the section on exemplary women, or *liệt nữ*, of court biographies, although another primary file for court biography, the *Nam Thiên Hiếu Hành Thực Lục* (Veritable records of exemplary behavior in Vietnam), does relate her story, as well as other stories of exemplary women of the Nguyễn dynasty. In the different narratives describing admirable women from the central and northern regions, similar patterns are found: they commonly feature a woman with a weak or deceased husband; a man with wealth and power, who desires to take her sexually; the resistance of the woman; and her subsequent death either as a result of the man's violence or by suicide. Minh Mạng chose which biographies to include in the *liệt nữ*, and apparently elected to exclude the southern woman, Dương, from this company, even though the stories of other exemplary women from northern and central regions are no more impressive than hers and, in fact, generally resemble hers.[17] The woman Dương of Gia Định was, in fact, in no way ill-suited to be the model of fidelity for the Vietnamese, but Minh Mạng's prejudices against southerners told against her.

"Lazy Sĩ of Southern Vietnam"

The most interesting point in the edict of Minh Mạng is his accusation that the intellectuals of southern Vietnam were lazy, which meant that they did not impress him as proper Confucian scholars. If we remember that the Gia Định Confucians contributed to the foundation of the Gia Định regime, then this comment seems somewhat off the mark, but it does tell us something about the region: that ongoing Confucian practice in Gia Định was sometimes obscured by the activities of diverse religious groups there. Even outside observers came away with this impression. Following his stay in Saigon, which lasted for several months during 1819-1820, the American John White wrote a report that makes no mention of

---

[16] DNTL2, 63:2a.

[17] For example, the court biography features a woman whose family name was Vũ, who lived in Hải Dương, the core region of the Red River delta. After her husband died, a son of a wealthy family fell in love with her for her beauty and proposed to her, but she committed suicide in order to maintain fidelity to her deceased husband. She was honored by Minh Mạng in 1836. *Đại Nam Chính-Biên Liệt Truyện Nhị Tập* (Second collection of the primary compilation of biographies of Imperial Vietnam) (hereafter *LTNT*) (1909. Tokyo: The Institute of Cultural and Linguistic Studies, Keio University, 1981), 44:3.

Confucian practice in the region, although this curious visitor left records elsewhere in his book of other religious features of Gia Định, such as Christianity, animism, and Buddhism, and the mixture of different religions.[18]

The relative lack of popularity of Confucian practices in the south affected the attitudes of Gia Định intellectuals towards scholars in northern and central Vietnam. Many felt inferior. Though he himself held a doctorate degree, the southern scholar Phan Thanh Giản (1796-1867), in his preface to Trương Đăng Quế's collection of works, insisted that his own accomplishments and talents were small compared to those of his colleague, Trương (1794-1865), who was from the central region, in Quảng Ngãi. We might interpret this as a mere act of politeness, but it is significant that Phan attributed his own inadequacies to the fact that he was a southerner[19]:

> I was born in *nam phương* [the southern part], and grew up there. I started my official career late,[20] and I did not have any chance to knock at the doors of great seniors. So my academic standard is quite humble. Especially in the field of literature, it is even more unskilled. My communication with other scholars did not reach beyond one district, and the range of things I saw did not pass over a hill or a mountain [in the south].[21]

Nevertheless, southerners did not always feel inferior. The southerners' humble laments concerning their own inadequacies were sometimes mixed, and complicated by, expressions of pride in their own particular heritage. They were even capable of expressing a degree of disdain towards people from other regions. To understand this, we need to examine the usage of two terms in nineteenth-century documents, the terms *bắc nhân* (people of north), and *nam nhân* (people of south), which came into frequent use from the middle of the 1830s.

---

[18] John White, *A Voyage to Cochin China* (1824. Kuala Lumpur: Oxford University Press, 1972).

[19] According to Phan's description of the history of his family's maternal line, his own sixth-generation grandfather, in the maternal line, was a Chinese who had moved to Vietnam from Fu Chien. Pierre Daudin, "Phan-Thanh-Gian 1796-1867 et sa famille d'aprés quelques documents annamites," *Bulletin de la Société des Études Indochinoises*, Tome 17 (1941): 27. The court biography says Phan's ancestor moved to Vietnam during the seventeenth century from China. *LTNT*, 26:21b. But I do not think these facts had affected Phan's identity as a southern Vietnamese man. Phan did not know the exact origins of his family until the 1830s. See Nguyễn Đức Dụ, *Gia Phả Khảo và Luận Thực Hành* (A study of genealogy and its compilation) (Hanoi: Nxb Văn Hóa, 1992), pp. 311-15.

[20] He was thirty years old in 1825 when he passed the local state examination. Trương Đăng Quế started his official career from 1819, when he was twenty-five years old. *LTNT*, 21:1a; Cao Xuân Dục, *Quốc Triều Hương Khoa Lục* (Record of regional examination graduates under the current dynasty) (hereafter *QTHKL*) trans. Nguyễn Thúy Nga, Nguyễn Thị Lâm (n.d. Ho Chi Minh City: Nxb Thành Phố Hồ Chí Minh, 1993), p. 110.

[21] Phan Thanh Giản, *Lương Khê Văn Thảo* (Prose of Luong Khe in manuscript form) (1876. Hanoi: Viện Hán Nôm A 2125), 2:6.

a) Bắc nhân and Nam nhân

Generally speaking, in Nguyễn dynasty chronicles *bắc* and *nam* were used to indicate the former Lê/Trịnh Đàng Ngoài, and the former Nguyễn Đàng Trong, respectively. *Bắc hà*[22] and *bắc hà nhân* had been used during the period of the Nguyễn state as official terms referring to Đàng Ngoài and the people of the Đàng Ngoài. Therefore, it is reasonable to conclude that *bắc nhân* was an abbreviation of *bắc hà nhân*, and that *nam nhân* was an abbreviation of *nam hà nhân*, so that the *bắc nhân* and the *nam nhân* were the people of former Đàng Ngoài and the people of former Đàng Trong, respectively. In 1837, Minh Mạng used the term *bắc nhân* to identify the people of former Đàng Ngoài, or the people to "the north of the Gianh River."[23] The court chronicle of 1843 offers obvious evidence that *nam nhân* referred to the people of former Đàng Trong, for it states that "only *nam nhân* had been appointed to the position of *nội vụ chủ thủ*," the court position in charge of royal property.[24] In a record concerning the same matter next year, the chronicle identifies the *nam nhân* as "the people of Quảng Bình south," in other words, people from the region formerly known as Đàng Trong.[25]

However, during Minh Mạng's reign, the two terms were also used in a different way: to indicate Bắc Kỳ and Nam Kỳ by the words *bắc* and *nam*. Only by grasping the nuances of this usage can we understand the central court's perceptions of the southerners' essential nature.

For example, the use of the phrase *nam nhân* is found in documents dating from 1834, written after the region of former Gia Định was swept by Lê Văn Khôi's revolt. At that time, the Huế court was looking for a means to appease the Gia Định people. What Minh Mạng found in the court's personnel record was a significant imbalance between southerners and northerners appointed to official positions at court level:

> As far as the number of court officials is concerned, there are fewer *nam nhân* than *bắc nhân*. As a rule, Nam Kỳ is the place where literature has recently begun to be developed, and so it is rare to see men pass the state examination. Since the title of doctor was installed, Phan Thanh Giản is the only man to have obtained the doctoral degree. If we use only the state examination as the means of recruitment, only *bắc nhân* will be recruited for several decades. If so, how can the *nam nhân* enter the court? From now on, select bright persons from *nam nhân* according to their talents to be used for the state, whether they have passed the state examinations or not.[26]

---

[22] It has the meaning, "north of the river." Here, the river is the Gianh River in present Quảng Bình province. North from Quảng Bình, there are Hà Tĩnh, Nghệ An, Thanh Hóa, Ninh Bình, and the rest of Bắc Kỳ.

[23] *DNTL2*, 184:22a.

[24] *Đại Nam Thực Lục Chính-Biên Đệ Tam Kỷ* (Primary compilation of the veritable records of the third reign of Imperial Vietnam) (hereafter *DNTL3*) (1894. Tokyo: Institute of Cultural and Linguistic Studies, Keio University, 1977), 32:21a.

[25] Ibid., 45:4b.

[26] *DNTL2*, 122:19b-20a.

In this statement, the phrase *nam nhân* was used as the abbreviation for *Nam Kỳ nhân* and apparently indicates the people of former Gia Định, or of Nam Kỳ. In other words, it was a new historical term, invented after Gia Định became Nam Kỳ. In 1835, just before Lê Văn Khôi's revolt was pacified, several Bắc Thuận and Hồi Lương captives, men formerly from Bắc Kỳ, ran away from the prisoners' camp in the region of Saigon. Minh Mạng's response to this news contains the term *nam nhân*: "They have nothing to rely on, and [their] facial appearance and language are clearly different from those of *nam nhân*, so it will be difficult for them to hide themselves properly."[27] The southern scholar, Phan Thanh Giản, also identified himself and his people as *nam nhân*. In praising Trương Đăng Quế's 1836 proposal to fortify a region called Tây Ninh,[28] northwest of Saigon, Phan Thanh Giản says: "it was an [excellent] idea we *nam nhân* never thought of [even though we live close to Tây Ninh]."[29]

It is not clear what Minh Mạng actually means by the term *bắc nhân* in his statement concerning the regional imbalance of southerners and northerners appointed to official positions at the central level. Another example, an argument on the same matter in 1838, may be clearer. Despite the fact that some attention had been paid to regional imbalances in the bureaucracy, the situation had not improved. Judging from the personnel record of the court, Minh Mạng was embarrassed when he found that northerners (*bắc nhân*) excessively outnumbered southerners on the Board of Justice. He gave the following reason as justification, and to vindicate himself:

> *Nam nhân* have been the object of promotion and transfer only in Nam Kỳ these days, so that the number of *nam nhân* in the central Boards is small. As a general rule, south [*nam*] and north [*bắc*] are one family. How can there be discrimination?[30]

In this example, it is again clear what the term *nam nhân* indicated: the people of former Gia Định. In the quote above, Minh Mạng states that "*nam* and *bắc* are one family." *Nam nhân* were the people of former Gia Định. Were the *bắc nhân*, then, the people of rest of Vietnam, i.e. regions to the north of Gia Định? It does not seem to be the case. It is highly possible that *bắc nhân* is the abbreviation for "Bắc Kỳ nhân," as *nam nhân* was for "Nam Kỳ *nhân*." It appears that, from the perspective of Minh Mạng in the central region, *bắc* and *nam*, north and south, constituted two opposite poles. Therefore, the *bắc* that appeared in the citations mentioned above should be identified as part of Bắc Thành, and of Bắc Kỳ during the period of Minh Mạng. The next example will provide us with further evidence concerning these two ways of identifying Vietnamese people by region during this time.

---

[27] Ibid.,154:12b-13a.

[28] Until 1837, it had been the region densely populated by Khmer people. Under the name of *đạo* Quang Hóa, it had been outside the range of Vietnam's direct administration. In 1837, Quang Hóa became a Vietnamese district. Along with another new district called Tân Ninh, this region formed Tây Ninh prefecture. Nguyễn Thu, *Hoàn Vũ Kỷ Văn*, vol. 3. Tây Ninh had the meaning of "to make the West (Tây, i.e. Cambodia) tranquil (Ninh)."

[29] Phan Thanh Giản, *Lương Khê Văn Thảo*, 2:7.

[30] DNTL2, 195:5b.

A court official of Minh Mạng found that a story highlighting the differences between *bắc nhân* and *nam nhân* was spreading in the regions of Hà Tĩnh and Nghệ An. According to his report to Minh Mạng, written at the end of 1835, the *nam nhân* had gained a reputation as rude and self-confident people, whose conversation and behavior were conducted as if they were standing on the heads of other people. On the other hand, *bắc nhân* always felt ashamed, and they always felt dissatisfied, despite having worked hard to achieve their goals.[31]

In his interpretation of geographical associations common during the period of the Nguyễn dynasty, Woodside also notes the above description and takes it into account. He identifies the *nam nhân* in the description as the people of former Đàng Trong, especially the people of the central region. He argues "many of these 'southerners' actually came from families resident in central Vietnam whose previous generations had fought with Gia-long in the south before 1802."[32] Inevitably, his definition of the *nam nhân* led to another conclusion: that the *bắc nhân* were the people from the region of Hà Tĩnh to the north, the former region of Đàng Ngoài;[33] he makes this argument despite the fact that it evidently contradicts his previous definition of *bắc nhân* as Chinese people resident in China.[34]

In my opinion, the phrase *nam nhân* here should be interpreted as referring to the Nam Kỳ people. I base my own conclusion on the following evidence. First, it was mainly the Nam Kỳ people "whose previous generations had fought with Gia-long." Gia Định had emerged as a clearly separate zone in politics and maintained that status until 1835, and it constituted a region distinguished from the core region of the former Đàng Trong territory, the central region of Vietnam. Secondly, we must consider the position of Thanh Hóa. Though it had belonged to the territory of Đàng Ngoài, it was quickly attached to the central region after the Nguyễn dynasty was formed. It is well known that Thanh Hóa was the "holy province" which produced Minh Mạng's ancestors and the core members of Nguyễn state. When Gia Long divided the territory of Vietnam into three regions, Thanh Hóa, Nghệ An, and Hà Tĩnh[35] were attached to the region under the direct rule of the central government. The regions of Thanh Hóa, Nghệ An, and Hà Tĩnh were identified as part of central Vietnam from the beginning of Gia Long's reign, and promotions of men from these areas to influential positions in the government bureaucracy were common.[36] Under these circumstances, there was no reason for the

---

[31] Ibid., 161:2a.

[32] Alexander Woodside, *Vietnam and the Chinese Model: A Comparative Study of Nguyễn and Ch'ing Civil Government in the First Half of the Nineteenth Century* (Cambridge: Harvard University Press, 1971), pp. 135-36.

[33] Ibid., p. 136.

[34] Ibid., p. 19.

[35] Hà Tĩnh was a new province that was made in the southern part of Nghệ An by the administrative reform of 1831. The names of Hà Nội and Hưng Yên also appeared for the first time from this year. To the north of Thanh Hóa, Ninh Bình had also been part of the central region. But Ninh Bình was absorbed into the region of Bắc Kỳ by the reform of 1831. Phan Thúc Trực, *Quốc Sử Di Biên* (A transmitted compilation of the state history) (hereafter *QSDB*) (n. d. Hong Kong: New Asia Research Institute, 1965), p. 210.

[36] See footnotes 40 and 42.

people of these regions to feel dissatisfied. The "dissatisfied attitude of the *bắc nhân*" described by the court official came about partly because they (the people of Bắc Kỳ) were more excluded from the central administration and politics of Vietnam than during any other previous century.[37] The contrast between *bắc* and *nam* sometimes generated a factionalism based on simmering conflicts between these two regions, Bắc Kỳ and Nam Kỳ. In 1834, the division between north and south emerged in an incident at the State college Quốc Tử Giám at Huế, where students came from all regions to prepare for the state examination. Students found that one official of this college was too sympathetic to students from Bắc Kỳ. In response to this "unfairness," the Nam Kỳ students expressed their displeasure, blaming the official, and even exchanging curses with his wife.[38]

b) Indifference of Southerners to Official Positions

Two purported characteristics of the *nam nhân*—their allegedly "rude and arrogant" behavior and their poor record in advancing to official positions—help us understand why Minh Mạng would have labeled them as "the lazy *sĩ*" in his edict of 1835.

To understand the first feature, we need to remember that Gia Định men were at the center of political power during the reign of Gia Long (1802-1820) and during the first half of Minh Mạng's reign (1820-1841). For the people of Huế and Hanoi, cities that had figured as Vietnam's political and cultural centers until the end of eighteenth century, it must have been astonishing to see the Gia Định people appear before them as high-ranking officials, generals, and unit commanders. The Gia Định elite, on the other hand, suddenly found themselves elevated to a new status, for their group effectively ruled all three regions of Vietnam during Gia Long's reign. At the beginning of the nineteenth century, numbers of Gia Định men and their families, speaking in a southern dialect that the local people of Huế and Hanoi found nearly incomprehensible, became a common sight in these cities.[39]

---

[37] In relation to this theme, Nola Cooke shows how much northerners of the Red River delta were excluded from core positions during the Nguyễn dynasty in "Southern Regionalism and the Composition of the Nguyen Ruling Elite," *Asian Studies Review* (Brisbane) 23,2 (1999), in the section titled "The Analysis."

[38] *QSDB*, p. 240.

[39] In Vietnam, "southward movement," or *nam tiến*, was common throughout history, yet many did migrate north during this period. For instance, we have the case of Tống Viết Phúc's family. Tống Viết Phúc was one of the Gia Định men whose ancestors had left from Thanh Hóa, and he participated in the Gia Định regime. He was killed by a Tây Sơn ambush in 1801. See *LTST*, vol. 13, Tống Viết Phúc. According to *Nam Thiên Hiếu Hành Thực Lục*, his wife was a woman from Bình Dương district near Saigon. In short, they were a couple of pure Gia Định descent. After the formation of the Nguyễn dynasty in 1802, Tống's wife moved north to Huế with her children. No doubt, Tống Viết Phúc was granted an award posthumously by the court. On land granted by the court, the family permanently settled in a village near Huế. In an interview with Tống Viết Sơn, a direct descendant of Tống Viết Phúc, Sơn identified himself to me as a man of Huế until he left his village to go to Saigon in the 1970s. Tống Viết Phúc's tomb and shrine are still in a village beside the Perfume River of Huế. See Choi, Byung Wook, "*Chào anh Việt Nam*" (Hello Vietnam, a collection of fieldwork notes) (Seoul: Narasarang, 1994), pp. 276, 282-83,

They were conquerors, especially in the region of Bắc Thành. Their reputation as "rude and self-confident southerners" was a reflection of their dominance during this time. As the people of Gia Định maintained their own territory and autonomous rule in southern Vietnam until 1832, that reputation must have lasted through a large part of Minh Mạng's reign.

The second characteristic of these southerners was that fewer of them advanced to central positions in the administration by passing the state examinations. At first glance, there would seem to be some incongruity between the southerner's arrogant attitude and their relative scarcity in official court positions. The quotations I've cited regarding the *nam nhân's* arrogance and their limited participation in the bureaucracy were made almost at the same time. The official's report of regional stereotypes common in Nghệ An and Hà Tĩnh .was written in 1835, while Minh Mạng's expressions of concern over the relatively low numbers of southerners in the government were recorded in 1834 and 1838. How could a self-confident attitude on the part of the southerners coexist with their simultaneous loss of influence? To find an answer, it is necessary to examine carefully shifts in the structure of power groups in central politics, and the reaction of southerners toward the state examinations.

The court biography, *Liệt Truyện*, mentions persons who played key roles in central politics. By comparing the biographies from the Gia Long reign contained in the *Đại Nam Chính Biên Liệt Truyện Sơ Tập*, and biographies from the period covering the reigns of Minh Mạng and Thiệu Trị, and part of the reign of Tự Đức, all recorded in the *Đại Nam Chính Biên Liệt Truyện Nhị Tập*, we discover a shift. I examined the regional backgrounds of people in each biography. The regional backgrounds of all 392 men who played prominent roles during the Gia Định regime and Gia Long's reign are shown below[40]:

Table 4: Regional Backgrounds of Gia Long's Men[41]

	North	Middle	South	Unknown	Total
Number	18	142	200	32	392
Ratio (%)	4.59	36.22	51.01	8.16	100

A drastic change took place during Minh Mạng's reign: the ratio of southerners was reduced from 51.01 to 6.39 percent.[42]

and 286. In the *Thực Lục* of Thiệu Trị, we read of a Gia Định man who had moved further north. A meritorious subject, Lê Văn Linh, hailed from Định Tường province. In 1842, the central court found that he had lived in Thanh Hóa after retirement. *DNTL3*, 16:6b.

[40] Following is a more detailed list showing the regional backgrounds of Gia Long's men. North: Hanoi (7), Hải Dương (1), Nam Định (4), Sơn Nam (1), Bắc Ninh (3), Quảng Yên (2). Middle: Thanh Hóa (16), Nghệ An (8), Hà Tĩnh (2), Quảng Bình (12), Thừa Thiên (44), Quảng Nam (10), Quảng Ngãi (9), Bình Định (37), Phú Yên (1), Khánh Hòa (2), Bình Thuận (1). South: Biên Hòa (23), Gia Định (122), Định Tường (21), Vĩnh Long (19). An Giang (11), Hà Tiên (4).

[41] *LTST.*

[42] The next table shows the regional background of the 219 men listed in the *Đại Nam Chính Biên Liệt Truyện Nhị Tập* who started to work as court officials during Minh Mạng's reign.

The results of central state examinations also show that southerners were much less likely to gain positions in the administration based on their success with those tests. According to *Quốc Triều Đăng Khoa Lục*, 75 men (*tiến sĩ* and *phó bảng*) passed the metropolitan examinations during the reign of Minh Mạng. Among them were only two southerners (2.63 percent), while thirty-five of the successful candidates (46.05 percent) were from the central region and thirty-seven (51.32 percent) from the north. During the same period, the relative numbers of graduates of regional examinations, identified by region of origin, more equitably reflected population distribution throughout the country. The average ratios for those graduates, identified by region of origin, was: 1 (south, 10.58 percent): 4.46 (middle, 47.21 percent): 3.65 (north, 42.20 percent). This result was reached by calculating all the graduates listed in *Quốc Triều Hương Khoa Lục* for the period of Minh Mạng's reign. The average ratio of southern graduates of regional examinations was quite reasonable if considered in relation to the population as a whole. The *Thực Lục* of Minh Mạng informs us that, countrywide, the number of registered male adults was 970,516 in the census of 1841,[43] and the population of southern Vietnam was 122,410, based on Nguyễn Thu's account.[44] The southern population thus constituted 12.61 percent of the whole population of Vietnam. This was close to the ratio (10.58 percent) of successful regional state examinees, *cử nhân*, who originated from southern Vietnam. Clearly, however, the result of the metropolitan examination was different. For southern Vietnam to have been fairly represented in that competition, the number of southerners who passed the metropolitan examination should have been between seven and eight, not just one.

	North	Middle	South	Total
Number	66	139	14	219
Ratio (%)	30.14	63.47	6.39	100

Reference: *LTNT*

It is not necessary for us to believe that the regional distributions of north and middle fully represent actual changes, because the organizing principles and selection criteria in the *Đại Nam Chính Biên Liệt Truyện Nhị Tập* for men north of Huế were substantially different from those used in the *Đại Nam Chính Biên Liệt Truyện Sơ Tập*. See the section, "The Sources," in Cooke, "Southern Regionalism and the Composition of the Nguyen Ruling Elite." I introduce this table to show the drastically reduced ratio for southern numbers, not only compared with the previous period (of Gia Long) but also compared with other regions during Minh Mạng's reign. The provincial origins of the 219 men are: North: Ninh Bình (1), Hanoi (16), Hưng Yên (7), Hải Dương (6), Nam Định (12), Sơn Tây (8), Bắc Ninh (16). Middle: Thanh Hóa (22), Nghệ An (18), Hà Tĩnh (19), Quảng Bình (14), Quảng Trị (11), Thừa Thiên (35), Quảng Nam (7), Quảng Ngãi (5), Bình Định (6), Phú Yên (1), Khánh Hòa (1). South: Biên Hòa (2), Gia Định (5), Định Tường (0), Vĩnh Long (3), An Giang (4), Hà Tiên (0).

It is interesting to note the promotions and marked advancement of men from three particular provinces: Thanh Hóa, Nghệ An and Hà Tĩnh. Fifty-nine men were from these three provinces. The number of men from each of these three provinces is higher than any other province with the exception of Thừa Thiên, the region of capital.

[43] *DNTL2*, 220:36a.

[44] Nguyễn Thu, *Hoàn Vũ Ký Văn*, vol. 3.

What was the reason for the *nam nhân's* failure to advance to central administrative positions, compared to the more successful *bắc nhân*? In part, it resulted from the central court's active bid to win northerners over to its side. An assessment of the extent to which the Nguyễn dynasty court succeeded in this work will have to wait for another study. The records do show, however, that Minh Mạng kept trying to achieve this goal. When he visited Hanoi in 1821, he meant not only to attend the official enthronement ceremony with the embassy from China, but also to make an appeal to the northerners, whom he hoped would participate in his court.[45] Occasionally, Minh Mạng's men were dispatched to the northern region for this same purpose, recruitment. In 1827, when one of his officials was sent to Sơn Nam and Nam Định, Minh Mạng asked him: "You have to visit any talented intellectual of Bắc Thành with a sincere mind. If you find any one who has any talent, you must remember to report his name to me."[46] Perhaps this was one way to appease the "dissatisfied" northerners.

Another reason for the northern candidates' relatively greater success had to do with that region's educational traditions and excellence in academic achievement. Northerners around the Red River Delta had a much richer experience in and longer tradition of preparing for the state examination than the southerners did.

Finally, the favorable economic situation of the southern land was a significant factor that helps to explain the relative "weakness" of *nam nhân* candidates in advancing to central positions, as well as their reported arrogance. Southern young men were greeted with a variety of opportunities that enabled them to lead a more comfortable life by conducting business rather than by serving as government officials. Young men throughout Vietnam commonly chose to make their living through the cultivation of rice, but it was easier for a southern farmer to accumulate wealth and land than it was for his counterparts in the central and northern regions. An example is Dũng (1794-1849), a member of the Trương family near Saigon. The second son of a peasant family, he chose to move to a different village, called Hòa Bình in Định Tường province, near the east bank of the Upper Mekong River (Tiền Giang), when he came of age. Though he started out with no property, he succeeded in accumulating sufficient wealth to be able to rise to a leading position in his new home. By the time of his death, he was a *thủ khoán*.[47] If he had been a man of the central or northern region, this kind of social advancement might have not been easily realized.

In fact, a position as a government official, at least during the Nguyễn dynasty, did not provide an individual with enough income to support an ordinary family. Unless an official (or his wife and family) was involved in earning money on the side in other ways, he had to suffer materially. For example, let us assume a certain southern Vietnamese passed the regional examination. After a while, he might be appointed as a head of a district, *tri huyện*. According to regulations, he

---

[45] *MMCY*, 4:3a.

[46] Ibid., 4:7b.

[47] *Trương Gia Từ Đường Thế Phả Toàn Tập* (Complete collection of the genealogy of the Truong family ancestry) (1886. Hanoi: Viện Hán Nôm A 3186), p. 6. *Thủ khoán* were in charge of guarding and lending village property. See Schreiner, *Les Institutions Annamites en Basse-Cochinchine avant la Conquête Française*, p. 27.

would be at the sixth rank second class, or *tùng lục phẩm*.[48] Another document informs us that until 1840, 22 *mân* (or *quan*) currency and 22 *phương* of husked rice made up the annual salary for an official of this rank.[49] During the middle of the 1820s, one *mân* was almost equal to one *phương* in Gia Định, according to the rice price found in the Châu Bản.[50] In this case, the total amount of this official's annual salary would be equal to 44 *phương* or 22 *hộc* of husked rice. To produce this amount of rice in Biên Hòa, it was enough to cultivate 2.88 *mẫu*.[51] In a more fertile land like Định Tường, they would have needed less land to produce the same amount of rice. But the natural conditions of southern Vietnam allowed a peasant family to cultivate more land. For instance, in the villages called Bình Đăng and Tân Mục of Định Tường province, 3-5 *mẫu* was the usual size for a plot of land for a peasant family.[52] Therefore, employment as a government official was not especially attractive to southerners, as far as salary was concerned. If those administrators relied only on their official salaries, even high-ranking officials would have found it difficult to lead a normal life. If an official insisted on living only on his salary and he was of fifth rank first class, he found that he could not afford enough clothes for himself and his family to live through the winter in Huế.[53] If he was an official of third rank first class, resolved to live on his salary alone in order to prove himself as man of integrity and fairness, he had to realize his family would probably starve if he were to be temporarily transferred to another post and forced to leave them behind.[54]

Not only were government officials paid relatively low salaries, they were also faced with temptations that led some to become involved in crime and to risk their lives, especially in the south. In the region of Gia Định, legal and illegal commercial activities were ongoing and brisk, compared with other regions, so that officials were tempted to become involved in profit-making ventures and to accept bribes offered by those engaged in the trade.[55] An epigram is found in the collection of Phan Thanh Giản's works, part of an argument regarding the thesis that civil officials do not love money, called "Ngự Chế Văn Thần Bất Ái Tiền Luận,"

---

[48] *Đại Nam Điển Lệ Toát Yếu* (A summary of the statutes of Imperial Vietnam) (hereafter *TY*) trans. by Nguyễn Sĩ Giác (1909. Ho Chi Minh City: Nxb Thành Phố Hồ Chí Minh, 1994), p. 24.

[49] *DNTL2*, 207:45a.

[50] Phan Huy Lê, "Châu Bản Triều Nguyễn và Châu Bản Năm Minh Mệnh 6-7," (Vermillion record of the Nguyen dynasty during 1825-1826) (manuscript), p. 33.

[51] Concerning rice productivity in southern Vietnam, see chapter six. Any discussion about land tax, when speaking of southern Vietnam during the 1820s and 1830s, is meaningless because large parts of the land were not registered. See chapter six.

[52] See my argument on the land size of a tenant in chapter six.

[53] In 1840, two officials of Huế court asked Minh Mạng: "Our families are too poor, please give us winter clothes." *DNTL2*, 218:36b.

[54] When Huỳnh Quýnh was appointed to a position in southern Vietnam, he revealed his financial difficulties to Minh Mạng in the following message: "This subject is to be posted away from the capital. My family is very poor and my children are still little. Thus, they do not have anything to live on. Please give me a permission to have the rice [the part of rice from his salary] paid directly to my family [here in Huế] to let them live on." *LTNT*, 18:7a.

[55] *DNTL2*, 78:17b-18a.

composed by a king of the Nguyễn dynasty. The epigram states that "[true] civil officials do not love money, and [true] military officials do not fear death [văn thần bất ái tiền, võ thần bất tích tử]."[56] This was a respectful and, ideally, heartening assertion that the officials of Nguyễn dynasty were meant to bear in mind, but it certainly also reflects how difficult it was for government administrators to resist the attractions of money.

In her article discussing the lax standards of Đàng Trong Confucianism, Nola Cooke introduces an interesting case that she found in *Quốc Triều Hương Khoa Lục*. Of eight Gia Định *cử nhân* graduates in 1813, none ever became officials.[57] *Bà Tâm Huyền Kính Lục* provides us with one of the likely reasons for this result. Among these eight graduates, there was a man whose name was Lưu Bảo Tâm. After he passed the regional examination, he firmly declined any position of the sort that was usually offered to successful candidates of the regional examination, asserting that, "if I became a government official, I would find it unavoidable to be involved in crime. It would be better to lead a more comfortable and wealthier life without becoming a government official." After making this declaration, he chose the occupation of broker and became wealthy.[58] There was another southerner called Trần Dã Lão (1797 - ?) who also showed no interest in becoming a government official despite his long investment in education. Before he decided to return home, he traveled to the capital of the Vĩnh Long province and to Saigon, where he spent time in study. According to Phan Thanh Giản's description, Trần completed his study of the Confucian Classics and reached a level of academic achievement sufficient to qualify him as a candidate for the state examination. Nevertheless, Trần Dã Lão returned to his home, not in order to pursue reclusive studies, but rather to engage in his family business.[59]

I think this indifference to government advancement was one of the significant reasons preventing the southern *sĩ* from advancing to central government posts during the 1820s-1830s. The "lazy *sĩ* of southern Vietnam" was a label that indicated southerner's indifference to official positions and to the successful completion of the state examinations that led to the central positions.

2. SPREAD OF EDUCATIONAL INSTITUTIONS

There is some evidence that Minh Mạng's interest in educating the people of Gia Định started in an earlier period of his reign, before the 1830s. I believe, nonetheless, that his main objective in sending educators south was to infiltrate the Gia Định government, which was dominated at that time by Lê Văn Duyệt's men,

---

[56] Phan Thanh Giản, *Lương Khê Văn Thảo*, 3:7.

[57] Nola Cooke, "Nineteenth-Century Vietnamese Confucianization in Historical Perspective: Evidence from the Palace Examinations (1463-1883)," *Journal of Southeast Asian Studies* 25,2 (1994): 307.

[58] Trần Tân Gia, *Bà Tâm Huyền Kính Lục* (An account of compassionate hearts and hanging mirrors) (1897. Hanoi: Viện Hán Nôm A 2027), pp. 75-78.

[59] Phan did not clearly say what Trần did, but it is certain that he did not choose any job typical for a Confucian scholar such as official, educator, or local doctor, for example. Phan mentions that Trần's work was "very accurate in arranging account books, and he never missed the timing of seeding and cultivating." Phan Thanh Giản, *Lương Khê Văn Thảo*, 3:194-20.

by sending his own civil officials into the region. In chapter two, I mentioned that Nguyễn Đăng Sở and an unnamed Nghệ An Confucian were appointed educational officers in 1821. Minh Mạng's purported reason for dispatching these two scholars was to educate southern students. The king made a statement in the same year explaining what factors prompted him to send these two men to Gia Định:

> Gia Định people, they are generally loyal and righteous. But they are short of learning. Therefore, they frequently let their temper show. If we send distinguished scholars to be teachers of Gia Định students and teach [them] manners, [they] will easily be influenced and will move to goodness.[60]

Minh Mạng's next action was more ambitious. In 1822, he recruited eight doctorate holders (*tiến sĩ*) for the first time in the Nguyễn dynasty. Four of them, Hà Quyền (Hanoi), Phan Hữu Tính (Nghệ An), Vũ Đức Khuê (Hải Dương), and Phan Bá Đạt (Hà Tĩnh) were appointed to the heads of four new prefectures, or *tri phủ* of Gia Định: Tân Bình, Định Viễn, Phúc Long, and Kiến An.[61] Minh Mạng said his intention was not only that they should administer these regions, but also that they should educate people:

> Gia Định people like righteousness and they can easily be influenced. Now we established *phủ*. You try to govern [them, but] the idea should be to educate and encourage good customs. That is my intention.[62]

But the results in both cases were frustrating for Minh Mạng. Faced with local solidarity on the part of Gia Định officials, Minh Mạng's officials found it impossible to perform their roles as "instructors." As noted in chapter two, Nguyễn Đăng Sở complained: "The emperor's order [on the matter of education and selection of educated men] was delivered from *thành* to *trấn*, and from *trấn* to *phủ* and *huyện*, but nobody asked me." The four doctoral degree holders also did not seem to have met with much success as the heads of new administrative units in the south. Before long, Phan Hữu Tính was transferred to an educational position in Định Tường military province.[63] His fate there may well have been the same as that of Nguyễn Đăng Sở. Another doctoral degree holder, Hà Quyền, was withdrawn to a civil position at Quảng Trị in the central region.[64] There is no evidence concerning the fates of the other two degree holders sent to help administer Gia Định during this time.

Before he could begin a truly effective campaign to reeducate the Gia Định people, Minh Mạng had to wait until Lê Văn Duyệt died. In 1832, following the old general's death, the Gia Định Thành Tổng Trấn was dismantled and a new governor-general, Lê Phúc Bảo, was appointed to rule the provinces of Định Tường and Vĩnh Long. It then became obvious that Minh Mạng's first priority in terms of

---

[60] *DNTL2*, 8:10b–11a.

[61] Ibid., 18:16b.

[62] Ibid., 18:17a.

[63] *LTNT*, 25:8a.

[64] Ibid., 25:8b.

ruling southern Vietnam was *giáo hóa*, or to "cultivate" the people: "In your position, you ought to make your first priority the work of *giáo hóa*."[65] At this time, Minh Mạng wanted to do more than "to teach Gia Định students, or to educate Gia Định people and encourage good customs," as he declared in the early 1820s. His desire from 1832 onward was to spread awareness of the central government that would secure southerners' loyalty to that government.

Schools

As soon as the southern land was brought under the direct control of the central authority in 1832, systems and tools for the education of southerners were established. *Đốc học, giáo thụ*, and *huấn đạo*, educational officers, were appointed to each administrative unit of *tỉnh, phủ, and huyện*, respectively. We know that the position of *đốc học* had been set up in each military province at the beginning of Minh Mạng's reign, while the positions of *giáo thụ* and *huấn đạo* appeared for the first time in 1823.[66] However, there is little documentary evidence to reveal how the education system at the lower level in southern Vietnam operated until Gia Định Thành Tổng Trấn was dismantled in 1832. Before this time, there seem to have been educational officers, but no organized school system. Not until 1834 did the central government started to fill the vacant positions of educational officers at the level of district in southern Vietnam.[67]

Beginning in 1832, schools were constructed at each local level. *Đại Nam Nhất Thống Chí*, compiled during 1865-1885, provides us with the locations of local schools. From this book, we can see how the number of schools increased from 1832 in southern Vietnam. Eight schools were listed of uniform size[68] at the level of prefecture, of which seven were built during the reign of Minh Mạng and one during Thiệu Trị's reign (1841-1847). Of the seven schools built during Minh Mạng's reign, six were evidently constructed after the dismantling of Gia Định Thành Tổng Trấn. Construction of a further eleven schools at district level commenced after 1835. The following table shows the figures.

---

[65] *MMCY*, 13:19b.

[66] Ibid., 4:23b.

[67] *DNTL2*, 127:7b.

[68] In 1835, the size of school at the levels of prefecture and district was standardized. *DNTL2*, 159:26b-27a.

Table 5: Establishment of Local Schools in Southern Vietnam[69]

	Biên Hòa p: 2 d: 7	Gia Định p: 3 d: 9	Định Tường p: 2 d: 4	Vĩnh Long p: 3 d: 8	An Giang p: 3 d: 9	Hà Tiên p: 1 d: 3
Province	1 (Minh Mạng)	1 (Gia Long)	1 (1836)	1 (1826)	1 (1842)	0
Prefecture	2 (Minh Mạng, 1837)	2 (1836, 1846)	2 (1833, 1838)	1 (1837)	1 (1832)	0
District	0	2 (1841, 1852)	2 (1835, 1838)	4 (1837, 1851, 1860, 1862)	2 (1837, 1839)	1 (1847)

(   ): year of establishment.

p: number of prefectures before 1865

d: number of districts before 1865

Because this data dates from 1865, the ratio of the number of local schools relative to the number of local units—prefectures or districts—does not accurately represent the situation in the first half of the nineteenth century. For example, the number of local schools in An Giang province looks quite small compared with the number of local units: there is only one prefecture school to serve three prefectures, and two district schools to serve nine districts. However, we have to remember that there were fewer local units at the beginning of the 1830s than indicated in the figures above. An Giang had one prefecture and two districts when it was created as a new province in 1832.[70] To judge to what extent Minh Mạng encouraged the spread of local schools, we need to select a province that was not affected by administrative reshuffling. Định Tường was the only stable province in terms of the number of administrative units and their locations; the number of prefectures and districts in 1865 in Định Tường, two and four respectively, was the same as that during Minh Mạng's reign. The chart shows us that five schools were established between 1833 and 1838, including two district and two prefecture schools. This might seem to be an insufficient number, since there were, in fact, a total of six prefectures and districts in the province. However it was unnecessary to build four district schools because the prefecture school located in a particular district could act as that district's school as well. For instance, in Định Tường, prefecture Kiến Tường had two districts, called Kiến Phong and Kiến Đăng, while prefecture Kiến An had two districts, called Kiến Hưng and Kiến Hòa. They needed to build district schools only at Kiến Đăng and Kiến Hòa to meet the needs of the four districts, because the districts of Kiến Phong and Kiến Hưng, where the offices of two prefectures were

---

[69] Viện Sử Học, trans., *Đại Nam Nhất Thống Chí* (Dai Nam gazetteer) (hereafter *DNNTC*) (Hue: Thuận Hóa, 1992).

[70] Nguyễn Thu, *Hoàn Vũ Kỷ Văn*, vol. 3.

located, already had prefecture schools. In the case of Định Tường province, we can say that local schools were fully established by Minh Mạng from the level of province to the level of district after the dismantling of Gia Định Thành Tổng Trấn.

From 1835, copies of Chinese classics, instructive literature, and exemplary suggestions of policy were distributed to provincial schools.[71] Needless to say, these copies were to help students prepare for the state examination. The copies were supposed to be distributed to the lower levels of schools. This was a method for disseminating the ideas of the central government downwards.

As with all educational materials, educational officers also had to be approved by the central government. A report from Định Tường province in 1836 describes the findings of central officers who had been dispatched to examine the quality of educational officers at the district level.[72] Two former *huấn đạo* in the districts of Kiến Đăng and Kiến Hòa were allowed to remain in their positions following the judgments of the central officials sent to this province. There were, however, no objective criteria for these assessments. These men were approved because, according to the records, "they have academic knowledge and are trusted and respected by students" and, perhaps more important to the court (which disliked "lazy" southerners) because "they work twice as hard as before."[73] The examinees' expressed willingness to help promulgate the ideas of the central court, as well as their evident loyalty to the central government, must have greatly influenced the judgment of the central officials who tested them.[74]

Minh Mạng's Instruction — Thập Điều, or Ten Moral Maxims

In 1835, Minh Mạng declared ten moral maxims to guide the Vietnamese people. These were: 1) *đôn nhân luận* (strengthen human duties); 2) *chính tâm thuật* (keep your thought right); 3) *vụ bản nghiệp* (work hard in your own occupation); 4) *thượng tiết kiểm* (respect frugality); 5) *hậu phong tục* (enrich worthwhile custom); 6) *huấn tử đệ* (cultivate youth); 7) *sùng chính học* (respect orthodox studies); 8) *giới dâm nặc* (make strict precautions against zest for lust); 9) *thận pháp thủ* (obey the law); and 10) *quảng thiện hành* (do more good works). An important result of this declaration was that villagers were now expected to listen to their king's instructions repeatedly, according to a predetermined schedule. Regulations stipulated that an original copy of these instructions was to be sent to each provincial government. From here, copies were made to be distributed to every village and every school, and these were to be read and lectured upon regularly. In the villages, people would gather in the communal house (*đình*) every three

---

[71] *MMCY*, 19:11b-12a.

[72] The officials at the district level were southerners.

[73] Châu Bản Triều Nguyễn (Vermilion Records of the Nguyen dynasty) (ANU Library, microfilm reels 60-4 [1836-1837]), lunar February 12, 1836.

[74] Though it was not a case involving *huấn đạo*, we do find records of another judgment by central officials assessing local officials. Phạm Như Tài, the head of district Tân Long, was forced to leave his position after he was judged inadequate: "he is too young and does not know administration." It was suggested that he should be sent to a central Board to learn administration. Châu Bản Triều Nguyễn, lunar December 9, 1836.

months and listened to lectures from elders concerning these maxims. The performance of this lecture was somewhat ritualized. At the center of a commune house a red table was located, and a copy of Minh Mạng's instructions was laid on this table. Everyone stood up and bowed to the copy five times. After the lecture was repeated, the copy of the maxims was replaced on the table. Both the lecturer and attendants bowed to the copy five times more, and then the lecture was concluded.[75] In 1841, a new position, *hương thân*, was established at the village level to oversee this ritual; it was the duty of the *hương thân* to lecture on the king's moral maxims four times a year.[76]

We cannot be certain whether these regulations and readings were actually practiced as stipulated in the villages, however there is evidence to suggest that the king's maxims, and the rituals established to broadcast them, were well known and even popular in the villages. A recent study has shown that, in the south, by the mid-1870s, the instructions were recited regularly. Their content became a source of controversy in negotiations between the French authorities and the Vietnamese court when those parties prepared the Second Saigon Treaty of 1874, because the instructions contained an item (*sùng chính học*) that opposed Christianity.[77] Of course, the instructions were intended not only for the southerners, but for all Vietnamese in every region, yet for our purposes the effect of the king's maxims on the people of Gia Định is most significant. Clearly the promulgation of these maxims in villages throughout the south was meant to strengthen the people's recognition of the central government and its king.

Plate 6. The Royal Library in the Hue Palace. The library was the symbolic center of the Hue court's intellectuals and ideology, from which educational institutions spread to southern Vietnam. Credit: the author, 1994.

---

[75] *DNTL2*, 129:8a.

[76] *QSDB*, p. 354.

[77] Youn, Dae Yeong, "Wanjo Sadeokje Sigi Daebulhyeopsang'eseoeui Kadolik Munje (A question of Catholicism in the process of Franco-Vietnamese negotiations during the period of Tu Duc) (MA thesis, Seoul National University, 1998), p. 45.

Obviously, in taking this action, the king was imitating similar cases in China, as Minh Mạng himself admitted.[78] Woodside also points out "his requirement was based upon precedents set by Ch'ing emperors like K'ang-hsi or Ming emperors like Hung-wu in China."[79] Nevertheless, Minh Mạng's ten instructional maxims contained original Vietnamese ideas that reflected, and now reveal, his own intent concerning the cultivation of the people of southern Vietnam.[80] In the first two items and the ninth item, loyalty to the central court, obedience to higher authority, and compliance with state law were emphasized. All of these had to do with the work of promoting awareness of the central government. The third item, *vụ bản nghiệp*, encouraged people to work hard in their own occupations, whether as *sĩ* (literati), *nông* (peasants), *công* (artisans), or *thương* (merchants). In the detailed comments that follow the maxims in this document, however, emphasis is only placed on the first two fields of endeavor, with particular attention paid to peasants. During this same period of time, in other contexts, Minh Mạng was warning that peasants should not fall into the occupations of artisans and merchants.[81] The word *bản nghiệp* had a dual meaning, signifying either one's own occupation, or an essential occupation, i.e. agriculture. Thus the phrase "*vụ bản nghiệp*," by implication, encourages the people to engage in agriculture. If we remember that southerners were frequently criticized by Minh Mạng for pursuing commerce, or *mạt nghiệp* (the lowest occupation), as he called it, then the true target audience for the third maxim becomes clear: southerners were being instructed to fix their rice fields. The seventh item, "*sùng chính học*," underscored the value of Confucianism and warned against acceptance of Christianity. Christianity had already proved a threat to the stability of his kingdom during 1833–1835 in southern Vietnam. I think Christians' active participation in Lê Văn Khôi's revolt prompted Minh Mạng to emphasize this item. The eighth item, "*giới dâm nặc*," was to warn against lust, or lecherous relationships between men and women. I cannot judge to what extent this maxim reflected a serious concern in Vietnamese society at that time, but I do think the king must have hoped this instruction would help curb the appetites of the southerners, whom he frequently criticized as lecherous.

---

[78] *DNTL2*, 129:5b.

[79] Woodside, *Vietnam and the Chinese Model*, p. 189.

[80] In 1398, the first emperor of the Ming dynasty of China promulgated six moral maxims popularly called *liu yu*. Examination shows how the original Chinese version of these maxims and the Vietnamese revisions differ from each other. The Chinese maxims are: 1. *hsiao shun fu mu* (hiếu thuận phụ mẫu, piety to parents) 2. *kung ching chang shang* (cung kính trưởng thượng, respect for elders) 3. *ho mu hsiang li* (hòa mục hương lý, harmony in the village) 4. *chiao hsun tzu sun* (giáo huấn tử tôn, cultivation of youth) 5. *ko an sheng li* (các an sinh lý, contentment in each field of living), and 6. *wu tso fei wei* (vô tác phi vị, avoidance of wrongdoing). Elders or disabled men were supposed to walk around the village singing these instructions. By order of the Ch'ing government in 1652, these items were carved into stone at several provinces in China. See Morobashi Tetsuji, *Daikanwajiten* (A Chinese-Japanese dictionary), vol. 2 (Tokyo: Taishukan Shoten, 1971), pp. 1157-58.

[81] *DNTL2*, 129:2a.

Cults

In each province of southern Vietnam, there were large numbers of shrines for different objects of worship, ranging from the state deities (*xã tắc*) to the Dragon King, Vietnamese, Khmer, and Chinese heroes, and mountain, river, and gods/goddesses of various origins. The following were commonly found in every province by the time *Đại Nam Nhất Thống Chí* was compiled during the second half of the nineteenth century: *đàn xã tắc*, or altar to the State deities; *đàn tiên nông*, altar for the god of agriculture; *đàn hội đồng* for soldiers who were sacrificed during the civil war with the Tây Sơn; *đàn sơn xuyên*, altar for the god of mountains and rivers; *văn miếu*, which was a shrine to Confucius; and a shrine for Thành Hoàng, the god of fortresses. Of these cults, the *văn miếu*, *đàn xã tắc*, and *đàn tiên nông* are directly relevant as evidence of the central government's work to cultivate southerners. We note especially the *đàn xã tắc* and the *đàn tiên nông* shrines, honoring state deities and the god of agriculture, respectively, which were established by Minh Mạng after the dismantling of Gia Định Thành Tổng Trấn. The following figure indicates shrines that existed in four provinces up to 1865 and shows when they were erected.[82]

Table 6: Shrines, and Year of Establishment[83]

	Biên Hòa	Gia Định	Định Tường	Vĩnh Long
văn miếu	1715	1824		1864
đàn xã tắc	1832	1832	1833	1836
đàn tiên nông	1832	1832	1832	1836

We can see that spreading Confucianism was not Minh Mạng's main consideration in his "cultivation" of southern Vietnam, as he built no shrines to Confucius (*văn miếu*) in southern Vietnam after 1832. He was mainly concerned with establishing places of worship to reinforce the dignity of the central court. He wished to remind the southerners that he and his family—not Lê Văn Duyệt—now ruled southern Vietnam; a necessary lesson because, as noted above, in his opinion southerners "only knew the existence of a frontier leader, but did not know the existence of the central court." Shrines dedicated to the state deities, and by extension, to the king's imperial ambitions, appeared in each province. The southerners also saw for the first time the altar for the god of agriculture, called Thần Nông, who, according to a legend from the Chinese classics, is said to have taught his people farming. Again, the central court was strongly recommending that southerners engage in the cultivation of rice rather than *mạt nghiệp*, or commerce.

Increased Numbers of Successful State Examination Candidates

As part of his campaign to press southerners toward acceptance of the central government, the king also chose to increase their opportunities to take the state

---

[82] None of those three kinds of shrines are found in An Giang or Hà Tiên provinces.

[83] *DNNTC*

examination. The creation of more qualified civil servants in the south would have increased the number of people who shared common ideas with the central government.

The examiners' requirements determined the number of successful candidates and their subsequent rank. As a rule, the regional examination was offered in four parts or stages.[84] If a candidate showed excellence in all four stages, he was honored as a graduate, or *cử nhân*. There were also second-degree graduates who had failed in showing excellence in one stage; they were called *tú tài*.

It would be difficult for the king to implement this part of his initiative unless potential candidates were willingly to respond to the government's offer. For this reason, the number of graduates was determined not only by the king, but also by the number of candidates who took the test. No exact regulation has been found describing this practice, but later evidence provides us with a clue that it had been going on. In 1841, the central government declared that one *cử nhân* was to be selected from each one thousand candidates, and one *tú tài* from every one hundred candidates.[85]

The next table provides information concerning the results of regional examinations during Minh Mạng's reign.

Table 7: Graduates of Regional Examinations in Minh Mạng's Reign[86]

	1821	1825	1828	1831	1834/ 1835[87]	1837	1840	Total
Vietnam	132	117	113	100	86	89	81	718
South	12 (16)	14 (15)	15 (16)	10	9	11	5 (6)	76 (83)
Ratio (%)	9.09	11.97	13.27	10	10.47	12.36	6.17	10.58

( ): number of graduates, including men from the central region[88]

The above figures reflect political changes in southern Vietnam. When Lê Văn Duyệt ruled Gia Định, both the number of southern graduates and the ratio of those graduates to the total number of graduates, were higher than those of previous

---

[84] Generally, there were four stages in the test during the Nguyễn dynasty: 1. *Kinh Nghĩa and Truyện*, or Chinese classics; 2. *Chiếu, Chế, and Biểu*, or composing official documents such as royal edicts or orders, and suggestions to the king; 3. *Thơ and Phú*, or composing literature such as poems and verse, and 4. *Văn Sách*, or suggestions for policy on certain matters. Cao Tự Thanh, *Nho Giáo ở Gia Định*, p. 124.

[85] *QSDB*, p. 356.

[86] *QTHKL, DNNTC*

[87] The regional examination of 1834 was postponed to 1835 in Nam Kỳ because Lê Văn Khôi's revolt was not yet quelled.

[88] Candidates from Bình Thuận and Khánh Hòa also took the examination in Gia Định. So it is very important to distinguish these men from others, even though their names were listed in the graduate group from the Gia Định site.

periods,[89] and continued to increase until 1828. When Lê Văn Duyệt's power was declining and Minh Mạng was about to abolish Gia Định Thành, both the numbers and ratio fell, as shown in the figure for 1831. After the suppression of Lê Văn Khôi's revolt, the proportion of southern graduates seems to have recovered. At the end of Minh Mạng's reign, however, the presence of southern graduates, both in number and ratio, dropped down to its lowest level. These patterns suggest that the stringency of the examiners' requirements and the numbers of candidates, especially from the southern region, must have varied in response to political changes and policies during the time.

Records suggest that Minh Mạng's campaign to "cultivate" the south bore fruit after the king's demise, during the reign of Thiệu Trị (1841-1847), when southern Vietnam appears to have produced a growing number of successful examination graduates. This result was due, in part, to the increased frequency of the exam. The regional examination was held every year throughout Thiệu Trị's reign, with a single intermission between 1844 and 1845. Of a total of five regional examinations held during this reign, two were regular exams and three "special," scheduled by the government in response to particular events or, perhaps, policy.

The same trend continued beyond 1847. In 1848, a special regional examination was held to commemorate Tự Đức's enthronement, and the following year a regular examination was scheduled. Table 8 below shows more detailed figures. During a span of twenty-eight years, from 1813–1840, the Nguyễn dynasty produced 912 graduates for the entire country. Amongst them, 94 graduates (10.31 percent) were from southern Vietnam.[90] During the next ten years (1841-1850), however, 113 graduates (11.92 percent of the total of 948) were from the south, and our evidence suggests that they were intensively recruited by the government. The increase in the ratio—which rose from 10.31 percent to 11.92 percent—was due to a new regulation of 1841 that fixed the Gia Định site's graduate quota at sixteen, which increased the ratio of Gia Định site graduates to 14.55 percent.[91] Because candidates from Bình Thuận and Khánh Hòa, two central provinces, also took examinations at the Gia Định site, not all sixteen candidates who received appointments would have been Gia Định men. Nevertheless, it is clear that the

---

[89] During the Gia Long period, there were three regional examinations, but they were temporary rather than regular. In 1807, the first regional examination was held, but was only designed to recruit graduates from the former Lê/Trịnh Đàng Ngoài region. From this examination, sixty-one graduates were produced in the region from Nghệ An north. Two more examinations followed.

	1813	1819	total
Vietnam	82	112	194
South	8	10 (12)	18 (20)
ratio (%)	9.76	8.93	9.28

( ): number of graduates including men from the central region

Reference: *QTHKL, DNNTC*

[90] See Table 7 and note 89.

[91] Hanoi: 23; Nam Định: 21; Nghệ An: 25; Thừa Thiên: 25; Gia Định: 16. *QTHKL*, p. 207.

overall number of graduates from this site increased, since the ratio of all graduates from this site (including the graduates from the two central provinces) to the total pool of graduates in Vietnam had been only 11.56 percent during Minh Mạng's reign.

Table 8: Number of Graduates during the 1840s[92]

	1841	1842	1843	1846	1847	1848	1849/ 1850[93]	Total
Vietnam	144	108	121	132	135	165	143	948
South	13 (15)	16	15	18	18 (20)	18 (20)	15 (17)	113 (121)
Ratio (%)	9.03	14.81	12.40	13.64	13.33	10.91	10.49	11.92

( ): total number of graduates, including men from the central region

During the reign of Thiệu Trị, the popularity of the state examination increased in southern Vietnam, and thereby further increased the number of candidates. The records show that, in 1847, the central government decided to recruit more graduates from the Gia Định site. When the examination was held in Gia Định that year, the court planned to approve sixteen graduates from the group of applicants, based on the regulations, but the number of candidates who appeared to take the exam at this site surpassed the government's expectations. Hearing this news, Thiệu Trị ordered examiners to pass four additional candidates.[94] As discussed previously, by this time the number of graduates reflected the number of candidates. In other words, the addition of four graduates meant that the number of candidates must have increased by 25 percent compared with the number in 1841, when the central government decided to recruit sixteen graduates from the Gia Định site.

It is possible to compute the total number of degree-holders (*cử nhân* and *tú tài*) from southern Vietnam who were produced during this period, from 1841–1850, when the exam was scheduled so frequently and the number of candidates appears to have been on the increase. Phan Thúc Trực writes that one graduate, *cử nhân*, was selected from one thousand candidates, and one *tú tài* from one hundred candidates, but his account surely describes the exceptional case of 1841, so it is not necessary to believe that one *cử nhân* was always selected from one thousand candidates. However, it is reasonable to assume that the proportion between the numbers of *cử nhân* and *tú tài* (1:10) would have been consistent from year to year. In other words, about ten *tú tài* degrees were probably awarded for each *cử nhân* degree. If this was true, we can assume that about 1,130 *tú tài* were produced during this period, along with the 113 *cử nhân*, making a notional total of 1,243 degree-holders. The number 1,243 is about 0.75 percent of the 165,598 registered male adults

---

[92] *QTHKL, DNNTC*.

[93] In 1849, a regional examination was held first only in Nam Kỳ. In other regions, examinations were postponed until 1850. The total number of graduates in this column, then, includes 1850 graduates from different regions.

[94] *DNTL3*, 71:1.

of southern Vietnam based on the 1847 census, when persons of all ethnic backgrounds were taken into account.[95] If we remember that the number of registered male adults in southern Vietnam was 122,410 at the end of Minh Mạng's reign,[96] when only ethnic Vietnamese were counted, then 1,243 degree holders would constitute approximately 1 percent of registered Vietnamese male adults of southern Vietnam during this period.

Plate 7. Statue of Nguyễn Hữu Huân, a southern *cử nhân*, famous for leading anti-French fighters. Credit: the author, 2002.

Minh Mạng's educational policies, which appear to have won the approval of his successor, Thiệu Trị, not only increased the number of schools throughout the south, but also enlarged the area from which scholars could be recruited. Until 1831, all southern graduates had come from only four of the southern provinces: from Biên Hòa, Gia Định, and Định Tường, located on the east of the Upper Mekong River (Tiền Giang); and from the main section of Vĩnh Long, the region situated between the Upper Mekong River and the Lower Mekong River (Hậu Giang). Beginning with the examination of 1835, however, we find that men from the western part of the Lower Mekong River also appeared as graduates of the regional examination. *Quốc Triều Hương Khoa Lục* informs us that five men from Vĩnh Long province became graduates in 1835. Amongst these, Bùi Hữu Nghĩa and Huỳnh Hữu Quang were from the Vĩnh Định district of Vĩnh Long province. Bạch Văn Lý and Nguyễn Văn Tấn, graduates in 1841 and 1843, were from the Phong Phú district, according to the *Quốc Triều Hương Khoa Lục*. Both the Vĩnh Định and

[95] Ibid., 67:10a.

[96] Nguyễn Thu, *Hoàn Vũ Kỷ Văn* vol. 3.

Phong Phú districts were located in the region of present Cần Thơ, on the west bank of the Lower Mekong River.[97]

CONCLUSION

After Gia Định Thành Tổng Trấn was dismantled in 1832, southerners were more exposed to central authority than they had been previously. Minh Mạng was determined to integrate the Gia Định people into the state so that they would better fit his understanding of "cultivated" Vietnamese pursuing their lives under his central authority. His stereotypes of southerners were not always based on reality, though they did have some basis in southern characteristics and actual economic conditions.

To carry out this broad and ambitious policy, the king relied on a number of strategies: the establishment of more educational institutions, such as schools; the promulgation of moral maxims; the establishment of new cults reinforcing state authority; and an increase in the number of state examinations. Though the increase in southern graduates of state examinations did not occur during the reign of Minh Mạng, but rather during his successor's, I think the popularity of the state examination among southerners was a significant result of Minh Mạng's "cultivation" campaign, which was meant to persuade southerners to accept Huế authority by spreading orthodox educational institutions throughout southern Vietnam. Groups of *cử nhân* and *tú tài* were produced by the regional examination, and they became not only the candidates for official government positions, but also government-qualified educated men or intellectuals in their own right at the village level. They acted as mediators who had already decided to stand at the side of the king and the central government, and they were ready to help link the king to the villagers. When the state examination was scheduled more frequently, and the number of successful graduates thereby increased, the exam apparently became more popular among southerners, so that the number of candidates who prepared for it rose in number. All of them could not be successful, but many of them became educated villagers.

The government had built prefecture- and district-level schools; it was the newly produced scholarly class, the groups of *nho sĩ*, who spread educational institutions to the village level. This process seems natural, but evidence suggests that the expansion of education in the villages did not take place effectively until after Minh Mạng's campaign to construct additional provincial schools throughout southern Vietnam. We can see this if we examine records left by earlier *nho sĩ*, who appear to have been more strongly oriented toward economic activities than their successors, and who did not leave any evidence of having invested their knowledge in their own villagers. Lưu Bảo Tâm, a 1810s *sĩ*, became a broker; the 1820s Confucian, Trần Dã Lão, returned home after completing his study to manage the

---

[97] From the *Đại Nam Nhất Thống Chí*, we find that the Vĩnh Định district and the Phong Phú district were, in fact, one. In 1839, the Vĩnh Định district was cut out from Vĩnh Long province and attached to a Khmer district called O Mon; together, these became the new Phong Phú district. This Phong Phú district belonged to An Giang province. *DNNTC*, p. 160. The Vĩnh Định district, or Phong Phú district, was located in the region around present Cần Thơ, on the west bank of Lower Mekong River. Huỳnh Minh, *Cần Thơ Xưa và Nay* (Can Tho, past and present) (Saigon, 1966), p. 24.

family business; and the earlier figure, Trịnh Hoài Đức, was obviously involved in commercial business. By contrast, after the 1840s we frequently meet southern *nho sĩ* who were working in schools at the village level.

The story of Hồ Huân Nghiệp (1828-1864), for example, shows how the value of a Confucian education became more valued and more popular in the villages of southern Vietnam during the period in question. Hồ Huân Nghiệp, a man of Gia Định province, was a local scholar who failed to pass the regional examinations. When his father died, he built a small house by the tomb of his father and opened a school. Nguyễn Thông (1827-1884), Hồ's colleague, reports that Hồ's small school was unfortunately located near a road frequented by burglars: "Burglars felt that Huân Nghiệp's house was an obstacle to their comings and goings, so they burnt his house. Huân Nghiệp and his students built it again, and did not cease teaching and learning. The burglars were touched by their hard work, so they chose a different road afterwards."[98] In the story of Phạm Văn Đạt, we meet another *nho sĩ* who dedicated himself to educating village students. Phạm Văn Đạt (1827-1861) was a man from Định Tường, who in 1848, at the age of twenty-one, passed his examination and became one of twenty successful *cử nhân*. In the court biography, he is only described as a fighter against the French, but Nguyễn Thông left a more detailed record of his life that reveals how this new generation of *nho sĩ* became closer to villagers: "When he was to go to Huế to see if it was possible to secure a government position after he had passed the regional examination, he did not have enough money, so his friends helped him. He went to Huế, but he gave up and returned home, as he was so strict and never susceptible to flattery. In his village, he was respected by people. Whoever had conflicts, they came to him to ask for a solution. There was a saying, 'if you are afraid of unbalance you ask a weight scale, if you want to stop conflict, ask Phạm.'"[99]

Certainly, the behavior and dedication of these local scholars, Phạm Văn Đạt and Hồ Huân Nghiệp, seems closer to Minh Mạng's ideals than does the behavior of their predecessors, who dedicated themselves to commerce. They stand as examples of the new southern *nho sĩ* who were educated to respect the central court. This new group of influential scholars rose to become local opinion leaders and accumulated respect and power in the villages that would enable them to mobilize their people under the banner of loyalty to the king when the French later advanced on southern Vietnam.[100]

---

[98] Nguyễn Thông, *Kì Xuyên Công Độc Sơ Biên* (First edition of Ki Xuyen's correspondence), vol. 2, Hồ Huân Nghiệp (1872. Hanoi: Viện Hán Nôm VHc 01719).

[99] Ibid. vol. 2, Phạm Văn Đạt.

CHAPTER FIVE

THE COSTS OF MINH MẠNG'S ASSIMILATION POLICY

The spread of educational institutions throughout southern Vietnam, implemented by Minh Mạng, continued simultaneously with another energetic policy of the central government's: the assimilation of other ethnic groups throughout the region. While Việt southerners were "cultivated" by the central government, their colleagues, the members of other ethnic groups, were to be Vietnamized.

In both Vietnamese and Cambodian histories, the Vietnamese annexation of Cambodia from 1835 has been featured as an important nineteenth-century historic event. Historians have tended to pay attention to Vietnamese assimilation policy towards Cambodia itself, and to Cambodians' resistance against Vietnamese colonial troops. The clash between Vietnamese and Cambodians from 1840 is often described as the result of Vietnam's attempt to abolish Cambodian traditions such as kingship, religion, and local leadership.[1] As a consequence, readers of both the histories of Vietnam and of Cambodia are preoccupied by the Vietnam government's assimilationist policies in Cambodia after 1835.

However, behind these tense interactions between the two countries, widely discussed by historians, other significant domestic events were taking place, notably Vietnam's simultaneous aggression against Khmer people in southern Vietnam starting in the same year.[2] We need to pay attention to a series of Khmer insurrections that occurred in southern Vietnam in conjunction with the rebellion in Cambodia from 1841 to 1845, insurrections that prevented Vietnamese troops from concentrating fully on military operations in Cambodia. Alexander Woodside argues that the Cambodian revolts quickly spread into southern Vietnam because of the Vietnamese government's tough actions against Cambodian leaders in that region: "Revolt among the Cambodians of southern Vietnam was stimulated by a quite specific process of sinicization called *cải thổ qui lưu*, changing from

---

[1] David P. Chandler, *A History of Cambodia* (Sydney: Allen & Unwin, 1993), p. 130.

[2] In his earlier work, David Chandler asserted "Minh Mang's policies toward Cambodia were an extension of those he applied in southern Vietnam." David P. Chandler, "Cambodia before the French: Politics in a Tributary Kingdom 1794-1848" (PhD dissertation, University of Michigan, 1973), p. 131. But he presented little evidence concerning Minh Mạng's ethnic policy in southern Vietnam.

[hereditary] aboriginal [chieftains] back to [appointed] circulating [bureaucrats]."[3] But it is hard for me to believe that the dissatisfaction of Cambodian leaders in southern Vietnam, by itself, could lead to Khmer insurrections in various places in southern Vietnam, ranging from Tây Ninh near to Saigon to An Giang and Hà Tiên, for a period of five years. To grasp what I believe to be the more significant reasons for the Khmer insurrections, we need to examine what happened not only to Khmer society, but also to other ethnic groups in southern Vietnam.

Concerning questions regarding the situation of southern ethnic groups during this period, studies by Vietnamese scholars have tended to reflect political considerations. Contemporary studies on ethnic minorities have been carried out in the fields of linguistics, anthropology, and folklore, but a systematic study, especially on the assimilation policy during the last century, has been avoided.[4] I think the main reason for this avoidance is related to contemporary political issues, for example, territorial claims by Cambodia which arose during the 1960s and 1970s. Under the present regime in Vietnam, which officially celebrates Vietnam's status as a multiethnic country composed of fifty-four ethnic groups, historical studies examining ethnic tensions are subtly discouraged, and therefore rare. To accommodate this ideology, Vietnamese historians of the present regime have developed a way to explain the ethnic tension of the nineteenth century as having arisen between peasants and a feudal government; that is, the ethnic insurrections of southern Vietnam are interpreted as peasant movements against the feudal government. In a collection of academic essays published in the early 1990s under the title, *Phong Trào Nông Dân Việt Nam Nửa Đầu Thế Kỷ 19* (Vietnamese peasant movements during the first half of the nineteenth century), Khmer insurrections are described as instances of peasant resistance against landlords and feudal government officials.[5] But we need to distinguish ethnic

---

[3] Alexander Woodside, *Vietnam and the Chinese Model: A Comparative Study of Nguyễn and Ch'ing Civil Government in the First Half of the Nineteenth Century* (Cambridge: Harvard University Press, 1971), p. 251.

[4] As one of a few tentative studies of assimilation, Phan An's book discusses the assimilation policy of the Nguyễn dynasty, but he mentions nothing about ethnic tensions. Instead, he only asserts that the assimilation policy brought about the successful incorporation of ethnic minorities into Vietnamese society. See Phan An, et al., *Những Vấn Đề Văn Hóa—Xã Hội Thời Nguyễn* (Social and cultural issues during the Nguyen Period) (Ho Chi Minh City: Nxb Khoa Học Xã Hội, 1993), pp. 69–70.

[5] Nguyễn Phan Quang, *Phong Trào Nông Dân Việt Nam Nửa Đầu Thế Kỷ 19* (Vietnamese peasant movements during the first half of the nineteenth century) (Hanoi: Nxb Khoa Học Xã Hội, 1986), p. 143. Chu Thiên's estimate of the number of peasant insurrections that took place during the Nguyễn dynasty has been cited occasionally to confirm the enormous number of insurrections that troubled that dynasty. In his article, written in 1960, which discusses peasant revolts during this period, Chu Thiên offered the following estimates: over seventy insurrections during the reign of Gia Long; over 230 during that of Minh Mạng; and over fifty during that of Thiệu Trị. Chu Thiên, "Mấy Nhận Xét Nhỏ về Những Cuộc Nông Dân Khởi Nghĩa Triều Nguyễn" (Some observations on peasant insurrections during the Nguyen dynasty), *Nghiên Cứu Lịch Sử* (hereafter *NCLS*) 19 (1960): 11-12. Though the numbers differ in some respects, later works concur with this author's basic contention that unrest increased markedly during Minh Mạng's reign. By citing Vietnamese works of 1962 and 1965, Woodside offers the following number: Gia Long, 105 and Minh Mạng, close to 200. Woodside, *Vietnam and the Chinese Model*, p. 135. Chu Thiên's numbers are still found in a relatively recent history book of Vietnam which emphasizes the instability of the nineteenth-century dynasty. See Nguyễn Phan Quang et al., *Lịch Sử Việt Nam Từ Nguồn Gốc Đến 1858* (History of Vietnam from its origins to 1858) vol. 2 (Ho Chi Minh City: Nxb Thành Phố Hồ Chí Minh, 1993), p. 136. But I think many of these

insurrections from peasant insurrections, for only in this way will we be able to understand both the ethnic and peasant issues during the first half of the nineteenth century in southern Vietnam.

In this chapter, I will discuss three issues: the nature of the court's assimilation policy; the ways in which the central government reorganized the ethnically diverse southern society; and how this process of assimilation contributed to strengthening the identity of southerners as Vietnamese.

1. THE IDEA OF ASSIMILATION

The Ethnic Circles of the Đại Nam Empire

Minh Mạng's ethnic policy was enabled, in part, by the expansion of his direct jurisdiction over not only southern Vietnam, but also over Cambodia during the 1830s. To understand the background of this situation, one must first understand the Nguyễn kingdom's titles and their implications.

From the beginning of the Nguyễn dynasty, the choice of a name for the country was considered significant because it would express, and confirm, the Vietnamese elite's concept of its newly unified territory. When the naming of the country was discussed at the beginning of the Nguyễn dynasty, the leaders of Gia Định regime were most concerned about the unification of the former Đàng Ngoài and Đàng Trong regions. But the unification was not only territorial; it also involved cultural expansion, in the sense that two differing cultural units were combined by the unification. In 1802, the name "Nam Việt" was chosen because, according to one argument:

> Our court possesses not only the land of An Nam [official name of the previous Lê dynasty in its dealings with the Chinese court], but also the land of Việt Thường [Đàng Trong region]. It cannot be compared with the [small] territories of Trần and Lê. The national title should be changed from An Nam to Nam Việt.[6]

The title "Nam Việt" takes a word each from the names An *Nam* and *Việt* Thường. Việt Thường was an ancient name for Champa.[7] The final title was fixed by the decision of the Chinese court as Việt Nam, a conversion of Nam Việt.[8] Though the Nguyễn dynasty preferred "Nam Việt" as the official title of the kingdom, the

---

insurrections were not due purely to peasant unrest, but were insurrections by ethnic minorities.

[6] *Đại Nam Chính-Biên Liệt Truyện Sơ Tập* (First collection of the primary compilation of biographies of Imperial Vietnam) (hereafter *LTST*) (1889. Tokyo: Keio Institute of Linguistic Studies, 1962), 11:2a.

[7] See *LTST*, vol. 33, foreign countries, Chiếm Thành, 14a.

[8] For a discussion of the process of conversion, see Woodside, *Vietnam and the Chinese Model*, p. 120. There is also a Vietnamese document that refers to this negotiation: *Đại Nam Thực Lục Chính-Biên Đệ Nhất Kỷ* (Primary compilation of the veritable records of the first reign of Imperial Vietnam) (hereafter *DNTL1*) (1848. Tokyo: The Institute of Cultural and Linguistic Studies, Keio University, 1968), 23:1b-2a. For the opinion of the Chinese court, see *Ch'ing Shih Kao Hsiao Chu*, (Outline history of the Ch'ing, with annotations) (Taipei: Quo Shih Kuan, 1990), p. 12103.

Nguyễn court apparently realized that changing it to "Việt Nam" did not alter the meaning; this title still implied that the Nguyễn dynasty was based on both An Nam and Việt Thường. On the contrary, as one prominent official of the period, Trịnh Hoài Đức, argued, the slightly revised title was more correct, because it showed that "we possessed the land of Việt Thường first, and the region of An Nam was added later."[9] As long as Nguyễn dynasty rulers were most concerned with establishing that they controlled the unified territories of Đàng Ngoài and Đàng Trong, "Việt Nam" seemed to them an appropriate national title.[10]

When Gia Định came under the direct control of the Nguyễn dynasty, however, the dynasty rulers started to feel that the national title of "Việt Nam" no longer adequately represented their expanded kingdom. This concern must have intensified after the territory of Cambodia was added to the southern part of Vietnam in 1835. As a consequence, the title "Vietnam" now indicated only one part of Vietnamese territory. To correct this discrepancy, the title of the kingdom had to be changed. The decision was made in 1838.

> This dynasty owns the whole southern part [*nam phương*]. The boundary to the east is linked to the Southern Sea, and to the west it encloses [land] beyond the sea. All creatures that move belong to our territory, and the whole land from beach to valley in the mountain is subordinate to our territory. If [the title] was changed to Đại Nam [Great South] from Việt Nam, the meaning will be clearer.[11]

As shown here, the choice of a new title, Đại Nam, basically had to do with territorial expansion to the south. To possess the south (*nam phương*) was equivalent to possessing Gia Định and Cambodia as well, because Cambodia had been under the jurisdiction of Gia Định Thành Tổng Trấn. The name "Đại Nam" reflected the dynasty's unification of three regions that had been separate before: An Nam of the Vietnamese, Việt Thường of Champa, and the former territory of Cambodia.

Before the appearance of Đại Nam, Minh Mạng's empire had included three basic ethnic categories, which we can picture as concentric circles of increasing width. At the center were the pure Vietnamese, or the Kinh people; next came other ethnic groups within the territory of Vietnam; last, were the indigenous peoples living in the so-called tributary countries such as three or four principalities in Laos, Jarai, and Cambodia.

---

[9] Trịnh Hoài Đức, *Cấn Trai Thi Tập* (The collected poems of Can Trai) (1819. Hong Kong: New Asia Research Institute, 1962), p. 132.

[10] In his argument concerning the term "Việt Nam," Woodside suggests a different idea: "The word *Việt* stood for the older part of the country, the northern and central areas, which had borne the name *Đại Việt* under the *Lê*. The word *Nam*, 'south,' referred to the newer areas, the colonized south, which had never previously been involved in the traditional Vietnamese kingdom." Woodside, *Vietnam and the Chinese Model*, p. 120. In his statement, Woodside argues that "the colonized south" seems to refer to the region of Gia Định. But in my opinion the court did not consider revising the state title to include reference to Gia Định until the later years of Minh Mạng's reign.

[11] *Đại Nam Thực Lục Chính-Biên Đệ Nhị Kỷ* (Primary compilation of the Veritable Records of the second reign of Imperial Vietnam) (hereafter *DNTL2*) (1861. Tokyo: Keio Institute of Linguistic Studies, 1963), 190:1b-2a.

Alexander Woodside has argued that the Nguyễn dynasty greatly desired to maintain a Chinese-style tribute system, to the extent that the court was even willing to confer the name of "king" on a Jarai sorcerer.[12] In reality, however, Minh Mạng does not seem to have been very concerned with maintaining a Chinese-style tribute system, as evidenced by the fact that he directly annexed Cambodia, Vietnam's most valuable tributary country, rather than maintaining it as a satellite kingdom. It appears that Minh Mạng also lost interest in small principalities. In 1827, Vietnam was involved in the internal troubles of Vạn Tượng, in Laos, but during that same year Minh Mạng withdrew his patronage of this country.[13] In 1838, he described Nam Chưởng (to the north of Vạn Tượng) as "only a small country located in a remote place beyond the frontier."[14] The Huế court stopped recognizing Nam Chưởng from 1838, and when an envoy of this country visited Vietnam in that year to pay tribute, Minh Mạng declined his offering.[15] It is true that Minh Mạng conferred the title of "king" on the Jarai sorcerer in 1834 and 1838, but this does not prove that he set great store in the country and its potential as a tributary region, for in 1834 he had described Jarai dismissively as: "located in a fairly remote place, and they rule people by knotting string." Towards the end of his reign, after Minh Mạng had sent deputies to visit the Jarai region, which was known to include two "countries," Thủy Xá and Hỏa Xá, the king established to his satisfaction that these two "countries" were little more than conglomerations of primitive tribes.[16] Looking at this evidence, I find it difficult to believe that Minh Mạng himself seriously considered Jarai as a tributary country, and that his actions regarding Jarai constitute evidence that the Nguyễn dynasty desired to maintain a Chinese-style tribute system. It is clear, at least, that the king himself was not committed to maintaining the tributary system. The annexation of Cambodia was the most significant evidence that he was more interested in expanding his territory.

Minh Mạng was more concerned with the Vietnamese and other ethnic groups within the territory of Đại Nam. His efforts to cultivate the southern Vietnamese engaged the first element, i.e., the pure Vietnamese, while his assimilation policy was directed at the second element, those who made up the ethnic circles of Đại Nam outside the center.

"Sĩ nông công thương" and *"Thân, biền, hán, thổ"*

Other phrases current during this period provide us with more evidence concerning the Nguyễn dynasty's attitude towards ethnic issues. For example, we note the phrase: *"sĩ, nông, công, thương"* (literati, farmers, artisans, merchants), a list of occupations adopted from the Chinese classics. Traditionally, this list was used to indicate the social groups, or the relative social values attached to different occupations.

Unlike in neighboring countries to the north, however, these kinds of social distinctions had little meaning in Vietnam, where social relations were less

---

[12] Woodside, *Vietnam and the Chinese Model*, p. 238.

[13] *LTST*, vol. 33, Vạn Tượng.

[14] *DNTL2*, 189: 9a.

[15] *LTST*, vol. 33, Nam Chưởng.

[16] Ibid., vol. 32, Thủy Xá, Hỏa Xá.

stratified, more egalitarian, than in other Northeast Asian countries. Especially in southern Vietnam during the first half of the nineteenth century, the classification of scholars and workers according to "*sĩ nông công thương*" was almost meaningless; in Vietnam, the phrase acted as no more than a rough list of occupations. We find evidence of this tendency in *Trương Gia Thế Phả*, the history of the Trương family in southern Vietnam, where various occupations are noted for different members of one family. Khánh (1792-1859) was a scholar and district official, but his father Mặc (1773-1846) was a musician (p. 5). Trương Minh Trung (1758-1823) was a peasant, and of his sons, one was a scholar, four were peasants, and one a merchant (pp. 3; 6-7). In this same extended family, the family of the peasant Trung, an artisan, also appears. Trung's third son, Trương Minh Đại (1800-1841), was a peasant, but Đại's second son, Trương Minh Phượng (1832-1874), became an artisan (pp. 6; 14). We even find a merchant from a scholar family. Trương Minh Nhượng (1793-1852) was the second son of a Confucian and government official named Trương Minh Thành (1767-1810). Trương Minh Nhượng and all his five brothers, including Trương Minh Giảng, were described as scholars or as ranking government officials. However, Nhượng's only son, Trương Minh Túc (1829-1886), became a merchant (pp. 10; 21).

Another phrase often used express the social reality of nineteenth-century Vietnam was "*thân, biền, hán, thổ.*"[17] The first two items describe types of officials and the second two describe types of commoners. The population of Vietnam was divided into officials (*quan*) and common classes (*dân*). Then the officials were divided into literati (*thân*), who included civil officials, and soldiers (*biền*), while commoners were categorized by ethnicity, as Vietnamese (*hán*) and other ethnic groups (*thổ*[18]). This list reflected a main concern of the central court in the early nineteenth century: how to deal with ethnic diversity. From Minh Mạng's reign, the trend was to Vietnamize other ethnic groups. As Minh Mạng admitted, "the court's policy towards barbarians [*man lieu*] has been one of indirect control [*ky my*]."[19] This policy of "indirect control" was, needless to say, part of his father's legacy, which Minh Mạng abandoned towards the end of the 1830s, after Gia Định Thành was dismantled; at this time he pursued, instead, with much more direct control, the "cultivation" of southern Vietnam and the assimilation of ethnic groups throughout the kingdom.

---

[17] *Đại Nam Thực Lục Chính-Biên Đệ Tam Kỳ* (Primary compilation of the veritable records of the third reign of Imperial Vietnam) (hereafter *DNTL3*) (1894. Tokyo: Institute of Cultural and Linguistic Studies, Keio University, 1977), 16:11a.

[18] Literally, *thổ* means local. So, in official records, *thổ dân*, or *thổ nhân* referred to local people in the central and southern regions of Vietnam who had lived in the plain prior to the arrival of the Vietnamese. Generally, *thổ dân*, or *thổ nhân* indicated the Khmer in southern Vietnam and the Cham in central Vietnam. Other ethnic groups on the hillsides were called "barbarians" (*man*). However, these two words were not always clearly distinguished from one another. During the nineteenth century, the Cham were mostly called *man*. Sometimes the Khmer were also called *man*. In contrast, *thổ*, by itself, was also used to indicate broadly other indigenous ethnic groups, so that its meaning contrasted with the meaning of *hán*.

[19] *Minh-Mệnh Chính-Yếu* (Abstract of policies of Minh Mang) (hereafter *MMCY*), trans. Ủy Ban Dịch Thuật Phú Quốc Vụ Khanh đặc-trách Văn-hoá (1897. Saigon: 1972-4), 24:6b.

Demand for the Assimilation Policy in Southern Vietnam

The assimilation policy was not introduced only in southern Vietnam; it was also ambitiously implemented in Cambodia, and other minorities inhabiting central Vietnam and the peripheral regions of northern Vietnam also found themselves subjected to this project. In 1838, the sons of ethnic leaders in the areas near Tuyên Quang, Cao Bằng, and Lạng Sơn were recommended to study at the national college, Quốc Tử Giám in Huế, reflecting Minh Mạng's intention to assimilate these ethnic groups.[20]

Nevertheless, the policy of assimilation was most significant in southern Vietnam, in large part because Gia Định was such an ethnically diverse region where various peoples had long lived together. As discussed in chapter one, Gia Định had been widely inhabited by the Khmer people, but was also dotted with settlements of Malays and other ethnic minorities, such as the Ma, Cho Ro, X'tieng, and M'nong. During the nineteenth century, the Cham people also were scattered around southern Vietnam. Based on *Việt Nam Dư Địa Chí* (A Vietnamese gazetteer),[21] which is believed to have been compiled during the nineteenth century, there were eight "barbarian and local ethnic groups" (*man thổ nhân chủng*) in Nam Kỳ, fifteen in Trung Kỳ, and twenty-two in Bắc Kỳ. The Ma, Cho Ro, X'tieng, M'nong, Khmer, and Cham must have constituted six of these eight ethnic groups. Additionally, Malays and other, now possibly assimilated, ethnic minorities in southern Vietnam might have been part of the eight ethnic groups noted in the gazetteer. Chinese immigrants had settled alongside these ethnic enclaves before the Vietnamese claimed Gia Định as Vietnamese territory. As the most recent settlers, the Vietnamese actively occupied the remaining regions, moving among the ethnic settlers already in residence.

According to *Hoàn Vũ Kỷ Văn* (Compendium on the [Vietnamese] world) written by Nguyễn Thu (1797-1854),[22] who observed the work of assimilation during the Minh Mạng and Thiệu Trị reigns, fourteen of the forty districts (35 percent) of southern Vietnam were established in regions that had earlier been populated largely by Khmer and other ethnic groups.[23] This account provides us with a convincing picture of southern Vietnam's ethnic diversity during the period before the assimilation policy was launched. In Vietnam today, the Khmer people live mainly in Sóc Trăng and Trà Vinh, to the west of the Upper Mekong River, but up until the 1840s there must have been many Khmer villages located also on the east side of the Upper Mekong River, in the Định Tường and Gia Định areas. To the northwest of Saigon, the prefecture of Tây Ninh was formed in 1836, and the records tell us that over one thousand Khmer and Cham households were located here before 1836.[24] Even the southern part of Định Tường, close to Gia Định province, was inhabited by the Khmer, as I discuss below. Gia Định was a fully

---

[20] *DNTL2*, 194:22b-23b.

[21] *Việt Nam Dư Địa Chí* (A Vietnamese gazetteer) (n.d. Hanoi: Viện Hán Nôm A 1829).

[22] Nguyện Thu was an 1821 graduate from Thanh Hóa. See *Đại Nam Chính-Biên Liệt Truyện Nhị Tập* (Second collection of the primary compilation of biographies of Imperial Vietnam) (hereafter *LTNT*) (1909. Tokyo: The Institute of Cultural and Linguistic Studies, Keio University, 1981), vol. 28.

[23] Nguyễn Thu, *Hoàn Vũ Kỷ Văn* (Compendium on the [Vietnamese] world) (n.d. Hanoi: Viện Hán Nôm A 585).

[24] *DNTL2*, 171:31a.

heterogeneous area, as far as ethnicity was concerned. For example, if a foreigner had visited the region of Hà Tiên in 1835, he would have found it hard to believe this region was actually a part of Vietnam, since the combined Khmer and Chinese population was over twice the Vietnamese population at this time.[25]

Minh Mạng's assimilation policy was a drastic shift for southerners. In the ethnically diverse Gia Định, they had learned to accommodate ethnic diversity, and under the Gia Định regime and Gia Định Thành Tổng Trấn, they had continuously been directed by rulers to do so. As discussed in Chapter One, Gia Long propounded a rule, *"hán di hữu hạn,"* which meant to "make clear the border between Vietnamese and barbarians." When a military governor of Hà Tiên rounded up non-registered Vietnamese, Chinese, Khmer, and Malays in 1811 in order to implement a land clearance project, Gia Long ordered that the members of different groups be forced to live separately in their new location.[26] But, under the new spirit of assimilation encouraged by Minh Mạng, southerners began to work as the cultural vanguard of the Vietnamese.

Sinicization, or Vietnamization?

When scholars examine Nguyễn dynasty documents in order to investigate the beginning of ethnic assimilation in Vietnam during this period, one term frequently draws their attention: *hán*. Literally, the word meant "Sinic," or "Chinese." There are references to *hán* people (*hán nhân* or *hán dân*), *hán* custom (*hán phong*), *hán* language (*hán âm*, or *hán ngữ*), and *hán* written characters (*hán chữ*). If we translate *hán* as "Chinese," these phrases would refer to Chinese people, Chinese custom, Chinese language, and Chinese characters, respectively. This translation is convenient for readers who wish to find evidence of Chinese influence in Vietnam. For example, the Huế court sent ten prefecture and district educational officers to Cambodia in 1835.[27] Their purpose was to teach the Cambodians *hán âm*, a task designated by Minh Mạng as one of the crucial responsibilities of Vietnamese officials in Cambodia.[28] Woodside contends that "The educational officers' task was to teach the Cambodians Chinese characters."[29] On the other hand, David Chandler believes that these deputies were meant "to teach Vietnamese language."[30]

To find the real meaning of the task these educational officers were charged with by Minh Mạng, it is necessary to examine further the use of the word *hán*. Most importantly, we need to remember that *hán* was the title of an ancient dynasty based in north China, from which Northeast Asian classical culture spread. Thus, the word *hán* was used by cultures who shared that heritage to mean "good," or "goodness," "prestige," "big," "largeness," "purity," and "center" or "middle." In Chinese, *Han tsu* (pronounced *hán tộc* in Vietnamese) does not refer to the Chinese people in general, but to the major Han ethnic group in China. In South

---

[25] Ibid., 159:12a.

[26] *DNTL1*, 43:5a.

[27] *DNTL2*, 160:20a.

[28] Ibid., 163:11a.

[29] Woodside, *Vietnam and the Chinese Model*, p. 250.

[30] David Chandler, "Cambodia before the French," p. 131.

Korea, the largest river that passes the capital is named Han Gang (the Han River, pronounced *Hán Giang* in Vietnamese), and the related names Han Seong (*Hán Thành*) and Han Yang (*Hán Dương*) have been alternately used in Korea to refer to the capital of that country's longest lasting dynasty, whose reign stretched from 1392-1910.

In nineteenth-century Vietnam, *hán* indicated Vietnamese, not Chinese, people, custom, and language. The word *hán* referred to a cultural space containing Confucianism, Mahayana Buddhism, and Chinese ideographs as common elements of Northeast Asian shared culture, in addition to the Vietnamese people's own heritage, including their customs and language. *Hán nhân*, or *hán dân* meant the Vietnamese people, differentiated from the Chinese (popularly called *đương nhân*, and *thanh nhân*), Khmer, and other ethnic minorities. *Hán phong* referred to Vietnamese custom or habit. *Hán ngữ* or *hán âm* was the Vietnamese language, including the Chinese writing system. *Hán chữ* referred basically to Chinese ideographs, as these constituted a universal writing system that was commonly used not only in China, but also in Vietnam, Korea, and Japan. At the same time, in Vietnam the system of Chinese ideographs was considered part of the Vietnamese *hán ngữ* or *hán âm*, because many of the characters had taken on Vietnamese pronunciations and usages.[31]

Ethnic minorities were also encouraged to learn the Vietnamese language. Inspired by the spirit of assimilation, one of Minh Mạng's men in Vĩnh Long province, Hà Quyền, proposed in 1838 to force Khmer people (*thổ dân*) in his province to learn Chinese characters (*hán chữ*), so as to make them familiar with Vietnamese custom (*hán phong*). According to his plan, he would first command a certain number of Vietnamese people (*hán dân*) to learn Khmer characters (*phiên chữ*) so that they would be able to communicate with the Khmer, and then he would encourage sons of Khmer people to study in Vietnamese prefecture and district schools. This was certainly an ambitious plan, but the direction of Minh Mạng's own assimilation policy was even more radical, because it discouraged Vietnamese from learning Khmer and it deprived the Khmer Buddhist temple of one of its traditional functions: education:[32]

> If Vietnamese [*hán nhân*] learn the Khmer characters [*phiên chữ*] first, it does
> not agree with our policy of changing barbarians through the influence of

---

[31] The *nôm* system, a Vietnamese adaptation of the Chinese characters, was used to refer to objects in writing. For example, let us assume that there was a man whose name was Đá, a local Vietnamese name that means stone. To write down his name, one might write "*Thạch*" using a Chinese character (*shih*) that means stone. This method could be viewed as a Sinicization of the Vietnamese name. But it was more popular to use a Vietnamized method of writing the name, which involved combining two Chinese characters: "*Thạch*" on the left side and "*đa*" (whose Chinese pronunciation is *tuo* with the meaning of much or many) on the right. The word on the left represents meaning, while the word on the right represents pronunciation. The new word that results from the combination is read in Vietnamese as *đá*, which has the same meaning and pronunciation as the word "*đá*" (stone) in the local vocabulary. It was a total Vietnamization of the Chinese characters.

[32] In addition, it is said that the Theravada Buddhist practice of the Khmer monks was forbidden, and Mahayana practice introduced. Instead of wearing their own orange surplices, monks were now required to use Vietnamese brown robes. See Mạc Đường, *Vấn Đề Dân Tộc ở Đồng Bằng Sông Cửu Long* (Ethnic issues in the Mekong Delta) (Ho Chi Minh City: Nxb Khoa Học Xã Hội, 1992), p. 160.

central culture [*dụng hạ*[33] *biến di*]. In An Giang and Hà Tiên provinces, as well as in Vĩnh Long province, force the sons of Khmer people [*thổ dân*] to go to officials in charge of education at the level of district and prefecture to learn *hán chữ*, not to stay in humble habits. Forbid them from going to their own monks to learn. Whoever learns *hán chữ* will be appointed head of the village, so let them know what is demanded. Afterwards, let them also learn the Vietnamese language [*hán nhân ngôn ngữ*], clothes, and food.[34]

However, education in the Vietnamese language was not sufficient to assimilate non-Vietnamese. An even more aggressive state policy recommended southerners live together with non-Vietnamese minorities, in an attempt to mix the peoples. By looking at the ways these ethnic groups mingled, we discover how deeply southerners were involved in the assimilation, and how enthusiastically the central government worked to Vietnamize other ethnic groups in southern Vietnam.

2. PATTERNS OF ASSIMILATION

The relevant ethnic minorities can be categorized into three large groups, each of which was approached in a slightly different manner by the state. First, there was the Khmer population, the largest group, settled predominantly in the delta. Next were ethnic minorities located in the region of Biên Hòa, in the open land running up to the highlands. Both of these groups cultivated rice, so that the government's attempts to merge these minorities with Vietnamese populations were mainly directed at the village (*thôn*, and *xã*), *tổng*,[35] and district levels. Finally, there were the Chinese settlers, who tended to be urban dwellers. In their case, the government sought to use the ethnic group's own associations, including the *xã* (of the *minh hương* Chinese) and *bang* (of the *thanh nhân* Chinese), to help further assimilation.

Khmer People

In seeking to assimilate the Khmer minority, Minh Mạng's government used a variety of methods, outlined below:

a) Combining Khmer villages and Vietnamese villages to make a Vietnamese *tổng*. Following this policy, the central government combined adjacent Khmer villages and Vietnamese villages to create a new Vietnamese administrative unit. In 1833, for example, when the district Tân Ninh of the prefecture Tây Ninh was formed, twenty-five Khmer villages of this region were combined with six Vietnamese villages that had previously been part of the Bình Dương and Thuận An districts. As a result of this action, two higher units, *tổng*, were created and

---

[33] Hạ was also the title of an ancient dynasty based in north China prior to the Hán Empire. Thus, *hạ* was occasionally used in Northeast Asian countries to mean "center" or "middle"; classical Chinese culture; and China or Chinese.

[34] DNTL2, 190:14b-15a.

[35] *Tổng* was a unit one level below, and smaller than, *huyện* (district). One *tổng* included ten to twenty villages (*xã* and *thôn*) in southern Vietnam.

made part of the district of Tân Ninh. Needless to say, the heads of both *tổng* were Vietnamese.[36]

b) Attaching Vietnamese villages to a Khmer district, and vice versa. The central government was also willing to redraw the boundaries of a pure Khmer district in order to make it part of an ethnically heterogeneous district. This method was used in the southern part of Vĩnh Long province, where the Khmer heritage was strong. Some of the adjacent Vietnamese villages were shifted under the jurisdiction of a Khmer district, while certain Khmer villages that had previously been part of that district were now cut off and attached to the neighboring Vietnamese district. In 1835, two neighboring Vietnamese *tổng*, including twenty villages that had belonged to the Vietnamese district of Vĩnh Trị, were attached to Trà Vinh, a predominantly Khmer district.[37] At the same time, according to Minh Mạng's *Thực Lục*, in the same year one *tổng* of Khmer villages in the Trà Vinh Khmer district was moved into the Vietnamese Vĩnh Trị district.[38]

c) Merging Khmer districts with Vietnamese districts. The government would also sometimes merge an entire Khmer district into a neighboring Vietnamese district. In 1839, for example, the Ngọc Luật Khmer district in An Giang province was joined to the neighboring Vietnamese district, Tây Xuyên.[39]

d) Building Vietnamese villages in the middle of Khmer villages. By command of the government, new Vietnamese villages were built among Khmer villages. In 1840, for example, when the government established two new districts, Hà Dương and Hà Âm, in An Giang province, in the midst of a former Khmer district, called Chân Thành, the king made this decree: "Let all Vietnamese [*hán dân*] in this area establish their own villages in new districts [. . .] so as make them [Vietnamese and Khmer people] live and cultivate [ricefields] together, so that they imitate each other."[40] Though he spoke of mutual "imitation," Minh Mạng actually expected the Khmer people to change their lifestyle and learn Vietnamese ways.

e) The Khmer diasporas. There is little doubt that the process of assimilation was usually tragic for the Khmer. Below, I note several cases which illustrate the disappearance of ethnic minorities from their own lands, and which, at the same time, provide evidence that the eastern bank of the Upper Mekong River had been largely inhabited by Khmer people until the 1830s and 1840s.

I note first the case of Chùa Bà Kết, a Buddhist temple originally built by Khmer people in the 1770s, located about three kilometers from present Chợ Gạo on the eastern side of the Upper Mekong river, and to the south of Mỹ Tho.[41] Since, according to Khmer custom, a Khmer village usually extends around a temple, the existence of a Khmer temple provides evidence that a village, populated by Khmers, once existed in that location. Sometime before the 1960s, the Khmer temple disappeared and a new Vietnamese temple was raised in its place, but the author of *Định Tường Xưa và Nay* does not provide us with information about what

---

[36] *DNTL2*, 171:33a.

[37] *Đại Nam Nhất Thống Chí* (Dai Nam gazetteer) (hereafter *DNNTC*), trans. Viện Sử Học (Hue: Thuận Hóa, 1992), vol. 5, 128.

[38] *DNTL2*, 155:20a.

[39] Ibid., 208:8b.

[40] Ibid., 208:9b.

[41] Huỳnh Minh, *Định Tường Xưa và Nay* (Dinh Tuong, past and present) (Saigon, 1969), p. 158.

happened between those two events: the construction of the Khmer temple in the eighteenth century, and, at some later date, the appearance of a Vietnamese temple and villages in that place.

Another piece of evidence collected by the scholar Việt Cúc provides clues concerning the fate of the Khmer residents in this area. Gò Công is located to the south of Chợ Gạo, in the southern part of Định Tường province. Two surviving regional names—Giồng Tháp, which means "the plain of *tháp*" (stupa) and Giồng Xe, which means "the plain of *xe*" (cart)—reveal that the Khmer once populated this land. According to the memories of local Vietnamese people, at one time a Khmer temple, with stupa, stood on Giồng Tháp, and Khmer-style buffalo carts (*xe trâu*) were once produced in Giồng Xe.[42] Việt Cúc records two stories about this region, formerly settled by the Khmer people; a careful reading of those stories sheds some light on the Khmer's departure from their homeland, and the timing of that departure.

According to Việt Cúc, in 1909 Giồng Tháp was visited by two Khmer Buddhist monks, traveling to visit the place where they had been born and had passed their childhoods. They were both over eighty years old, but their age did not prevent them from making a pilgrimage to the land of their ancestors.[43] Their ages, and the year of their visit to Giồng Tháp, indicate that they left their homeland, Giồng Tháp, sometime in the decade between 1830-1840. Of course, they could not find any surviving marks of their own village and temple because the sites had already been Vietnamized by the time they returned.

Another story describes the situation of an old Khmer man who longed for his hometown, but had never been able to return for a visit. When a musician from Gò Công was traveling around the south of Vietnam in 1929, he was visited by this man, who was over eighty years old at that time. Because the old man had heard that this musician was from Gò Công, he approached the musician to ask for news about his hometown, where his umbilical cord had been buried. The old man was born in Giồng Tháp and left it when he was seven or eight years old,[44] sometime in the ten years between 1840 and 1850. The two stories introduced above indicate that the families of all these men abandoned their villages located east of the Upper Mekong River when the central government's assimilation program was accelerated. I believe that the Khmer villagers situated around the temple of Chùa Bà Kết probably also left their homes at this time. Some Khmers would have stayed behind, but they or their children would have been assimilated.

f) Vietnamization of Khmer cults. The basic and most characteristic means of assimilation used by the Nguyễn dynasty was to suppress, or even more typically, subsume and domesticate the religious and ancestral cults of ethnic minorities. Ceremonies for dead rulers of the ethnic minorities were carried out by Vietnamese in the Vietnamese way. For example, in 1840 a shrine for the Cambodian kings was built in Huế.[45] From this time, the souls of these dead kings were honored with a Vietnamese ceremony, their altars filled with Vietnamese food and incense smoke, their tablets placed in a shrine built to match Vietnamese architecture they never

---

[42] Việt Cúc, *Gò Công Cảnh Cũ Người Xưa* (Go Cong, its environs and people in the past) vol. 2 (Saigon, 1969), pp. 32–33.

[43] Ibid., p. 33.

[44] Ibid., p. 34.

[45] *DNTL2*, 213:26.

had seen, and located in Huế, a city which they had never visited. Before long the cult of Champa followed the same fate.[46] This was the time when the remnants of the Champa state completely disappeared from the map of Vietnam.[47]

Plate 8. An extant Khmer temple in Trà Vinh province. Credit: the author, 1997.

The Vietnamization of ethnic cults was conducted not only by the central government, but also by common people in southern Vietnam, who would often build a Vietnamese temple over the remains of a Khmer temple. We have already noted such a case: the Khmer Buddhist temple, Chùa Bà Kết, near Chợ Gạo,

---

[46] *DNTL3*, 13:2a.

[47] According to Hoàng Côn's *Chiếm Thành Khảo* (A study of Champa) (1914. Hanoi: Viện Hán Nôm A 970), Champa's royal heritage ended at this time. A critical reason was that the Cham leader, Nguyễn Văn Thừa, was involved in the Lê Văn Khôi revolt. After that, the remaining Chams in Phan Rang (present-day central Vietnam) were subjected to the full force of the Vietnamization project. Po Dharma describes the situation: "Hindu Chams were forced to eat beef, Muslim Chams were forced to eat pork and lizard. Political jurisdictions and offices were renamed in Vietnamese, and Vietnamese codes and judicial procedures were introduced. Onerous new taxes and labor demands were levied in an attempt to treat the Chams like conquered rebels and then to transform them into Vietnamese." Cited from William Collins, "Interdisciplinary Research on Ethnic Groups in Cambodia," (for discussion at the National Symposium on Ethnic Groups in Cambodia held in Phnom Phen, Centre for Advanced Study, Phnom Phen, July 18-19, 1996), p. 39. In 1835, the Vietnamese established complete control of the Cham land under their administrative authority, and it is believed this defeat prompted the migration of Chams to Cambodia. Ibid., p. 41. Afterwards, when Vietnam occupied Cambodia, they were again subjected to Vietnamese rule. Some of these Cham refugees returned to southern Vietnam at that time. In 1843, 2,383 Malays and Chams were planted in a region beside Khmer people in the prefecture Ba Xuyên of An Giang province. They were allowed to move to prefecture Tây Ninh of Gia Định province if they wished. *Khâm Định Đại Nam Hội Điển Sự Lệ* (Official compendium of institutions and usages of Imperial Vietnam) (hereafter *KDDNHDSL*) (1851. Hanoi: Viện Hán Nôm VHv 1570), vol. 38, Phiên Dân Qui Hóa, 22-23.

disappeared, and a Vietnamese temple now stands in its place. There are other similar examples. Phụng Sơn Tự is a Buddhist temple in Cây Mai, originally built by the Vietnamese monk, Liễu Thông (1753-1840), on the site of a former Khmer temple. It continued to develop as a Vietnamese temple during his lifetime.[48]

At times, the Vietnamese people did not actually raze religious buildings, but instead altered and adopted the cults, and even the icons, of their ethnic neighbors. In Châu Đốc, a border area in An Giang province, at Sam Mountain, a place popularly visited by Vietnamese, the Bà Chúa Sứ temple contains a stone statue of a woman. According to Lê Hương, a southern historian who bases his argument on a legend he came across during the 1960s, the woman after whom the temple is named was a Cambodian who traveled to Vietnam long ago to locate her husband, and who afterwards was transformed into a sacred stone on Sam Mountain. According to Lê Hương, the Vietnamese living in this region had respected this Khmer woman for over one hundred years, believing that she was either Vietnamese or Chinese.[49] If so, this indicates that Vietnamese may well have outfitted this Khmer statue in a Vietnamese costume after the assimilation policy was initiated during the 1830s.

Ethnic Minorities in Biên Hòa

In Biên Hòa, the usual method of assimilation was to pull the ethnic minority community into the Vietnamese administrative unit. This method is clearly outlined in a statement by Minh Mạng in 1837:

> Barbarians of this province have lived in remote and mountainous places. Until now, the court's policy towards them has been one of indirect rule [ky my]. But they have already established households within my land, so they are my people, too. Therefore, we have to teach them everything from the way of cultivation [of ricefields] to language [ngôn ngữ] and clothes. Let them gradually forget barbarian habits [di tập] and let them be affected by the Vietnamese way [hán phong]. Afterwards, consider a place [for them] to build villages, and register them. It is the cardinal way to change barbarians by using central culture [dụng hạ biến di].[50]

The process of assimilation has several stages. First, the ethnic minority communes were regarded as a part of Vietnamese territory. At this stage, however, they were still "barbarians," waiting to become Vietnamese, living beyond the reach of the Vietnamese state. But they were evidently people of Đại Nam kingdom. Next, Vietnamese culture was to be introduced to these "barbarians." After that, their communes were to be reorganized as Vietnamese villages with Vietnamese names. Finally, the people themselves would be made Vietnamese by being officially registered on government documents. The entire assimilation process, as it was carried out in Biên Hòa, involved the following steps.

---

[48] Nguyễn Lang, *Việt Nam Phật Giáo Sử Luận* (History of Buddhism in Vietnam), vol. 2 (Hanoi: Văn Học, 1994), p. 334.

[49] Lê Hương, "Địa Danh, Di Tích Lịch Sử, Thắng Cảnh Trong Vùng Người Việt Gốc Mien" (Names of places, historic sites, and beautiful places in the region of Vietnamese of Khmer origin), *Tập San Sử Địa* 14-15 (1969): 50-1.

[50] *DNTL2*, 182:2.

a) Creating a transitional unit—*thủ* from *sách*. First, the Biên Hòa minorities were to be organized into autonomous communes, called *thủ*. Before they were absorbed into Đại Nam, their small villages had been called *sách*. When some of the X'tieng people yielded themselves to become part of Đại Nam during the years 1840 to 1849, their *sách* were officially erased and the population organized into four *thủ*. In 1840, thirty-three X'tieng *sách* were reorganized as two *thủ* called Tân Lợi and Tân Định. In 1841, twenty-eight X'tieng *sách* were consolidated to form the *thủ* Tân Bình, and twenty-two other X'tieng *sách* became the *thủ* Tân Thuận.[51] Drawing on Nguyễn Thu's explanation, it appears that 409 male X'tieng adults with their families formed the Tân Định (1840), Tân Lợi (1840), Tân Bình (1841), and Tân Thuận (1849) communes. As a consequence, Biên Hòa province was officially declared to constitute two prefectures and four communes (*thủ*). At this stage relatively early stage in the assimilation process, the newly absorbed and reorganized ethnic minorities still maintained their own way of life.[52]

Another example will show us a more detailed picture of the *thủ*. In 1842, it was reported from Biên Hòa that the residents of twenty-eight X'tieng villages, or *sách*, "wanted" to be registered and to pay tax. Their payment was to be made in honey. At the suggestion of province officials, a *thủ* called Thông Bình was formed to accommodate these villagers, and Vietnamese officials were sent to rule them. The newly appointed *thủ ngụ*—an official position filled by a Vietnamese—would act as head of this semi-Vietnamized commune. Below the *thủ ngụ*, there was one assistant Vietnamese official, and four Vietnamese soldiers.[53] This consolidation of village-level administrative units and appointment of a small cadre of bureaucrats and soldiers was the first step in the process meant to bring ethnic minorities into direct and daily contact with Vietnamese culture.

In some cases, these administrative positions were not filled by Vietnamese individuals sent by provincial authority, but were given as rewards to any Vietnamese volunteer who contributed to this assimilation project. Biên Hòa officials sent a man and his five colleagues to different X'tieng regions to persuade ethnic minorities to enter the Vietnamese administrative system. This man was successful in his mission, so that twenty villages (*sách*) with ninety male adults were reorganized in 1843 as one *thủ*, called Tân Thuận. Because of his success, this man was appointed to be the *thủ ngụ*, and his colleagues were allowed to stay on as government representatives in the newly formed *thủ*, Tân Thuận.[54]

b) Creating a Vietnamese unit—*tổng*. Before long, each *thủ* was to be reorganized as a *tổng*, the equivalent Vietnamese administrative unit. Since the several *thủ* mentioned above were established in the 1840s, only a short time before 1859, when the Hue court began to lose control over this region to French troops, there is no evidence that these *thủ* were converted to *tổng*. But if we look at another

---

[51] *KDDNHDSL*, vol. 44, *man nùng thổ*, pp. 18-19. Each *sách* is believed to have become a village called either *xã* or *thôn*. It appears that this process took place, for example, from 1835 in Vĩnh Long province (though it involved a Khmer commune, the case is still suggestive). Several *trang* and *sách* of the Khmer people in Lạc Hóa prefecture were removed from the Trà Vinh and Tuân Nghĩa districts and annexed to two Vietnamese districts called Vĩnh Trị and Vĩnh Bình. At this time, the bigger *trang/sách* became a *xã*, while the smaller *trang/sách* became a *thôn*. *DNTL2*, 155:19b-20a; vol. 44, *man nùng thổ*, p. 20.

[52] Nguyễn Thu, *Hoàn Vũ Ký Văn*, vol. 3.

[53] *DNTL3*, 14:4.

[54] Ibid., 30:22b.

thủ that had existed prior to the five *thủ* discussed above, we find evidence of a typical administrative transformation. In 1838 when Phúc Bình district was formed in Biên Hòa, the former three *thủ* of that area—Bình Lợi, Định Quan and Phúc Vĩnh—became four *tổng*: Phúc Thành, Bình Sơn, Bình Tuy, and Bình Cách.[55] At this stage, their own villages, which at this point were still called *sách* by the Vietnamese, also became *xã*, or *thôn*. This was the final step taken to absorb ethnic minority communes into Vietnamese administrative units. Vietnamese citizens became the heads of the new *tổng*. I believe that the Vietnamese *thủ ngự*, head of the former *thủ*, would have been likely to take over as head of the new *tổng*.

c) Creating a Vietnamese district consisting of several ethnic groups. Another method of assimilation was to establish a new Vietnamese district in the region populated by ethnic minorities. This method was used when Long Khánh district of Biên Hòa province was formed in 1837. Two X'tieng communes (*thủ*) called Long An and Phúc Khánh were dismantled and reorganized as Vietnamese units. Five *tổng*, including thirty-six villages (*xã* and *thôn*), were created by the two communes, with a population of 541 taxpayers.[56]

d) Creating a Vietnamese district with both Vietnamese and ethnic minorities. Administrative units were also manipulated to form an ethnically heterogeneous district. The villages of ethnic minorities in marginal areas were incorporated into Vietnamese villages cut off from an adjacent Vietnamese region. The villages of the Vietnamese and the villages of the ethnic minorities formed a district together. For example, Phúc Bình district was formed this way in 1838. Sixteen villages of the Vietnamese, with 635 taxpayers, were taken off from Phúc Chính district and formed Phúc Bình district together with three communes (*thủ*) of the ethnic minority that had resided in places called Bình Lợi, Định Quan and Phúc Vĩnh. These three communes became four *tổng* and forty-eight villages with 519 taxpayers belonging to the Phúc Bình district.[57]

e) Encouraging villagers to become Vietnamese. After they became members of a *tổng*, the next step for most ethnic villagers was to accept the Vietnamese way. Though it was not necessary for all members to know the Vietnamese language, some of their leaders had to have knowledge of it. To be Vietnamese, first of all, their names needed to follow Vietnamese custom. For example, the residents of six *tổng* of Long Khánh district, four *tổng*—Phúc Thành, Bình Sơn, Bình Tuy, and Bình Cách—in the Phúc Bình district, and two *tổng*—Quang Lợi, and Cựu An—in the Bình An district, all in Biên Hòa province, all had to change their family names; for the residents of these twelve *tổng*, thirteen new family names were assigned by the government.[58] The given family names were common nouns with meanings related to trees and animals. Some of them, such as Lâm (forest), Lý (plum), Dương (willow), and Mã (horse), had long been popular family names not only in Vietnam, but also in China and in Korea.

Once these residents became members of the Vietnamese community, they also had to fulfill their duties to the kingdom. One of the essential duties was to pay taxes and to undertake mandatory military service in the same way as Vietnamese. During the process of assimilation, Vietnamese language, clothes, customs, food,

---

[55] *DNNTC*, vol. 5, p. 38.

[56] *DNTL2*, 186:11b-12a.

[57] Ibid., 195:2b-3a.

[58] Nguyễn Thu, *Hoàn Vũ Kỷ Văn* vol. 3.

methods of cultivation, and even the way of eating (using chopsticks, for example[59]) were introduced to the newly naturalized people. Finally, they were registered as Vietnamese. From 1846, the government started to compile the land cadastre of Long Khánh district for the purpose of charging land tax.[60]

f) Raising children to be new Vietnamese. Although I have outlined many of the central government's typical assimilation strategies, the patterns hardly show us a vivid picture of how Biên Hòa ethnic minorities were assimilated. Even more important than administrative strategies, I think, was physical encroachment on the part of the Vietnamese villagers. Once Vietnamese villages and ethnic minority villages stood side by side, Vietnamese encroachment into ethnic minority villages must have occurred.[61] As time passed, the boundary between Vietnamese and ethnic minorities surely became unclear, and substantial assimilation would have taken place from this time. The major consequence, of course, was the extinction of the ethnic minority's identity, unless members of the group moved to a different place to escape being subsumed. At a certain point, the remaining ethnic minorities would have found themselves surrounded by Vietnamese. Their only options were to be assimilated or to withdraw.

There is evidence concerning the fate of some of the children whose parents chose to leave their homes. Judging from the story of a man who lived later, in the first half of next century, but whose memories are nonetheless revealing, it appears that when Biên Hòa minorities abandoned their villages, children who were left behind quickly adapted themselves to Vietnamese customs. Bình Nguyên Lộc, an author who was born and raised in Biên Hòa province, remembered that there had been strange men in his family's village when he was around six years old. They were called *mọi*, a Vietnamese word to indicate savages. Relying in part on the memories of his father, who was ninety-two years old at the time this story was recalled, in 1970, Bình Nguyên Lộc described these "barbarians." In 1913, they had been servants:

> They [barbarians in general] had built a village and had lived by rice cultivation, but they did not know plowing. Yet they used cultivation equipment made with bronze and iron. They gradually retreated to the forest, but they never resisted us. When I turned six years old, I only saw servants,

---

[59] The Vietnamese often regarded the use of chopsticks—a common custom in four Northeast Asian countries—to be evidence of proper civilization and etiquette. When a court official Trương Quốc Dụng described unique Khmer habits of Lạc Hóa in Vĩnh Long province and Ba Xuyên in An Giang province, the habit he noted, which he found most unusual, was that they did not use chopsticks. Trương Quốc Dụng. *Thoái Thực Ký Văn* (or *Công Ha Ký Văn*) (After-dinner recollections, or recollections beyond the office) (n.d. Hanoi: Viện Hán Nôm A 1499), p. 95.

[60] Nguyễn Đình Đầu, *Nghiên Cứu Địa Bạ Triều Nguyễn: Biên Hòa* (Researching land cadastres of the Nguyen dynasty: Bien Hoa) (Ho Chi Minh City: Nxb Thành Phố Hồ Chí Minh, 1994), p. 351.

[61] One of the reasons the Vietnamese found it relatively easy to encroach upon the land previously claimed by ethnic minorities was because the non-Vietnamese were less competitive as cultivators. In 1843 and 1844, the Phúc Bình district and the Long Khánh district suffered from a lack of food, and nearly all of the victims were members of ethnic minority communities. See *DNTL3*, 33:15a; 37:16b. Once they had been hit by famine, it was normal for members of these communities to abandon their plots and travel to more remote places. Vietnamese were then able to move into the vacant land.

their village did not exist any more. But they were not servants whom we took by force, as we did in ancient times, but we bought children. Whenever they had a bad harvest, they sold children in exchange for rice and salt.

According to this observer, the "barbarians" were Ma tribespeople who had lived in this region before the Vietnamese arrived. Though the main population of this minority village had retreated to a more remote place, some of their children had remained with the Vietnamese. All of them were extremely poor, and only one of them had married, to a disabled daughter of a rich Vietnamese family. By the time this storyteller had grown into adulthood, he found that these people had drastically changed. Now the descendants of the Ma spoke fluent Vietnamese, married Vietnamese women, and some of them were very fond of learning Chinese characters.[62]

Assimilation of Chinese Settlers

Chinese settlers were not exempt from assimilation. However, the process of assimilation for these non-"barbarian" residents was not direct, but more cautious.
a) Abolition of *thanh nhân* associations. Previously, I mentioned that *thanh nhân* associations suffered significant discrimination in the field of commerce. Towards the end of the Gia Định Thành period, they were prohibited from trading by sea, and from 1837, no *thanh nhân* could deal in overseas trade. In addition, the following year the king decreed that no member of a *thanh nhân* association would be allowed to work on any foreign trade ship in any form:

As for all *thanh nhân* who immigrate [to my country] and live here, only allow them to trade by river, but do not permit them to trade by sea. No maritime traders may hire *thanh nhân*, either as helmsman or as crew.[63]

In 1839, Minh Mạng experimented with a significant new technique to further assimilation: he decided to abolish the *thanh nhân*'s insular shelter, the *thanh nhân* associations (*bang*). Cambodia, a land newly absorbed by Vietnam, was chosen as a test site for this strategy; in that region, *thanh nhân* were not allowed to organize any new branch of their own association. If new Chinese immigrants arrived in Cambodia, they had to live with the Vietnamese in Vietnamese villages in order to become Vietnamese:

If you [Vietnamese officials in Cambodia] have Vietnamese and *thanh nhân* who recently immigrated to your place and live around the administrative center, have them [Vietnamese and Chinese immigrants] build villages according to their number. Have them influence each other to make all of them Vietnamese [*hán dân*]. You do not need to organize separately the *thanh nhân* by *bang*.[64]

[62] Bình Nguyên Lộc, "Việc Mãi Nô Dưới Vòm Trời Đông Phố và Chủ Đất Thật của Vùng Đồng Nai" (Being slaves a long time under the sky of Dong Pho and the real owners of Dong Nai region), *Tập San Sử Địa* 19-20 (1970): 249-52.
[63] *DNTL2*, 196:26a.
[64] Ibid., 205:8b.

Had the central court seen a positive result in Cambodia, the same method might have been implemented in Vietnam afterwards. However, it was not possible for the nineteenth-century Vietnamese government to destroy the Chinese immigrants' *bang* system totally. Nonetheless, it should be regarded as an extremely ambitious trial by the central government to Vietnamize Chinese settlers.

b) Conversion of *thanh nhân* to *minh hương*. The government's attempts to assimilate the Chinese continued throughout the reign of Thiệu Trị (1841-1847), who implemented a number of different strategies. We can assume the court recognized that it would be difficult to force the *thanh nhân* to abandon their identity within a short period. To encourage assimilation, the Vietnamese government devised another method which sought to establish an intermediate agency to facilitate interaction with the Chinese. The association of the *minh hương* Chinese was to be a mediating body between the *thanh nhân* Chinese and the Vietnamese. In 1842, a new regulation was decreed, intended to convert *thanh nhân* members into members of *minh hương* associations. According to this law, a *thanh nhân* Chinese who had newly immigrated to Vietnam could live as a member of one of the *thanh nhân* associations. If he had a son or grandson born after he had immigrated, however, that son or the grandson would not be allowed to wear a pigtail, as his father or grandfather had. Once the child reached eighteen years of age, the head of the appropriate *thanh nhân* association had to register the child as a member of a *minh hương* association. If, in that region, a *minh hương* association did not exist, then a new *minh hương* association had to be established when at least five male children of *thanh nhân* members reached maturity.[65]

c) Discrimination against *minh hương* Chinese, and the possibility of assimilation. Scholars have not discovered in the Vietnamese records any specific regulations calling for general discrimination against the *minh hương* Chinese. Nevertheless, careful examination of government documents does provide us with some evidence of discrimination. We note, for example, the court's response towards a *minh hương* official, Vương Hữu Quang, who was part of the central government. From this case, the attitude of Vietnamese officials towards their *minh hương* colleagues can be inferred.

Vương Hữu Quang was a Gia Định *minh hương* who had passed the regional examination in 1825. When persistent cold rain fell during the spring of 1840, threatening agriculture in the region, he was ordered by Minh Mạng to pray for the rain to cease. The weather failed to improve, however, and Vương blamed the situation on the king, asserting that Minh Mạng had provoked Heaven with his inappropriate behavior: first, allegedly giggling with his subjects in his office (about certain amusing things), and second, reading a disreputable book. Minh Mạng admitted the first mistake, but denied the second, and in time Vương's second accusation was proved to be untrue, at which point Vương immediately submitted his apology. The usual punishment for such an error was demotion, yet Vương discovered that the court was considering the most severe punishments: decapitation, or exile.[66] The extreme response of court officials may have had to do with the fact that Vương was a Chinese.

---

[65] *KDDNHDSL*, vol. 44, *thanh nhân*, p. 8.

[66] *DNTL2*, 212:7a-11a.

Evidence of discrimination against *minh hương* Chinese can also be found if we examine the results of state examinations. While Lê Văn Duyệt was ruling Gia Định, two *minh hương* became *cử nhân* graduates in 1825 and 1831, during a period—from 1821 to 1831—when four regional examinations produced a total of fifty-seven graduates. After Gia Định Thành Tổng Trấn was abolished and the assimilation policy launched, no *minh hương* graduate emerged from the remaining three regional examinations offered at the Gia Định site from 1835 to 1840, during Minh Mạng's reign. During eleven years, from 1835 to 1846, the Gia Định site produced ninety graduates, but there was not a single successful *minh hương* candidate among them. In 1847, when Thiệu Trị recruited four additional graduates from among the candidates who were tested at the Gia Định site—the king took this action due to the sharp increase in the number of candidates—one *minh hương* Chinese was able to join the other nineteen laureates. After this time, no other *minh hương* candidate who tested at the Gia Định site was listed among the graduates. From 1835 to 1858, out of a total of 182 graduates who had come to the Gia Định site for their examination, only one was a *minh hương*.[67]

The decrease in the number of *minh hương* Chinese who successfully took and passed the state examinations can be interpreted in different ways. It is very possible that many Chinese settlers made an attempt to camouflage their ethnicity and declared themselves publicly to be Vietnamese, not *minh hương*, when they applied to take the state examinations. The court chronicle of 1844 supports this hypothesis. Without revealing his origins, a young *thanh nhân* called Dương Quang Tô registered in Quảng Nam province to take a regional examination. To hide his identity as *thanh nhân*, he only declared that he was the son of his Vietnamese mother (Quảng Nam was his mother's birthplace). He passed the examination with the rank of *tú tài*. Then, for some reason, he confessed his deception, and, as a result, was deprived of his *tú tài* title, registered as a member of a *minh hương*, and punished by flogging; he received one hundred lashes.[68]

This example suggests that many individuals in this new generation of Chinese settlers probably continued to attempt to assimilate by "passing" as Vietnamese. We read of Dương Quang Tô, who was called *thanh nhân*, which meant he was one of the Chinese settlers who could be expected to maintain a Chinese appearance, of the sort that had been standard in China under Manchu-Ch'ing rule, with the appropriate hairstyle, language, and clothes. Nevertheless, this man completed three or four stages of the regional examination, which means his appearance must have been indistinguishable from that of other ordinary Vietnamese candidates. In other words, he had already successfully altered his appearance before arriving to take the examination. For *minh hương* members, who were much closer to Vietnamese in their outlooks than were the *thanh nhân*, it would have been even easier to "pass." In order to hide one's ethnic identity more completely, a youthful *minh hương* candidate could have chosen Dương Quang Tô's method, for example.

---

[67] See Cao Xuân Dục, *Quốc Triều Hương Khoa Lục* (Record of regional examination graduates under the current dynasty) (hereafter *QTHKL*) trans. Nguyễn Thúy Nga, Nguyễn Thị Lâm (n.d. Ho Chi Minh City: Nxb Thành Phố Hồ Chí Minh, 1993).

[68] *DNTL3*, 36:20b.

Marriage

During this period in southern Vietnam, assimilation was a widespread trend, facilitated by the government, as we have seen, and its impact on the lives of Việt and ethnic southerners was substantial. Since Việt families in the heterogeneous south tended to live closer to ethnic minorities than before, it was a natural consequence to mix with them, and frequent social contact led to a new pattern in marriage. Intermarriage between Vietnamese and the members of other ethnic groups became more common from this time. The *Trương Gia Thế Phả* vividly illustrates the new trend.

The family records contained in the *Trương Gia Thế Phả* cover approximately two centuries (from the eighteenth to the end of the nineteenth century), and seven generations, and list nine Việt men and women who married non-Vietnamese: four who married "barbarians," three who married *minh hương*, and two who married *thanh nhân*. Until the beginning of Minh Mạng's reign, there had not been any case of ethnic intermarriage in this family. Towards the middle of Minh Mạng's reign, however, reports of intermarriage begin to appear, and the numbers increased from 1835.

An analysis of ethnic intermarriages in this family illuminates several interesting points. Firstly, we see that intermarriages for the thirty-four years between 1825 and 1859 outnumbered those that took place during the half-century that followed. Next, we find that the diversity of these ethnic intermarriages increased over time. Additionally, analysis shows the degree of ethnic intimacy in assimilation: In the beginning of this period, a "barbarian" was absorbed into this family. *Minh hương* Chinese were next, and *thanh nhân* Chinese were the last group to be linked with this family.

Using the ages of each couple and the years of birth and death of their children, I was able to calculate roughly the year of each marriage. The results appear below.

Table 9: Trương Family Members' Marriages with other Ethnic Members[69]

Year	Before 1825	1825-1830	1830-1835	1835-1859	After 1859
Number	0	1 "barbarian": 1	1 *minh hương*: 1	4 "barbarian": 2 *minh hương*: 1 *thanh nhân*: 1	3 "barbarian": 1 *minh hương*: 1 *thanh nhân*: 1

a) "Barbarians." Trương Minh Sắc (1806-1835), of the third generation, was the first recorded member of this family to marry a non-Việt woman: he married a "barbarian" woman with the family name of Nguyễn.[70] The couple had two sons, the eldest of whom died in 1831 during childhood (p. 24). Their second son, Trương Minh Mẫn, was born in 1832 (p. 15). Given these facts, I assume this marriage probably took place slightly before 1830.

---

[69] *Trương Gia Thế Phả.*

[70] Unfortunately, I cannot identify her regional background by the *chữ nôm* writing in the original document. The only thing I can recognize is that she was "barbarian [*man*], Nguyễn Văn Khẩn's [?] daughter." (p. 7)

There were also cases of Vietnamese women who married men of other ethnic groups. A woman called Trương Thị Bôi (born in 1819) married a "Rạch Giá,[71] of Hà Tiên province, a barbarian [*man nhân*] called Nguyễn Văn Nga," whom I believe to have been a Khmer, though he might have been from another ethnic group; it is clear he was not a Chinese settler. Two children, Nguyễn Văn Vĩnh and Nguyễn Văn Bảo, were born from this marriage (p. 18). As this was Trương Thị Bôi's second marriage, it probably did not take place when she was between the ages of fifteen and twenty, the normal range for Vietnamese woman in the past. If this second marriage took place before the woman was forty-one years old, as was probably the case, then the date of the marriage falls before 1859.

The next case involves an intermarriage which presumably took place before 1850. Trương Thị Như (1830-1854) was the second daughter of a village leader, Trương Minh Tuấn. Her father chose "a Đồng Nai barbarian [*man nhân*] called Nguyễn Văn Dưỡng" as a husband for his unmarried daughter. A son, Nguyễn Văn Chi, was born from this union (p. 19). As Đồng Nai was another name for Biên Hòa province, this "barbarian" man would have belonged to one of the ethnic minorities of Biên Hòa.

A man of the fourth generation, Trương Minh Yến (1820-1889), married a woman called Đặng Thị Thuận, who was from another ethnic group and who had been born in 1830, in the region of Rạch Kiến.[72] They had one son and one daughter. This was Yến's second marriage; evidently he married after his first wife (1821-1867) died (pp. 18-19). Considering that both the children born from this second marriage died in 1883 and in 1885, when they were still young (pp. 36-37), and taking into account the span of Đặng Thị Thuận's childbearing years, I calculate that the marriage took place during the 1870s. Unfortunately this woman was not identified with a particular ethnic group. The records say only that she was "a widowed daughter of a Rạch Kiến barbarian [*man nhân*]." If the city of Rạch Kiến noted here is the same as the present-day city of Rạch Kiến, located between Saigon and Gò Công, it suggests that that Khmer people, or people of other ethnic minorities—other than Chinese settlers—could still be found in the region by that time. This woman's family name was Đặng Văn, one of the common family names among the Vietnamese, indicating that she may well have come from an ethnic group that was in the process of being assimilated.

b) Chinese settlers. Marriage between Chinese settlers and Vietnamese was quite common in Vietnam, so much so that one visitor from China, Ts'ai, writing in the mid-1830s, claimed that "Vietnamese women love to marry Chinese men."[73] The fact that Ts'ai's information on the Vietnamese relied mostly on his experiences with his own people, the *thanh nhân* Chinese, during his stay in Vietnam,[74] suggests that we need not accept his assertions concerning the inclinations of Vietnamese women at face value. It is likely that intermarriages of this kind were often expedient, rather than romantic, for it might well have been

---

[71] Thanks to Nguyễn Đình Đầu, who helped me identify this name, which was written in *nôm*.

[72] Ibid.

[73] Ts'ai T'ing Lan, *Hải Nam Tạp Trứ* (Various records of the land beyond the southern ocean) (1836. Hanoi: Viện Hán Nôm HVv 80), p. 36.

[74] From his arrival in Quảng Ngãi to the time of his departure through Lạng Sơn, he was continuously guided by Chinese settlers from their own *thanh nhân* associations, such as the Fu Chien *bang*, the Kuang Tung *bang*, and the Ch'ao Chou *bang*.

necessary for Chinese settlers to take on Vietnamese wives or concubines in order to settle successfully in Vietnam. In any case, marriage between Chinese men and Vietnamese women was not uncommon in Vietnam.

However, it is interesting that the Trương family's history (*Trương Gia Thế Phả*) shows us a different picture. While marriages with other ethnic members and with *minh hương* Chinese are commonly reported in this history, it appears that no member of this family had married a *thanh nhân* Chinese by the middle of the nineteenth century. Intermarriages with *minh hương* Chinese settlers began from 1830-1835. For example, a man from the third generation, called Đồng (1808-1865), married a *minh hương* woman, whose family name was Trịnh (1814-1888) (p. 7). Since the eldest son of this couple was born in 1835 (p. 15), I believe them to have married slightly before 1835. A man from the fourth generation, called Trương Minh Huân (1826-1866), also married a *minh hương* woman, named Đỗ Thị Vạn (p. 18). Though this family history does not give the year of Đỗ Thị Vạn's birth, we can infer that this marriage took place during the assimilation period before 1846, taking into account the age of her husband and the fact that this couple's eldest daughter was born in 1846 (p. 32). The last case of marriage with a *minh hương* woman is found far later in these documents; this union involved a man of the fourth generation, born in 1855, and a *minh hương* woman born in 1862 (pp. 26-27). All marriages with *minh hương* Chinese in this family united Vietnamese men and *minh hương* women.

Marriages with *thanh nhân* were quite different from those with *minh hương* members. All of this family's marriages involving the *thanh nhân* Chinese matched Vietnamese women with *thanh nhân* Chinese men, and appear to have taken place rather late, when the period of assimilation was coming to an end, due to the French advance in Vietnam from 1859. It was just after the middle of the nineteenth century when two women from this family married Chinese men who belonged to *thanh nhân* associations. Fourth-generation Trương Thị Sách married a *thanh nhân* Chinese from Kuang Tung *bang*. As she was born in 1843, she could have married either before or after 1859. Trương Thị Tài was born in 1848, and married a *thanh nhân* Chinese from Fu Chien *bang* (p. 16). Considering her age, this marriage probably took place after 1859.

I do not intend to use these marriages between Trương women and *thanh nhân* Chinese as evidence of ethnic assimilation. On the contrary, they show us that the ethnic or cultural distance between the Vietnamese and the Chinese was comparatively large relative to the distance between the Vietnamese and members of any other ethnic groups. For this reason, intermarriages between the Vietnamese and *thanh nhân* Chinese rarely took place during the first half of the nineteenth century.

3. ETHNIC CONFLICT AND SOUTHERNERS

Insurrections

The court's radical assimilation policy led to an outbreak of resistance by non-Việt ethnic groups in southern Vietnam. Towards the end of Minh Mạng's reign in 1841, through 1845, southern Vietnam was swept by a series of ethnic insurrections.

Dissatisfaction exploded in the Cambodia region first, but then insurrections quickly spread throughout southern Vietnam as well. By the beginning of Thiệu

Trị's reign (1841-1847), Hà Tiên, An Giang, and Vĩnh Long provinces had experienced insurrections by the Khmer people.[75] The provinces of Gia Định, Định Tường, and Biên Hòa were relatively calm compared with the three provinces to the west of the Upper Mekong River (Tiền Giang), where a large proportion of the population was Khmer. Nevertheless, this does not mean the former areas escaped ethnic turbulence. The potential for ethnic conflict existed everywhere. Up until 1845, Vietnamese people, including local officials, were frequently abducted or killed by the Khmer people in Tây Ninh, a recently established prefecture of the Gia Định province with a large Khmer population, so that even the central government, while committed to assimilation and the expansion of its territories, prohibited the *hán nhân* southerners from intruding into the regions predominantly inhabited by Khmer people.[76] Định Tường province was less exposed to potential trouble from the Khmer population, but Khmer villages were still scattered throughout that province at this time. Biên Hòa province was another region into which numbers of ethnic minority groups had been absorbed as a result of the central administration's redistricting policies, but some of these newly formed villages were about to break apart due to opposition from ethnic minorities. In 1839, an ethnic minority village leader in Phúc Bình district of Biên Hòa province made plans to flee the area with his people. His appeal to his followers was reported as follows:

> Since *cải thổ qui lưu*, they have charged a head tax every year, and have forced us to sell local products at a lower price. In addition, they have conscripted soldiers from us, and have measured our land [in an arbitrary way]. How can we cope with this?[77]

The dissatisfaction of *thanh nhân* Chinese during this time was also expressed in various forms. Interestingly, they often cooperated with the Khmer minority in battles against Vietnamese; documents report that *thanh nhân* Chinese were frequently discovered among Khmer insurgents.[78] Furthermore, in 1845, a central official complained that many Chinese of Gia Định province had fled to Cambodia during this time and were working as spies against the Vietnamese.[79]

The insurrection in the prefecture of Lạc Hóa in Vĩnh Long province deserves particular mention here, because it not only illustrates the development of ethnic conflict, but also provides an example of a cultural confrontation between the Vietnamese and a particular ethnic group. Occupying land that stretched between two main streams of the Mekong River, the Khmer inhabitants of this region had maintained their own community up until the reign of Minh Mạng. Because they had contributed soldiers to the forces of Nguyễn Phúc Ánh, the future Gia Long, they had been allowed to maintain their own community under their own leadership. Nguyễn Văn Tồn, a Khmer, had been honored as a meritorious subject of Gia Long, and since that time his family had ruled this region, which was

---

[75] For general information about Khmer insurrections of these regions, see Nguyễn Phan Quang, *Phong Trào Nông Dân Việt Nam Nửa Đầu Thế Kỷ 19*, pp. 133-59.

[76] *DNTL3*, 47:4b.

[77] *DNTL2*, 204:12b.

[78] *DNTL3*, 3:27; 11:24a; 23:9b; 25:16.

[79] Ibid., 46:17b.

called Đồn Uy Viễn, or the Uy Viễn military post.[80] In 1825, the name of the region was changed from Đồn Uy Viễn to *phủ* Lạc Hóa, at the suggestion of Lê Văn Duyệt,[81] but despite its new designation as a *phủ*, this remained an autonomous Khmer region. Then the inhabitants joined Lê Văn Khôi's revolt against the central government, and their autonomous rule ended abruptly in 1834.[82] In other words, the region of Lạc Hóa exemplifies the end of the mutual coexistence between the Vietnamese and Khmer people that had existed since the Gia Định regime.

In 1841, the Khmer people of Lạc Hóa rose up in an attempt to reclaim their autonomous rule and traditional way of life. Inspired by a former Cambodian official called Lâm Sâm,[83] thousands of Khmer people took part in this insurrection. According to Vietnamese officials, the rebels made use of aspects of indigenous Khmer beliefs to mobilize the Khmer against the Vietnamese. Lâm Sâm used magic spells, religious apparel, and magic flags to assist his followers, claiming these instruments would help them fight against the Vietnamese. In both Tuân Nghĩa and Trà Vinh districts, Khmer people took part in this insurrection, and their first operation was to destroy the office of the Vietnamese governor of Lạc Hóa prefecture, to which these two districts belonged.[84]

Polarization between Southern Vietnamese and Non-Vietnamese

a) Exposure of southerners to ethnic conflict. The southerners were the first Vietnamese to be involved in the assimilation policy after it was launched by the central government. The inhabitants of all the Vietnamese villages which were joined with Khmer villages for the purpose of assimilation were affected, and their Việt leaders faced new challenges as a result of the reorganization. Typically, after Gia Định Thành Tổng Trấn was dismantled, the king appointed high-ranking officials from the central and northern regions to all province-level positions, and he left southern men in charge of newly assimilated units located within those provinces. Regional bureaucratic units such as *tổng*, *huyện*, and *phủ*, that contained both Vietnamese and ethnic minority communes, were most often headed by southerners. In other words, officials from the central and northern regions held higher level appointments which made them responsible for "cultivating" southerners, while southerner officials, who held less prestigious positions, were largely responsible for assimilating other ethnic groups.[85] The case

---

[80] Ibid., 6:8a.

[81] *MMCY*, 24:7a.

[82] *DNTL3*, 6:8a.

[83] In his work on this insurrection, Nguyễn Phan Quang suggested Lâm Sâm's Khmer name is Sa Sam, but the court recorded his name as Lâm Sâm. Nguyễn Phan Quang contends that a court scribe arbitrarily chose Lâm for this man's family name. See Nguyễn Phan Quang, *Phong Trào Nông Dân Việt Nam Nửa Đầu Thế Kỷ 19*, p. 133. But I believe the family name Lâm had probably already been assigned to him during the assimilation period. Before the insurrection, he had been a Cambodian official, holding a title as an official with sixth rank. *DNTL3*, 6:8b. To be designated a government official under the Vietnamese protectorate, it was necessary to have a Vietnamese family name. Lâm was one of the family names given to ethnic minorities during assimilation.

[84] *DNTL3*, 6:8.

[85] The same pattern can be seen in Cambodia. Trương Minh Giảng (1792-1841), a southerner, was in charge of the assimilation project in Cambodia, and he became the first target of the

of Bùi Hữu Nghĩa (1807-1872) may be representative. As an 1835 graduate and the first graduate from the west bank of the Lower Mekong River (Hậu Giang), he was appointed to be magistrate of a district in Phúc Long prefecture of Biên Hòa province. Before long, he was transferred to Trà Vinh district, a Khmer district in Vĩnh Long province, whose governor-general, Trương Văn Uyển, was from the central region.[86] We also find records of the official, Nguyễn Khắc Điều, an 1837 graduate from Gia Định province. In 1844, he was magistrate of Bình An district[87] in Biên Hòa. Thiệu Trị's *Thực Lục* informs us that this man worked with a provincial administration commissioner (*bố chính*) named Đỗ Huy Cảnh, and with a surveillance commissioner (*án sát*) named Phan Văn Xưởng.[88] According to the *Quốc Triều Hương Khoa Lục*, Đỗ Huy Cảnh was from the north (Nam Định province), and Phan Văn Xưởng was from the central region (Quảng Nam province).

In addition to Việt officials and villagers, southern convicts were also called on to cooperate in the state's ambitious assimilation project. In 1836, the central court decided to plant southern convicts in military plantations in Cambodia, for reasons described by Minh Mạng: "[southern convicts] will live among Cambodians, then they will make them learn and be affected by Vietnamese custom (*hán phong*). That will also be a way of changing barbarians through the use of *hán*."[89] Apparently, the king was willing to include any southerners, even convicts, in the category of *hán* when it was posed against the *di*, or barbarians.

As assimilation proceeded, more southerners were exposed to ethnic conflicts. Under the new regulation of 1836, one-fifth of southern male adults were conscripted as soldiers in the provinces of Biên Hòa (number of conscripts 1,813), Gia Định (6,143), Định Tường (3,575), and Vĩnh Long (6,465), making a total of 17,996 conscripts.[90] Before Gia Định Thành Tổng Trấn was dismantled, southern military conscripts had been dispatched not only to areas throughout southern Vietnam, but also to the central and northern regions. From 1836 on, however, they were sent only to Cambodia and Hà Tiên province, where they mainly came in contact with Khmer people.[91] For the southern soldiers, this was a significant change. From this time, their main responsibility was to control the Khmer. When Khmer insurrections broke out in 1841, four thousand additional southerners were conscripted as soldiers from Gia Định (1,500), Định Tường (1,000), Vĩnh Long

---

outraged Khmer people. A Khmer manifesto collected by Vietnamese spies in 1841 revealed strong enmity towards Trương, and also revealed the people's suspicion that Trương wanted to make their queen, Ngọc Vận, his wife. *DNTL2*, 220:12b-13a.

[86] Huỳnh Minh, *Cần Thơ Xưa và Nay* (Can Tho, past and present) (Saigon, 1966), p. 71.

[87] This district was formed in 1808. In 1837, it was enlarged based on a pattern of assimilation. The ethnic minority of the *thủ An Lợi* were absorbed into this district, and reorganized as a *tổng*. Mixed with three former Vietnamese *tổng*, this reorganization made five *tổng* of mixed ethnicity. *DNNTC*, p. 38.

[88] *DNTL3*, 42:24b-25.

[89] *DNTL2*, 172:20a.

[90] Châu Bản Triều Nguyễn, lunar January 27, 1836; *DNTL2*, 165:17b-18b. As far as the number of conscripted soldiers is concerned, these two documents show slight discrepancies for most provinces, but the discrepancy for Vĩnh Long province is considerable. When the Châu Bản record shows that 6,465 soldiers were conscripted from Vĩnh Long province, *DNTL* lists 5,400 as the correct number. As the Châu Bản is an original record and more detailed in its figures, I prefer to accept the information found in the Châu Bản.

[91] *DNTL2*, 165:18b-19a.

(1,000), and An Giang (500). In 1842, 3,500 were added to this number, from Biên Hòa (500), Gia Định (1,000), Định Tường (500), Vĩnh Long (1,000), and An Giang (500).[92] To determine the ratio of the conscripted population to the taxpaying population, I will choose three eastern provinces (of southern Vietnam) that had relatively stable populations[93] during Minh Mạng's reign: Biên Hòa, Gia Định, and Định Tường. Next is the registered number of taxpayers of each province at the end of Minh Mạng's reign, based on Nguyễn Thu's record[94] and the ratio of conscripted southerners who were directly exposed to ethnic conflicts. As Nguyễn Thu's population figures did not include ethnic minorities,[95] they enable us to figure out the ratio of Vietnamese soldiers to the Vietnamese population:

Table 10: Southern population and soldiers in 1836-1841

	Biên Hòa	**Gia Định**	**Định Tường**
Taxpayer Population	11,100	31,790	26,330
Soldiers	2,313	8,643	5,075
Ratio (%)	**20.84**	**27.19**	**19.27**

As shown in the above table, between 19.27 percent and 27.19 percent of registered southern taxpayers on the eastern side of the Upper Mekong River would be directly involved in ethnic conflicts as soldiers. This is already an impressive figure, but in fact the actual ratio of conscripted soldiers to the entire population of eligible males was even higher, for "taxpayers" included male adults between eighteen and sixty years old, while the maximum age for military service was officially fifty years old during the Nguyễn dynasty.[96] The percentage of soldiers among southern men eighteen to fifty years old, then, would have been higher than

---

[92] *DNTL3*, 16:19a.

[93] As I discussed in the previous chapter, administrative reshuffling was frequent from the end of Minh Mạng's reign. Thus, it is difficult to compare the allocated number of soldiers in 1836 with the whole population during that time. For example, the number of soldiers in 1836 from Vĩnh Long was listed as 6,465, but we must keep in mind the fact that, when these numbers were calculated, Vĩnh Long province included a substantial portion of land along the western Lower Mekong River. This land and its villages would be shifted into An Giang province three years later, in 1839. The taxpayer population of Vĩnh Long was 28,020 during Minh Mạng's reign, based on Nguyễn Thu's information, but it is possible that this figure was calculated after the land along the western part of the Lower Mekong River was incorporated into An Giang province.

[94] Nguyễn Thu, *Hoàn Vũ Kỷ Văn*, vol. 3.

[95] By contrast, the taxpayer population of 1847 under Thiệu Trị's reign included ethnic minorities. *DNTL3*, 67:10a. Therefore, the population figures for 1847 are less appropriate to be used as a source from which to calculate the ratio of soldiers relative to the pure Vietnamese population. The registered taxpayer population of 1847 is as follows:

Biên Hòa	Gia Định	Định Tường	Vĩnh Long	An Giang	Hà Tiên	Total
16,949	51,788	26,799	41,336	22,998	5,728	165,598

[96] *Đại Nam Điển Lệ Toát Yếu* (A summary of the statutes of Imperial Vietnam) (hereafter *TY*) trans. Nguyễn Sĩ Giác (1909. Ho Chi Minh City: Nxb Thành Phố Hồ Chí Minh, 1994), p. 452.

the percentages noted above.[97] Ratios of conscripts to taxpayers in the western region were probably not very different from comparable ratios in the eastern region, but western soldiers were more likely to be exposed to ethnic conflict, because the western provinces of Vĩnh Long, An Giang, and Hà Tiên were more often disrupted by ethnic insurrections, especially those carried out by the Khmer.

b) Ethnic polarization. Southerners were to be the first Vietnamese who directly experienced ethnic conflict, and they were the first victims of the animosity many ethnic groups came to feel against the Vietnamese. Conflicts of this sort actually strengthened the southerners' identification with Vietnam as a whole and reinforced their sense of identity as Vietnamese people.

One example of this psychological transition caused by ethnic tension is found in a story originating from this period. Among the exemplary women introduced in *Nam Thiên Hiếu Hành Thực Lục*, we meet one whose case is relevant to our study of the ethnic problem during the assimilation period.

> Nguyễn Thị Liệu was a woman of Kiến Đăng district, [to the northern side of Mỹ Tho], in Định Tường province. One day she was going alone along a small path. On the way, she encountered a Khmer man called Giao. He tried to rape her. She committed suicide, so that she kept her chastity and was not contaminated by force.[98]

This book goes on to say that Nguyễn Thị Liệu was rewarded posthumously by the central court in 1845. Considering that the central court elected to highlight this story and the year in which she was rewarded, we can conclude that the alleged incident happened during the time of ethnic conflict.

Several points can be drawn from this anecdote. Firstly, it appears that Khmer people were still to be found in the northern part of Định Tường during the 1840s, as well as in the southern part of this province. Secondly, two ethnic groups, Vietnamese and Khmer, appear to have existed close to each other in normal daily life. In other words, these villagers appear to have been following Minh Mạng's recommendation that ethnic minorities and Vietnamese "live and cultivate together, so that they may imitate each other."[99] Related to this is a third point: that this Khmer man had a Vietnamese name, Giao. Taken as a whole, this example offers some information about the situation of the Khmers in the process of assimilation during Minh Mạng's reign.

There is also evidence of ethnic tension in this story, which involves confrontation between two ethnic groups: a Khmer man's attack versus a Vietnamese woman's resistance and death. After the incident was recorded by the court, it grew in fame and was elaborated upon by southerners; a different version of this same story can be found in a collection of legends and tales compiled by Huỳnh Minh and published in 1969.[100] My main concern in introducing this latter version is

---

[97] To the number of soldiers, convicts should be added, too. Occasionally, southern convicts were conscripted to combat Khmer people. For example, in 1845, convicts from six provinces were organized as soldiers to fight against Khmer insurgents in front of the Vietnamese troops. *DNTL3*, 48:12a.

[98] *Nam Thiên Hiếu Hành Thực Lục* (Veritable records of exemplary behavior in Vietnam) (1869. Hanoi: Viện Hán Nôm VHv 1240), vol. 5, Định Tường.

[99] *DNTL2*, 208:9b.

[100] Huỳnh Minh, *Định Tường Xưa và Nay*, pp. 137-39.

not to initiate a debate about the source or content of the story, but to use the tale as evidence of the sentiments of southerners, who apparently maintained the strong emotions of ethnic conflict evoked during this period, revised their memories of these ethnic conflicts over time, and carried those collective memories over into the next century. It is also possible, of course, that the tale was further revised by southerners during the twentieth century, so that we cannot judge what was the real content of this story. However, what is important is that in the series of stories of southerners collected and published during the 1960–70s by Huỳnh Minh, only this 1840s story was used to symbolize the ethnic split between Vietnamese and Khmer people. In other words, the Vietnamese considered the 1840s, even after more than a century, to have been an era marked by serious ethnic conflict.

If we compare the original story in *Nam Thiên Hiếu Hành Thực Lục* to the elaborated version of the 1960s, we will see how sharply the ethnic clash made southerners turn towards their own ethnic identity and heightened the division of the two peoples into Vietnamese and "barbarian."

According to *Định Tường Xưa và Nay*, the Khmer man's name was Thạch Giao. The woman's name was Liệu. Her father engaged in trade with Khmer people, sailing along the streams of the Mekong River to the border area next to Cambodia, as was common among southern Vietnamese during that time. This time he departed for his business trip after informing his daughter that this would be his final trip because of the troubles between Vietnam and Cambodia. Unfortunately, he was caught by Khmer bandits. Hearing about her father's capture, Liệu left her village to seek any news about him. On the way, she fell into Thạch Giao's trap and committed suicide (p. 137).

At this point, a careful interpretation of the documents is necessary concerning the Khmer man, Giao. *Nam Thiên Hiếu Hành Thực Lục* informs us that he lived near Liệu's village, but in the newer version of the tale, elaborated over years, the heroine fell into Giao's trap as she travels to seek her father. Considering the sources of the two stories, I would conclude that Giao was Liệu's acquaintance, and that he had lived near her family, and may well have been guiding her to find her father. The situation in Cambodia was threatening at this time, so it may well have been necessary for a young woman to secure a guide. If the guide were reliable, he could have helped shield her from the hostile curiosity of the Khmer, his own people. The fact that this Khmer man is so clearly identified supports my assumption, for if she had met him for the first time—a complete stranger—on the road, it is unlikely his name would have been identified in the official document, *Nam Thiên Hiếu Hành Thực Lục*.

It is the conclusion of this story that best represents the southerners' sentiments at this time (1960s). Once the woman was attacked, a clear division emerged: the division into Vietnamese and barbarian. According to the twentieth-century version of this tale, when the Khmer man turned on her and began to press her, this Vietnamese woman declared: "Now, you reveal the habits of barbarians. I will die, but I certainly will remain a ghost in order to eradicate vices for [my] people [*dân*]." With that, she bashed her head against a rock. With the suicide, this story divided the characters into representative Vietnamese and Khmer. The southerners created the story of the woman's ghost, a ghost who would begin to help the Vietnamese defeat the Khmer people (pp. 138-39).

c) More evidence of ethnic division. The appearance of a local religion, Bửu Sơn Kỳ Hương, during this time provides more evidence that southerners were preoccupied with and concerned by ethnic issues. Founded by a southerner, Đoàn Minh Huyên (1807-1856), this new religion actively spread from 1849 through 1856, in the region around Châu Đốc in An Giang province, where serious ethnic disturbances had occurred. In many ways, this religion showed Buddhist influences, but it also involved elements that can be traced directly to the contributions of the *hán nhân* southerners. Unlike normal Buddhist priests, Bửu Sơn Kỳ Hương priests were not required to shave their heads, reflecting the strong Vietnamese concern with keeping their hair long. Priests did not rely on followers' donations, but instead supported themselves by clearing land and cultivating rice, occupations which had always been strongly recommended by the central government, especially under the reign of Minh Mạng. In addition, piety to parents and respect for ancestors were main elements of this religion, both practices much more typical of Vietnamese than of Khmer cultures. Lastly, the religion strongly advocated allegiance to one's country and gratitude to one's countrymen, attitudes that were no doubt both necessitated and intensified by ethnic tensions.[101]

In her study of this religion, Huệ Tâm Hồ Tai also offers evidence that we may interpret as relevant to our examination of ethnic conflicts between the Vietnamese and two different ethnic groups: the Khmer and the Chinese. According to this scholar, Trần Văn Thành, born in 1820 or 1821, was the greatest of Đoàn Minh Huyên's twelve well-known disciples. When trouble with the Khmer minority erupted in 1840, he headed a company of fifty men and acted as a successful military leader until 1846, so that he surely had direct experience of ethnic conflicts in the region. As the contest between Vietnam and Cambodia drew near a resolution, he returned home and converted to Bửu Sơn Kỳ Hương in 1849. We note this story of his actions following his conversion:

> As the earliest and most trusted of the Buddha Master's [Đoàn Minh Huyên] disciples, Trần Văn Thành was given the task of planting amulets throughout the Seven Mountains to counteract the effect of the evil tablets that were said to have been left there by Chinese emigrés. The traditional Vietnamese suspicion of the Chinese was exacerbated by proximity and by competition for scarce resources in the South. The Vietnamese accordingly believed that the Chinese, motivated by a desire to prevent the Vietnamese from achieving the greatness that was their destiny, had planted evil tablets to that effect in the one area which was linked in the sectaries' mind with this glorious national future.[102]

I would argue that it was during the period of Vietnam's assimilation project, and following years of ethnic turmoil, when "the traditional Vietnamese suspicion of the Chinese" intensified. And this new religion, the Bửu Sơn Kỳ Hương, grew out of ethnic differentiation, which was made possible by the southerner's realization of their ethnic identity as Vietnamese.

---

[101] For information on the practices and doctrines of this religion, I am indebted to Huỳnh Minh, *Vĩnh Long Xưa và Nay* (Vinh Long, past and present) (Saigon, 1967), p. 278; and Đinh Văn Hạnh, "Bửu Sơn Kỳ Hương Với Cuộc Kháng Chiến Chống Pháp " (Buu Son Ky Huong and anti-French movement) (PhD dissertation, Viện Khoa Học Xã Hội TPHCM, 1996).

[102] Huệ Tâm Hồ Tai, *Millenarianism and Peasant Politics in Vietnam* (Cambridge: Harvard University Press, 1983), pp. 14-15.

CONCLUSION

I have discussed assimilation as an important policy of the central government in southern Vietnam. As a result of this policy, peaceful coexistence between different groups, which had been part of the Gia Định heritage, was thoroughly abandoned. The assimilation project aimed to Vietnamize all ethnic groups of southern Vietnam, and in this effort, southerners were assigned—and also volunteered—to act as part of the vanguard. As long as they were ethnically Vietnamese, the court considered them appropriate tools for furthering Vietnamization. Lower-level officials, peasants, soldiers, and even convicts were used to Vietnamize other ethnic groups in southern Vietnam. It was during this time that a higher percentage of the southern Vietnamese population experienced conflict with other ethnic groups, more than at any previous time.

As a result of the extreme policy of assimilation, the central court saw another rupture in southern Vietnam. For five years, southern Vietnam was swept by ethnic turmoil between Vietnamese and ethnic minority groups. It was during this time that Việt southerners began to acknowledge their identity as *hán nhân* Vietnamese, as the country was polarized and southern Vietnamese came to stand on the side of the central court. They were the first victims of the resentment and rage directed towards the Vietnamese "aggressors" by members of the ethnic groups that had suffered from Vietnamese policies. They had to choose where they belonged: were they chiefly southerners, who enjoyed a cooperative relationship with other ethnic groups, as had been the case from the Gia Định regime, or were they, rather, Vietnamese subjects living under the rule of the king in Huế? They would be driven to choose the latter.

CHAPTER SIX

LAND MEASUREMENT AND THE PROTECTION OF PRIVATE LAND OWNERSHIP

Along with the spread of educational institutions and the assimilation of ethnic groups into the Viet state and culture, another significant action was launched from 1836 in southern Vietnam. It was *đạc điền*, or land measurement. Literally, this project was intended to measure regional and property boundaries, to clarify land borders and land ownership. For this work, land cadastre was introduced in 1836 for the first time in southern Vietnam. Units of land were standardized following the example of other regions of Vietnam, by *mẫu, cao* (or *sào*), *thước*, and *thốn*.[1] The central government created public land (*công điền, công thổ*) by confiscating private land (*tư điền, tư thổ*); in southern Vietnam, most land had been owned privately.

Vietnamese scholars have produced two studies on land measurement based on solid data: Nguyễn Đình Đầu's *Chế Độ Công Điền Công Thổ Trong Lịch Sử Khẩn Hoang Lập Ấp ở Nam Kỳ Lục Tỉnh* (The public land system in the history of opening land and establishing villages in the Six Provinces of southern Vietnam), and Trần Thị Thu Lương's *Chế Độ Sở Hữu và Canh Tác Ruộng Đất ở Nam Bộ Nửa Đầu Thế Kỷ 19* (Land ownership system and rice cultivation in southern Vietnam during the first half of the nineteenth century). By examining the 1836 land cadastre, both of these authors illuminate the pattern of land ownership during the nineteenth century. These authors identify the creation of public land as the most important result of land measurement, and they judge that project to have been a significant achievement of the Nguyễn dynasty, writing: "Minh Mạng clearly did not want southern Vietnam developed with private land ownership any more," and "public land could appear only by the will of the ruling class from the first half of the nineteenth century."[2] Nguyễn Đình Đầu contends that the creation of public land facilitated a tendency towards equalization (*bình quân hóa*) in nineteenth-century

---

[1] *mẫu* (150 thước * 150 *thước*): 4,894.4016 square meters; *cao* (or *sào*, 1/10 *mẫu*): 489.44016 square meters; *thước* (1/15 *cao*): 32.639344 square meters; *thốn* (1/10 *thước*): 3.263934 square meters. See Nguyễn Đình Đầu, *Nghiên Cứu Địa Bạ Triều Nguyễn: Định Tường* (Researching land cadastres of the Nguyen dynasty: Dinh Tuong) (Ho Chi Minh City: Nxb Thành Phố Hồ Chí Minh, 1994), p. 26.

[2] Trần Thị Thu Lương, *Chế Độ Sở Hữu và Canh Tác Ruộng Đất ở Nam Bộ Nửa Đầu Thế Kỷ 19* (Land ownership system and rice cultivation in southern Vietnam during the first half of the nineteenth century) (Ho Chi Minh City: Nxb Thành Phố Hồ Chí Minh, 1994), pp. 57 and 205.

Vietnamese society.[3] In other words, this effort was meant to extend an important aspect of the Vietnamese heritage—the public land system—into southern Vietnam.[4]

However, a more careful examination of documents raises questions about their conclusion that the most important result of, and motivation for, the central government's land measurement project was to create public land. In dealing with detailed historic evidence, Nguyễn Đình Đầu and Trần Thị Thu Lương relied mainly on a few sources: the 1836 land cadastre and several declared decisions by the central court, which can be found in the court chronicle. While the 1836 cadastre is a document of great value, and certainly contributes to our understanding of this period, it is not enough to give us a comprehensive picture of the situation during these years. A large amount of private land was not registered in this cadastre, as will be shown below, and that land must be taken into account by scholars seeking to comprehend the impact of this policy. Also, a more careful examination of the court chronicles shows that arguments, disagreements, or friction existed between Minh Mạng and his officials at this time, and I would argue that the two authors in question neglected to consider significant details in the record concerning these disagreements.

Most importantly, Nguyễn Đình Đầu and Trần Thị Thu Lương fail to explain an inconvenient statistic that prevents us from accepting their opinion that the

[3] Nguyễn Đình Đầu *Chế Độ Công Điền Công Thổ Trong Lịch Sử Khẩn Hoang Lập Ấp ở Nam Kỳ Lục Tỉnh* (The public land system in the history of opening land and establishing villages in the Six Provinces of southern Vietnam) (Hanoi: Hội Sử Học Việt Nam, 1992), pp. 102 and 104-5. A similar opinion is found in Sơn Nam's work on Gia Định. He claims, "the Nguyễn dynasty actively developed public land during the first half of the nineteenth century." Sơn Nam, *Đất Gia Định Xưa* (Land of Gia Dinh in the past) (Ho Chi Minh City: Nxb Thành Phố Hồ Chí Minh 1993), p. 73. This general view has led some scholars to conclude that the Nguyễn government deprived its people of private property by confiscating and converting it into public land. In their work on land clearance in southern Vietnam during the first half of the nineteenth century, Nguyễn Cảnh Minh and Dương Văn Huề claim: "After people had cleared land through years of hard work and made it cultivable, the land they had cleared could not become their private property because of the government. They only had the right of usage; the land became public land." Nguyễn Cảnh Minh, Dương Văn Huề, "Chính Sách Chiêu Dân Khai Hoang Lập Ấp ở Nam Kỳ của Nhà Nguyễn Nửa Đầu Thế Kỷ 19" (Policies of recruitment of people, opening land and villages in southern Vietnam during the first half of the nineteenth century), *Nghiên Cứu Lịch Sử* (hereafter *NCLS*), 3, 274 (1994): 15. This general conclusion is based on two themes: one, that the Nguyễn dynasty kept trying to increase public land; two, that the Nguyễn dynasty was essentially reactionary, a common assessment among Hanoi historians. For some of them, the Nguyễn government's work to increase public land in southern Vietnam was also a work of exploiting its people.

[4] The *đạc điền* had been done in 1618 at Quảng Nam and Thuận Hóa. *Đại Nam Thực Lục Tiền-Biên* (Primary compilation of the veritable records of Imperial Vietnam, premier period) (hereafter *TB*) (1844. Tokyo: Keio Institute of Linguistic Studies, 1961), 2:4a. By 1663, land was measured as far south as the region of Khánh Hòa. *TB*, 5:5. Slightly after the measurement of land in southern Vietnam was completed, the land of Bình Thuận province was measured. *Đại Nam Thực Lục Chính-Biên Đệ Nhị Kỷ* (Primary compilation of the veritable records of the second reign of Imperial Vietnam) (hereafter *DNTL2*) (1861. Tokyo: Keio Institute of Linguistic Studies, 1963), 172:14b-15a.

creation of public land was the most important result of land measurement. In fact, the ratio of public land produced in 1836 was only 3.58 percent of registered cultivated land in southern Vietnam.[5] As *quan điền* (previously existing government land) was included in this figure, the amount of newly created public land must have been less than 3.58 percent of registered land. Moreover, this percentage is strongly influenced by figures from Vĩnh Long province, that had a ratio of public land over 10 percent; in other provinces, the range was only 0.07-1.5 percent. We need to remember the case of Bình Định province in the central region as well. When in 1838 the central government found that the amount of private land significantly exceeded the amount of public land, it recommended redistribution of land.[6] An 1839 report from the Board of Finance shows that the ratio of public land to private land had been around 10 percent in this province. Due to the land redistribution policy instituted earlier that year, the ratio of public land rose to over 60 percent in this province.[7] Compared with this result, the amount of private land newly claimed as public land in southern Vietnam—3.58 percent—is obviously quite small.

Given these figures, two different explanations might be suggested: either the central government was not deeply committed to creating public land in southern Vietnam, or it made the attempt, but failed. I think it is necessary to consider both possibilities in order to understand the actions of the court and the response in southern Vietnam. At the beginning, the central government obviously had intended to create public land on a large scale, but it was confronted by a number of situations that forced it to moderate those plans. Eventually, by 1840, the original intention to create public land was abandoned. The government adopted a different policy that encouraged private land ownership in the region and sought to link southern landowners to the government hierarchy by offering official titles and status as awards. I demonstrate this process in my main discussion.

In this chapter, three matters are dealt with. I review the pattern of land ownership that had dominated in Gia Định until 1836. Unless the strong tradition of private land ownership in Gia Định is understood, the cause and result of the 1836 land measurement cannot be perceived properly. Next, I consider the content of the land measurement policy and its consequences. Finally, I evaluate Minh Mạng's policy on land ownership. Because the king was obviously a decision maker, his

---

[5] The following table is recreated based on figures found by Nguyễn Đình Đầu. See Nguyễn Đình Đầu, *Chế Độ Công Điền Công Thổ Trong Lịch Sử Khẩn Hoang Lập Ấp ở Nam Kỳ Lục Tỉnh*, p. 127.

	Biên Hòa	Gia Định	Định Tường	Vĩnh Long	An Giang	Hà Tiên	Total
Cultivated Land (*mẫu*)	13,420.2	165,464.9	137,007.3	178,817	96,579.2	2,750.8	594,037.4
Public Land (*mẫu*)	39.7	2456.7	156	18,521.4	7	28.7	21,209.5
Ratio (%)	0.3	1.5	0.1	10.4	0.007	1.04	3.58

[6] *DNTL2*, 196:23.

[7] Before reform, about six to seven thousand *mẫu* were designated as public land in this region, while private land made up about seventy thousand *mẫu*. Following the reform, about forty thousand *mẫu* of that private land had been converted to public land. See *DNTL2*, 207:40b.

attitude towards land ownership will provide us with a clue to understanding the nature of land measurement in Vietnam more generally. In this chapter, I will refer to several local documents, in addition to the court chronicle and land cadastre. Papers of land trade and property distribution, and tenantship contracts involving southerners are new sources that illuminate southern practices relevant to land ownership. As these agreements were made among villagers, but not shown to officials beyond their own villages, they contain more accurate information than official documents.

1. FORMS OF LAND OWNERSHIP

Private Land Ownership in Gia Định

a) Settlement in Gia Định, and family labor. After Gia Định came to be inhabited by increasing numbers of Vietnamese during the sixteenth and seventeenth centuries, private land ownership became the major form of land ownership. Several reasons help explain this pattern. Most of all, it had to do with the process of settlement in Gia Định. At the time when immigrant Vietnamese began to appear, this land was sparsely populated by other ethnic groups, especially Khmer people. The sparse population and wide availability of land helped preserve the peace between the indigenous villagers and immigrant Vietnamese. Thus, the process of Vietnamese immigration into Gia Định was relatively peaceful, undisturbed by any serious clashes, until the middle of the seventeenth century, when wars started to occur between the Nguyễn state and Cambodia.

Plate 9. Thatched house beside a stream of the Mekong River.
Credit: the author, 1997.

Earlier interactions between indigenous settlers and Vietnamese newcomers in the central region had been much more troubled. In a part of that region, the Cham population that had cultivated and occupied the land was forcefully removed and Vietnamese settlers introduced in their place. This action was a consequence of the serious confrontation between the Vietnamese and the Cham people in this region. As shown by the case of Lê Thánh Tông in the late fifteenth century, it was a common practice to import a Vietnamese population into a former Cham area, often by introducing new *đồn điền*, or military plantations, one of the most popular forms of settlement. Frequently, the immigrant Vietnamese did not clear virgin land for themselves, but instead appropriated Cham property, which became available after Vietnamese military pressure forced out the villagers who previously inhabited the area. In the central region, during the period of the Nguyễn state, this practice was still followed. When thirty thousand Trịnh overlord soldiers were captured in a battle in 1648, they were sent to settle in the region of present day Phú Yên. The Nguyễn state's main consideration was to fill this land, formerly occupied by Cham villagers who had fled the Vietnamese military incursions: "previously, this land was of Cham barbarians (*Chiêm liêu*). Now, the population is small but land is large [. . .] we insert [the captured Trịnh soldiers] into this land [. . .] and let them clear *gian điền*." Here, the *gian điền* was not virgin land; it was land that had been abandoned by the Cham, but which lay among plots of cultivated land. Fifty men were tied into one group to make a village and provisions for half a year were given to them. From this time the region of Phú Yên was home to organized Vietnamese villages.[8]

In this case, the villages of central Vietnam were supposed to be under the state's control from the beginning. Under these circumstances, it is to be expected that the distribution of land was more orderly than in Gia Định. Moreover, we must remember that the majority of Vietnamese settlers in this area were former northerners who still kept the memory of the public lands common in the north. Although the geographic landscape around Phú Yên was different from that of northern Vietnam, the two regions did share one condition in common: there was limited arable land available. In this situation, the establishment of public lands was readily justified. In the mid-1830s, the government noted that an excess of public land had been accumulated in Bình Định, leading to an imbalance that ought to be corrected. Yet documents show that the tradition favoring public land still existed in Bình Định in 1838, when the ratio of public to private land was 1:10.[9]

Gia Định saw a different pattern of settlement compared to the central region. In 1698, the Nguyễn state calculated there were already forty thousand Vietnamese households in Gia Định, established by Vietnamese immigrants who had moved to Gia Định on their own initiative. In that year, the Nguyễn government recruited non-registered people from the central region and sent them to Gia Định.[10] This was the first and last action of the Nguyễn state to increase the Vietnamese population in the region.

---

[8] *TB*, 3:14b-16a.

[9] *DNTL2*, 207:40b.

[10] *TB*, 7:14.

The majority of Gia Định people were spontaneous immigrants from the central region, peasants who elected to leave their villages of their own free will, for their own reasons. Normally the unit of emigration was a family; sometimes a family would be joined by other families. Once these immigrants entered Gia Định, land for cultivation was available everywhere, but it was land that had to be cleared. Because wild animals, such as tigers, poisonous snakes, and crocodiles, posed a danger to anyone attempting to clear plots in the watery forest, this labor was usually carried out in groups for safety.[11] But the unit of labor for land clearance was still a single family. As Nguyễn Thị Thạnh pointed out, "for the peasants who went south on their own, their family members were the main source of labor."[12] Land that had been prepared for cultivation belonged to the family who did the work, especially the head of family and his wife. Eliacin Luro left us an account of the normal pattern of settlement in southern Vietnam in his book, *Cours d'Administration Annamite* (1877): "Every family occupied one part of land that [the members of each family] would be able to clear. From this time, private land ownership by peasants was established."[13]

We have earlier evidence that supports Luro's observation and provides us with more detailed information concerning the extent of private land that was cleared by family labor. It is a document of property distribution produced in a village of Định Tường region in 1818.[14] In that year, a man called Nguyễn Văn Cụ and his wife Phạm Thị Quan, both in their seventies, made a will outlining the distribution of their property. Their land was to be distributed between their two sons and three daughters. According to the will, the bulk of land had been cleared and worked by family members. The parents' decision was to divide the land into six pieces, *sở*, or *thửa*. A piece of land facing a small stream was allocated as rice fields intended to support ceremonies of ancestor worship (*điền hương hỏa*). This land was bequeathed to their eldest son. The remaining five pieces of the land were equally distributed among his five children. A visual representation of this land distribution is given below.

Based on this sketch, we can make certain assumptions. When the Nguyễn Văn Cụ couple arrived in this region, probably by boat, they might well have begun clearing land in the location now designated for the *điền hương hỏa*. Afterwards, their growing children added to the labor force. As the silkworm nibbles away at mulberry leaves, they would have cleared land to the north and east until they met the land that had been claimed by other families. The cleared land in this parcel had belonged entirely to the parents. When a child reached the age to form a separate family, a certain amount of land could be given to the new couple for their own house and fields. This sort of distribution could take place as land clearance continued, however, at this stage only usage rights, not actual ownership of the property, were being distributed. Considering that this husband and wife were in their seventies, we can assume that most of the five children had already

---

[11] Việt Cúc, *Gò Công Cảnh Cũ Người Xưa* (Go Cong, its environs and people in the past), vol. 1 (Saigon, 1968), p. 35.

[12] Nguyễn Thị Thạnh, "The French Conquest of Cochinchina, 1858-1862" (PhD dissertation, Cornell University, 1992), p. 42.

[13] Cited in Nguyễn Đình Đầu, *Chế Độ Công Điền Công Thổ*, p. 119.

[14] Appendix 1.

formed their own families by 1818, the year the will was written. The first child could have reached his fifties by this time. Still, the parents remained official owners of the whole land.

Diagram: Land distribution of the Nguyễn Văn Cụ couple to their children in 1818

North

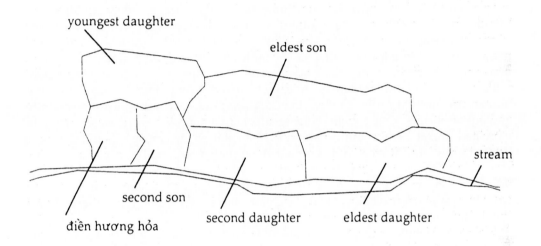

youngest daughter

eldest son

stream

second son

second daughter   eldest daughter

điền hương hỏa

South

Nevertheless, the parents could not maintain absolutely exclusive rights over the cleared land. As the land had been cleared by family labor, each family member had rights over the property to some extent, even while the parents officially owned the land. A typical pattern in land trade documents of southern Vietnam makes it clear that certain rights accrued to sons and daughters regarding their parents' land. Bills of land trade found in Định Tường province declared, without exception, that the purpose of the document itself was to avoid possible quarrels between a buyer and any members of the seller's family. For example, an 1830 land-trade bill ends with the following notation: "If anyone [of the sellers' family] disputes this deal later, we [sellers] will be happy to pay the price." Each family member signed the document.[15] Notes of this kind reflect the value of family labor that had been invested when the land was first cleared. In case the official owner of the land sold that property without first consulting and winning

---

[15] See Appendices 2–7. From 1861, this process was accepted by the central government as the general rule of Vietnam. *Đại Nam Điển Lệ Toát Yếu* (A summary of the statutes of Imperial Vietnam) (hereafter *TY*), trans. Nguyễn Sĩ Giác (1909. Ho Chi Minh City: Nxb Thành Phố Hồ Chí Minh, 1994), p. 162. For the signature, the finger-joint print (*điểm chỉ*) was used among villagers.

the agreement of other family members, such as his wife, children and even daughters-in-law, those relatives might claim a portion of the land.

b) Villages. The next reason for the prevalence of private land ownership had to do with the relationship among members of a village. In the case of a village formed by several families, it is hardly to be expected that members of all the households would have maintained strong solidarity at the beginning, when land was first being cleared. At this stage, the village was merely a unit that consisted of several nuclear families. No doubt there was intimacy and perhaps a sense of mutual allegiance among some of the villagers, as they were pioneers who had overcome hardship together in a new land, but village solidarity would still have been weak. Until stronger relationships, such as marriage, began to link the families more closely to one another, most of these people would have been strangers to each other. As Trần Văn Giàu described, "each home was a bamboo-hedged area."[16] In addition, villages in southern Vietnam were generally open to newcomers, a condition that facilitated mobility. Especially at the beginning of settlement in southern Vietnam, people often moved several times before choosing a permanent place to settle,[17] and various kinds of refugees continuously moved into and out of villages. Consequently, the relationship among villagers was relatively loose and frail at the beginning. Once a dispute started up among village members, it often grew until it created a serious rift, so that occasionally an entire village was split.[18] The spirit of private land ownership was developed in this way, because villagers in southern Vietnam could not trust that their claims to land would always be respected by their neighbors and so wished to have those claims clearly defined and even documented.

c) Local Habits of Land Ownership. Another reason for widespread private land ownership in southern Vietnam is thought be related to the habits of ethnic groups who came into contact with the Việt settlers. As the most populous local ethnic group, the Khmer people need to be considered and their local system of land ownership taken into account. Basically, Khmer villages did not have public land. A big village, called *sóc*, was divided into several smaller units, called *phum*, each

---

[16] *Vietnam Cultural Window* 4 (1998): 9.

[17] We saw earlier that Võ Tánh's family had lived in Biên Hòa until his grandfather moved to Gia Định, probably from the end of the seventeenth century to the beginning of the eighteenth century. *Đại Nam Chính-Biên Liệt Truyện Sơ Tập* (First collection of the primary compilation of biographies of Imperial Vietnam) (hereafter *LTST*) (1889. Tokyo: Keio Institute of Linguistic Studies, 1962), 6:1a. A son of the Trương family called Dũng (1794-1849) moved from Gia Định to Định Tường before he married. See *Trương Gia Từ Đường Thế Phả Toàn Tập* (Complete collection of the genealogy of the Truong family ancestry) (1886. Hanoi: Viện Hán Nôm A 3186), p. 6. Lê Hương provides us with several more cases. For example, Nguyễn Thị Tự had lived in Bến Tre before she moved to Cao Lãnh in 1819; another family, Nguyễn Văn Luân, moved from Biên Hòa to Cao Lãnh in 1820. Lê Hương, "Những Người Việt Tiền Phong Trên Bước Đường Nam Tiến Tại Cao Lãnh-Kiến Phong" (Vietnamese at the front of southward movement in Cao Lanh-Kien Phong), *Tập San Sử Địa*, 19 & 20 (1970): 229.

[18] For example, Bình Tiên village and Tân Phú Trung village in present Sa Đéc were previously united as one village, but the households were divided into two camps by a quarrel over the village anniversary. A portion of Tân Phú Trung's inhabitants built the new village of Bình Tiên. See Huỳnh Minh, *Sa Đéc Xưa và Nay* (Sa Dec, past and present) (Saigon, 1971), p. 223.

of which consisted of five to ten families. But the *phum* was, in fact, constituted of an extended family, including parents and the families of their married daughters.[19] The unit of one family was the basic element of a village, and cultivation was possibly carried out through family labor on the private land around the *phum*. This was a common practice observed by Vietnamese who came to live alongside Khmer people, and it may well have influenced the new immigrants. The habits of the Chinese may also have been influential. The Chinese began arriving in Gia Định in 1679, and by the time large numbers of Vietnamese began emigrating to the region, Chinese had already been clearing land, establishing villages, and developing private land ownership for a number of years. Thus, the Khmer and Chinese models of private land ownership might have influenced the Vietnamese.

Significantly, the geography of the region, the natural conditions in Gia Định, which had helped shape the Khmers' approach to land ownership, must have also played a role in reshaping typical Vietnamese practices. In Gia Định, a comparatively sparse Khmer population had access to large areas of land. Around a village, sufficient land existed in the shadow of the forest. By means of the family's labor, additional land could be cleared whenever it was needed, and the work of clearing any new parcel started from the point where a family had settled. Thus, land was extended as the manpower of a family increased. The Vietnamese met the same natural conditions, and under these conditions, they might well have turned to methods of land ownership that resembled the Khmer methods. If we remember the pattern of land distribution exemplified by the estate of the Nguyễn Văn Cụ couple, described above, we find that the Vietnamese settlement pattern was quite similar to that of the Khmer people. From the point where parents had settled, the land was extended by clearance. Though this was not mentioned in the will, I believe Nguyễn Văn Cụ's sons built their houses, after they married, on the edge of land they later inherited from their parents. Possibly his daughters did, too.

Land Accumulation by Trade

Wherever virgin land was cleared to form a new village in Gia Định, that village came to be made up of several families, each of whom owned land privately. After this initial phase, land must have begun to be accumulated as time passed. Additional land clearance, land trade, occupation of other people's land, inheritance, and marriage could all be expected to transfer increasing portions of land into the hands of certain families. Among these, land clearance and land trade were the two most common ways for families to accumulate land, to the extent that these methods became characteristic features of Gia Định. Land trade, especially, was dominant by the beginning of the nineteenth century in this region where private land ownership had come to be the norm, rather than the exception.

Several land trade bills show us how actively private land was traded in Gia Định. Though the following example of a land trade took place between the years 1830-1836, I think it represents a normal pattern that had existed in Gia Định long before the 1836 land measurement initiative. According to this bill of trade, a man

---

[19] Mạc Đường, *Vấn Đề Dân Tộc ở Đồng Bằng Sông Cửu Long* (Ethnic issues in the Mekong Delta) (Ho Chi Minh City: Nxb Khoa Học Xã Hội, 1992), pp. 130 and 150.

called Trần Văn Phiên and his wife, who lived in a region of Định Tường, purchased three *dây* (strings) from a man called Thắng and his brothers in 1830, and one *dây* from his stepbrother in 1831.[20] The *dây* was a unit of measurement for land used in Gia Định up to 1836, and we do not know exactly how much land one *dây* encompassed, yet this bill of trade enables us to guess the area represented by one *dây*, for when Trần Văn Phiên and his wife distributed their property to their children, the relation between *dây* and *mẫu* was revealed. In their will, written in 1857,[21] seven cases are noted that show measurements in both *dây* and *mẫu* for the same piece of land, a precaution that was necessary because some of the land had probably been purchased before 1836 and the extent of the parcel originally recorded in *dây*. Thus, in the will, we find: 3 *dây* or 23 *mẫu*; 4 *dây* or 27 *mẫu*; 3 *dây* or 45 *mẫu*; 3 *dây* or 26 *mẫu*; 1 *dây* or 8 *mẫu*; 3 *dây* or 25 *mẫu*; and 6 *dây* or 48 *mẫu*. Based on these examples, with the exception of the "3 *dây* or 25 *mẫu*," we can conclude that one *dây* equaled between seven and eight *mẫu* in this region. So the area of land Trần Văn Phiên and his wife accumulated between 1830 and 1831 was about thirty *mẫu*, at least. As the average area of one *mẫu* in Gia Định was about five thousand square meters, this means they accumulated at least fifteen hectares during those two years.

Each land trade bill of these two years also reveals that land trade had already been a popular practice before the 1830s. According to the two bills of 1830 and 1831, both three *dây* of land and one *dây* of land sold to Trần Văn Phiên and his wife had been traded previously from the former owners to Thắng and his brothers and Trần Văn Phiên's stepbrother, who in turn traded them to Trần Văn Phiên and his wife. Trần Văn Phiên and his wife left another document recording a land trade that occurred in 1834.[22] According to this bill, the couple bought one *dây* of land that had been owned by a woman and her children. The land trade bill shows that this land had also been acquired by the woman's family through trade.

Mobility of Southerners

The mobility of settlers within Gia Định helped to generate land trade and land accumulation among southerners. A great deal of spontaneous movement seems to have occurred. The reasons were varied; families might relocate to seek a better place, to escape a quarrel with a neighbor, or to escape military corvée. Amongst these possible reasons, it was especially common for villagers to relocate in order to avoid military corvée. To understand this feature, we need to look at the military situation in southern Vietnam at the end of the eighteenth century.

When the Gia Định regime was established in 1788, conscription increased to the highest level in the history of Gia Định. According to a regulation issued by the regime in 1788, half of Gia Định's men were required to perform military service.[23] If a man was conscripted to become a soldier, he was often accompanied to

---

[20] Appendices 2–3.

[21] Appendix 8.

[22] Appendix 5.

[23] *Đại Nam Thực Lục Chính-Biên Đệ Nhất Kỷ* (Primary compilation of the veritable records of the first reign of Imperial Vietnam) (hereafter *DNTL1*) (1848. Tokyo: The Institute of Cultural and Linguistic Studies, Keio University, 1968), 3:21b.

the military camp by his wife and children.[24] Therefore, conscription of a soldier could lead to the disappearance of a whole family from a village. If he and his family fled their home village before being conscripted, they would not come back to their original village. This situation lasted into the next century.

Another reason that provoked Gia Định men to try to leave their village involved the terms of conscription. As a compensation for Gia Định people, Gia Long significantly loosened the ratio of conscription after he took control of the whole territory of Vietnam. From 1814, only one in eight men was supposed to be conscripted, which meant that eligible male villagers faced a much lower chance of being mustered into service. For the man conscripted, however, the burden was the same. If he became a soldier, this man had to stay in military service until the age of fifty[25] or even fifty-five,[26] earning a low monthly salary of one *quan* that could only buy about twenty to thirty liters of rice.[27] The Gia Long regime also ruled that the conscription would not take place if the number of male adults in a village numbered less than eight.[28] This condition must have caused males potentially eligible for military service to seek another village with less than eight men.

In 1822, soon after Lê Văn Duyệt started to work as the governor-general of Gia Định Thành, he was rewarded by Minh Mạng for identifying ten thousand additional male adults, or households, in southern Vietnam. According to Nguyễn Thu, the total number of registered households in Gia Định was around 100,000

---

[24] *Đại Nam Thực Lục* left us two pieces of evidence for this common practice. In 1798, it was found that soldiers' wives and children had been under custody at a military camp because their husbands or fathers had run away. *DNTL1*, 10:4b. In 1799, soldiers were forbidden to bring their wives and children, in case the soldiers were sent on long-term expeditions. According to a decision from this year, the families of officers were supposed to be cared for by local officials, and the families of soldiers were to be cared for by local people near the military base. *Thực Lục* informs us some soldiers' families had been engaged in commercial trade with soldiers taking part in long-term expeditions. See *DNTL1*, 10:26a.

[25] *TY*, p. 452.

[26] *Đại Nam Thực Lục Chính-Biên Đệ Tam Kỳ* (Primary compilation of the veritable records of the third reign of Imperial Vietnam) (hereafter *DNTL3*) (1894. Tokyo: Institute of Cultural and Linguistic Studies, Keio University, 1977), 4:8b.

[27] In 1836, for instance, the monthly salary of one soldier was one *quan*. *TY*, p. 451. The rice price for one *phương* (about thirty-eight liters) in 1840 was one and a half *quan* in the west part of the Mekong delta. Đỗ Bang, *Kinh Tế Thương Nghiệp Việt Nam Dưới Triều Nguyễn* (The commercial economy of Vietnam during the Nguyen dynasty) (Hue: Nxb Thuận Hóa, 1996), p. 37. Thus, a soldier's monthly salary could purchase about twenty-five liters of husked rice. But the rice price had been about one *quan* per *phương* during the 1820s. I think a soldier's monthly salary was originally set to equal the value of one *phương* of husked rice per month. Based on Nguyễn Công Trứ's calculation, a family with six members could survive one year on seventy-two *hộc* of unhusked rice at that time. *DNTL2*, 167:21a. Roughly this would have provided one *hộc* (two *phương*) of unhusked rice for one person per one month. Usually, two *phương* of unhusked rice yields one of husked rice or a bit more. In short, the monthly salary for one soldier was a minimum amount, just sufficient to feed up to one person for one month. Basically, one *hộc*=two *phương*; one *phương*=13 *thăng*. One *thăng* was 2.932 liters; one *phương* was 38.133 liters; and one *hộc* was 76.226 litres. Đỗ Bang, *Kinh Tế Thương Nghiệp Việt Nam Dưới Triều Nguyễn*, p. 20.

[28] *DNTL1*, 48:15.

during the period of Gia Long.[29] If so, we can conclude that at least 10 percent of the male adults of Gia Định had lived unregistered, without the government being aware of them, and we can surmise that a substantial proportion of these unregistered men kept on the move because they hoped to elude government notice and in that way escape conscription. Lê Văn Duyệt noted this problem in his observation to the central court in 1829:

> In this region, people lead an easy life as land is rich and fertile. In addition, it is easy for them to move to any place because rivers and streams run in every direction. Therefore, people are easygoing, arrogant, and lazy   [. . .] when they worry the military duty will claim them, they immediately leave their own village, and they throw themselves into another village that has not been filled [with enough number of male adults]. If there is a family, father and sons, and grandfather and grandsons live in different villages.[30] So they do not have any fixed registration forever. We even have a case in which a man moves to three or four different villages in a year.[31]

As this quote makes clear, circumstances favored those southerners who elected to leave their village and relocate. First of all, the transportation system was convenient to anybody who decided to take a long journey in any direction. People who moved settled quickly in new places, because abundant rich land awaited them. Trịnh Hoài Đức informs us of a custom in Gia Định that would have favored migrant families:

> [Gia Định] has huge numbers of streams. Therefore, nine out of ten people are familiar with crossing water and operating boats [. . .] villagers do not consider whether a relationship is close or not when they serve visitors [. . .] Therefore, people do not bring provisions with them when they travel. That is one of the reasons why people who secretly leave their villages are easily accepted and are raised in different villages.[32]

What would have happened when a family departed from their village and abandoned their land? There were several possible results. Firstly, their land might be occupied by a different person, a practice described in a report from 1857: "If a family who possesses land hears that conscription is likely, the [family head] runs away to a different place with his family. Village power holders

---

[29] Nguyễn Thu, *Hoàn Vũ Kỷ Văn* (Compendium on the [Vietnamese] world) (n.d. Hanoi: Viện Hán Nôm A 585), vol. 3.

[30] In a report of 1857, we discover that it was fairly common for southern men to change their name to disguise their identity: "if there are three male adults of a family, all of them change their family name to different family names, and leave to different places to avoid military service." *Đại Nam Thực Lục Chính-Biên Đệ Tứ Kỷ* (Primary compilation of the veritable records of the fourth reign of Imperial Vietnam) (hereafter *DNTL4*) (1892. Tokyo: The Institute of Cultural and Linguistic Studies, Keio University, 1980), 19:2b.

[31] *DNTL2*, 61:5b-6a.

[32] Trịnh Hoài Đức, *Gia Định Thành Thông Chí* (Gia Dinh gazetteer) (n.d. École Française d'Extrême Orient microfilm A 1561), 4:7-8.

[*hào lý*] do not report it because they wish to take their chances with the land."[33] The next result was to see a new tenant in this village. Whoever took over the land abandoned by the runaway family would seek another person to cultivate it. The land might be loaned to the new owner's family members, to his neighbors, or to another person or family who may have moved to this village. What would happen to the man who had left his village? He might find a place in a different area and start to clear land there, or he might become a tenant farmer in a different village. In such a case, the population structure of Gia Định as a whole would be changed: one landowner has disappeared (the man who left his village) and two tenants have appeared (the tenant who was to cultivate the abandoned land, and the migrant who settled as a tenant in another village).

Plate 10. Typical scene of southern Vietnam life: water, boats, rice, and women.
Credit: the author, 1997.

Though I have made some assumptions and simplified the process, I believe the mobility of southerners was one of the most important conditions facilitating the accumulation of land in the hands of certain property owners and an increase in the number of tenant farmers engaged to help work that land in Gia Định.

Hidden Land

Though a number of bills can be found documenting land trades throughout southern Vietnam, land trades were probably not always recorded on paper. Some of these negotiations might have been settled by oral contract, as well. In case the

---

[33] *DNTL4*, 19:2b-3a.

piece of land to be traded had not been registered previously, paperwork would only have caused trouble, because it would make the hidden land visible in public, to bureaucrats of the government. To comprehend the full extent of private land ownership in southern Vietnam, we must consider the existence of hidden land.

When central officials began trying to implement their land measurement policy, they had a picture of Gia Định in mind, a picture based on their own records, which led them to believe that rice fields throughout the south were occupied entirely by a handful of landowners. To these officials, who had come mainly from northern and central regions, these extensive private holdings, and apparent scarcity of public lands, were evidence of vicious practices in Gia Định. From their point of view, the accumulation of land by a few property owners had gone too far. Trương Đăng Quê was the central official in charge of land measurement in southern Vietnam. After a two-month stay in southern Vietnam, he asserted, "There is not any piece of land for the poor to insert an awl, as the rich have occupied [all the land in southern Vietnam]."[34]

However, his rather simplistic assessment (which echoed the history classic *Shih Chi*) did not accurately reflect the real situation in southern Vietnam, because large amounts of unregistered land existed behind the scenes. Some hidden land was controlled by "the rich," but "the poor" must have possessed some as well. For example, if a peasant cleared land in a new place after he had secretly left his own village in order to escape detection by the government, it seems unlikely that he would have willingly declared the existence and location of this newly cleared land to that same government.

Even Trương Đăng Quê noted the existence of hidden land. Although he wrote "there is not any piece of land for the poor to insert an awl" in order to critique widespread private land ownership and land accumulation in southern Vietnam, other statements by this official reveal that he understood that land in the region had not been entirely possessed by landlords. He listed the following categories of hidden, unregistered land:

> [1.] Originally, it was charged [for tax] as a rice field, but the land has been changed to the site of a house and attached to the field for vegetables or fruits; [2.] There is cultivated land but it has not been registered; [3.] land is located in another village, but it was registered to this village; [4.] Tax was charged on one piece of land, but the land has been divided into tens of pieces and sold to others; [5.] It is said that a piece of land is located in one place, but it is extended further and further by a meandering path. Therefore, you cannot reach the main field [he/she] really cultivates until you go for half a day.[35]

Among the five cases introduced above, the second provides us with an example that certainly demonstrates why central officials' calculations (based on official documents) of the exact amount of land being cultivated in the region should not be trusted. The fourth case also provides us with a clue concerning the existence of hidden land. If a piece of land was divided into tens of pieces and then sold without informing the authorities, each new owner of a small parcel would have little motivation to declare his/her acquisition. If hidden land located far from

---

[34] *DNTL2*, 168:1.

[35] Ibid., 168:2a.

the village was uncovered by the central official, as described in the fifth case, the owner of this property would have been a particularly unlucky man or woman. As part of popular vocabulary still, southerners use the phrase *ruộng ma*, which means "ghost rice field." This practice of cultivating and maintaining fields in out-of-the-way locations is part of Gia Định's heritage.

Given the existence of hidden land, it can be assumed that by 1836 land accumulation had not progressed to the level described by Trương Đăng Quê, so that "there is not any piece of land for the poor to insert an awl." Ironically, it was the government's push for land measurement that accelerated land accumulation in Gia Định. An examination of the process of land measurement and of Minh Mạng's ideas concerning land ownership will help clarify this point.

2. LAND MEASUREMENT AND ITS CONSEQUENCES

The Question of Tax

The following was part of Minh Mạng's edict declared in 1836 when land measurement was launched in the south:

> It is very important to clarify the borders of fields. Until now, fields have been measured by *mẫu, cao, thước, thốn*. This is a common system that has been used in all provinces within the country without exception. How can only the six provinces of Nam Kỳ be different? [Because people in these provinces are] familiar with old habit, it has been very rare [that they] record clearly [land] by *mẫu* and *cao*, but [instead] in eight or nine cases out of ten [land] has been calculated by *thằng* and *sở*. This way is not only close to a primitive humble habit, but also follows a non-standardized rule.[36]

Land measurement was yet another policy instituted by Minh Mạng as part of his larger effort to bring southern Vietnam under the same system as the rest of Vietnam. Southern Vietnam had not typically used *mẫu*, the unit of measurement common in other regions of the country, to calculate land area, but had instead recorded area in units of *thằng* (or *dây*, string) and *sở* (or *thửa*, place). In addition, based on 1833 observations, Minh Mạng's official Doãn Uẩn said that *khoảnh*[37] and *sở* had been used as land measurement units in Gia Định.[38] Even inside one *tổng*, different units were employed. In Đông Thịnh village, close to Bình Cách village, land had been measured by *sở* or *thửa*.[39] In Đông An village, *khoảnh* was used along with *sở* or *thửa*.[40]

Not only were there many different local units in use, but each local unit was apt to be applied inconsistently. For example, one *dây* was equal to seven to eight *mẫu* in Bình Cách village in Định Tường province, as we learned from the case discussed above. But this definition was not common throughout Gia Định. As

---

[36] Ibid., 166:15a.

[37] Chinese *ch'ing*, to indicate one hundred patches of field.

[38] Doãn Uẩn, *Doãn Tướng Công Hoạn Tích*, p. 13.

[39] Appendix 4.

[40] Appendix 1.

shown in another document (see Appendix 12), the amount of one *dây* could be as much as fifteen *mẫu* even in the same village. What I assume is that the exact amount of one *dây* varied according to the shape of the land, productivity, quality, location, and regional differences. For the central officials who were pursuing unification of measurements throughout Vietnam, these discrepancies were unacceptable.

However, more practical reasons existed for the new land measurement policy. The central government was looking for stable and increased revenue from southern Vietnam. One of the main reasons for the increased demand for revenue was to maintain the recently annexed land of Cambodia. According to a report from a Vietnamese official in Cambodia, Vietnam had to maintain five or six thousand military posts in that region, so that annual expenditure was seventy or eighty thousand *hộc* of unhusked rice, or the same amount of *quan* in money.[41] Without repairing the tax system, the central government could not find any effective way to keep up with the continued expense of maintaining control over Cambodia.

Before the government's new land measurement policy was introduced, land was graded according to quality and tax charged according to three different grades: "one *hộc* per one *dây* of land of first grade," for example. But probably the tax had not been charged consistently, since the land was not measured consistently, as noted above. What's more, it is likely that many parcels of land had not been properly rated. For example, the amount of annual tax for the three *dây* of land that Trần Văn Phiên and his wife purchased in 1830 had been one *hộc*, while annual tax for only one *dây* of land purchased in the next year was also set at one *hộc*.[42] The discrepancy apparently resulted from the different assessments of the two parcels: the first piece of land had been rated as third grade, whereas the latter had been assessed as first grade property. However, it is not clear that the different grades assigned in this case accurately reflected qualitative differences in the two pieces of land traded to this couple; in fact the prices they paid for the land suggest otherwise. The three *dây* of land purchased in 1830 were bought for 1,150 quan, whereas the one *dây* purchased in 1831 cost 400 *quan*. According to the price of these two pieces of land, we find the small parcel of land had almost the same value per *dây* as the large one. In short, the owner of land valued at 1,150 *quan* and the owner of land valued at 400 *quan* were paying the same tax, despite the fact that they both were cultivating land of similar quality. Doãn Uẩn describes the general situation: "There is one *khoảnh* of land registered. In several cases, the size of one *khoảnh* is even equal to 300 *mẫu*. But the amount of tax levied [for this land] is only the amount for a three to five *mẫu* portion of land."[43]

As development of the new land measurement policy neared completion, an elaborate tax system was suggested by Trương Đăng Quê, and examined by court officials in Huế. The court decided that southern land should be divided into detailed grades and that taxes were to be charged in amounts ranging from twenty *thăng* to forty *thăng* per *mẫu*, according to grade. But ultimately Minh Mạng chose to

---

[41] *DNTL2*, 198:7a.

[42] Appendices 2 and 3.

[43] Doãn Uẩn, *Doãn Tướng Công Hoạn Tích* (or *Tuy Tĩnh Tử Tạp Ngôn*) (Minister Doan's chronicle of office, or Tuy Tinh Tu's miscellaneous notes) (1842. Hanoi: Viện Hán Nôm A 2177), p. 13.

simplify the tax system and do away with assessments of "grades" altogether. For one *mẫu* of all privately owned wet rice fields, regardless of grade, twenty-six *thăng* (about seventy-eight liters) of unhusked rice was to be charged as tax.[44] The basic idea behind this decision was that southern land should be regarded as uniformly fertile. This decision also incorporated Minh Mạng's desire to encourage land clearance: "If the amount of tax is different [according to different grades], troubles over newly cleared land will unavoidably occur in the future."[45] The twenty-six *thăng* of tax imposed by this decision was smaller than before, considering that there had been previous cases in which over fifty *thăng* had been charged per one *mẫu* of land in southern Vietnam, as claimed by Minh Mạng.[46] Despite the lower

---

[44] *DNTL2*, 172:10b-12b.

[45] *DNTL2*, 172:11b-12a. In 1836, tax per *mẫu* was fixed as follows:

From Nghệ An Northward		
Grade	Public Land	Private Land
1	80 *thăng* unhusked rice	26 *thăng* unhusked rice
2	56	20
3	33	13
Khánh Hòa to Quảng Bình		
Grade	Public Land	Private Land
1	40 *thăng* unhusked rice	40 *thăng* unhusked rice
2	30	30
3	20	20
Southern Vietnam and Bình Thuận		
	Public Land	Private Land
Wet Rice Field	26 *thăng* unhusked rice	26 *thăng* unhusked rice
Dry Rice Field	23	23

from Nguyễn Thế Anh, *Kinh Tế và Xã Hội Việt Nam Dưới Các Vua Triều Nguyễn*, pp. 102-3.

[46] *DNTL2*, 172:13b. Here we need to consider the productivity of land in southern Vietnam. Exact evidence has not yet been found that would establish with certainty the productivity of rice fields in this period. However, two records documenting rice production in Biên Hòa and An Giang will help us to calculate annual productivity. In 1840, it was reported that soldiers and convicts in a military plantation located in Biên Hòa province produced 4,600 *hộc* of unhusked rice from three hundred *mẫu* of land, while another group of military plantation soldiers in An Giang produced nine thousand *hộc* of unhusked rice from 770 *mẫu*. *DNTL2*, 210:24. An average yield in the first case was 15.3 *hộc* per one *mẫu*; in the second case, it was 11.7 *hộc*. If we use these two ratios as benchmarks of annual productivity, then the twenty-six *thăng* of annual tax assessed by the central government was 1/11.7 – 1/15.3 (6.5 percent – 8.5 percent) of annual productivity, because twenty-six *thăng* was equal to one *hộc* at that time. Based on some 1899 productivity figures for southern Vietnam, Ngô Vĩnh Long assumes that the twenty-six *thăng* annual tax was less than 4 percent of estimated yield. Ngô Vĩnh Long, *Before the Revolution: The Vietnamese Peasants under the French* (New York: Columbia University Press, 1991), p. 56. But I think 1899 productivity figures cannot be used automatically to

tax, the central government obviously achieved its goal to increase its revenue by means of land measurement. Three years after land measurement was launched, the central government found the annual revenue from southern Vietnam had increased by three times compared with the amount collected in 1825, when this land was under the rule of Lê Văn Duyệt.[47]

By means of this policy, the central government also meant to clarify the ownership of land, above all to uncover individuals who had avoided paying taxes on their land. Until the land measurement project was completed, it was impossible for the central government to identify the actual owner of a specific parcel. In many cases, a portion of land had already been divided into pieces and those pieces sold to different people, yet the government had not been informed of these changes in ownership. For example, in Bình Phục Nhất village of Định Tường province, the land cadastre of 1836 informs us that only forty-three pieces of wet rice field were known to the government, but the land measurement initiative revealed that these parcels had been divided into 143 pieces. For example, a piece of land that had been claimed in the name of Nguyễn Văn Hán was found to have been divided and sold, so that it was now owned by two different persons called Đinh Văn Hội and Ngô Thị Hoa. Trần Văn Miển was an original owner of a piece of land, but that parcel had been divided into eleven pieces and was now owned by seven different persons.[48] Without land measurement, hidden ownership of this kind would never have been discovered by the central government.

Conscription

There was another reason for the central government to measure the land throughout Gia Định: it wished to determine the size of the population more exactly in order to know how many persons could be mobilized as soldiers. As Vietnamese troops advanced into Cambodia from 1835, more manpower was required, and Minh Mạng looked to the south for additional conscripts because he understood that the area had received preferential treatment during Gia Long's reign. While one man had been conscripted among three or five in the central and the northern regions, since 1814 only one among eight had been conscripted in southern Vietnam. As the demand for manpower increased, and with the intention of unifying the conscription system, the Huế government decided to conscript one man among five in this region,[49] so that, theoretically, the ratio of southern men bound to serve the military should have increased by 60 percent. But the 1836 Châu Bản provides us with more realistic figures, as follows:

---

calculate the productivity of the 1840s, and Ngô Vĩnh Long's generalization concerning productivity is an unacceptable because yields varied by region in the south during the 1840s.

[47] *DNTL2*, 198:17a.

[48] See Địa Bạ of Bình Phúc Nhất village of Định Tường province; Nguyễn Đình Đầu, *Nghiên Cứu Địa Bạ Triều Nguyễn: Định Tường*, pp. 312 and 323-25.

[49] *DNTL2*, 165:17a.

Table 11: The Quotas for 1836 Conscriptions [50]

	Biên Hòa	Gia Định	Định Tường	Vĩnh Long	An Giang	Hà Tiên	Total
Taxpayer Population	10,242	34,124	20,167	27,457	15,136	1,481	108,607
Soldiers before 1836	483	1,658	1,229	3,322	926	87	7,705
New quota of 1836	1,813	6,143	3,575	6,465	2,860	237	21,093
Rate of Increase (%)	275.3	270.5	190.9	94.6	208.9	172.4	173.8

Apparently, the quota for the total number of soldiers (21,093) from the registered male adult population (108,607) in the south was about 20 percent, a ratio conforming to Minh Mạng's regulation to conscript one soldier from five adult men. But the number who were now being called to serve represents an increase of 173.8 percent, not 60 percent, of the total number of men who were mustered into the army previously, because in actuality fewer than one in eight men had been conscripted in Gia Định before this time. If one man in eight had been conscripted, the total number of soldiers before 1836 should have been around 13,570 (12.5 percent of the male adult population). But the above table shows that only 7,705 (7.1 percent of the male adult population) men had been conscripted.

The rate of increase in the total number of soldiers conscripted should have been higher. As a matter of fact, Minh Mạng came to the decision to conscript one in five eligible men in southern Vietnam slightly before his land measurement project was implemented. Therefore, the numbers of soldiers called up from the southern region in 1836 was calculated based on the previous registration system. As land measurement progressed, the central government discovered more landowners to provide additional manpower for the army. Consequently, the quota for the total number of soldiers should have increased with the increased number of men (landowners), leading to a rate of increase greater than 173.8 percent.

Disputes about Land Measurement

Despite the many practical reasons for instituting a land measurement program, certain obstacles ultimately prevented the central government from completing its work on southern land. First of all, disagreements occurred between officials in the central court and the officials who had been appointed to positions in southern Vietnam. Trương Văn Uyển was one of the latter. When he heard of the new project, he expressed dissatisfaction with the decision. In his report to Minh Mạng, he asserted that land measurement would cause trouble with southerners. Southern Vietnam had only recently settled down following the revolt

---

[50] Châu Bản Triều Nguyễn, lunar January 27, 1836.

of Lê Văn Khôi, and a land measurement program threatened to provoke southerners once again.[51] The southerners' responses toward the new program were described in other statements by Minh Mạng's officials. When two officials came back from southern Vietnam, Minh Mạng asked them about the situation. Đỗ Bá Đại, an advocate of land measurement, cautiously declared: "all the learned [*thức giả*] want it to be done, while one or two ignorant people do not want it."[52] The second report came closer to fulfilling Trương Văn Uyển's prediction, and may well have been more accurate. According to Mai Viết Trang, "all people are shaking and sighing."[53] Thus, the king was warned that this plan would meet with some resistance.

In addition, it became clear that there was not enough time to prepare or implement such a large program effectively. It was February of 1836 when Trương Đăng Quê went to Saigon to start land measurement, and its completion was declared in August. For proper work, seven months was not enough time. As Trương Đăng Quê admitted, officials from the provincial level down to the village level needed more time in order to learn the exact way to measure land.[54] Yet Minh Mạng was resolved that the plan be carried out. Soon after completion of the project, the central court received evidence that the effort had been sloppy and the information collected was unreliable. Even in the province of Gia Định, where Trương Đăng Quê's office was located, the governor-general complained that the measurement of land had not been done in appropriate ways. For example, the measurements of land represented in *mẫu* were not always correct; abandoned land was registered as cultivatable land in many cases; and the names of landowners in land cadastres were often wrong—these were not the real owners.[55] Deceptive or confused reports from villagers concerning ownership of land made it impossible for central officials to grasp the situation. If the central officials had secured the support of local lower-ranking officials, this effort might have been easier, but this had not been the case, and local officials were inclined to collude with villagers. Tống Hữu Tài was a local official in Định Tường province accused by a Huế official of "extorting money from villagers when he was doing land measurement."[56] Though the accuser chose to characterize these transactions as "extortion," I assume the money the local official received from villagers was offered as payment for favors. This incident suggests that deals were being made and favors exchanged between local officials and villagers in cases involving land measurement.

Therefore, the official land cadastres (*địa bạ*) compiled in 1836 in southern Vietnam are not believed to represent reality. Let me introduce an example. If we look at the 1836 land cadastre of Bình Cách village in the province of Định Tường, it appears that Trần Văn Phiên, a resident of the village, owned land totaling fifty-one *mẫu*, three *cao*, five *thước*, and five *thốn*. It was divided into two parcels: one piece of land with the size of twenty-seven *mẫu*, five *cao*, six *thước*, and the

---

[51] Ibid., 167:16b.

[52] Ibid., 167:30b.

[53] Ibid.

[54] Ibid., 168:2a.

[55] Ibid., 188:33b.

[56] Ibid., 169:6.

other piece with an area of twenty-three *mẫu*, seven *cao*, fourteen *thước*, five *thốn*.[57] Was this all the land he possessed in 1836? The answer is no. If we examine his will,[58] we learn more about the nature of this man's property, for in the will he mentions these two pieces of land. He had maintained the former (three *dây* of land) in one place, the latter (four *dây* of land) in another place. Since he did not mention from whom he purchased these two pieces of land, it can be guessed they were not procured from the land trade. How then did he get them? There were two possibilities: clearance or inheritance. If we remember that the former land was allocated by him to be *điền hương hỏa* (land for his and his wife's sacrificial rites), while the latter was left as *điền từ đường* (land for the sacrificial rites of his parents and grandparents), we can conclude the smaller piece of land had very possibly been cleared through labor, under the supervision of Trần Văn Phiên and his wife, while the larger parcel had been inherited. According to the records of 1836, the three-*dây* plot was measured at twenty-three *mẫu*, while the four-*dây* plot was measured at twenty-seven *mẫu*. These two pieces of land made up the fifty-one *mẫu*, three *cao*, five *thước*, and five *thốn* total recorded on the land cadastre of 1836. However, we have at least three pieces of evidence that Trần Văn Phiên had purchased land before 1836. Had all of these parcels been sold before 1836? Another land cadastre formed in 1855 provides us with the answer. On this cadastre, Trần Văn Phiên still did not declare all the land he possessed, but he revealed that in 1855 he owned two pieces of land that had been purchased in 1830 and 1834. The size of the two pieces of land at 1855 totaled forty-four *mẫu* two *cao*, seven *thước*.[59] At very least, this amount of land had been kept secret and not reported at the time of the 1836 cadastre.

What then were the chief results of the government's land measurement program? Evidently it played a role in expanding tax revenue and increasing conscription rates, but even more importantly, it facilitated the process that the northerners had meant to discourage: the accumulation of land by private landowners throughout the south. The government's effort introduced standardized land measurement units into the region,[60] so that borders of land were defined in more detail, more sharply than before. As a result, ownership of land became more clear, more easy to confirm or disprove. The clarification of land ownership made it easier to trade land, and this would have led to additional accumulation of land by those who had the means to engage in purchase or trade. In addition, as noted above, the king chose to simplify the land tax system as part of the measurement program, and this revision of the tax system also facilitated the purchase and trading of land. As the tax became simpler—and even lighter, as far as registered land was concerned—families found it easier to maintain larger areas of land than before. The new tax system must have encouraged the acquisition of more and more land by capable landowners, who would have gained their new property either by clearance or by trade.

---

[57] Địa Bạ of Bình Cách village (1836).

[58] Appendix 8.

[59] Địa Bạ of Bình Cách village (1855).

[60] On any trade bill after 1836, land was traded by *mẫu* (Appendix 6). From Trần Văn Phiên's will, dated 1857, one can easily determine whether any piece of his land was purchased before or after 1836 depending on the measurement units employed. See Appendix 8.

These conditions would probably have been enough to insure that the private holdings of landowners throughout the south increased in size, but one further development would speed the process: the central government itself began to recognize private land ownership.

3. MINH MẠNG AND PRIVATE LAND OWNERSHIP

While a number of court officials disapproved of the extent to which land was controlled by private owners throughout the southern regions, Minh Mạng himself was an advocate of private land ownership and land accumulation, at least in the case of southern Vietnam. The king had concluded that the basic way to create public land in that region was to avoid touching private land. The following examples from 1836 reveal how public land was created in southern Vietnam. Usually officials chose abandoned land, land previously owned by the government, land cleared by laborers under the patronage of the government, or the land of former military plantations to convert into public land.[61] In addition, some confiscated private land was made public. The land belonging to Lê Văn Duyệt's father was appropriated in this way,[62] but this was an exceptional, even punitive action, carried out by a regime that wished to sully Lê Văn Duyệt's memory and exact payment from his family.

While Minh Mạng's officials were occupied trying to implement an idealistic model of land reform, the monarch kept raising the issue of private property, as evidenced by several arguments between Minh Mạng and his officials concerning land reform in Bình Định province, further north. His officials were fascinated by the prospect of creating public land through land redistribution in Bình Định province, and they hoped to accomplish the same thing in southern Vietnam, but Minh Mạng kept trying to temper the enthusiasm of his officials.

His ideas on private land are clearly expressed in an argument with an official called Võ Xuân Cẩn. Võ was the first man who had suggested land reform in Bình Định province. Originally he recommended that any landowner possessing over five *mẫu* would have to forfeit the surplus and see it converted to public land.[63] This suggestion was made in 1838, when Minh Mạng and his men were disputing whether they ought to confiscate private land to produce public land as the next step in the land measurement project that had already begun in Gia Định. Minh Mạng responded to Võ's recommendation in this way:

> In ancient times, rulers made their people lead lives by the means of *quân điền* [equal distribution of land], and let them have stable property and stable minds. It was a pretty idea. The past and the present, [however] are different. After the *tỉnh điền* [well-field system] was abandoned by the Ch'in dynasty, it was not able to be recovered through Han, T'ang, Sung, and afterwards. It is mainly because the world is different and the work cannot be the same. Though it [*quân điền*] has been done, there has not been any place which saw any result. Again, private land has been possessed for a long time, and ownership has

---

[61] *DNTL2*, 171:25.

[62] *LTST*, 23:29b.

[63] *DNTL2*, 196:23a.

already been recognized. Now, [you say we should] cut away and take their private property. Basically, bloodshed is not the thing to make people feel comfortable. Once [the conflict] happens, it will spread more and more. I am afraid we would not see profitable results.[64]

If we remember that Minh Mạng had actively been implementing harsh strategies, such as the policy to incorporate Gia Định and Cambodia into greater Vietnam, a policy that cost the lives of many Vietnamese, as well as Khmers and others, then we understand that this king did not fear "bloodshed" or "conflict" very much and would not have been dissuaded from any course of action by the prospect of "bloodshed." Therefore, given the response quoted above, we can conclude that the main consideration that prevented him from advocating Võ's proposal was his own concept of "private property." On this point, he sharply distinguished himself from his subordinates. He also does not appear to have agreed with them that the landlord-tenant relationship deserved serious criticism. For him, "it is natural to see the rich provide the land and the poor provide the labor."[65]

Tempered by this skeptical response from Minh Mạng, the reform ultimately carried out in Bình Định province was less radical than a number of officials had proposed. In any village where the total area of public land exceeded that of private land, or the areas of public land and private land were equal, land reform did not need to be implemented. Reform was only carried out in any village where there was more private than public land.[66] Though Minh Mạng finally agreed that there should be land reform in Bình Định province, he never seemed to be enthusiastic about it.

As far as southern land was concerned, the records show that Minh Mạng hardly expressed any interest in creating public land throughout that region. His main goal was to create more arable land in order to produce more rice. In his opinion, land accumulation was not a vicious practice so long as land was cleared and rice production increased; his attitude was reinforced by a respect for private property. Some of his officials were eager to implement the same sort of policy in the south that had been applied in Bình Định province; in fact, they were ready to propose an even more radical program of land reform for the south. In 1840, an official named Lê Khánh Trinh, who was a native of Huế who had passed the regional examination in 1831, suggested that half of all private land be converted to public land.[67]

From Minh Mạng's point of view, however, the problem was not the lack of land, but the fact that the land available was not fully cultivated. In a region like southern Vietnam, where the population was sparse but land plentiful and fertile, the main problem was scarcity of labor: "In every province of Nam Kỳ, land is fertile and rice fields are abundant. [I] do not worry whether the amount of rice fields is small for each peasant, but [I] only worry that people are not diligent [enough to fully cultivate their land]."[68] To him, the accumulation of land was not a

---

[64] Ibid., 196:23b.

[65] Ibid., 195:15b.

[66] Ibid., 204:8a.

[67] Ibid., 210:5.

[68] Ibid., 210:5b.

problem *per se*, although if an owner accumulated land that exceeded his capacity to cultivate it, that was a real crime. As long as the land was cultivated, the size of land holdings did not matter. Lê Khánh Trinh's proposal for creating public land in Gia Định province had to be revised in order to satisfy the king. Minh Mạng outlined a compromise:

> If there is any land that has been abandoned in any village, order villagers to clear it again, and make the cleared land into public land [. . .] or, if there is any village that has any owner who has relatively too much land to be able fully to cultivate it [. . .] then, take half or 30 percent to 40 percent of his [fallow] land.[69]

As a result of this instruction, six or seven thousand *mẫu* of public land was created by government appropriations exacted from six or seven hundred private landowners in the province of Gia Định.[70] As the rice fields of Gia Định province registered in 1836 totaled 165,464.9 *mẫu*,[71] newly created public land in 1840 constituted 3.6 to 4.2 percent of all registered land. But, as Minh Mạng's instruction shows, the newly created public land was converted from land that had been abandoned or uncultivated because of the shortage of manpower.

For Minh Mạng, the creation of public land by this means had two goals: first, he wished to establish public land in southern Vietnam to effect a symbolic transformation, so the south would more closely resemble the northern and central regions; second, he intended to warn landowners that they would not be allowed to leave their land uncultivated. The latter goal was not met, however, for though public land was created by the new policy, this land was often left uncultivated or abandoned once again, because few volunteers were available to till it. We find evidence of this pattern in a case from Vĩnh Long province, in a record dated one month earlier than the record of Lê Khánh Trinh's recommendation for land reform. According to this document, certain Vĩnh Long landowners agreed to offer up part of their land to be converted into public land because they did not have enough laborers to cultivate the land. Yet villagers did not want to accept this gift, despite the fact that 70 to 80 percent of them were tenant farmers.[72] Minh Mạng's official in this province, Trần Tuyên, claimed that it was due to the landlords' resistance to losing their laborers, implying that the landlords were threatening the tenant farmers, and warning them not to accept the public land.[73] However, Minh Mạng's interpretation was different. According to him, it was evidence that land was fertile and abundant in southern Vietnam.[74] Minh Mạng's interpretation

---

[69] Sometimes, this decision is misinterpreted as evidence that the Nguyễn dynasty chose radical methods to create public land. Following is an example: "three-tenths of the private land in the south was ordered to be made into communal (public) land." Nguyễn Thị Thạnh, "The French Conquest of Cochinchina, 1858-1862," p. 85.

[70] *DNTL2*, 210:6b.

[71] Nguyễn Đình Đầu, *Chế Độ Công Điền Công Thổ Trong Lịch Sử Khẩn Hoang Lập Ấp ở Nam Kỳ Lục Tỉnh*, p. 127.

[72] *DNTL2*, 209:24b-25a; 210:5b.

[73] Ibid., 209:24b-25a.

[74] Ibid., 210:5b.

was closer to reality. But this reality was what frustrated Minh Mạng's initial intention to warn landowners who did not fully cultivate land, and it is what persuaded him not to cling for long to the initial policy of creating public land.

Creation of Private Land

The basic goal of Minh Mạng was to guarantee private land ownership and allow that mainstream practice to continue in southern Vietnam. He was working to create private land rather than to increase public land. Generally, land cleared by soldiers and convicts was government land (*quan điền*), which up until 1840 had often been selected as suitable to convert to public property. From this year, however, the government land was offered for sale to villagers. In Biên Hòa province, new cultivable land had been produced by the labor of convicts, who had thereby completed their compulsory service period and were waiting to be released. Minh Mạng elected to offer this property to the convicts, who would then become small landowners, or to sell it to other willing villagers. He instructed his officials to convert these cleared plots into public land only as a last resort:

> Secretly visit them [convicts]. If they want to stay there, insert them into the village [adjacent to the cleared land] and register them to do corvée service. And give the cleared land to them as the form of private land to live on. If they want to go back home, sell the cleared land to others so that the land would become private land. In case there is no one who wants to buy this land, let the villagers manage this land as public land. From now on, this decision will be the example of [what to do with] land cleared like this by convicts.[75]

Minh Mạng was even trying to sell off government land to create private land. To him, the only land suitable to be made public in southern Vietnam was that which did not attract anybody.

In this context, the new approaches to land clearance that started from 1837 can be better understood. Prior to this time, two forms of land clearance—initiated by individuals and sponsored by the government—had existed separately in Gia Định. As discussed earlier, private land had been cleared by individuals without any government involvement, whereas military plantations, or *đồn điền*, had been opened under the command and supervision of the government.

After the land measurement project was completed in southern Vietnam, however, the central government became involved in land clearance projects initiated by individuals. Firstly, it sought to pressure those individuals already aligned with the government. From the village up to the provincial level, the head of each unit was to be rewarded or punished according to the amounts of land cleared under his jurisdiction.[76] Under this regulation, bureaucrats at each level of government were supposed to be responsible for land clearance by individual residents in their area. In other words, the purpose of this regulation was to connect enterprising southerners who sought to clear land for themselves with central government authority. The second form of intervention meant to encourage

---

[75] Ibid., 215:8a.

[76] Ibid., 171:27b-28a; 208:10a.

southerners to extend their private holdings. If a man wanted to clear land, he could now ask the local government for support, and buffalo, tools, and seeds would be provided. To encourage the cultivation of additional land, taxes on land were not charged for six years.[77] Perhaps even more important, farmers were allowed to range beyond the boundaries of their own villages, and even into the domains of neighboring villages, to seek new property. As long as he/she had the intention to clear land, he/she was allowed to enter a different village to do so.[78] In this way, 4,936 *mẫu* of land was cleared and registered in 1839, for instance.[79] The former village head Trần Văn Thiện (1795-1883) of Gia Định province provides an example of an enterprising man who took advantage of Minh Mạng's new policies. In 1844, Trần Văn Thiện decided to clear land that was located close to his village but belonged to a different prefecture. He asked permission from the official of *phủ* Tây Ninh, and cleared the region of Bến Cầu. This man continued to clear land and attract cultivators until he had built four villages.[80]

Because the king not only recognized but encouraged private land ownership in southern Vietnam, land was also continuously accumulated by trade. If we examine the will of Trần Văn Phiên again, we find that the total amount of land he accumulated by 1857 was about 282.5 *mẫu* (thirteen plots), excluding his original property totaling fifty-one *mẫu*, three *cao*, five *thước*, and five *thốn*. The record shows that he purchased 133 *mẫu* (eight plots) of this land after 1836, but the actual amount he purchased was even more than that. We have two more pieces of evidence that he purchased forty-four *mẫu*, nine *cao*, three *thước*, 8 *thốn* of land in 1839, and about twenty-seven *mẫu* in 1846.[81] In the cadastre of 1855, we find more evidence that he purchased seventy-four *mẫu*, eight *cao*, ten *thước* in 1844.

He accumulated land more energetically after 1836, and he purchased land located in different villages. Of his land, five plots totaling 121 *mẫu* were located in two different villages called Dương Xuân and Song Thịnh. All 121 *mẫu* were obviously purchased after the 1836 land measurement.[82]

Landlords and Tenants

Another element that contributed to the increase in private land throughout Gia Định was the increasing number of runaway soldiers and of men who had fled their village to escape conscription. Clearly the government had not foreseen this development, which was the result of its own failure in mobilizing and holding onto their soldiers. As discussed in the previous section, deserters from the military had been one of the main sources of labor for landlords in southern Vietnam before the land measurement program was initiated. However, the number of deserters and men fleeing conscription sharply increased after land measurement began. As a court official stated, "[after 'the conscription of soldiers' (*giản binh*)] we began to

---

[77] Ibid., 182:2a.

[78] Ibid..

[79] *DNTL2*, 215:32b.

[80] Huỳnh Minh, *Tây Ninh Xưa và Nay* (Tay Ninh, past and present) (Saigon, 1972), pp. 104-5.

[81] Appendices 6 and 7.

[82] Appendix 8.

see the vicious influence of *giản binh*. Soldiers or candidate soldiers disappeared more frequently than before."[83]

One of the safest alternatives for such runaways was to become tenant farmers in a new village. A report from Vĩnh Long province in 1840 illuminates a common situation at the village level: "In a village in this province, the number of landowners is two or three among ten people. Whenever there is conscription, landless people claim they cannot be conscripted as they do not have land [. . .], so they are pleased to be tenants."[84] Being a tenant was clearly preferable to being a soldier. Probably the villagers who frustrated the central officials by refusing to accept public land were motivated by these same considerations.

There was an additional reason behind the southern peasants' willingness to become tenants: the work was not as hard as in many other regions. This was an unusual facet of life in southern Vietnam, mainly due to the "lack of labor in a large and rich land." Under these conditions, the relationship should not always be interpreted as the "heavy extraction from the peasantry [by southern landlords]."[85] A former communist leader of southern Vietnam, Trần Văn Giàu, recently acknowledged that southern Vietnam before French occupation was "the land where landlords needed cultivators more than cultivators needed landlords."[86] The relatively advantageous situation of southern tenants can be demonstrated by an examination of the rents they paid for land, the productivity of their fields, and the areas of land they usually rented.

An estimate of the amount of rent can be made by reference to the will of Trần Văn Phiên. This landlord left us the amount of annual income from his rented land as follows: 290 *giạ* unhusked rice from twenty-three *mẫu*; 320 *giạ* from twenty-seven *mẫu*; five hundred *giạ* from forty-five *mẫu* [. . .].[87] Based on these figures, the amount of annual rent per one *mẫu* of land was approximately twelve to thirteen *giạ*. According to the interpretation of Sơn Nam, who also analyzed this document, one *giạ* equaled thirty-seven liters,[88] equal to one *phương*. If the annual rent in this region was twelve to thirteen *phương* or 6–6.5 *hộc* of unhusked rice per *mẫu*, then the base rent was obviously much higher than the government tax of 26 *thăng* (about one *hộc* or two *phương*), by about 6-6.5 times, in fact.

However, in order to be able to judge whether this amount of rent posed a burden for a typical tenant farmer, we need to consider the productivity and the amount of land one tenant family could cultivate in southern Vietnam. As discussed above, we have evidence that one *mẫu* of land in Biên Hòa province produced about 11.7 *hộc* annually, and in An Giang province in 1840, soldiers and convicts were able to produce 15.3 *hộc* of unhusked rice on the same amount of land. Almost surely productivity in the region around Bình Cách village, where Trần Văn Phiên lived,

---

[83] *Binh Chế Biểu Sớ* (Memorials and commentaries on the military system) (n.d. Hanoi: Viện Hán Nôm A 1543), p. 243.

[84] *DNTL2*, 209:24b-25a.

[85] Nguyễn Thị Thạnh, "The French Conquest of Cochinchina, 1858-1862," p. 88.

[86] Trần Văn Giàu, "Người Lục Tỉnh (The people of Six Provinces)," *Xưa và Nay* (Past and present) No. 44B (Ho Chi Minh City, 1997), p. 4.

[87] Appendix 8.

[88] Sơn Nam, *Đất Gia Định Xưa*, p. 84.

was higher than those two figures,[89] however let us choose 11.7 *hộc* of unhusked rice as the minimum annual harvest per *mẫu* in the region around Bình Cách village. If 6 to 6.5 *hộc* (twelve to thirteen *giạ*, which would constitute 51.28 percent to 55.55 percent of the annual product) of unhusked rice was deducted as annual rent, then 5.2 to 5.7 *hộc* of unhusked rice was left. In the discussion above, I noted that a soldier's monthly salary was set at one *hộc* of unhusked rice, so that annually he would have received the equivalent of twelve *hộc* of unhusked rice. To produce a surplus that would provide him with this amount of unhusked rice annually, it was enough for a tenant to rent two to three *mẫu*. If we consider the fact that productivity was generally higher than 11.7 *hộc* per *mẫu* in this region, this tenant might well have been able to rent less than two to three *mẫu*, yet still earn an income equal to a soldier's. If we use the figure 15.3 *hộc* to represent annual rice productivity, then 8.8 to 9.3 *hộc* of unhusked rice would be left as a surplus for the tenant's own use after he paid rent. To earn twelve *hộc* of unhusked rice for one year, he only needed to rent about 1.5 *mẫu*. In this region, however, it was common for one small tenant family to rent three to five *mẫu* of land, as will be shown in Table 12 below, which lists tenants' rents in Bình Đăng and Tân Mục villages near Bình Cách village. The average amount of land rented by every tenant was over 3.5 *mẫu*, with the exception of tenant "I." Among the nine tenants noted here, four of them cultivated 3.6 to 5.2 *mẫu*, the most common size of land for a tenant in this region, and five of them paid rent of 12.2 to 15.2 *giạ* per one *mẫu*. Tenants "B" and "H" paid 18.2 *giạ* and 17.5 *giạ* respectively, a bit higher than the norm, but the difference was not considerable and could have been related to higher productivity of their land.[90]

Tenants who could call on additional labor, for instance by recruiting more family members or perhaps subtenants, could rent more land. Let us consider tenant "C," who rented 17.1 *mẫu*, as an example. If an annual harvest of 11.7 to 15.3 *hộc* of unhusked rice per *mẫu* is assumed, his 17.1 *mẫu* of land would have yielded between 200.07 to 261.63 *hộc* a year. After paying his rent of 260 *giạ* or 130 *hộc*, about 70 to 131 *hộc* of unhusked rice would have been left. His available surplus was then at least five to ten times the annual salary of a soldier.

---

[89] There are two reasons for my assumption. Firstly, the soil in this region is much more fertile than in any region of the two other provinces. This village was located in a place between Mỹ Tho and Saigon. By the first half of the nineteenth century, this region encompassed the most productive land in southern Vietnam. Kiguchi Kazumasa, *Betonamu no Nomin* (Vietnam's peasants) (Tokyo: Kokon Shoin, 1966), p. 189. Secondly, the productivity of civilian cultivators must have been higher than that of military plantation soldiers and convicts.

[90] Only tenants "E" and "G" paid exceptionally high rent to their landlords. There are two possible explanations for these exceptions. One is that the productivity of these two tenants' land was extremely high. The other possibility is that these two tenants were exploited by their landlord. I think it likely that high productivity explained the comparatively high rents. I make this conclusion in part because both "E" and "G" rented their fields from a major landlord, Dương Văn Uy, who also employed other tenants. In the cases of tenants "A," "B," "C," "D," and "I," this landlord charged average rents. Secondly, tenant "G" was deputy head of this village. It is not likely this village leader would accept unfair or inequitable conditions from his landlord.

Table 12: Tenants and Their Rents (1860)[91]

Tenant	Total Size of Rented Land (*mẫu*)	Pieces of Land	Landlords	Total Rent (Unhusked Rice)	Additional Rent: Wax-husked Rice-ducks
A	9	1	Dương Văn Uy	110*giạ* (12.2*giạ / mẫu*)	2pieces-1*giạ*-2
B	11	1	Dương Văn Uy	200*giạ* (18.2*giạ / mẫu*)	2pieces-1*giạ*-2
C	17.1	2	Dương Văn Uy, Nguyễn Văn Thống	260*giạ* (15.2*giạ/mẫu*)	4pieces-2*giạ*-4
D	8.1	1	Dương Văn Uy	100*giạ* (12.3*giạ/mẫu*)	2pieces-1*giạ*-2
E	3.6	2	Dương Văn Uy, Nguyễn Văn Phương	100*giạ* (27.7 *giạ/mẫu*)	2pieces-1*giạ*-2
F	4.1	1	Hồ Thị Phú	60*giạ* (14.6*giạ/mẫu*)	1pieces-1*giạ*-2
G	5.2	3	Huỳnh Văn Tài, Nguyễn Văn Phương, Dương Văn Uy	140*giạ* (26.9*giạ/mẫu*)	3pieces-2*giạ*-2
H	4	1	Hà Văn	70*giạ* (17.5*giạ/mẫu*)	1pieces-1*giạ*-2
I	1.4	1	Dương Văn Uy	20*giạ* (14.2*giạ/mẫu*)	0pieces-0*giạ*-2

Under these circumstances, to be a tenant was not always a tragedy for the peasants of southern Vietnam. Furthermore, as tenants they still could claim exemption from conscription because they owned no land. If they were forcibly conscripted, it was easier for tenants to flee their villages and go into hiding than it was for landowners; this must have been one of the main considerations for deserters from the military and for those men who left their villages in order to avoid conscription. Though as tenants they had to pay additional rent, in the form of wax, ducks, and husked rice,[92] and they also had to provide labor called *công lễ*

---

[91] From Appendix 9

[92] See Appendix 9.

to their landlords, they still enjoyed better lives as tenant farmers than they would have as soldiers. From the perspective of landlords, the strangers who appeared in their villages and volunteered to become tenants were a valuable labor force. A central official in Vĩnh Long province complained of this situation: "the rich continuously accept the poor but they never ask where these strangers came from."[93] The more men who showed up seeking work as tenant farmers, the better the conditions for landlords who wished to accumulate land.

The Government-Landlord Connection

The central government meant to take advantage of the wealth of landlords in southern Vietnam and to enlist them as officials in the government hierarchy. According to a decision in 1839, anyone who donated over 2,500 *hộc* of unhusked rice and transported it to Cambodia or An Giang province, where Vietnamese soldiers were concentrated, was awarded a government rank of eighth to ninth level and the official title *bá hộ* (hundred doors). At that time, Minh Mạng was expecting to see volunteers who would donate and transport as much as five thousand *hộc* of unhusked rice.[94] In other words, he anticipated that wealthy southerners would be able to donate and transport an amount of rice equal to the monthly salary of 7,500 soldiers, or enough to feed over six hundred soldiers for one year.

Afterwards, this policy was perpetuated as the means to open new *đồn điền*. *Đồn điền* had originally been military units organized by the government, but these new *đồn điền* were settlements, generally farming settlements, organized by landowners and based on land accumulation. From the beginning of Tự Đức's reign (1848-1883), the most popular types of *đồn điền* were organized by individuals. According to a regulation of 1852, the formation of a village was entrusted to any individual, and this person was expected to be linked to the government hierarchy. If a man collected fifty families and established a military plantation called a *đội* (platoon, a unit of military plantation), he was titled a *đội trưởng* (head of platoon) with seventh government rank. If he could collect one hundred families, he could build a bigger *đồn điền* called a *cơ* (battalion), and in such a case he was titled *cai cơ* (head of battalion) with sixth government rank. Later, a *đội* was expected to be converted to a village called an *ấp*, and a *cơ* was to become a *tổng*. Both *đội trưởng* and *cai cơ* became the heads of these newly created villages. If a man could build a village by mobilizing fifty families, he was titled *bá hộ* with ninth government rank; if he mobilized one hundred families, he was titled *bá hộ* with eighth government rank. The rule of each village was also entrusted to these men.[95] They were the wealthy southerners popularly called (by the government) *thổ hào* or *cường hào* (powerful local families), *hương mục* (notables), and *chức sắc* (government rank holders), who collected families and built villages.[96]

The *Trương Gia Thế Phả* genealogy frequently lists government titles from the fourth generation of peasant families onward. A lady called Hoa (1829–1865) was the daughter of a peasant. She married a *bá hộ* Nguyễn Văn An. (p. 18) Trương

---

[93] *DNTL2*, 195:15a.

[94] Ibid., 201:8b.

[95] *DNTL4*, 9:4b-6b.

[96] *Binh Chế Biểu Sớ*, p. 73.

Minh Sở (1825–1891) was the son of peasant, and he was also listed as a farmer, yet he became a *đội trưởng* of Cơ Gia Tá. (p. 19) Trương Minh Trừ (1827–1885), his younger brother, became a *bá hộ* by the "donation of capital to official work." (p. 20) These individuals must have accumulated property by farming, and they were absorbed into the bottom rungs of the government hierarchy.

Other evidence will provide us with a clearer idea of the process. In the will of Trần Văn Phiên, written in 1857, his eldest son Trần Văn Học (1819-1879) and his brother Trần Văn Đinh (1823- ?),[97] another landlord, were also mentioned as *bá hộ*.[98] Judging from their titles, we can make draw of two conclusions: either that they had donated and transported over 2,500 *hộc* of unhusked rice, or they had been involved in the formation of a new village. At any rate, they were examples of how a family of southern landlords came to be engaged as members of the central government's bureaucracy. Trần Văn Học was later to "supply provisions and ammunition for the anti-French righteous army" during the 1860s,[99] an action that might have not been irrelevant to his status as a government rank holder.

CONCLUSION

Land measurement was one of the central government's initiatives designed to help implement a unified system throughout southern Vietnam. Those who were dispatched to carry out this project measured southern Vietnam's rice fields anew, employing units of measurement common in northern and central Vietnam, and produced land cadastres. At the same time, the project also created some public land of the sort that had traditionally existed in the northern and central regions of Vietnam.

In the face of the traditional land ownership practices of southern Vietnam, the original intention of the government's land measurement initiative—to create public land—was diluted. Southerners' dissatisfaction with the government's redistribution of land also served to undermine the project and frustrate its original advocates, many of them high-ranking members of the court. Perhaps the most important factor that prevented the widespread confiscation of private land and creation of new public land in the south was Minh Mạng's attitude toward land ownership. Essentially, he was an advocate of private land ownership, and his main concern was to continue land clearance and to increase rice production and tax collections in southern Vietnam. To achieve this goal, Gia Định's tradition of private land ownership was to be protected and encouraged.

In sum, the consequence of government land measurement was officially to recognize private land ownership and the practice of land accumulation. Facilitated by the establishment of clear boundaries, secure ownership, and a more consistent system for measuring area, landlords found themselves able to purchase, hold, and cultivate more land, so that the practice of accumulating land was encouraged, rather than discouraged, in the south by the new government measures.

---

[97] For the genealogy of this family, see Nguyễn Hữu Hiếu, *Võ Duy Dương với Cuộc Kháng Chiến Đồng Tháp Mười* (Vo Duy Duong and resistance movement in Dong Thap Muoi) (Dong Thap Province: Nxb Tổng Hợp Đồng Tháp, 1992), pp. 66-67.

[98] Appendix 8.

[99] Ibid., p. 70.

Minh Mạng's objective was to win these landlords over to the central government. Those landlords who gained status as a result of their association with the central government rose to become influential public opinion leaders in southern society and came to support the authority of Huế.

CONCLUSION

I have examined the central government's policies in southern Vietnam during the first half of the nineteenth century and, in my early chapters, discussed Gia Định as a peripheral region which, from the end of the eighteenth century, maintained its own identity based on distinctive political units called the Gia Định regime and Gia Định Thành Tổng Trấn. In 1788, the Gia Định regime was formed, based in Saigon, to oppose the regime of the Tây Sơn to the north. Nguyễn Phúc Ánh, a remnant prince of the Nguyễn state, was the leader of this regime; he won authority and allegiance because he had grown up in Gia Định and learned how to deal with Gia Định people on their own terms, rather than by asserting his status as a royal prince. The Gia Định regime consisted of independent military groups drawn from the people of that region. In the course of its term, this southern regime concluded over two hundred years of conflict between north and south Vietnam, including the Tây Sơn struggle against Gia Định, and eventually formed the last dynasty which ruled the first unified territory corresponding to present-day Vietnam. Within the Gia Định regime, we can find extremely flexible relationships between subjects and king, among the members of the regime, and between ethnic groups including Chinese, Khmer, and Westerners. Christians were also important members of this regime.

This heritage continued into the next century, under the rule of a semi-autonomous Gia Định local government. Gia Định became one of the three administrative regions (northern, central, and southern) created by the Nguyễn dynasty. With exclusive rights over Gia Định, the governors-general (all Gia Định men) of this local government ruled the region until 1832. Among the three governors-general of Gia Định, Lê Văn Duyệt was the most influential. He was the leader of the pro-Minh Mạng faction when Minh Mạng was designated as the second king of the Nguyễn dynasty. But he was also one of the core members of the Gia Định regime who faithfully preserved its heritage. Under his rule, Christians enjoyed religious freedom, and Chinese settlers held their place at the center of Gia Định's ruling group, just as they had during the previous Gia Định regime. Personal relationships between individuals close to the governor-general were more important than bureaucratic affiliation to the central government, so that even ex-convicts became members of the power group. However, the king Minh Mạng began to regard the Gia Định heritage as a force that threatened to undermine the unity of Vietnam. The king and his court regarded Christians, Chinese settlers, and ex-convicts as the most significant, and potentially disruptive, groups closely linked to the power of Lê Văn Duyệt. In the 1820s, tension between the central government and the southern regime developed over their different policies towards these three groups.

The central government finally asserted direct control over the southern region with the 1832 administrative reform. Gia Định was divided into six provinces, and these six provinces together were categorized as Nam Kỳ, or the southern part of

Vietnam. As a result, we see a drastic change in the composition of southern Vietnam's leadership. First, bureaucrats appointed by the Huế court replaced the Gia Định officials who had maintained personal links to the governors-general. Next, civil officials took precedence over military generals in the governmental hierarchy of each province; most significantly, civil officials recruited by the state examination from the northern and central regions came to occupy top leadership positions in southern Vietnam. Yet Minh Mạng had to pay a price for this reforms. A revolt by the Gia Định people broke out the next year and lasted until 1835, when it was suppressed by the central government, an action that cost thousands of Gia Định lives. The main participants of the revolt were Christians, Chinese settlers, and ex-convicts, but evidence shows that large numbers of southerners from the level of local officials down to villagers were also found among the rebels. After the revolt had been quelled, Gia Định became more like a colony. Mass murders and other acts of repression followed, causing tensions that could have led to another revolt if there had been no further responses by the central government.

The second part of this book looked at these policies pursued by Minh Mạng in southern Vietnam. Following the incorporation of southern Vietnam into the kingdom as a whole, Minh Mạng initiated a program to "cultivate" southerners. Minh Mạng's view of southerners was complicated, based on a certain personal bias, as well as on the actual traditions prevailing in Gia Định. Not only the "contaminated ethics" and "lazy literati" frequently noted by Minh Mạng, but also the pursuit of commerce and indifference to official positions and state examinations were characteristic of southerners. However, the most serious problem, from Minh Mạng's point of view, was southerners' ignorance and disregard of the central government and royal authority. Minh Mạng's main techniques for "cultivation" involved increasing the numbers of educational institutions, such as schools, instituting ceremonial readings of his moral maxims, and establishing shrines to the state deity (*xã tắc*). The purpose was to make southerners aware of Huế's authority. In a short period of time, Minh Mạng's decision to increase the number of educational institutions was followed by the central government's efforts to increase the number of degree holders of the state examinations. During the 1840s, about 1 percent of all registered male adult Vietnamese in Nam Kỳ were recruited as degree holders, men who were to serve as intermediaries between the king and southern villagers.

At the same time, the assimilation policy was launched. Under this initiative, Chinese, Khmer, and other ethnic groups of southern Vietnam were forced to assimilate with the Vietnamese. Việt southerners were encouraged by Minh Mạng to take an active role in the process of assimilation. Backed by the central government's support and recognition, they were in the vanguard of the government campaign to Vietnamize other ethnic groups. It is difficult to assess the results of this policy because an analysis of the change in the relative proportions of ethnic non-Việt and Việt groups throughout the south must wait for evidence that will be enable us to compare exact populations (including other ethnic groups) in 1836 and 1855, for example. But I believe southern Vietnam, which previously had been ethnically heterogeneous, with about 30 to 35 percent of its territory populated by non-Vietnamese, and probably a similar proportion of the total southern population constituted of non-Vietnamese, began to be more actively Vietnamized from the middle of the 1830s. This radical assimilation policy resulted in widespread insurrections by other ethnic groups from the end of Minh Mạng's reign, and a serious rift between Vietnamese and other ethnic groups resulted. Minh Mạng's assimilation policy sparked insurrections that devastated southern Vietnam, draining resources and energy from the region. In the process, it also sharpened ethnic tensions that would isolate southern Vietnamese from other ethnic groups in the anti-French movement during 1860s-1870s. When the Việt southerners found themselves increasingly alienated from their non-Việt neighbors, they turned to the north. Together with Minh Mạng's cultivation efforts, his assimilation policies led southerners to stand with the Huế authority.

The central government's efforts to win the allegiance of the southerners, and the results of those efforts, can be traced by examining the 1836 land measurement program, which was instituted after the revolts of the early 1830s had been quelled. If "cultivation" and assimilation were two policies implemented to change southern society, in some sense the land measurement policy can be understood in the same context. The introduction of standardized land units to southern Vietnam and creation of public land were two aspects of this policy. But Minh Mạng was not simply a neo-Confucian fanatic; he often took a pragmatic approach to state-building. He needed tax revenue and conscripts above all. In the same way, he did not want to cause another conflict with southern Vietnam by challenging its tradition of private land ownership and thus alienating southern landlords. Most of all, he aimed to encourage farmers to clear southern land and increase rice production; unlike some of his own officials, he was not very eager to implement land redistribution by confiscating private land. Minh Mạng was prepared to compromise with southern Vietnam's landlords. Private land ownership was respected and facilitated by Minh Mạng's decisions after the land measurement project was completed. At the same time, southern landlords were offered incentives to become part of the government hierarchy.

From the end of Minh Mạng's reign, groups of Confucian scholars (*nho sĩ*), and landlords (*điền chủ*) emerged as opinion leaders in a southern Vietnam that had been ethnically reorganized under Việt initiative. I think these two groups were the main elements that led the anti-French movements during the 1860s–1870s; these resistance movements were mainly carried out by the Vietnamese, without any significant contribution from other ethnic groups. Famous anti-French leaders, such as Nguyễn Đình Chiểu (1822-1888), Nguyễn Thông (1827-1884), Phạm Văn Đạt (1827-1861), Nguyễn Hữu Huân (1830-1875), and Phan Văn Trị (1830-1910), were all born and educated during Minh Mạng's reign and later. Except for Nguyễn Hữu Huân, all were graduates from the 1840s,[1] the boom period for state examinations in southern Vietnam.

Some recent Vietnamese scholars have tried to demonstrate the participation of other ethnic groups in the "righteous armies" (*nghĩa quân*).[2] Admittedly, members of other ethnic groups must have played a role in the resistance. Some could have been mobilized by force, and it would also have been possible for ethnic minorities to participate willingly in the resistance movements because they had come to identify themselves as Vietnamese as the result of assimilation. However,

---

[1] Nguyễn Đình Chiểu, 1843; Nguyễn Thông, 1849; PhạmVăn Đạt, 1848; Nguyễn Hữu Huân,1852; Phạm Văn Trị, 1849.

[2] Nguyễn Phan Quang et al., *Khởi Nghĩa Trương Định* (Truong Dinh's upspring) (Ho Chi Minh City: Nxb Thành Phố Hồ Chí Minh, 1989), pp. 77-78; Nguyễn Hữu Hiếu, *Võ Duy Dương với Cuộc Kháng Chiến Đồng Tháp Mười* (Vo Duy Duong and resistance movement in Dong Thap Muoi) (Dong Thap Province: Nxb Tổng Hợp Đồng Tháp, 1992), p. 138.

studies of this kind have failed to collect substantial evidence that would show that other ethnic groups took part voluntarily in the resistance. In particular, we cannot find any evidence of participation by *thanh nhân* Chinese in the resistance movements. I believe their reluctance to ally with the Việt rebels resulted, in large part, from ethnic conflicts that stemmed from the assimilation policy of Minh Mạng.

Concerning landlords who participated in the resistance, I have mentioned the *bá hộ* Trần Văn Học, who financially supported the anti-French "righteous armies." In addition, there was the famous anti-French leader, Trần Thị Sanh,[3] Trương Định's second wife, who provided Trương Định with financial support; she was the daughter of a landlord, Trần Văn Đồ, titled a *bá hộ* in Gò Công.[4] According to a report written by a collaborator with the French army, Lê Phát Đạt, he arrested seven resistance movement leaders in An Vĩnh village in 1875.

Plate 11. Painting depicting Trương Định and southern leaders of the anti-French resistance. The Hanoi National History Museum. Photograph by the author, 1994.

Among the seven leaders, two were landlords titled *bá hộ*.[5] In addition to these landlords, whose names have been recorded, there were surely other landlords who

---

[3] Trương Định married this woman possibly in 1862, when he decided to continue to lead the resistance movement. In 1997, when I visited Gò Công, I learned the year of Trương Định's second marriage from a local researcher, Nguyễn Tri Nha, a member of "Ban Tuyên Giáo Thị Ủy Gò Công." My thanks to him.

[4] Nguyễn Phan Quang et al., *Khởi Nghĩa Trương Định*, p. 61.

[5] PhạmThiều et al., *Nguyễn Hữu Huân, Nhà Yêu Nước Kiên Cường Nhà Thơ Bất Khuất* (Nguyen Huu Huan, a persistent patriot and indomitable poet) (Ho Chi Minh City: Nxb Thành Phố Hồ Chí Minh, 1986), p. 129.

participated in this resistance movement but who have disappeared, leaving no record behind them. For example, a resistance movement leader, Đặng Khánh Tinh, was the son of a rich family in Gò Công region. After he was arrested and executed, his family was also destroyed and there was even a relative who changed the family name from Đặng to Nguyễn.[6] The first wife of Trương Định was "the daughter of a *"hào dân* [wealthy local person]."[7] Her family "contributed their property to help Trương Định fight the French. After Trương Định failed, the Lê family was destroyed and scattered."[8] I believe that many of the landlord families of southern Vietnam which had emerged and prospered during the first half of the nineteenth century then collapsed during the 1860s-1870s because they were involved in the failed resistance movement. The participation of southern landlords in the anti-French movement will be more clearly illustrated when more of the landlord's families that disappeared at this time are rediscovered through further research.

During the second half of the nineteenth century, new leadership for southern society was formed from groups that had not participated in the resistance movements, notably Christians, Chinese settlers, and Vietnamese landlords who collaborated with French rule.[9] In a sense, this shift seems to have revived the diverse society that had been characteristic of the Gia Định regime one century earlier. However, an important difference at the end of the nineteenth century was that southerners in particular, and Vietnamese in general, already had experienced the consequences of Minh Mạng's successes and failures in regard to regionalism, religion, ethnic questions, and land ownership. This experience would influence their historical decisions in the twentieth century.

---

[6] Hồ Văn Hiếu, "Hoạt Động của Nghĩa Quân Trương Định Vùng Gò Công Tây" (Activities of Truong Dinh's righteous army in the region of Western Go Cong), *130 Nam Nghìn Lại Cuộc Đời và Sự Nghiệp Trương Định* (Tien Giang Province: Kỷ Yếu Hội Thảo Khoa Học Sở Văn Hóa Thông Tín Tiền Giang, 1995), pp. 97-98.

[7] Nguyễn Thông, *Kì Xuyên Công Độc Sơ Biên* vol. 2, Trương Định.

[8] Nguyễn Phan Quang et al., *Khởi Nghĩa Trương Định*, p. 58.

[9] Milton Osborne divides the categories of Vietnamese collaborators into property owners and Catholics of the precolonial period. Milton Osborne, *The French Presence in Cochinchina and Cambodia: Rule and Response (1859-1905)* (Bangkok: White Lotus, 1997), p. 66. As the majority of the property owners had been landlords before the French conquest, the collaborator landlords can be regarded as having their roots in the precolonial period. In regard to the collaborator landlords, Pierre Brocheux affirms that "the origins of the large landowners date primarily from the French conquest, for then the conquerors wished to reward Vietnamese who had collaborated with them." Pierre Brocheux, *The Mekong Delta: Ecology, Economy, and Revolution, 1860-1960* (Wisconsin: Center for Southeast Asian Studies, 1995), p. 109. From the arguments of the two authors, the readers of Vietnamese history may receive the impression that precolonial landlords, collaborators, and the landlords of the colonial period were all of one lineage. But it should be noted that the landlords of precolonial southern Vietnam and those of colonial period were separate groups of people. In fact, Milton Osborne does not provide us with clear evidence that would show whether the well-known collaborators such as Tran Tu Ca ("a village notable") and Do Huu Phuong ("probably a man of some wealth"), whom he listed as the only examples of "property owners," were actually southern landlords.

APPENDICES

- All information for the appendices was provided to the author in October 1997 by Trương Ngọc Tường, an independent scholar from the Tiền Giang province of Vietnam, in the original form of handwritten papers.

- The will of the Trần Văn Phiên couple exists in two versions, both of which are included here.

◯: Unclear letter

▢: Vietnamised Chinese letter, or Nôm

* ▢ (者・廾) (*"gia" in Vietnamese)

* 點▢ (指・⋯) (*"điểm chi" in Vietnamese)

WILL OF THE NGUYỄN VĂN CỤ COUPLE (1818)

建安府　建和縣　建盛總　寓東安村　柴裕　阮文具　夫妻等

計

一立詞相分由前前年　夫妻二命配室和諧生獲衆子　長男阮文於次男阮文茹女子阮
氏□(衤+鬼)阮氏低阮氏□(卄+禾)同相造田　○家財等物規矩成結　立家居　須臾運　彼
至茲忽見年高七旬數等來　生死不期　嗟牟○長腸消慮彼等衆子不調　請本村本族
同知爲証乃立詞　相分田○　家財分許衆子　領年庚　彼等存見面口傳來筆記書云生
長男勝壹分香火　富者同兮賤也　男女同平等均分　若某子反惡不顧親言　○○不許
分食之內　宜廢爲他人之列　言顧行○如文誠行顧言依法而行爲此茲詞

所開田○家財各物列陳于后

一草田壹所稅三項　坐落在東安村簿在平公西村　所田分爲陸分　置爲香火壹分　存
五分均分爲分食

一內所田壹頃有梽○櫚壹頃南至小溪　西至名証田　東至內所名茹分　北至內所氏
□(卄+禾)分置爲香火嫦阮文於任食奉祀

一內所田壹頃　南至氏□(衤+鬼)氏低分　西至名茹氏□(卄+禾)分　東北至次酒田嫦阮文
於分食

一內所田壹頃　西至香火分　北至內所氏□(卄+禾)分　東至內所氏低分　南至小溪
　　　由名茹有立○櫚壹頃　嫦阮文茹分食

一內所田壹頃　南至小溪　西至內所名茹分　北至內所名於分　東至氏□(衤+鬼)分　嫦
阮氏低分食

一內所田壹頃　南至小溪　西至內所氏低分　北至內所名於分　東至次酒田
　　　嫦阮氏□(衤+鬼)分食

一內所田壹頃　南至香火分　西至名証田　北至次酒田　東至內所名於分　嫦氏□(卄+
禾)分食

一雜家壹座參間貳厦以爲奉祀

一大銅鍋壹口

一半銅鍋壹口　由有蓋

一銅○唾貳口

一中土○壹口

一大土○壹口

一飯碗龍形參拾口

一石磁參拾口

一共各文契放債錢參百貫

一栗子五百□（舊・斗）

一奴女壹俘　名昆屋

以上自雜家壹座以至奴女壹俘　總共指壹物夫妻養老　若彼夫妻　彼運臨命故事安
旬祀畢　衆子男女同平等均分　如奴壹俘則立詞宜放　此奴俘爲此茲詞

本村視誠人　名〇手記
　　　　　　名〇點□（指・一）　　　　　　　　同爲証

嘉隆拾柒年參月初捌日
　　　立詞人　阮文具手記　　妻范氏貫點□（指・一）

本族視誠人　名書手記
　　　　　　名〇手記
　　　　　　名〇手記
　　　　　　名罷點□（指・一）

作詞人　名爵字記

LAND TRADE BILL, BÌNH CÁCH VILLAGE (1830)

建安府 建和縣 盛光總 平格村

名勝 名細 名川等 為絕賣田事

由愚等父 名勝 有造買草田 放 名謝 氏理 氏達 分食田 各現文契○ 愚等父○

田今成三繩 田舊租稅壹斛從參項 坐落在本村 東至內所放氏從分食田 西至內所

名岐香火田 南至名寶放氏□名壽田 北至俚綿田 肆至依然 而愚父命放留伊田

許愚等○○ 今愚等絕賣伊田許村長番夫妻實價錢壹千壹百五拾貫永為己田 愚等

不得返言回贖 若後何人爭阻伊田 則愚等甘受所損各○ 為此茲賣

証見二人　　里長 府 手記

　　　　　　鄉師 宣 手記

　　　　　　鄉禮 寶 手記　　　　　　　　　　　同為証

　　　　　　守本 法 點□(指+⺗)

　　　　　　守券 論

　　　　　　　　　　　　　　　　　　　名細點□(指+⺗)

明命拾壹年肆月初捌日立絕賣人　　　　名勝點□(指+⺗)

　　　　　　　　　　　　○○○拾玖年　名川點□(指+⺗)

　　鄰田人 名岐點□(指+⺗)

　　　　　　　　作文字人名□(言+背)記

LAND TRADE BILL, BÌNH CÁCH VILLAGE (1831)

建安府　建和縣　盛光總　平格村

氏□　及親子名晃夫妻　名正等　爲絶賣田事
由前年　彼等　有造買草田壹項壹繩稅一斛　坐落本村　此田東至彼田　西至俚然田
南至俚然田　北至小溪　通行肆至依然　今彼等　應絶賣此田許親子村長番夫妻實價
錢肆百貫永爲己田　若後日彼等反言　何理甘受所損　各○　爲此茲賣

証見人　　鄉師　宣　手記
　　　　　該亭　○　手記　　　同爲証

　　　　　　名正　點□（指＋灬）
　　　　　　妻　氏實　點□（指＋灬）
　　　　　　親子　名晃　手記

明命拾貳年肆月初參日立賣人　　　　　　氏□　點□（指＋灬）

　　　　　作　文契　名晃　字記

LAND TRADE BILL, ĐÔNG THỊNH VILLAGE (1831)

建安府 建和縣 盛會總 東盛村

名小夫妻 親子 名□等 爲絶賣田事

由前父母彼有造買 草田壹所 稅參項 坐落在本村 稅納平公西村 如此 田已相分

爲陸分 艮爲香火壹分 存五分 歸彼壹分 任食田貳頃 東至氏艷田中畔爲限 西至

氏輝內所分食田 南至小溪通行 北至主買分食田 東西肆至 依如契內 今絶賣許

里長安夫妻 依價回錢壹百柒拾貫 是記永爲己物 傳子留孫 如後日內族何人爭徂

此分食田 則彼等甘受所損 各○ 爲此 茲絶賣

証見人　名書 手記

　　　　合(名?)信 手記　　　同爲証

　　　　　　　　　　　親子 名□(犭+苟) 點□(指+‥)

明命拾貳年五月貳拾肆日　　其妻 氏獻 點□(指+‥)

　　　　　立賣人　名小 點□(指+‥)

　　　　　　　　　　　親子 名○ 點□(指+‥)

　　　由抄文契名華字記

　　　　　代寫按長盛字記

LAND TRADE BILL, BÌNH CÁCH VILLAGE (1834)

建安府 建和縣 盛光總 平格村

名義 及子名東 名燕 名□(亻‧罷) 名〇 氏問等 為絕賣田事
由彼有造買草田壹項壹繩 坐落在本村 此田東至師宣田 西至故參永田 南至師宣
名寶田 北自園榔至小江 通行肆至依然 今彼等同應絕賣伊田許副總番夫妻 實價
回錢陸百貫 永為己田 若後日本族何人爭阻伊田 則彼等受〇所損各〇 為此茲賣

証見人 勾魏點□(指‧⌣)
　　　　村長法記

　　　　　　　　　　　　　　　　名東點□(指‧⌣)
明命拾五年五月初拾日　　　　　名燕手記
　立賣人　　　　名義點□(指‧⌣)　　名□(亻‧罷)點□(指‧⌣)
　　　　　　　　　　　　　　　　名〇點□(指‧⌣)
　　　　　　　　　　　　　　　　氏問點□(指‧⌣)

作文契本字名〇記

LAND TRADE BILL, BÌNH CÁCH VILLAGE (1839)

南漕義利壹幇水平邏　親妹氏正氏偶等　爲絶賣田事

緣民　內祖妣　故氏誠　有造買草田原參繩　坐落在平格村地分　今度成肆拾肆畝玖

篙參尺捌寸　現著故父阮文誼分耕　此田東近嘉定省新春村地分氏合田　西近日新

村地分前氏數田　南近主買並前氏艶　氏從　氏□(重+見)　名岐田　北近名寶田　肆至依

然　今民等應絶賣此田　許該總番夫妻　的價回錢　貳千貳百貫　永爲己田　受納官稅

若何人爭徂此田則民等甘受償所損各項茲絶賣

視誠人　　　　　村長　阮文魏記

　　　　　　　　役且　阮文法　點□(指+灬)

　　　　　　　　里長　吳文傷手記

明命貳拾年參月拾陸日　　　　水平邏手記

立絶賣人　　　　　　　　　　親妹氏正　點□(指+灬)

　　　　　　　　　　　　　　親妹氏偶　點□(指+灬)

　　　　　　　　○文契本○記

LAND TRADE BILL, BÌNH CÁCH VILLAGE (1846)

建安府　建和縣　盛光總　平格村

名晃夫妻外孫名於等　爲絶賣田事

由民父母　有留來　原草田壹繩坐落在本村　承度成原肆繩爲壹所貳拾柒畝餘　簿著

陳文番分耕內　原民田壹繩　東西各近文番田　南近范文寶田　北近民居土　連至小

○　各有畔○爲限　肆至依然　今民等　應絶賣此田　許胞弟文番夫妻　的價錢貳百貫

永爲己田納租　若後日民等爭阻此田　甘受所損各○　茲絶賣

証見人

紹治陸年陸月拾柒日

　　　　　　　立絶賣人　妻氏寔　點□(指+…)

　　　　　　　　　　　名晃　點□(指+…)

　　　　　　　　　　　名於　點□(指+…)

　　　　　作文契人　名晃本字記

WILL OF THE TRẦN VĂN PHIÊN COUPLE (1857), VERSION ONE

建安府 建和縣 盛光總 平格村

鄉主 番夫妻等 爲立囑書 前定家財田土事
由民夫妻下生衆子五名氏 及妾子貳名氏 有造賣草田 等所坐落在本村 並雙盛
陽春貳村 該田參百參拾五畝零 茲民年已至陸旬 生死不期 恐衆子後日不和生心
雀角 爰請本村本族立囑書 前定相分
內祀堂壹座參屋 正堂壹間貳厦 客堂參間貳厦 廚屋參間貳厦 並家財祀器及儲器
各項無幾應充祀堂 從香火監奉 毋須分定
內田土民爲香火壹分 充祀堂壹分 存數干相分許衆子等 等其分用食
言顧行據如父敎 行顧言遵法而行 若某名氏 不遵前定 鳴鼓而攻之 除爲人外 收
其分食 充祀堂所有香火分食田各數干在何村東西肆近壹壹開

列于後茲囑書

嗣德拾年拾月拾陸日

　　　　　　立囑書人　鄉主　番　手記
　　　　　　妻氏創　點□(指+…)

　　　　　　　　　　代寫囑書　名揚　字記

一艮香火田　原參繩　度成壹所貳拾參畝餘　民分耕　坐落在本村　東西肆近依如薄
地　臨辰忌民夫妻　　　　由田粟貳百玖拾□(者+斗)
一充祀堂田　原肆繩　度成壹所　貳拾柒畝餘　民分耕　坐落在本村　東西肆近依如薄
地　忌民內祖考祖妣　顯考顯妣等肆日　及民胞兄胞弟胞姉胞妹等會忌　壹期參月貳
拾貳日　由田粟參百貳拾□(者+斗)　以上香火二所田　交許長男百戶學　認領奉祀
一長男百戶學分食田　原買阮文誼田參繩　度成壹所　肆拾五畝　民分耕　坐落在本

村　東西肆近依如薄地　　　由田粟五百囗(者+斗)

一次男　秀才昭分食田　原買黎文廩田參繩　度成分受貳拾陸畝　民分耕　東西肆近
依如薄內　北近內所氏奎分田　又補壹分原買黎氏盛田壹繩捌畝　壹分原買名雄　壹
分原買名囗田　此參分田並原分均坐落在本村　東西肆近各照文契
　　　　　　由田粟五百五拾囗(者+斗)

一次次男　百戶錠　分食田　參繩原買黎氏盛田　度成分受貳拾五畝　坐落在本村　東
西肆近照內文契　又補壹分原買黎氏好田捌畝　坐落在陽春村　東西肆近依如文契
　　　　　　由田粟五百五拾囗(者+斗)

一女子氏魁分食田　原買黎氏山田　共肆拾參畝　坐落在陽春村　東西肆近各有文契
　　　　　　由田粟五百五拾囗(者+斗)

一次女氏奎分食田　原買黎文廩田陸繩　度成稅受　肆拾捌畝　民分耕　坐落在本村
東西北依如薄內　南近內所秀才昭分田　　　由田粟五百柒拾囗(者+斗)

一妾子文敎分食田　原買阮文勇田半所原簿參拾壹畝五篙零　坐落在雙盛村　東西
肆近現有契內　又補壹分原買武文擇　武輝宣田拾畝零　坐落在雙盛村　東西肆近
現有契內　　　　　由田粟參百五拾囗(者+斗)

一妾女氏妥分食田　原買阮文勇田半所原簿參拾壹畝五篙零　坐落在雙盛村　東西
肆近現有契內　又補壹分　原買陳文論田五畝零　坐落在雙盛村　東西肆近現有契內
　　　　　　由田粟參百參拾囗(者+斗)

百戶學點囗(指+一)　　　　　　妻氏妙點囗(指+一)

壻杜公揚點囗(指+一)　　　　　妻氏魁點囗(指+一)

壻范弘道點囗(指+一)　　　　　妻氏奎點囗(指+一)

次子文敎點囗(指+一)　　　　　妻氏第點囗(指+一)

由嗣德拾玖年陸月拾貳日衆男女名氏各現認領

分食田用食〇下玆由　　　　　　內孫文養點囗(指+一)

本族人視誠陳文集手記　　　　　內次孫文弘點囗(指+一)　由年庚壬子拾五歲

　　　　　　　　　　　　　　　內次次孫文弼點囗(指+一)由年庚乙卯拾貳歲

由囑書貳本壹本支許本族人執守　次女氏妥點囗(指+一)

WILL OF THE TRẦN VĂN PHIÊN COUPLE (1857), VERSION TWO

建安府 建和縣 盛光總 平格村

鄉主 番夫妻等 爲立囑書 前定家財田土事
由民夫妻下生衆子五名氏 及妾子貳名氏 有造賣草田 等所坐落在本村 並雙盛
陽春貳村 該田參百參拾肆畝五篙零 茲民年已至陸旬餘 生死不期 恐衆子後日不
和生心雀角爰請本村本族立囑書 前定相分
內祀堂壹座參屋 正堂壹間貳厦 客堂參間貳厦 廚屋參間貳厦 並家財祀器及儲器
各項無幾應充祀堂 從香火監奉 毋須分定
內田土民爲香火壹分 充祀堂壹分 存數干相分許衆子等 等其分用食
言顧行據如父教 行顧言遵法而行 若某名氏 不遵前定 鳴鼓而攻之 除爲人外 收
其分食 充祀堂所有香火分食田各數干在何村東西肆近壹壹開

列于後茲囑書

証見人　里長 武文智 點□(指+…)
　　　　村長 杜文本記

嗣德拾年拾月拾陸日
　　　　　　　立囑書人 鄉主 番 手記
　　　　　妻氏創 點□(指+…)
　本族視誠人 陳文毛 點□(指+…)
　　　　　陳文集 點□(指+…)
　　　　　　　　代寫囑書 范弘道 字記

一香火田 原參繩 度成壹所貳拾貳畝五尺零 民分耕 坐落在本村地分 東西肆近
依如薄地 臨辰忌民夫妻　　　　　由田粟貳百玖拾□(者+斗)
一充祀堂田 原肆繩 度成壹所 貳拾畝零 民分耕 坐落在本村 東西肆近依如薄地
忌民內祖考祖妣 顯考顯妣等肆日 及民胞兄胞弟胞姉胞妹等同會忌 壹期參月貳

拾貳日 由田粟貳百捌拾□(者+斗)　向上香火二所田　交許長男百戶學　認領奉祀

一長男百戶學分食田　原買阮文誼田參繩　度成壹所　肆拾貳畝五篙　民分耕　坐落
在本村地分　東西肆近依如薄地　　　由田粟五百□(者+斗)

一次男　秀才昭分食田　原買黎文廪田參繩　度成分受貳拾陸畝　民分耕　東西肆近
依如薄地　北近內所氏奎分田　又補壹分原買黎氏盛田壹繩捌畝　壹分原買黎文雄
田貳畝餘　壹分原買阮文□田參畝　此參分田並原分均坐落在本村　東西肆近各照
文契　　　　　　由田粟五百五拾□(者+斗)

一次次男　百戶錠　分食田　參繩原買黎氏盛田　度成分受貳拾五畝　坐落在本村　東
西肆近照內文契　又補壹分原買黎氏好田柒畝　坐落在陽春村　東西肆近依如文契
　　　　　　　由田粟五百五拾□(者+斗)

一女氏魁分食田　原買黎氏山田共肆拾參畝　坐落在陽春村　東西肆近各有文契
　　　　　　　由田粟五百五拾□(者+斗)

一次女氏奎分食田　原買黎文廪田陸繩　度成稅受　肆拾捌畝　民分耕　坐落在本村
東西北依如薄內　南近內所秀才昭分田　　　　　由田粟五百柒拾□(者+斗)

一妾子文孝分食田　原買阮文勇田半所簿參拾壹畝五篙零　坐落在雙盛村　東西肆
近現有契內　又補壹分原買武文擇　武輝宣田拾畝餘　坐落在雙盛村　東西肆近現有
文契　　　　　　由田粟參百五拾□(者+斗)

一妾女氏妥分食田　原買阮文勇半所原簿參拾壹畝五篙零　坐落在雙盛村　東西肆
近現有文契　又補壹分　原買陳文論田五畝　坐落在雙盛村　東西肆近現有文契
　　　　　　由田粟參百拾□(者+斗)

由嗣德拾參年陸月拾貳日　眾子男女各現認領香火分食田　以下茲由

　　　　　　　　長男陳文學　認領點□(指+一)
　　　　　　　　女陳氏魁　　認領點□(指+一)
　　　　　　　　女陳氏奎　　認領點□(指+一)
　　　　　　　　內孫男陳文養　認領點□(指+一)
　　　　　　　　內孫男陳文弘　認領點□(指+一)
　　　　　　　　次妾女陳氏妥認領點□(指+一)
　　　　　　　　次妾孫陳文委　認領點□(指+一)

TENANT RENTS, BÌNH ĐĂNG AND TÂN MỤC VILLAGES (1860)

嗣德拾參年拾貳月貳拾壹日列編民借田粟並礼田數于在後

⋮

平登新睦貳村田以下

鄉眸借壹所田 玖畝貳篙拾貳尺 原簿楊文威 價借粟壹百拾□(者+斗)

　　蠟貳片米壹□(者+斗)鴨壹雙

汾疆借壹所田 拾壹畝原簿著楊文威 價借粟貳百□(者+斗)

　　蠟貳片米壹□(者+斗)鴨壹雙

名盛借壹(參)所田 共拾柒畝壹篙貳尺貳寸 原簿楊文威阮文統 該借粟貳百陸拾□(者+斗)

　　蠟肆片米貳□(者+斗)鴨貳雙

名□(r+栗)借壹所田 捌畝拾貳尺捌寸 原簿楊文威 價借粟壹百□(者+斗)

　　蠟貳片米壹□(者+斗)鴨壹雙

名知借貳所田內壹所壹畝貳篙柒尺五寸原簿楊文威, 內壹所貳畝肆篙拾參尺原簿阮文芳該價借粟壹百□(者+斗)

　　蠟貳片米壹□(者+斗)鴨壹雙

名觴借壹所田 肆畝貳篙柒尺五寸 原簿胡氏富 價借粟陸拾□(者+斗)

　　蠟壹片米壹□(者+斗)鴨壹雙

副村盛借參所田內壹所壹畝貳篙柒尺寸簿黃文財, 內壹所貳畝肆篙拾參尺壹寸簿阮文芳, 內壹所壹畝陸篙簿著楊文威該價借粟壹百肆拾□(者+斗)

　　蠟參片米貳□(者+斗)鴨貳雙

名埋借壹所田 肆畝 原簿何文〇 價借粟柒拾□(者+斗)

　　蠟壹片米壹□(者+斗)鴨壹雙

名餃借壹所田 壹畝肆篙 原簿著楊文威 價借粟貳拾□(者+斗)

　　鴨壹雙

BIBLIOGRAPHY

Annales de L'association de la Propagation de la Foi (Paris/Lyon) 17 (1826) through 34 (1833) stored in the State Library of Sydney.

Binh Chế Biểu Sớ (Memorials and commentaries on the military system). n.d. Hanoi: Viện Hán Nôm A 1543.

Bình Nguyên Lộc. "Việc mãi nô dưới vòm trời Đồng Phố và chủ đất thật của vùng Đồng Nai" (Being slaves a long time under the sky of Dong Pho and the real owners of Dong Nai region). In *Tập San Sử Địa* (Saigon) 19 and 20 (1970).

Brown, Edward. *Cochin-China, and my Experience of it. A Seaman's Narrative of His Adventures and Sufferings during a Captivity among Chinese Pirates, on the Coast of Cochin-China, and Afterwards during a Journey on Foot Across that Country, in the Years 1857-1858.* 1861. Taipei: Ch'eng Wen Publishing Company, 1971.

Brocheux, Pierre. *The Mekong Delta: Ecology, Economy, and Revolution, 1860-1960.* Wisconsin: Center for Southeast Asian Studies, 1995.

Cao Tự Thanh. *Nho Giáo ở Gia Định* (Confucianism in Gia Dinh). Ho Chi Minh City: Nxb Thành Phố Hồ Chí Minh, 1998.

Cao Xuân Dục. *Quốc Triều Đăng Khoa Lục* (Record of metropolitan examination graduates under the current dynasty). Translated by Lê Mạnh Liêu. n.d. Saigon: Trung Tâm Học Liệu, Bộ Văn Hóa Giáo Dục Thanh Niên, 1961.

Cao Xuân Dục. *Quốc Triều Hương Khoa Lục* (Record of regional examination graduates under the current dynasty). Translated by Nguyễn Thúy Nga and Nguyễn Thị Lâm. n.d. Ho Chi Minh City: Nxb Thành Phố Hồ Chí Minh, 1998.

Chandler, David P. "Cambodia before the French: Politics in a Tributary Kingdom 1794-1848." PhD dissertation, University of Michigan, 1973.

———. *A History of Cambodia.* Sydney: Allen & Unwin, 1993.

Châu Bản Triều Nguyễn (Vermilion Records of the Nguyen dynasty). ANU Library, microfilm reels 60-64 (1836-1837).

Ch'en Chingho. "Gencho Shoki no 'Kashukomu' ni Tsuite" (Comments on 'The Official affairs of the Ha Chau' [Regions below Vietnam]). *Sodaiajiakenkyu* (Tokyo) 11 (1990).

Ch'ing Shih Kao Hsiao Chu (Outline history of the Ch'ing, with annotations). Taipei: Quo Shih Kuan, 1990.

Ch'oe Sang Su. *Han'gukkoa Weolnamgoaeui Kwan'gye* (Relations between Korea and Vietnam). Seoul: Hanweolhyeophoe, 1966.

Choi, Byung Wook. "Wanjo Ch'ogieui Kajeongseongch'ongjin: Myeongmyeongjewa Ch'ongjin'gwan Yeomunyeol'eui Kwan'gyereul Chungsimeuro" (Gia Dinh thanh tong tran, and relations between Minh Mang and Le Van Duyet, in the early Nguyen Dynasty). MA thesis, Korea University, 1993.

———. *"Chào anh Việt Nam"* (Hello Vietnam, a collection of field-work notes). Seoul: Narasarang, 1994.

————. "Shipgusegi Cheonban (1823-1847) Betnameui Tongnamashia Kwanseon Muyeok" (Vietnamese court vessel trade in Southeast Asia during the first half of the nineteenth century). *Dongyang Sahak Yongu* (Journal of Asian historical studies) (Seoul) 70 (2000).

————. "Shipgusegi Chungban Nambu Betnameui Taeoemuyeokgoa Betnam Sang'incheung' eui Hyeongseong" (The Rise of Vietnamese Overseas Traders during the middle of the nineteenth century). *Dongyang Sahak Yongu* 78 (2002).

Chu Thiên. "Mấy Nhận Xét Nhỏ về Những Cuộc Nông Dân Khởi Nghĩa Triều Nguyễn" (Some observations on peasant insurrections during the Nguyen dynasty). *Nghiên Cứu Lịch Sử* (Hanoi) 19 (1960).

Collins, William. "Interdisciplinary Research on Ethnic Groups in Cambodia." For discussion at the National Symposium on Ethnic Groups in Cambodia, Centre for Advanced Study, Phnom Phen, July 18-19, 1996.

Cooke, Nola. "Nineteenth-Century Vietnamese Confucianization in Historical Perspective: Evidence from the Palace Examinations (1463-1883)." *Journal of Southeast Asian Studies* (Singapore) 25,2 (1994).

————. "Regionalism and the Nature of Nguyen Rule in Seventeenth-Century Vietnam." *Journal of Southeast Asian Studies* 29 (1998).

————. "Southern Regionalism and the Composition of the Nguyen Ruling Elite." *Asian Studies Review* (Brisbane) 23,2 (1999).

Crawfurd, John. *Journal of an Embassy from the Governor-General of India to the Courts of Siam and Cochin China.* 1828. Singapore: Oxford University Press, 1987.

Đại Nam Chính-Biên Liệt Truyện Nhị Tập (Second collection of the primary compilation of biographies of Imperial Vietnam). 1909. Tokyo: The Institute of Cultural and Linguistic Studies, Keio University, 1981.

Đại Nam Chính-Biên Liệt Truyện Sơ Tập (First collection of the primary compilation of biographies of Imperial Vietnam). 1889. Tokyo: Keio Institute of Linguistic Studies, 1962.

Đại Nam Điển Lệ Toát Yếu (A summary of the statutes of Imperial Vietnam). 1909. Translated by Nguyễn Sĩ Giác. Ho Chi Minh City: Nxb Thành Phố Hồ Chí Minh, 1994.

Đại Nam Liệt Truyện Tiền-Biên (Collection of biographies of Imperial Vietnam, premier period). 1852. Tokyo: Keio Institute of Linguistic Studies, 1961.

Đại Nam Nhất Thống Chí (Dai Nam gazetteer). Translated by Viện Sử Học. Hue: Thuận Hóa, 1992.

Đại Nam Thực Lục Chính-Biên Đệ Nhất Kỷ (Primary compilation of the Veritable Records of the first reign of Imperial Vietnam). 1848. Tokyo: The Institute of Cultural and Linguistic Studies, Keio University, 1968.

Đại Nam Thực Lục Chính-Biên Đệ Nhị Kỷ (Primary compilation of the Veritable Records of the second reign of Imperial Vietnam). 1861. Tokyo: Keio Institute of Linguistic Studies, 1963.

Đại Nam Thực Lục Chính-Biên Đệ Tam Kỷ (Primary compilation of the Veritable Records of the third reign of Imperial Vietnam). 1894. Tokyo: Institute of Cultural and Linguistic Studies, Keio University, 1977.

Đại Nam Thực Lục Chính-Biên Đệ Tứ Kỷ (Primary compilation of the Veritable Records of the fourth reign of Imperial Vietnam). 1892. Tokyo: The Institute of Cultural and Linguistic Studies, Keio University, 1980.

Đại Nam Thực Lục Tiền-Biên (Primary compilation of the Veritable Records of Imperial Vietnam, premier period). 1844. Tokyo: Keio Institute of Linguistic Studies, 1961.

Daudin, Pierre. "Phan-Thanh-Gian 1796-1867 et sa famille d'aprés quelques documents annamites." *Bulletin de la Société des Études Indochinoises* (Saigon) Tome 17 (1941).

Địa Bạ (Land cadastre) of Bình Cách village (1836). Hanoi: National Archives No. 2.

Địa Bạ (Land cadastre) of Bình Phục Nhất village (1836). Hanoi: National Archives No. 2.

Địa Bạ (Land cadastre) of Bình Cách village (1855). Ho Chi Minh City: Viện Hán Nôm at Viện Khoa Học Xã Hội, Serial No. 13.

Đinh Văn Hạnh. "Bửu Sơn Kỳ Hương Với Cuộc Kháng Chiến Chống Pháp." (Buu Son Ky Huong and anti-French movement) PhD dissertation, Viên Khoa Học Xã Hội Thành phố Hồ Chí Minh (TPHCM), 1996.

Đinh Xuân Lâm, Nguyễn Phan Quang. "Bốn Bang Thư, Một Tài Liệu Có Giá Trị Về Cuộc Khởi Nghĩa Lê Văn Khôi (1833-1835)" (Bon Bang's statement, a valuable document about Le Van Khoi's revolt). *Nghiên Cứu Lịch Sử* 178 (1978).

Đỗ Bang. *Kinh Tế Thương Nghiệp Việt Nam Dưới Triều Nguyễn* (The commercial economy of Vietnam during the Nguyen dynasty). Hue: Nxb Thuận Hóa, 1996.

Doãn Uẩn. *Doãn Tướng Công Hoạn Tích* (or *Tuy Tĩnh Tử Tạp Ngôn*) (Minister Doan's chronicle of office, or Tuy Tinh Tu's miscellaneous notes). 1842. Hanoi: Viện Hán Nôm A 2177.

Dương Bảo Vận. "Một vài nghiên cứu về sách Gia Định Thành Thông Chí" (Some research into the book Gia Dinh Thanh Thong Chi). *Xưa và Nay* (Ho Chi Minh City) 53B (1998).

Dương Thị The, et al. *Tên Làng Xã Việt Nam Đầu Thế Kỷ 19—thuộc các tỉnh từ Nghệ Tĩnh trở ra* (Names of Vietnamese villages in the beginning of the nineteenth century—places belonging to each province from Nghe An and Ha Tinh northward). Hanoi: Nxb Khoa Học Xã Hội, 1981.

Finlayson, George. *The Mission to Siam and Hue, the Capital of Cochin China, in the Years 1821-22*. 1826. Singapore: Oxford University Press, 1988.

Fujiwara, Riichiro. "Vietnamese Dynasties' Policies toward Chinese Immigrants." *Acta Asiatica* (Tokyo) 18 (1970).

———. *Tonanajiashi no Kenkyu* (Study on Southeast Asian history). Kyoto: Hozokan, 1986.

Hát Đông Thư Dị (Hat Dong's records of curiosities). n.d. Hanoi: Viện Hán Nôm VHc 01749.

Hồ Văn Hiếu. "Hoạt Động của Nghĩa Quân Trương Định Vùng Gò Công Tây" (Activities of Truong Dinh's righteous army in the region of western Go Cong). *130 Nam Nghìn Lại Cuộc Đời và Sự Nghiệp Trương Định*. Tien Giang Province: Kỷ Yếu Hội Thảo Khoa Học Sở Văn Hóa Thông Tín Tiền Giang, 1995.

Hoàng Anh. "Chợ Bình Tây Xưa" (Binh Tay Market in the past). *Xưa và Nay* 36B (1997).

Hoàng Côn. *Chiếm Thành Khảo* (A study of Champa). 1914. Hanoi: Viện Hán Nôm A 970.

Huỳnh Minh. *Địa Linh Nhơn Kiệt, Tỉnh Kiến Hoà (Bến Tre)* (Land and people, Kien Hoa Province [Ben Tre]). Saigon, 1965.

————. *Bạc Liêu Xưa và Nay* (Bac Lieu, past and present). Saigon, 1966.

————. *Cần Thơ Xưa và Nay* (Can Tho, past and present). Saigon, 1966.

————. *Vĩnh Long Xưa và Nay* (Vinh Long, past and present). Saigon, 1967.

————. *Gò Công Xưa và Nay* (Go Cong, past and present). Saigon, 1969.

————. *Định Tường Xưa và Nay* (Dinh Tuong, past and present). Saigon, 1969.

————. *Sa Đéc Xưa và Nay* (Sa Dec, past and present). Saigon, 1971.

————. *Tây Ninh Xưa và Nay* (Tay Ninh, past and present). Saigon, 1972.

————. *Gia Định Xưa và Nay* (Gia Dinh, past and present). Saigon, 1973.

Khâm Định Đại Nam Hội Điển Sự Lệ (Official compendium of institutions and usages of Imperial Vietnam). 1851. Hanoi: Viện Hán Nôm VHv 1570.

Khâm Định Tiễu Bình Lưỡng Kỳ Nghịch Phỉ Phương Lược (Official compendium of rebel suppression in northern and southern territories of the empire). 1836. Hanoi: Viện Hán Nôm VHv 2701.

Kiguchi, Kazumasa. *Betonamu no Nomin* (Vietnam's peasants). Tokyo: Kokon Shoin, 1966.

Lamb, Alastair, ed. *The Mandarin Road to Old Hue: Narratives of Anglo-Vietnamese Diplomacy from the Sevententh Century to the Eve of the French Conquest.* Hamden, Connecticut: Archon Books, 1970.

Langlet, Philippe. *L'Ancienne historiographie d'état au Vietnam.* Paris: École Française d'Extrême Orient, 1990.

Launay, Adrien Charles. *Histoire générale de la Société des Missions Etrangères* Tome 2. Paris: Téqui, Libraire-Editeur, 1894.

Lê Công Văn Duyệt Sự Trạng (Accounts of matters for Le Van Duyet). n.d. Hanoi: Viện Hán Nôm A 540.

Lê Hương. "Địa Danh, Di Tích Lich Sử, Thắng Cảnh Trong Vùng Người Việt Gốc Mien" (Names of places, historic sites, and beautiful places in the region of Vietnamese of Khmer origin). *Tập San Sử Địa* 14-15 (1969).

————. "Những Người Việt Tiền Phong Trên Bước Đường Nam Tiến Tại Cao Lãnh-Kiến Phong" (Vietnamese at the front of southward movement in Cao Lanh-Kien Phong). *Tập San Sử Địa* 19-20 (1970).

Lê Quý Đôn. *Phủ Biên Tạp Lục* (Records of border appeasement). Translated by Lê Xuân Giào. Saigon: Phủ Quốc Vụ Khanh Đặc Trách Văn Hóa, 1973.

Mạc Đường. *Vấn Đề Dân Tộc ở Đồng Bằng Sông Cửu Long* (Ethnic issues in the Mekong Delta). Ho Chi Minh City: Nxb Khoa Học Xã Hội, 1992.

McLeod, Mark. *The Vietnamese Response to French Intervention, 1862-1874.* New York: Praeger, 1991.

Miller, Robert Hopkins. *The United States and Vietnam, 1787-1941.* Washington DC: National Defense University Press, 1990.

Minh-Mệnh Chính-Yếu (Abstract of policies of Minh Mang). Translated by Ủy Ban Dịch Thuật Phú Quốc Vụ Khanh đặc-trách văn-hoá. 1897. Saigon, 1972-74.

Mục Lục Châu Bản Triều Nguyễn (Vermilion Record abstracts of the Nguyen Dynasty), vol. 1. Hue: Hue University, 1960.

Mục Lục Châu Bản Triều Nguyễn (Vermilion Record abstracts of the Nguyen Dynasty, Minh Mang reign to 1823) vol. 2. Hue: Hue University, 1962.

Nam Thiên Hiếu Hành Thực Lục (Veritable records of exemplary behavior in Vietnam). 1869. Hanoi: Viện Hán Nôm VHv 1240.

Nam Xuân Thọ. *Võ Trương Toản* [biography]. Saigon: Tân Việt, 1957.

Ngô Vĩnh Long. *Before the Revolution: The Vietnamese Peasants under the French.* New York: Columbia University Press, 1991.

Nguyễn Bảo. *Sử Cục Loại Biên* (Editions from the history bureau). 1833. Hanoi: Viện Hán Nôm A 9.

Nguyễn Cảnh Minh, Dương Văn Huề. "Chính Sách Chiêu Dân Khai Hoang Lập Ấp ở Nam Kỳ của Nhà Nguyễn Nửa Đầu Thế Kỷ 19" (Policies of recruitment of people, opening land and villages in southern Vietnam during the first half of the nineteenth century). *Nghiên Cứu Lịch Sử* 274 (1994).

Nguyễn Đình Đầu. *Chế Độ Công Điền Công Thổ Trong Lịch Sử Khẩn Hoang Lập Ấp ở Nam Kỳ Lục Tỉnh* (The public land system in the history of opening land and establishing villages in the Six Provinces of southern Vietnam). Hanoi: Hội Sử Học Việt Nam, 1992.

———. *Nghiên Cứu Địa Bạ Triều Nguyễn: Biên Hòa* (Researching land cadastres of the Nguyen dynasty: Bien Hoa). Ho Chi Minh City: Nxb Thành Phố Hồ Chí Minh, 1994.

———. *Nghiên Cứu Địa Bạ Triều Nguyễn: Định Tường* (Researching land cadastres of the Nguyen dynasty: Dinh Tuong). Ho Chi Minh City: Nxb Thành Phố Hồ Chí Minh, 1994.

Nguyễn Đức Dụ. *Gia Phả Khảo và Luận Thực Hành* (A study of genealogy and its compilation). Hanoi: Nxb Văn Hóa, 1992.

Nguyễn Gia Cát. *Đại Nam Hoàng Triều Bi Nhu Quận Công Phương Tích Lục* (The record of outstanding achievements of the Commandery Duke Bi Nhu [Pigneau de Béhanie] of the Dai Nam imperial court). Hanoi: Viện Hán Nôm A 1178.

Nguyễn Hữu Hiếu. *Võ Duy Dương với Cuộc Kháng Chiến Đồng Tháp Mười* (Vo Duy Duong and resistance movement in Dong Thap Muoi). Dong Thap Province: Nxb Tổng Hợp Đồng Tháp, 1992.

Nguyễn Lang. *Việt Nam Phật Giáo Sử Luận* (History of Buddhism in Vietnam) vol. 2. Hanoi: Văn Học, 1994.

Nguyễn Minh Tường. *Cải Cách Hành Chính Dưới Thời Minh Mệnh (1820-1840)* (Administrative reform under the reign of Minh Mang). Hanoi: Khoa Học Xã Hội, 1996.

Nguyễn Phan Quang, et al. "Tìm hiểu một điểm lien quan đến nguyên nhân cuộc bạo động Lê Văn Khôi—vấn đề Lê Văn Duyệt" (Understanding one point relating to the cause of the Le Van Khoi insurrection—the problem of Le Van Duyet). *Nghiên Cứu Lịch Sử* 105 (1967).

Nguyễn Phan Quang. "Thêm mấy điểm về cuộc bạo động Lê Văn Khôi (1833-1835)" (Several additional points concerning Le Van Khoi's revolt [1833-1835]). *Nghiên Cứu Lịch Sử* 147 (1972).

———. "Vấn đề Cố Du (Marchand) trong cuộc bạo động Lê Văn Khôi (1833-1835)." (The problem of Father Marchand in the Le Van Khoi revolt) *Nghiên Cứu Lịch Sử* 158 (1974).

———. *Phong Trào Nông Dân Việt Nam Nửa Đầu Thế Kỷ 19* (Vietnamese peasant movements during the first half of the nineteenth century). Hanoi: Nxb Khoa Học Xã Hội, 1986.

———, et al. *Khởi Nghĩa Trương Định* (Truong Dinh's upspring). Ho Chi Minh City: Nxb Thành Phố Hồ Chí Minh, 1989.

———. *Cuộc Khởi Binh Lê Văn Khôi ở Gia Định (1833-1835)* (Le Van Khoi's raising an army [1833-1835]). Ho Chi Minh City: Nxb Thành Phố Hồ Chí Minh, 1991.

———, et al. *Lịch Sử Việt Nam Từ Nguồn Gốc Đến 1858* (History of Vietnam from its origins to 1858) vol. 2. Ho Chi Minh City: Nxb Thành Phố Hồ Chí Minh, 1993.

Nguyễn Thế Anh. *Kinh Tế và Xã Hội Việt Nam Dưới Các Vua Triều Nguyễn* (Vietnam's economy and society under kings of the Nguyen dynasty). Saigon: Lửa Thiêng, 1971.

———. "Quelques aspects économiques et sociaux du problème du riz au Vietnam dans la prèmier moitié du 19 siècle." *Bulletin de la Société des Études Indochinoises* (Paris) 42,1-2 (1967).

Nguyễn Thị Thạnh. "The French Conquest of Cochinchina, 1858-1862." PhD dissertation, Cornell University, 1992

Nguyễn Thông. *Kì Xuyên Công Độc Sơ Biên* (First edition of Ki Xuyen's correspondence). 1872. Hanoi: Viện Hán Nôm VHc 01719.

Nguyễn Thu. *Hoàn Vũ Kỷ Văn* (Compendium on the [Vietnamese] world). n.d. Hanoi: Viện Hán Nôm A 585.

Nguyễn Văn Hầu. "Sự Thôn Thuộc và Khai Thác Đất Tầm Phong Long—Chặng Cuối Cùng của Cuộc Nam Tiến" (The claiming and opening of Tam Phong Long region—the final stage of southward movement). *Tập San Sử Địa* (Saigon) 19-20 (1970).

Nguyễn Văn Mại. *Việt Nam Phong Sử* (A history of the Vietnamese road). n.d. Hanoi: Viện Hán Nôm AB 320.

Osborne, Milton E. *The French Presence in Cochinchina and Cambodia: Rule and Response (1859-1905)*. Bangkok: White Lotus, 1997.

Phạm Đình Hổ. *Tang Thương Ngẫu Lục* (Tang Thuong's occasional records). 1836. Hanoi: Viện Hán Nôm A 218.

Phạm Thiểu, et al. *Nguyễn Hữu Huân, Nhà Yếu Nước Kiên Cường Nhà Thơ Bất Khuất* (Nguyen Huu Huan, a persistent patriot and indomitable poet). Ho Chi Minh City: Nxb Thành Phố Hồ Chí Minh, 1986.

Phan An, et al. *Những Vấn Đề Văn Hóa—Xã Hội Thời Nguyễn* (Social and cultural issues during the Nguyen period). Ho Chi Minh City: Nxb Khoa Học Xã Hội, 1993.

Phan Huy Chú. *Hải Trình Chí Lược* (Récit sommaire d'un voyage en mer) (1833). Translated and edited by Phan Huy Lê, Claudine Salmon and Tạ Trọng Hiệp. Paris: Cahier d'Archipel 25, 1994.

Phan Huy Lê. "Châu Bản Triều Nguyễn và Châu Bản Năm Minh Mệnh 6-7" (Vermilion record of the Nguyen dynasty during 1825-1826). Manuscript, 1998.

Phan Phát Huồn. *Việt Nam Giáo Sử* (History of Christianity in Vietnam). Saigon: Cứu Thế Tùng Thư, 1965.

Phan Thanh Giản. *Lương Khê Thi Thảo* (Poetry of Luong Khe in manuscript form). 1876. Hanoi: Viện Hán Nôm VHv 151.

———. *Lương Khê Văn Thảo* (Prose of Luong Khe in manuscript form). 1876. Hanoi: Viện Hán Nôm A 2125.

Phan Thúc Trực. *Quốc Sử Di Biên* (A transmitted compilation of the state history). n.d. Hong Kong: New Asia Research Institute, 1965.

Schreiner, Alfred. *Les Institutions Annamites en Basse-Cochinchine avant la Conquête Française*, Tome 2. Saigon: Claude & Cie, 1901.

Shimao, Minoru. "Meimeiki (1820-1840) Betonamu no Nankichiho Tochi ni Kansuru Ichi Kosatsu" (A study on Vietnamese rule of the South during the reign of Minh Mang). *Keio Gishokudaigoku Gengobunka Kenkyusho Kiyo* (Tokyo) 23 (1991).

Silvestre, Jean. "L'insurrection de Gia-Dinh, la révolte de Khoi (1832-1834)." *Revue Indochinoise* (Hanoi) 7-8 (1915).

Smith, Ralph B. "Politics and Society in Viet-Nam During the Early Nguyen Period (1802-1862)." *Journal of the Royal Asiatic Society* (London) 2 (1974).

Sơn Nam. "Việc Khẩn Hoang Vùng Rạch Giá" (Opening of Rach Gia region). *Tập Sản Sử Địa* 19-20 (1970).

———. *Đất Gia Định Xưa* (Land of Gia Dinh in the past). Ho Chi Minh City: Nxb Thành Phố Hồ Chí Minh, 1993.

Tạ Chí Đại Trường. "Những Bức Thư Chữ Nôm của Nguyễn Ánh Do Giáo Sĩ Cadière Sưu Tập" (Chu Nom letters of Nguyen Phuc Anh collected by Father Cadiere). *Tập Sản Sử Địa* 11 (1968).

Taboulet, Georges. *La geste Française en Indochine: histoire par les textes de la France en Indochine des origines à 1914*, Tome 1. Paris: Librairie D'Amérique et D'Orient, Adrien-Maisonneuve, 1955.

Tai Huệ Tâm Hồ. *Millenarianism and Peasant Politics in Vietnam*. Cambridge: Harvard University Press, 1983.

Taylor, Keith W. "Surface Orientations in Vietnam: Beyond Histories of Nation and Region." *The Journal of Asian Studies* 57,4 (1998).

Thạch Phương et al. *Địa Chí Bến Tre* (Gazetteer of Ben Tre Province). Hanoi: Nxb Khoa Học Xã Hội, 1999.

Thái Bạch. *Bốn Vị Anh Hùng, Kháng Chiến Miền Nam* (Four heroes of the southern resistance movements) vol. 2. Saigon: Tủ Sách Sông-Mới, 1957.

Thompson, Claudia Michele. "A Negotiated Dichotomy: Vietnamese medicine and the intersection of Vietnamese acceptance and resistance to Chinese cultural influence." PhD dissertation, University of Washington, 1998.

Trần Tân Gia. *Bà Tâm Huyền Kính Lục* (An account of compassionate hearts and hanging mirrors). 1897. Hanoi: Viện Hán Nôm A 2027.

Trần Thị Thu Lương. *Chế Độ Sở Hữu và Canh Tác Ruộng Đất ở Nam Bộ Nửa Đầu Thế Kỷ 19* (Land ownership system and rice cultivation in southern Vietnam during the first half of the nineteenth century). Ho Chi Minh City: Nxb Thành Phố Hồ Chí Minh, 1994.

Trần Văn Giàu, et al. *Địa Chí Văn Hóa Thành Phố Hồ Chí Minh* (Cultural gazetteer of Ho Chi Minh City), vol. 1. Ho Chi Minh City: Nxb Thành Phố Hồ Chí Minh, 1987.

Trần Văn Giàu. "Người Lục Tỉnh" (The people of Six Provinces). *Xưa và Nay* 44B (1997).

Trịnh Hoài Đức. *Gia Định Thành Thông Chí* (Gia Dinh gazetteer). n.d. École Française d'Extrême Orient microfilm A 1561.

———. *Cấn Trai Thi Tập* (The collected poems of Can Trai). 1819. Hong Kong: New Asia Research Institute, 1962.

Trương Bá Cần. *Công Giáo Đàng Trong: Thời Giám Mục Pigneau (1771-1799)* (Catholicism of Dang Trong: The period of Pigneau de Béhaine [1771-1799]). Ho Chi Minh City: Tủ Sách Đại Kết, 1992.

Trương Gia Từ Đường Thế Phả Toàn Tập (Complete collection of the genealogy of the Truong family ancestry). 1886. Hanoi: Viện Hán Nôm A 3186.

Trương Quốc Dụng. *Thoái Thực Ký Văn* (or *Công Ha Ký Văn*) (After-dinner recollections, or recollections beyond the office). n.d. Hanoi: Viện Hán Nôm A 1499.

Ts'ai T'ing Lan. *Hải Nam Tạp Trứ* (Various records of the land beyond the southern ocean). 1836. Hanoi: Viện Hán Nôm HVv 80.

Việt Cúc. *Gò Công Cảnh Cũ Ngươi Xưa* (Go Cong, its environs and people in the past), vol. 2. Saigon, 1969.

———. *Gò Công Cảnh Cũ Ngươi Xưa* (Go Cong, its environs and people in the past), vol. 1. Saigon, 1968.

Vietnam Cultural Window (Hanoi) 4 (July 1998).

Việt Nam Dư Địa Chí (A Vietnamese gazetteer). n.d. Hanoi: Viện Hán Nôm A 1829.

White, John. *A Voyage to Cochin China*. 1824. Kuala Lumpur: Oxford University Press, 1972.

Wong, Lin Ken. "The Trade of Singapore." *Journal of the Malayan Branch of the Royal Asiatic Society* (Singapore) 33,192 (1960).

Woodside, Alexander Barton. *Vietnam and the Chinese Model: A Comparative Study of Nguyễn and Ch'ing Civil Government in the First Half of the Nineteenth Century*. Cambridge: Harvard University Press, 1971.

Youn, Dae Yeong. "Wanjo Sadeokje Sigi Daebulhyeopsang'eseoeui Kadolik Munje (A question of Catholicism in the process of Franco-Vietnamese negotiations during the period of Tu Duc). MA thesis, Seoul National University, 1998.

INDEX

SOUTHEAST ASIA PROGRAM PUBLICATIONS

Cornell University
Studies on Southeast Asia

Number 37   *Sumatran Sultanate and Colonial State: Jambi and the Rise of Dutch Imperialism, 1830-1907*, Elsbeth Locher-Scholten, trans. Beverley Jackson. 2003. 332 pp. ISBN 0-87727-736-2.

Number 36   *Southeast Asia over Three Generations: Essays Presented to Benedict R. O'G. Anderson*, ed. James T. Siegel and Audrey R. Kahin. 2003. 398 pp. ISBN 0-87727-735-4.

Number 35   *Nationalism and Revolution in Indonesia*, George McTurnan Kahin, intro. Benedict R. O'G. Anderson (reprinted from 1952 edition, Cornell University Press, with permission). 2003. 530 pp. ISBN 0-87727-734-6.

Number 34   *Golddiggers, Farmers, and Traders in the "Chinese Districts" of West Kalimantan, Indonesia*, Mary Somers Heidhues. 2003. 316 pp. ISBN 0-87727-733-8.

Number 33   *Opusculum de Sectis apud Sinenses et Tunkinenses (A Small Treatise on the Sects among the Chinese and Tonkinese): A Study of Religion in China and North Vietnam in the Eighteenth Century*, Father Adriano de St. Thecla, trans. Olga Dror, with Mariya Berezovska. 2002. 363 pp. ISBN 0-87727-732-X.

Number 32   *Fear and Sanctuary: Burmese Refugees in Thailand*, Hazel J. Lang. 2002. 204 pp. ISBN 0-87727-731-1.

Number 31   *Modern Dreams: An Inquiry into Power, Cultural Production, and the Cityscape in Contemporary Urban Penang, Malaysia*, Beng-Lan Goh. 2002. 225 pp. ISBN 0-87727-730-3.

Number 30   *Violence and the State in Suharto's Indonesia*, ed. Benedict R. O'G. Anderson. 2001. Second printing, 2002. 247 pp. ISBN 0-87727-729-X.

Number 29   *Studies in Southeast Asian Art: Essays in Honor of Stanley J. O'Connor*, ed. Nora A. Taylor. 2000. 243 pp. Illustrations. ISBN 0-87727-728-1.

Number 28   *The Hadrami Awakening: Community and Identity in the Netherlands East Indies, 1900-1942*, Natalie Mobini-Kesheh. 1999. 174 pp. ISBN 0-87727-727-3.

Number 27   *Tales from Djakarta: Caricatures of Circumstances and their Human Beings*, Pramoedya Ananta Toer. 1999. 145 pp. ISBN 0-87727-726-5.

Number 26   *History, Culture, and Region in Southeast Asian Perspectives*, rev. ed., O. W. Wolters. 1999. 275 pp. ISBN 0-87727-725-7.

Number 25   *Figures of Criminality in Indonesia, the Philippines, and Colonial Vietnam*, ed. Vicente L. Rafael. 1999. 259 pp. ISBN 0-87727-724-9.

Number 24   *Paths to Conflagration: Fifty Years of Diplomacy and Warfare in Laos, Thailand, and Vietnam, 1778-1828*, Mayoury Ngaosyvathn and Pheuiphanh Ngaosyvathn. 1998. 268 pp. ISBN 0-87727-723-0.

Number 23   *Nguyễn Cochinchina: Southern Vietnam in the Seventeenth and Eighteenth Centuries*, Li Tana. 1998. Second printing, 2002. 194 pp. ISBN 0-87727-722-2.

Number 22   *Young Heroes: The Indonesian Family in Politics*, Saya S. Shiraishi. 1997. 183 pp. ISBN 0-87727-721-4.

Number 21 *Interpreting Development: Capitalism, Democracy, and the Middle Class in Thailand*, John Girling. 1996. 95 pp. ISBN 0-87727-720-6.

Number 20 *Making Indonesia*, ed. Daniel S. Lev, Ruth McVey. 1996. 201 pp. ISBN 0-87727-719-2.

Number 19 *Essays into Vietnamese Pasts*, ed. K. W. Taylor, John K. Whitmore. 1995. 288 pp. ISBN 0-87727-718-4.

Number 18 *In the Land of Lady White Blood: Southern Thailand and the Meaning of History*, Lorraine M. Gesick. 1995. 106 pp. ISBN 0-87727-717-6.

Number 17 *The Vernacular Press and the Emergence of Modern Indonesian Consciousness*, Ahmat Adam. 1995. 220 pp. ISBN 0-87727-716-8.

Number 16 *The Nan Chronicle*, trans., ed. David K. Wyatt. 1994. 158 pp. ISBN 0-87727-715-X.

Number 15 *Selective Judicial Competence: The Cirebon-Priangan Legal Administration, 1680–1792*, Mason C. Hoadley. 1994. 185 pp. ISBN 0-87727-714-1.

Number 14 *Sjahrir: Politics and Exile in Indonesia*, Rudolf Mrázek. 1994. 536 pp. ISBN 0-87727-713-3.

Number 13 *Fair Land Sarawak: Some Recollections of an Expatriate Officer*, Alastair Morrison. 1993. 196 pp. ISBN 0-87727-712-5.

Number 12 *Fields from the Sea: Chinese Junk Trade with Siam during the Late Eighteenth and Early Nineteenth Centuries*, Jennifer Cushman. 1993. 206 pp. ISBN 0-87727-711-7.

Number 11 *Money, Markets, and Trade in Early Southeast Asia: The Development of Indigenous Monetary Systems to AD 1400*, Robert S. Wicks. 1992. 2nd printing 1996. 354 pp., 78 tables, illus., maps. ISBN 0-87727-710-9.

Number 10 *Tai Ahoms and the Stars: Three Ritual Texts to Ward Off Danger*, trans., ed. B. J. Terwiel, Ranoo Wichasin. 1992. 170 pp. ISBN 0-87727-709-5.

Number 9 *Southeast Asian Capitalists*, ed. Ruth McVey. 1992. 2nd printing 1993. 220 pp. ISBN 0-87727-708-7.

Number 8 *The Politics of Colonial Exploitation: Java, the Dutch, and the Cultivation System*, Cornelis Fasseur, ed. R. E. Elson, trans. R. E. Elson, Ary Kraal. 1992. 2nd printing 1994. 266 pp. ISBN 0-87727-707-9.

Number 7 *A Malay Frontier: Unity and Duality in a Sumatran Kingdom*, Jane Drakard. 1990. 215 pp. ISBN 0-87727-706-0.

Number 6 *Trends in Khmer Art*, Jean Boisselier, ed. Natasha Eilenberg, trans. Natasha Eilenberg, Melvin Elliott. 1989. 124 pp., 24 plates. ISBN 0-87727-705-2.

Number 5 *Southeast Asian Ephemeris: Solar and Planetary Positions, A.D. 638–2000*, J. C. Eade. 1989. 175 pp. ISBN 0-87727-704-4.

Number 3 *Thai Radical Discourse: The Real Face of Thai Feudalism Today*, Craig J. Reynolds. 1987. 2nd printing 1994. 186 pp. ISBN 0-87727-702-8.

Number 1 *The Symbolism of the Stupa*, Adrian Snodgrass. 1985. Revised with index, 1988. 3rd printing 1998. 469 pp. ISBN 0-87727-700-1.

SEAP Series

Number 19 *Gender, Household, State: Đổi Mới in Việt Nam*, ed. Jayne Werner and Danièle Bélanger. 2002. 151 pp. ISBN 0-87727-137-2.

Number 18 *Culture and Power in Traditional Siamese Government*, Neil A. Englehart. 2001. 130 pp. ISBN 0-87727-135-6.

Number 17 *Gangsters, Democracy, and the State*, ed. Carl A. Trocki. 1998. Second printing, 2002. 94 pp. ISBN 0-87727-134-8.

Number 16 *Cutting across the Lands: An Annotated Bibliography on Natural Resource Management and Community Development in Indonesia, the Philippines, and Malaysia*, ed. Eveline Ferretti. 1997. 329 pp. ISBN 0-87727-133-X.

Number 15 *The Revolution Falters: The Left in Philippine Politics after 1986*, ed. Patricio N. Abinales. 1996. Second printing, 2002. 182 pp. ISBN 0-87727-132-1.

Number 14 *Being Kammu: My Village, My Life*, Damrong Tayanin. 1994. 138 pp., 22 tables, illus., maps. ISBN 0-87727-130-5.

Number 13 *The American War in Vietnam*, ed. Jayne Werner, David Hunt. 1993. 132 pp. ISBN 0-87727-131-3.

Number 12 *The Political Legacy of Aung San*, ed. Josef Silverstein. Revised edition 1993. 169 pp. ISBN 0-87727-128-3.

Number 10 *Studies on Vietnamese Language and Literature: A Preliminary Bibliography*, Nguyen Dinh Tham. 1992. 227 pp. ISBN 0-87727-127-5.

Number 9 *A Secret Past*, Dokmaisot, trans. Ted Strehlow. 1992. 2nd printing 1997. 72 pp. ISBN 0-87727-126-7.

Number 8 *From PKI to the Comintern, 1924–1941: The Apprenticeship of the Malayan Communist Party*, Cheah Boon Kheng. 1992. 147 pp. ISBN 0-87727-125-9.

Number 7 *Intellectual Property and US Relations with Indonesia, Malaysia, Singapore, and Thailand*, Elisabeth Uphoff. 1991. 67 pp. ISBN 0-87727-124-0.

Number 6 *The Rise and Fall of the Communist Party of Burma (CPB)*, Bertil Lintner. 1990. 124 pp. 26 illus., 14 maps. ISBN 0-87727-123-2.

Number 5 *Japanese Relations with Vietnam: 1951–1987*, Masaya Shiraishi. 1990. 174 pp. ISBN 0-87727-122-4.

Number 3 *Postwar Vietnam: Dilemmas in Socialist Development*, ed. Christine White, David Marr. 1988. 2nd printing 1993. 260 pp. ISBN 0-87727-120-8.

Number 2 *The Dobama Movement in Burma (1930–1938)*, Khin Yi. 1988. 160 pp. ISBN 0-87727-118-6.

Cornell Modern Indonesia Project Publications

Number 75 *A Tour of Duty: Changing Patterns of Military Politics in Indonesia in the 1990s*. Douglas Kammen and Siddharth Chandra. 1999. 99 pp. ISBN 0-87763-049-6.

Number 74 *The Roots of Acehnese Rebellion 1989–1992*, Tim Kell. 1995. 103 pp. ISBN 0-87763-040-2.

Number 73 *"White Book" on the 1992 General Election in Indonesia*, trans. Dwight King. 1994. 72 pp. ISBN 0-87763-039-9.

Number 72   *Popular Indonesian Literature of the Qur'an*, Howard M. Federspiel. 1994.
170 pp. ISBN 0-87763-038-0.

Number 71   *A Javanese Memoir of Sumatra, 1945–1946: Love and Hatred in the
Liberation War*, Takao Fusayama. 1993. 150 pp. ISBN 0-87763-037-2.

Number 70   *East Kalimantan: The Decline of a Commercial Aristocracy*, Burhan
Magenda. 1991. 120 pp. ISBN 0-87763-036-4.

Number 69   *The Road to Madiun: The Indonesian Communist Uprising of 1948*,
Elizabeth Ann Swift. 1989. 120 pp. ISBN 0-87763-035-6.

Number 68   *Intellectuals and Nationalism in Indonesia: A Study of the Following
Recruited by Sutan Sjahrir in Occupation Jakarta*, J. D. Legge. 1988.
159 pp. ISBN 0-87763-034-8.

Number 67   *Indonesia Free: A Biography of Mohammad Hatta*, Mavis Rose. 1987.
252 pp. ISBN 0-87763-033-X.

Number 66   *Prisoners at Kota Cane*, Leon Salim, trans. Audrey Kahin. 1986. 112 pp.
ISBN 0-87763-032-1.

Number 65   *The Kenpeitai in Java and Sumatra*, trans. Barbara G. Shimer, Guy Hobbs,
intro. Theodore Friend. 1986. 80 pp. ISBN 0-87763-031-3.

Number 64   *Suharto and His Generals: Indonesia's Military Politics, 1975–1983*, David
Jenkins. 1984. 4th printing 1997. 300 pp. ISBN 0-87763-030-5.

Number 62   *Interpreting Indonesian Politics: Thirteen Contributions to the Debate,
1964–1981*, ed. Benedict Anderson, Audrey Kahin, intro. Daniel S. Lev.
1982. 3rd printing 1991. 172 pp. ISBN 0-87763-028-3.

Number 60   *The Minangkabau Response to Dutch Colonial Rule in the Nineteenth
Century*, Elizabeth E. Graves. 1981. 157 pp. ISBN 0-87763-000-3.

Number 59   *Breaking the Chains of Oppression of the Indonesian People: Defense
Statement at His Trial on Charges of Insulting the Head of State, Bandung,
June 7–10, 1979*, Heri Akhmadi. 1981. 201 pp. ISBN 0-87763-001-1.

Number 57   *Permesta: Half a Rebellion*, Barbara S. Harvey. 1977. 174 pp.
ISBN 0-87763-003-8.

Number 55   *Report from Banaran: The Story of the Experiences of a Soldier during the
War of Independence*, Maj. Gen. T. B. Simatupang. 1972. 186 pp.
ISBN 0-87763-005-4.

Number 52   *A Preliminary Analysis of the October 1 1965, Coup in Indonesia (Prepared
in January 1966)*, Benedict R. Anderson, Ruth T. McVey, assist.
Frederick P. Bunnell. 1971. 3rd printing 1990. 174 pp.
ISBN 0-87763-008-9.

Number 51   *The Putera Reports: Problems in Indonesian-Japanese War-Time Cooperation*,
Mohammad Hatta, trans., intro. William H. Frederick. 1971. 114 pp.
ISBN 0-87763-009-7.

Number 50   *Schools and Politics: The Kaum Muda Movement in West Sumatra
(1927–1933)*, Taufik Abdullah. 1971. 257 pp. ISBN 0-87763-010-0.

Number 49   *The Foundation of the Partai Muslimin Indonesia*, K. E. Ward. 1970. 75 pp.
ISBN 0-87763-011-9.

Number 48   *Nationalism, Islam and Marxism*, Soekarno, intro. Ruth T. McVey. 1970.
2nd printing 1984. 62 pp. ISBN 0-87763-012-7.

Number 43   *State and Statecraft in Old Java: A Study of the Later Mataram Period, 16th to 19th Century*, Soemarsaid Moertono. Revised edition 1981. 180 pp. ISBN 0-87763-017-8.

Number 39   Preliminary Checklist of Indonesian Imprints (1945-1949), John M. Echols. 186 pp. ISBN 0-87763-025-9.

Number 37   *Mythology and the Tolerance of the Javanese*, Benedict R. O'G. Anderson. 2nd edition, 1996. 104 pp., 65 illus. ISBN 0-87763-041-0.

Number 25   *The Communist Uprisings of 1926–1927 in Indonesia: Key Documents*, ed., intro. Harry J. Benda, Ruth T. McVey. 1960. 2nd printing 1969. 177 pp. ISBN 0-87763-024-0.

Number 7   *The Soviet View of the Indonesian Revolution*, Ruth T. McVey. 1957. 3rd printing 1969. 90 pp. ISBN 0-87763-018-6.

Number 6   *The Indonesian Elections of 1955*, Herbert Feith. 1957. 2nd printing 1971. 91 pp. ISBN 0-87763-020-8.

Translation Series

Volume 4   *Approaching Suharto's Indonesia from the Margins*, ed. Takashi Shiraishi. 1994. 153 pp. ISBN 0-87727-403-7.

Volume 3   *The Japanese in Colonial Southeast Asia*, ed. Saya Shiraishi, Takashi Shiraishi. 1993. 172 pp. ISBN 0-87727-402-9.

Volume 2   *Indochina in the 1940s and 1950s*, ed. Takashi Shiraishi, Motoo Furuta. 1992. 196 pp. ISBN 0-87727-401-0.

Volume 1   *Reading Southeast Asia*, ed. Takashi Shiraishi. 1990. 188 pp. ISBN 0-87727-400-2.

Language Texts

INDONESIAN

Beginning Indonesian through Self-Instruction, John U. Wolff, Dédé Oetomo, Daniel Fietkiewicz. 3rd revised edition 1992. Vol. 1. 115 pp. ISBN 0-87727-529-7. Vol. 2. 434 pp. ISBN 0-87727-530-0. Vol. 3. 473 pp. ISBN 0-87727-531-9.

Indonesian Readings, John U. Wolff. 1978. 4th printing 1992. 480 pp. ISBN 0-87727-517-3

Indonesian Conversations, John U. Wolff. 1978. 3rd printing 1991. 297 pp. ISBN 0-87727-516-5

Formal Indonesian, John U. Wolff. 2nd revised edition 1986. 446 pp. ISBN 0-87727-515-7

TAGALOG

Pilipino through Self-Instruction, John U. Wolff, Maria Theresa C. Centeno, Der-Hwa V. Rau. 1991. Vol. 1. 342 pp. ISBN 0-87727—525-4. Vol. 2. 378 pp. ISBN 0-87727-526-2. Vol 3. 431 pp. ISBN 0-87727-527-0. Vol. 4. 306 pp. ISBN 0-87727-528-9.

THAI

A. U. A. Language Center Thai Course, J. Marvin Brown. Originally published by the American University Alumni Association Language Center, 1974. Reissued by Cornell Southeast Asia Program, 1991, 1992. Book 1. 267 pp. ISBN 0-87727-506-8. Book 2. 288 pp. ISBN 0-87727-507-6. Book 3. 247 pp. ISBN 0-87727-508-4.

A. U. A. Language Center Thai Course, Reading and Writing Text (mostly reading), 1979. Reissued 1997. 164 pp. ISBN 0-87727-511-4.

A. U. A. Language Center Thai Course, Reading and Writing Workbook (mostly writing), 1979. Reissued 1997. 99 pp. ISBN 0-87727-512-2.

KHMER

Cambodian System of Writing and Beginning Reader, Franklin E. Huffman. Originally published by Yale University Press, 1970. Reissued by Cornell Southeast Asia Program, 4th printing 2002. 365 pp. ISBN 0-300-01314-0.

Modern Spoken Cambodian, Franklin E. Huffman, assist. Charan Promchan, Chhom-Rak Thong Lambert. Originally published by Yale University Press, 1970. Reissued by Cornell Southeast Asia Program, 3rd printing 1991. 451 pp. ISBN 0-300-01316-7.

Intermediate Cambodian Reader, ed. Franklin E. Huffman, assist. Im Proum. Originally published by Yale University Press, 1972. Reissued by Cornell Southeast Asia Program, 1988. 499 pp. ISBN 0-300-01552-6.

Cambodian Literary Reader and Glossary, Franklin E. Huffman, Im Proum. Originally published by Yale University Press, 1977. Reissued by Cornell Southeast Asia Program, 1988. 494 pp. ISBN 0-300-02069-4.

HMONG

White Hmong-English Dictionary, Ernest E. Heimbach. 1969. 8th printing, 2002. 523 pp. ISBN 0-87727-075-9.

VIETNAMESE

Intermediate Spoken Vietnamese, Franklin E. Huffman, Tran Trong Hai. 1980. 3rd printing 1994. ISBN 0-87727-500-9.

* * *

Southeast Asian Studies: Reorientations. Craig J. Reynolds and Ruth McVey. Frank H. Golay Lectures 2 & 3. 70 pp. ISBN 0-87727-301-4.

Javanese Literature in Surakarta Manuscripts, Nancy K. Florida. Vol. 1, *Introduction and Manuscripts of the Karaton Surakarta*. 1993. 410 pp. Frontispiece, illustrations. Hard cover, ISBN 0-87727-602-1, Paperback, ISBN 0-87727-603-X. Vol. 2, *Manuscripts of the Mangkunagaran Palace*. 2000. 576 pp. Frontispiece, illustrations. Paperback, ISBN 0-87727-604-8.

Sbek Thom: Khmer Shadow Theater. Pech Tum Kravel, trans. Sos Kem, ed. Thavro Phim, Sos Kem, Martin Hatch. 1996. 363 pp., 153 photographs. ISBN 0-87727-620-X.

In the Mirror: Literature and Politics in Siam in the American Era, ed. Benedict R. O'G. Anderson, trans. Benedict R. O'G. Anderson, Ruchira Mendiones. 1985. 2nd printing 1991. 303 pp. Paperback. ISBN 974-210-380-1.

To order, please contact:

Cornell University
SEAP Distribution Center
369 Pine Tree Rd.
Ithaca, NY 14850-2819 USA

Online: http://www.einaudi.cornell.edu/southeastasia/publications/
Tel: 1-877-865-2432 (Toll free – U.S.)
Fax: (607) 255-7534

E-mail: SEAP-Pubs@cornell.edu
Orders must be prepaid by check or credit card (VISA, MasterCard, Discover).